Exploring Science and Mathematics in a Child's World

Genevieve A. Davis
Kent State University

J. David Keller
Kent State University

PEARSON

Merrill
Prentice Hall

Upper Saddle River, New Jersey
Columbus, Ohio

Library of Congress Cataloging-in-Publication Data

Davis, Genevieve A.
    Exploring science and mathematics in a child's world / Genevieve A. Davis and J. David Keller.
        p. cm.
    Includes bibliographical references and index.
    ISBN 978-0-13-094522-8
        1. Science—Study and teaching (Elementary).   2. Mathematics—Study and teaching (Elementary)   3. Science—
Mathematics. 4. Learning, Psychology of. I. Keller, J. David. II. Title.
    LB1585.D34 2009
    372.35'044—dc22   2007028018

Vice President and Executive Publisher: Jeffery W. Johnston
Publisher: Kevin M. Davis
Acquisitions Editor: Julie Peters
Development Editor: Ben Sullivan Prout
Editorial Assistant: Tiffany Bitzel
Senior Project Manager: Linda Hillis Bayma
Production Coordination: Norine Strang, S4Carlisle Editorial Services
Design Coordinator: Diane C. Lorenzo
Photo Coordinator: Valerie Schultz
Cover Designer: Ali Mohrman
Cover images: Top three, courtesy of Kent State University Child Development Center; bottom, Kurt Keller Photography
Production Manager: Laura Messerly
Director of Marketing: Quinn Perkson
Marketing Manager: Amy Judd
Marketing Coordinator: Brian Mounts

This book was set in Berling by S4Carlisle Publishing Services. It was printed and bound by R.R. Donnelley & Sons Company. The cover was printed by R.R. Donnelley & Sons Company.

Pearson Education Ltd.
Pearson Education Singapore Pte. Ltd.
Pearson Education Canada, Ltd.
Pearson Education–Japan

Pearson Education Australia Pty. Limited
Pearson Education North Asia Ltd.
Pearson Educación de Mexico, S.A. de C.V.
Pearson Education Malaysia Pte. Ltd.

10 9 8 7 6 5 4 3 2 1
ISBN-13: 978-0-13-094522-8
ISBN-10:   0-13-094522-6

To my children, Anthony, Elizabeth, and Andrew, who continue to nourish me with love, happiness, and inspiration.

Genevieve A. Davis

To Brandon, Jackson, Peyton, and Parker, who taught their grandfather how to explore the world of science and mathematics.

J. David Keller

About the Authors

GENEVIEVE A. DAVIS received her Ph.D. from the University of Connecticut. Dr. Davis is an Associate Professor of Mathematics Education in the College of Education, Health and Human Services at Kent State University. She has had experiences teaching elementary, middle school, and college mathematics in New Jersey, Connecticut, and Amsterdam in the Netherlands. While teaching and consulting in the Netherlands, she worked in Amsterdam and Geneva, Switzerland, on the International Schools Curriculum Project. She has also given numerous presentations and has worked collaboratively with educators in China, South Africa, Russia, and England. Dr. Davis has received many honors and awards for her teaching and innovative work in the schools. Among them are the Distinguished Teaching Award from the Kent State Alumni Association, the Burton Gorman Teacher Impact Award from Kent State, and the Ohio Best Practices Award from the State of Ohio for her work on a National Science Foundation Grant in Mathematics Education. Her current research, writing, and grant work is focused on professional development of teachers and mathematics teaching and learning in the elementary and middle grades.

J. DAVID KELLER received his Ph.D. from the University of Texas at Austin. Dr. Keller joined Kent State University (KSU) in 1990. He worked with the Akron (Ohio) public schools for 26 years as a classroom teacher, curriculum developer, and coordinator for the Gifted and Talented Program. He was codirector of the KSU/NASA Global Robotic Observatory System with observatories at Kent State University and the Western Australia State Observatory, Perth, Australia. He has served as a member of the National Science Education Association Committee for Gifted Education. He has given several international presentations including such places as Moscow, Beijing, and several cities in Turkey. He has been a Visiting Professor at Delhi University, New Delhi, India, and at Edith Cowan University in Perth. He was Visiting Astronomer at the Western Australia State Observatory in Perth. His book *Teacher's River Guide: A Curriculum Handbook for Educators* received the First Place National Award from the Corporation for Public Broadcasting in 1995. In 2000, Dr. Keller received the Distinguished Teaching Award from the Kent State Alumni Association. Dr. Keller is currently serving as interim chair of Teaching, Leadership and Curriculum studies in the College of Education, Health and Human Services at Kent State University.

Preface

In this book, you will learn ways to explore the natural world of the young child and examine how science and mathematics can provide contexts for curiosity, creativity, and discovery. We provide the research-based information and ways to invite inquiry, encourage problem solving, and introduce the scientific and mathematical thinking that is essential for young learners. This text also includes foundational information about how young children learn, and ideas on how to create environments that promote learning. The philosophies of the National Science Teachers Association (NSTA) and the National Council of Teachers of Mathematics (NCTM) form the foundation for the approaches to inquiry described in this book. These approaches involve encouraging creative scientific and mathematical explorations for young children that are based on children's interests. This motivational approach leads to sense-making about the world and is at the core of current reform movements in science and mathematics.

PURPOSE

This book is a resource for adults who spend time exploring the world with young children. Its purpose is to provide concrete ways to engage children in inquiry about the natural world. The book helps to spark interest in and give ideas for exploration about the natural, universal phenomena that everyone experiences in their day-to-day lives. Thus, the ideas for exploration found in this book cover universal topics such as sunshine and shadows, clouds, water, wind, seeds, leaves, insects, birds, rocks, light, and color. If we are to cultivate learners who think critically and solve problems creatively, we need to find ways to tap into their natural curiosities to discover all the "whys" they ponder and provide a culture where new "whys" are pondered and exploration is permitted.

AUDIENCE

The audience for this book includes anyone who spends time with young learners, anyone who is curious and interested in natural phenomena, and anyone who is interested in the current reform movements in science and mathematics. Students and professionals in early childhood education can benefit from learning about how to engage children, from infancy through the primary grades, in scientific and mathematical inquiry in and out of school settings. Parents and caregivers of young children can find ways to explore their surroundings and become critical thinkers and solvers of problems about our natural world. Agencies and educational organizations who work with parents can use this book as a resource to help with parenting ideas that promote and support exploration of the natural world. This book will be a valuable resource for all intended audiences.

ORGANIZATION OF TEXT

This text is organized in two parts: Part I: Theoretical Foundations for Teaching Science and Mathematics has six chapters and Part II: Concept Explorations, has twelve. The first two chapters provide a theoretical foundation for teaching young children and for understanding how young children learn. Understanding how children think, learn, and feel is an important part of preparation for early childhood education. In this part, we also provide information about how young children learn to make sense of their world, how they learn to think, and how language and scientific and mathematical thinking (inquiring, exploring, and constructing knowledge) are important parts of cognitive development. Along these lines, Chapter 3 provides information about designing experiences that promote good problem-solving skills.

Also within Part I, we provide a chapter titled "Measurement—A Way to Capture Observation in Mathematics and Science" and a chapter titled "Organizing Data in Science and Mathematics." These two chapters are designed to give specific ideas about how to help children use tools of mathematics and science to capture and share their observations and discoveries. The last chapter in Part I, "Criteria for Developing Concept Explorations," gives specific information about how to structure environments that support natural inquiry and investigation across the 12 Concept Explorations that follow in Part II. In each of these chapters, review and discussion questions are offered as springboards for conversation and reflection.

Part II: Concept Explorations identifies 12 natural themes that exist in the world of children. These themes are called Concept Explorations and all have several common features:

- They are part of the child's immediate environment.
- They utilize children's interests and curiosities to develop related skills in science and mathematics.
- They are related to national standards in science and mathematics.
- They allow children to collaborate and co-inquire with their teachers, fellow students, and other adults on interesting explorations.

These Concept Explorations help children uncover what they know and spark interest in determining what they want to find out.

Each Concept Exploration has several criteria that cause it to be a productive experience for children. These criteria include the following:

- Incorporates solid science and mathematics content.
- Considers the appropriate level of child development.
- Truly integrates science and mathematics.
- Is guided by the child's world.
- Incorporates children's literature.
- Involves children exploring with basic materials.
- Is founded on safe environments.

General science and mathematics content are provided for the reader as background information as they engage in the activities described in each Concept

Exploration. Bibliographies are included for additional exploration and support across all Concept Explorations.

ACKNOWLEDGMENTS

We are deeply appreciative for all the help and inspiration we received while writing this book. We offer thanks to the Kent State University Child Development Center, Kent State University early childhood students, their cooperating teachers, and the children who field tested the Concept Explorations. We thank the editors at Merrill/Prentice Hall, Julie Peters and Ben Prout, and photo manager Carol Sykes, for their guidance, direction, and encouragement as we worked through every aspect of the book. We would also like to thank our reviewers: Sara Jane L. Adler, Washtenaw Community College; Susan Anton, Hostos Community College of the City University of New York; Sarah J. Carrier, Auburn University; Diane Cerreto, Eastern Connecticut State University; Susan H. Christian, Patrick Henry Community College; Mary Larue, J. Sargeant Reynolds Community College; Cynthia A. Lundeen, Florida State University; and Jana Sanders, Texas A&M University–Corpus Christi, and RoseMary Weaver, Arkansas State University. Their thoughtful and helpful comments were appreciated as we worked through the development of this book. We wholeheartedly thank our friend, colleague, and mentor, Dr. Trish Yourst Koontz, for her inspiration and support throughout our work at Kent State University.

I am grateful for the inspiration and support I have received from my parents, Anthony and Edith LaRusso, for their immeasurable love and encouragement, and my family for teaching me what it means to find wonder in the world. Appreciation is also expressed to my husband, Walter, for his encouragement and support.

I am also indebted to my mentor, Dr. Vincent J. Glennon, who served as my graduate advisor at the University of Connecticut. In his memory, my work reflects the many contributions he made to my development as a mathematics educator.

Genevieve A. Davis

Appreciation is expressed to my wife Ginny for her encouragement, patience, and understanding during the development of this book.

Obviously, many people have contributed to my development as a scientist and educator. Particular appreciation is given to two mentors, Dr. Jim Jackson and Dr. Rolland Bartholomew, who directed me through my graduate studies. In addition, Richard Nelson has been a close colleague and friend. All three of these people will recognize that their contributions to my knowledge have taken root.

J. David Keller

Brief Contents

Contents

CHAPTER 5 **Organizing Data in Science and Mathematics**   **70**

CHAPTER 6 **Criteria for Developing Concept Explorations**   **86**

PART II   CONCEPT EXPLORATIONS

CHAPTER 7   Astronomy and Space Science   115

CHAPTER 8   **Birds**   **141**

CHAPTER 11   Leaves   197

CHAPTER 12   Light and Color   213

CHAPTER 13   **Rocks**   **235**

CHAPTER 14   **Seeds**   **253**

CHAPTER 16   Toys and Tools   289

Note: Every effort has been made to provide accurate and current Internet information in this book. However, the Internet and information posted on it are constantly changing, so it is inevitable that some of the Internet addresses listed in this textbook will change.

CHAPTER 1

A Child's World—*How Young Children Learn*

There are only two ways to live your life. One is as though nothing is a miracle. The other is as if everything is.—Albert Einstein

Babies live in a completely perceptual world, as all their knowledge comes through their available senses. They begin their lives with an impressive ability to take in, organize, and process these perceptions, and thus make sense of their world (Gonzalez-Mena & Widmeyer Eyer, 2001). Infants are responsive to touch and pain and are able to respond to objects placed in hand. They are able to distinguish between sweet, sour, and bitter tastes and smells, preferring the sweet ones. They adapt their head movements as their eyes move and scan their environment for interesting sights and moving objects. Infants will also turn in the direction of a sound. They prefer complex sounds to pure tones and are capable of distinguishing certain sound patterns (Berk, 2006).

As infants perceive the world around them, they pay attention and make sense of their perceptions. Thus, their attention is interwoven with what they perceive (Bruning, Schraw, Norby, & Ronning, 2004). It is the attention to these perceptions that gives infants experiences that will lead to *memory*, which is the retaining of impressions and experiences, and *conceptual knowledge*, which is nothing the construction of meaning about the impressions and experiences. This development is short of miraculous.

> As infants perceive their world, they experience many interesting things. It is through these experiences that they begin to make sense of their world and construct knowledge.

At birth, the world of each child consists of only their immediate surroundings: the sounds of commotion and peacefulness that the infant senses in the environment, the security of being held by a parent or caregiver, the bright rays of light from a lamp, or a cool breeze from the window. Infants are quite captivated by people's actions. They learn and remember by perceiving such actions in their world. Infants do not need to be as physically active to acquire new information as they will later, when motor activity will facilitate certain aspects of perception and cognition (Berk, 2006).

1

The only reality infants know about this small world is what they gain by using their available senses: sight, touch, sound, smell, and taste. These five senses will be their tools for a lifetime of learning. Infants' first experiences are simply the joy of sensing and observing. As they grow and develop, their experiences help them make sense of their world. As infants experience predictable events, they become better able to understand logical patterns (Poole, 1998).

As infants receive stimuli they can be either pleased or distressed by them. It is important that infants have rich and varied positive personal interactions, perceptual events and items with which to interact. Through careful, individualized observation, teachers can determine how much stimulation is appropriate for each child, as both overstimulation and understimulation are risks. Through their world perceptions, infants develop impressions, attitudes, and ideas about people and life. Sharp and loud sounds may startle and concern them. The sound of a pleasant voice causes them to smile, giggle, or respond with arm and leg movements. Infants are extremely sensitive to temperature and currents of air that cause them to be too warm or too cold. Their sensations and responses are quite immediate. What do they need to know for their basic comforts from minute to minute? How do they communicate their basic needs to adults? What actions invite certain kinds of interaction with others?

Most infants today live in a sensually exciting world. The experiences of hearing a parent sing, a rattle shake, or a rubber toy squeak are being replaced, in some instances, by electronic devices. The touch of an electronic toy can initiate a medley of children's songs accompanied by sounds of animals and locomotives. Young children are flooded with sounds and sights of music and videos. They observe more, but these observations are part of a distant and imaginary world, one created by such media as television and DVDs featuring Elmo, Big Bird, or Barney. These experiences can be positive in developing understanding of relationships about cause and effect, how things work, and how people relate to each other. Conversely, children also must have many firsthand, personal experiences observing and manipulating items in their immediate and real environment. Authentic experiences with caring people and hands-on explorations provide infants opportunities to learn (e.g., National Council of Teachers of Mathematics [NCTM], 2000; National Research Council [NRC], 1996). As children continue to experience their world, they are continually filled with curiosity, wonder, and amazement.

IMPLICATIONS FOR ADULTS

It is critical when working with children to direct their experiences and observations to their immediate world. Children must experience the feeling of getting wet or cooled off by a breeze; of stacking blocks and knocking them down; of watching clouds float in the sky; and of seeing trees fluttering in the breeze. Actual experiences in which children can see, feel, hear, smell, and taste contributes to their developing impressions, knowledge, and understanding of their world. It is their perceptual world, the source of all they know, that will continue to impact what they understand about the unseen, imperceptible abstractions of the world.

Educational experiences for young children should emphasize meaning making and the construction of knowledge (Chaille & Britain, 1997). As we help children explore and inquire about their own theories and ideas related to mathematics and science, we are invited to reawaken our own senses and experience the perceptual world of the child.

In this book, we will explore the perceptual world of the child and examine how mathematics and science can provide the contexts for curiosity, creativity, discovery, and delight. The explorations described in this book will help us to provide environments and social interactions that support and value children's natural curiosities and interests. The mathematical and scientific contexts of these explorations are essential in helping children understand how their world works. If we are to cultivate learners into critical thinkers and creative problem solvers, then we must tap into their natural curiosities and desires to find out about the "whys" they ponder and to provide a culture in which children can discover new questions to ponder and explore.

Herein we also identify several authentic themes of major childhood influence. These themes, called *Concept Explorations*, provide sources of timeless fascination for young children. Each Concept Exploration has several commonalties (see Figure 1.1). They are part of the children's immediate environment. They utilize children's interests and curiosities to develop related skills in mathematics and science such as patterns, classification (sorting by common characteristics), seriation (placing items in a sequenced series or gradation), measurement, and questioning. They are related to the national standards in mathematics and science. They allow children to collaborate and co-inquire with their teachers and other adults on interesting explorations, to uncover what they know and to spark interest in determining what they want to learn.

A guiding principle for this book is reflected in Vygotsky's notion that "the interaction between the adult and the child, for Vygotsky, is like a dance—the child leads and the adult follows, always closely in tune with the child's actions" (Berk & Winsler, 1995, p. x). In this sense, teachers become co-inquirers alongside children in their quest for understanding their world.

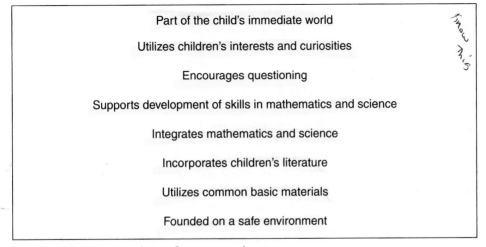

Part of the child's immediate world

Utilizes children's interests and curiosities

Encourages questioning

Supports development of skills in mathematics and science

Integrates mathematics and science

Incorporates children's literature

Utilizes common basic materials

Founded on a safe environment

FIGURE 1.1 Commonalities of concept explorations.

A CHILD'S WORLD OF CAUSE AND EFFECT

From the very beginning of his education, the child should experience the joy of discovery.—Alfred North Whitehead

Children are naturally curious and continually engage in exploration and play. They are intrigued by cause-and-effect phenomena and delight in being surprised. *Cause and effect* simply refers to the relationship between an action and its outcome. For example, if a child pushes a certain button on a toy, she may hear a "moo" sound; or if a child drops a ball off a high chair, it may bounce. Piaget (1952) theorized that children learn through play when they can cause things to happen or change. Through their exploration and play, children are intrigued by the incongruous events that they experience (Rogers & Sawyers, 1992). Play enhances learning and development for children of all ages and cultures. The Association for Childhood Education International, in their position statement about play, states that "play is a powerful, natural behavior contributing to children's learning and development and that no program of adult instruction can substitute for children's own observations, activities and direct knowledge" (Isenberg & Quisenberry, 2002).

Early in development, before most children are 2 years of age, their curiosity expands beyond basic needs. They begin to understand that they can have interesting experiences with basic toys. They are learning about cause and effect, or means and ends, when they can cause a ball to roll simply by placing it somewhere on a slanted surface. They find that they can shake a rattle and hear sounds. Pushing a yellow button on a toy causes a song to be heard. Pushing a blue button causes the sound of a bird chirping or a dog barking. Toys can activate the senses, and children learn that they can "test" toys to see what sensations and observations they can create. Through their exploration, experimentation, and play, children learn that they can cause things to change or happen. This is the beginning of their understanding of cause-and-effect relationships. Observation becomes the tool for understanding relationships, making predictions, and figuring out why things happen. They learn to cause situations so that related events can be observed and enjoyed. Similarly, young children will pull at a mobile to cause it to chime or play music. They will push a roly-poly penguin off their high chair to see and hear it fall. They squeeze their teddy bears to create sounds. As they repeat these actions, young children begin to remember and learn how to make interesting things happen and last (Piaget, 1952). They also may initiate interactions with others to get attention and receive stimulation or look away to discourage interactions. These experiences are examples of how a young child builds memory of the impressions and experiences in life.

Cause-and-effect relationships are social too. If a caregiver always sings a particular song as she feeds the baby, the baby begins to anticipate the song and the feeding. Likewise, if a baby shakes a blanket and the cat comes running, the baby begins to associate this cause-and-effect relationship and repeats the actions, because the young child remembers the patterns.

Social contexts are also filled with numerous cause and effect occurrences. As children interact with others, they quickly learn how to make someone smile by opening their mouth or clapping their hands. As children engage in feeding, oftentimes certain patterns of care are comforting and predictable. It is important for us to be aware of how we interact with and respond to little ones. These experiences and interactions will set the stage for symbolic learning and language.

As discussed, many toys for young children are designed to nurture their development for understanding these interesting cause-and-effect relationships. Playing with these toys gives them a feeling of control and allows them to predict and anticipate events. They can control making sounds and causing lights to flash. Soon they learn that they can control other aspects of their environment on their own. They can drop the cracker from their highchair or open and close a cabinet door. They learn that they are able to manipulate their world. They pull a blanket to bring a toy closer to them or they push aside a barrier to get a toy (Gordon & Williams Browne, 2004). Making giggly sounds sometimes brings the attention of others nearby. Similarly, crying is a way to get the attention of a parent or caregiver. Infants who experience such predictable events and routines by a responsive caregiver at this stage will be better able to understand logical patterns later (Poole, 1998). Mathematical and scientific thinking is closely related to a child's ability to search and discover patterns.

As we become accustomed to watching children develop, our observations of these senses tend to become secondary. As parents educators, and caregivers, we become much more interested in the direct communication we have with the children in our care. We tend to not notice specific stimuli that cause children's responses. We must remember, however, that each child's environment is critical in nurturing mathematical and scientific reasoning and thinking processes. It remains, as it shall for their lifetime, that everything they learn and do is a product of using their five senses. Our task is to help these children develop and utilize these senses and observation skills in a nurturing environment that leads to sound mathematical and scientific thinking.

CREATING ENVIRONMENTS THAT SUPPORT DEVELOPMENT

The world we create in our classrooms and in our indoor and outdoor play spaces determines the nature of learning for each child. These environments are the catalysts that determine what the children experience and observe. For our purposes, we will define our *classroom* as any and all locations that teachers use for facilitating the learning process. The classroom includes the central environment that is home to our students, as well as the outdoor play spaces and perhaps a nearby grassy area or meadow where we can walk and observe flowers and butterflies, trees and squirrels, water and rocks.

The classroom must be as authentic and exciting as possible. This place and its surrounding environment is part of the child's real world. It should include interesting materials and experiences that activate all five of the child's senses and provide things that capture interest and curiosity. It is the process of exploration and play that not only is quite enjoyable but also sparks discovery. It is through these processes that children are able to learn about learning. They channel their curiosity and they persist, discover, and invent. Therefore, we must strive to provide interesting, engaging, and thought-provoking environments for our curious children.

In the remainder of this chapter we continue to look at how young children learn to make sense of their world, how they learn to think, and how language and mathematical and scientific thinking are important parts of cognitive structuring.

HOW EMERGENCE OF LANGUAGE SUPPORTS MATHEMATICS AND SCIENCE LEARNING

. . . language is a major instrument of thought.—Jerome Bruner (1966)

The perception of sounds begins before birth. In the womb, the child can hear sounds. The mother's voice resonates throughout her body. The child recognizes her voice and at birth feels an attachment to it. Over the next several months the child learns to recognize attitudes from voices. A pleasant voice initiates giggles; a harsh voice causes flinching or crying. Soon it is obvious that the child recognizes voices of familiar people.

Experiences of infancy occur with limited verbal development. Although infants have not yet developed the mental processes that allow them to verbalize with words what they are thinking, they do respond to a variety of stimuli. They are learning how to react to the world around them and how the world reacts to them.

Observing small infants' vocalizations, body movements, and gestures gives us clues about what they are internalizing (e.g., Piaget, 1954). The differentiated crying gives us clues to what they are trying to tell us. They are "saying" that they are hungry, cold, wet, lonely, or frightened. When you talk animatedly or lovingly and soothingly to infants, they sometimes respond excitedly with their whole body.

Adults have wonderful "conversations" with infants by soliciting their reactions to pleasant, enthusiastic talks and actions. Infants respond with laughter and giggles and many physical movements. We view this as the child taking in the experience and appreciating the interchange. The child views this as a form of attention and communication that they are important, involved, cared for, and loved.

Although the development of speech comes between 2 and 6 years of age (Gordon & Williams Browne, 2004), infants have an amazing ability to respond and communicate verbally to people before that time. From crying, to cooing, to babbling, to using one-word utterances, babies experiment with gestures and making sounds with their mouth to communicate meaning for things. For example, a baby may open and close the hands to mean "pick me up," twist the hand at the wrist to mean "all gone," or make a sniffing sound to mean "flower." Adults replicate these gestures and sounds to communicate with the infant.

Later, babies will imitate the words they hear. They must experiment with making verbal sounds to imitate these words; and they must also develop meaning and understanding for what words represent. In this way, the words they speak communicate their ideas. Words are vehicles for young children as they form and communicate concepts to others. Young children begin to recognize that certain sounds relate to particular activities and meanings. When we analyze the first appearance of *syntax*, the structure of grammar in a language, we observe an interesting construction—the holophrase (Bruner, 1966) or the one-word utterance. Examples of holophrases are "up," "drink," "dog," "ball," or "boo." Oftentimes, these holophrases are emphasized by body movements and gestures, such as pointing or waving. Perhaps "book" is accompanied by holding hands together with the palms up.

When young children put together two or more holophrases such as "allgone," "gobyebyeinthecarcar," or "byebye," they have discovered a newfound power of communication. They have discovered two important properties of language: The *combinatorial property* pertains to how things or words combine to produce new meaning. The *productive property* pertains to causing or bringing about action (Bruner, 1966). Toddlers become increasingly capable of using many forms of representation to communicate. Oftentimes they may use body movements and actions if they are struggling for words to represent their thinking. They simply will show in action what they mean. Toddlers represent their ideas about the world through symbolic play (Gordon & Williams Browne, 2004; Trepanier-Street, 2000). Their actions "speak" volumes about what their impressions and experiences mean to them.

It is amazing that children learn to talk so quickly without formal instruction. By age 2 years, most children can verbally communicate with others; and by age 5 years, their language structure is similar to adult language. Children's first words tend to be nouns such as *ball, mama, dada, up,* or *cracker.* At this stage, young children will generalize meaning with the words they use. For example, a 1-year-old may say "cracker" for many different foods. Eventually, "cracker" will be used for only crackers. Or, "doggie" may refer to all four-legged animals. This is the beginning of the development of a broad classification scheme—hallmarks of mathematical and scientific thinking.

Children then develop verb concepts such as "smile" and "drink." Their verbalization of these terms confirms that they recognize a relationship between the sound of the term and a specific object, person, or event. Making sounds is having a cause-and-effect relationship for children. Such ability to integrate experience and develop concepts with communication is reflected in Dewey's (1959) conceptualization of learning as "a continuing reconstruction of experience."

Having developed the skill of verbalizing specific terms, children soon combine words requiring even higher level thinking processes. They can tie nouns and verbs together into a phrase or sentence, such as "Get ball" or "Eat cookie." These statements indicate that children are using words to form ideas or processes. They can put several terms together to create ideas and relationships. They can start to verbalize the cause-and-effect relationships they have observed and experimented with during their earlier development. They might ask, "How grow?"

Young children also use incorrect forms of words to express themselves. A young child, for example, may say to his grandmother, "Mom-Mom, you are a good cooker." This evidences the child's use of adding *-er* to a word to express action such as *player, singer,* or *worker.* The generalization to the word *cooker* is an interesting phenomenon considering the child, most likely, has never heard *cooker* used in this way. Making sense of these patterns in the use and form of words is an example of the logic required to understand mathematical and scientific concepts and ideas.

Moreover, comprehension for spoken language is evident when a child hears the word *ball* and then looks for a particular ball. Learning to link language to impressions and experiences is also important in the development of mathematical and scientific thinking, and requires the same interpretations, understandings, and meanings.

EMERGENCE OF SYMBOLIC LANGUAGE

Symbolic or written language develops similarly to oral language. Both develop as children see and hear language as they interact and explore with others who use the same language. An example of children beginning to recognize written language is when they learn the alphabet or numbers. Children enjoy saying their ABCs and singing the familiar ABC song as well as rote reciting of numerals. *Rote recitation* does not involve conceptual meaning or understanding; it is an example of learning a verbal pattern. There is a *stable order* in its recitation, similar to reciting the numbers: C always comes after *B*; or *eight* always comes after *seven*. Young children do not always evidence their knowledge of this stable order because it lacks conceptual meaning. For the child, however, just being able to say the ABCs provides a sense of accomplishment.

Young children begin to recognize shapes of letters and numbers through constant play with blocks and plastic or magnet representations of them, or by seeing them on interactive toys or electronic media. They see each letter and numeral as a separate entity. Learning these arbitrary letters or numeral names is a necessary step in learning how to represent *conceptual understandings* of letters and numerals. A preschooler, for example, asks a teacher how to make the letter *B*. In response, the teacher asks why it is important to know how to make the letter *B*. The preschooler then shows the teacher a drawn picture and explains that the creature is saying "Boo!" This use of the letter *B* illustrates the difference between rote learning of a symbol and applying the conceptual meaning to a symbol for sounding out an important word.

It will be the knowing of the letter sounds that will help the young child learn how to construct and read combinations of letters. Recognizing the sounds that the letters make and that letters can be combined to form new sounds marks a readiness for further language development. The child begins to understand that letters are grouped into words, then words can be grouped into sentences. Children's ability to actually write the alphabet and write words and sentences cannot occur until they have internalized the shapes of the letters and can duplicate their sounds.

Children become increasingly competent in representing their ideas and understandings through language as they communicate with others. Peers and adults become models for language use and enhance children's opportunities to communicate. Continual, active, concrete experiences encourage and support children's ability to represent their experiences with oral and written language. Indeed, education is, as Dewey theorized, active and constructive. As early-child educators, we must be continually aware of the many ways children represent their thinking.

Providing young children with interesting toys allows the necessary scaffolding for their language learning and development. Such toys include stacking cups and rings, puzzles and mosaics, animals and farm houses, blocks and building toys, various pull toys, and real things from the environment. As children play and pretend, they use actions, props, and words to create symbols for what they are doing and experiencing.

MATHEMATICS DEVELOPMENT

The foundation for children's mathematical development is established in the earliest years. Mathematics learning builds on the curiosity and enthusiasm of children and grows naturally from their experiences. Mathematics at this age, if appropriately connected to a child's world, is more than "getting ready" for school or accelerating them into elementary arithmetic. Appropriate mathematical experiences challenge young children to explore ideas related to patterns, shapes, numbers, and space with increasing sophistication.—(NCTM, 2000, p. 73)

Mathematics is a particular way of thinking and all children everywhere do it quite naturally. From their earliest encounters, children explore the abstractions of mathematics. Parallel to the development of language skills is the development of concepts related to basic areas of mathematics. We can follow the development of mathematical concepts as we look at infants and toddlers. The basic mathematical concepts addressed here are pattern, sequence, seriation, spatial relationships, object permanence, sorting, comparing, classifying, and one-to-one correspondence.

Pattern

An important mathematical concept that infants develop is pattern. Pattern is the underlying theme of all mathematics and science. It is our ability to discover and recognize patterns that helps us understand how our world works in logical and predictable ways. Experiences with observing and making sense of patterns are what helps young children become logical thinkers who can reason and think critically.

As infants are cared for in predictable ways, they experience the idea of patterns. They easily begin to recognize and anticipate the rhythm or pattern of their care. As they experience this daily routine, infants come to anticipate the sequence of events. Such experiences are important to the development of recognizing the logical patterns that will be discovered later in their mathematical and scientific experiences. As babies approach their first birthday, they anticipate sequences and patterns in games that include patty-cake, peek-a-boo, singing, dancing, touching of the nose and toes, and feeling different textures. These rich experiences help children to develop the ability to predict and anticipate events.

Sequence

Sequence, like pattern, is a mathematics concept that children internalize early in life. Sequence refers to the organization and order of successive events and experiences. Recognizing sequ-ences helps young children's developing sense of order, logic, and reason. They begin to recognize the sequencing of their day and are able to predict what may happen next. They may also observe the sequence of seeds growing into plants, the sun rising and setting, the melting of snow, or the leaves falling from the trees. Each of these events involves sequences in nature. As children become more sophisticated observers, they can discover sequences in daily activities and involvements.

Before the age of 2 years, children tend to involve themselves in activities that require sequencing, such as taking turns, following a certain order when doing a task, or learning how to get dressed. Children may also use

Dan Floss/Merrill

Activity: Observe children doing self-directed construction playing. Watch and listen to their discussions. How do they describe the sequence of their role-playing events?

sequencing in play; for example, they may push all the blocks off the table and then one by one pick them up and put them back on the table, only to knock them all off again. Young children often repeat a sequence of events numerous times, because the predictability of these actions is enjoyable.

As children listen to stories either from books or other people, they begin to build concepts for sequence: what comes first in the story, next, and how the story logically unfolds. They often like to predict what may happen next. This type of activity helps to build a mind-set for rational and logical thinking, which again are important skills for budding mathematicians and scientists.

When children play in a sandbox they are constructing. When they use building blocks they set goals for what they want to build. Playing with dolls and figures requires that the children develop story lines about what the dolls are doing. Playing with racing cars promotes decisions about which car comes in first. Each of these activities designed by children requires an understanding of the concept of order and sequence. We can evaluate children's true understanding of sequence better by watching their actions than we can by listening to their verbalization. A child might be using sequence skills in many activities, but because of their developing language skills, may not be able to describe to you the process they are doing through play.

Soon after children start to make sentences, they give great detail about processes they use to make play-doh cookies, paint a picture, or create roads in the sandbox. They tell about how they will plant seeds in the garden or in the flower box.

Children will act out sequences of events with toy figures that may represent family members—Mom-mom, Poppy, Daddy, Mommy, Aunt Rachel, and cats Shadow and Sunshine. This type of play illustrates how a child makes sense out of events. Such active play fosters personal meaning (Isenberg & Quisenberry, 2002). Children can also be encouraged to put photographs of the family vacation at the seashore in order according to what happened first, second, and so forth. Such observations are valuable in evaluating the developmental level of children.

Seriation

Seriation is a mathematics concept that involves organizing or ordering things in a logical way. Consider toys that can be manipulated, such as different-sized stacking rings or blocks. Early in the use of these types of toys, children do not attend to the seriated relationship, of which ring or block goes on first. Over a period of time, however, the child will try to put the largest item on the bottom, as the rings are seriated by size. Exploring and discovering this

A 24-month-old explores the concept of seriation with a set of nesting toys.

Darci Houser

seriated set of rings is important for logical mathematical thinking. In addition, these types of investigations are interesting, engaging, and motivational.

Other types of seriated toys and tools include cookie cutters in different sizes and pie plates in varying diameters. These toys can be explored for seriation of their nesting attributes. Such explorations can prompt children to tell stories relating to the seriated sizes of the toys, with encouragement from teachers. For example, a young child playing at a play-doh center with a seriated set of bunny cookie-cutter shapes could be asked about the "baby bunny" and the "mommy bunny," and eventually she might tell a story about them. Children's self-directed play often develops and utilizes seriation skills. Seriation becomes more natural as children enter school as kindergartners and continues to become more sophisticated through the primary grades.

Spatial Relationships

Another important concept developed in mathematics is spatial relationships. The games and interactions that comprise play in infancy also help babies become aware of their body parts and develop a sense of their physical self. Such exploration helps them to know where they are in relation to their world. As toddlers become more skilled with moving about their world, a concept called navigation, they experience spatial relationships firsthand. They navigate themselves through a play tunnel or space fort, they begin to climb on play structures and equipment. These experiences will be the foundation for more mathematics concepts to follow involving directionality and position in space, such as the concepts of *up, down, over, next to, under, above, beside, in between, first,* and *last.*

Object Permanence NB

Babies can discover the important concept of object permanence in a simple game of peek-a-boo. For very young babies, this is a fun game because it elicits an element of surprise when someone appears and then disappears. Learning that the person or object does not actually disappear is a major accomplishment for a little one. Such a discovery is important for the mathematics concepts that will follow. Once babies know, by about 9 months of age (Piaget, 1963), that something is still there even when it is hidden, they will begin to be more observant and notice similarities and differences among the objects themselves. Such observations and experiences of objects lead to sorting and classifying. Piaget explains that knowledge arises neither from objects nor the child, but from interactions between the child and those objects.

Sorting NB

Sorting occurs when things with like attributes are grouped together. As Poole (1998) reports, if you give an 18-month-old five blocks and one ball, the child will handle and examine the ball (the different object) for a longer time than the blocks. This activity suggests that the child feels the difference between the blocks and the ball and wants to explore the different one longer to make sense of the difference. As such, the concept and process of sorting begins to be evident. When young children put the blocks in the block corner, the books on the book shelf, their socks in the big box, or the toy animals in the wooden barn, they are sorting.

Toddlers are likely to group similar objects together quite easily, whereas seriating or sequencing objects by a specific characteristic is more difficult. For example, if you give 4-year-olds a group of stuffed teddy bears and ask them to arrange them by size, they will focus on the big bears and the little bears without considering the seriation or the ordering by size.

Comparing

When toddlers sort items and put them into two groups, such as the big teddy bears and the little teddy bears, they are demonstrating the concept of comparing. In comparing, children identify and examine specific properties of different objects or ideas and then make judgments about how they are similar and how they are different. Comparing causes a person to look at details and specifics instead of generalities, to observe and study more carefully. Noting that some things are big and some things are little requires a judgment about attributes or qualities of things.

Having children make comparisons is valuable because it requires them to actively make observations related to specific items. They must look for divergent ideas, to go beyond the obvious. Beginning activities that involve comparing tend to be of objects common to the children's environment. They can compare cars and trucks, dogs and cats, apples and oranges, or cookies and crackers. These activities are important for children in that they promote the use of the five senses.

After a child has developed and used the skill of comparing concrete objects, teachers can extend this to comparing ideas. Children can compare sunrises and sunsets, seasons, a pumpkin and an apple, a carrot and cucumber, story lines from Eric Carle books, or songs and poetry. Charting their ideas about the similarities and differences of two things or events is helpful in developing expressive language.

Classifying

Classifying is a way of comparing. Classification refers to putting like things together and naming the group, such as big bears, little bears; shiny shells, dull shells; round buttons, square buttons; or smooth rocks, rough rocks. Classification schemes are important for young children to construct, as they are central to scientific thinking. Rocks, seashells, birds, seeds, and just about everything in nature has a classification system defining it.

More specifically, classifying is the division of items into groups by identifying a specific attribute that we recognize. We identify specific attributes or pertinent discrete characteristics that distinguish items within the collection. We can classify cars and trucks, dogs and cats, meats and vegetables.

What is your favorite collection? Does it remind you of something?

Classifying is a natural activity for young children. They love to collect items from nature. Rocks, leaves, acorns, seashells, and pinecones become important collections. Children separate their treasures by texture, color, shape, size, and favorites. *Attributes* are inherent characteristics of objects. Classification is often explored with commercial manipulatives called attribute blocks. Typical attribute block sets classify by color (red, blue, yellow), size (big, small), shape (square, circle, rectangle, triangle), and

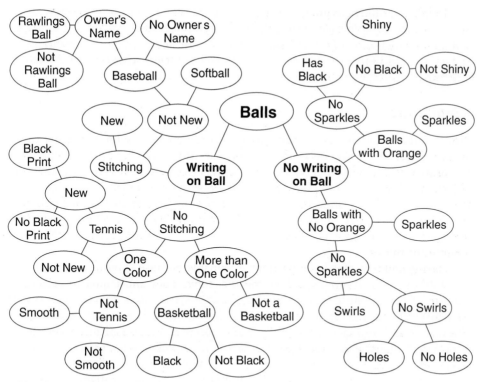

FIGURE 1.2   Classification chart of balls. (Keller & Brickman, 1998)

thickness (thick and thin). Attribute blocks are valuable for initiating classification development because the attributes are discernable.

It is also good to use more natural objects than attribute blocks, objects that are real aspects of the child's world. As mentioned, young children can gather, play with, and sort items such as seashells, leaves, seeds, rocks, and other natural objects from their backyard, nearby park, or other natural area.

Classification is an extension of sorting. In a classification, the collection of items continues to be divided into subgroups until each item is unique. Children can design classification of common objects around them. Classifications tend to be based on more obvious characteristics so that all can agree on how the items fit in the classification. See Figure 1.2.

One-to-One Correspondence

As toddlers have experiences with authentic hands-on learning, and with counting and sharing, they begin to develop the concept of one-to-one correspondence. When distributing a snack, for example, toddlers can give each child one mini muffin or one orange section. In this way, they are learning to relate to the notion of one for each person: "One for you, one for you, one for you, and one for me." Teachers can provide many opportunities to distribute "one" to "each child" and model this concept.

One-to-one correspondence extends as toddlers count a collection of items. Toddlers learn the counting sequence of numbers but are not always consistent in their ability to name the numbers in order. Toddlers seem to enjoy practice counting and know "how" to count although the actual sequence of naming numbers is not always followed. Teen numbers are often confused or left out. Teachers can model the stable order principle and keep track of counted items when counting a collection of things (e.g., 1, 2, 3, 4, . . .).

Learning to count is a similar process to learning the alphabet. Wanting to show what they know, children take great pride counting aloud. They seem to enjoy reciting the counting numbers and will attempt to count objects in their environment. They may not have one-to-one correspondence or stable order, but practicing these skills is important. We must recognize, however, that children's verbal counting does not indicate real conceptual numeric understanding, only that they can sequence particular sounds. We may ask toddlers how many blocks they have, and they may give a number that seems to be selected at random. By about age 4 or 5 years, however, they are able to understand the logical concepts for numbers under 10.

As their skills develop, children relate the rote counting sequence to rational counting. They might have a stack of blocks in front of them and start pointing to particular blocks and, at the same time, start the counting sequence. However, close observation indicates that they might count at a different rate than that at which they point. It is also common for them to point to the same items more than once.

For children to be able to count rationally, they need to demonstrate one-to-one correspondence. This is demonstrated when a child actually relates the counting to specific individual items. Touching each item only one time as the child recites the counting sequence illustrates this concept. "This is car 1. This is car 2. This is car 3." Children can confirm their one-to-one correspondence by keeping track of each item counted.

Relating the concept of one-to-one correspondence to rational counting is a complex skill. Young children must be able to keep track while reciting a stable order of numerals to their one-to-one counting. This skill often does not occur until the kindergarten years.

The mathematical concepts highlighted here are important components of rational and logical thinking. As children interact with their environment and with people in their world, they begin to see order in and make sense of their world.

J. David Keller

Observe the child counting the toys. Is the child using one-to-one correspondence?

THINKING SKILLS

Raths, Wasserman, Jonas, and Rothstein (1986) define thinking as a way of learning. Thinking is different from memorizing in that it requires decision making by the learner. Thinking causes one to not simply memorize "facts" but to understand and "acquire facts" through the process of making judgments based on available information.

Making a cause-and-effect relationship is a basic thinking operation. When children discover that they can cause a change, they model that process at every opportunity. When they find that pushing a button on the television causes the television to light up and make noise, this is what they choose to do. Children test an idea based on observing other people doing similar activities, and thus continue to test the idea until they learn that this is not a good idea, usually from a parent or caregiver.

Using thinking skills such as examining cause-and-effect relationships also promotes the development of questioning. Words that children use, such as *how, why,* and *where,* indicate they are examining cause-and-effect relationships. These words are critical in development, because they allow children to wonder, probe, explore, and ask questions as well as request tools, information, and knowledge. As language skills develop, children quickly become virtual questioning machines asking hundreds of questions each day: "Can I paint?" "Why do I have to do this?" "Will you help me?" "How can I do that?"

How we respond to these questions is critical to the formation and development of a child's attitude toward their active thinking and inquiring. If they are met with criticism and admonishment, they will infer that adults do not want them to think and ask questions. If they are met with answers, they will infer that questioning is a good way of learning what they want to know. If they are met with conversation, discussion, and available resources and materials, they will infer that questioning is a good way to promote and examine ideas. These opportunities are critical for their development of inquiry skills and confidence in analyzing ideas on their own. For every question that children verbalize, they internalize several more questions. Opportunities for children to play on their own terms give them the freedom to explore their own ideas at their own pace. Nondirected play is critical to the early development of questioning skills. Through play, children do not have to develop a formalized verbal question. They can formulate a concept and test it without trying to verbally share their ideas with others. They can repeat and revise the process at their own will. Individual nondirected play has no time constraints.

It is difficult to comprehend what is going on in the mind of a child. Consider the following example. Grandma and Grandpa had that great opportunity to take their grandson, Brandon, for an afternoon drive. Not wanting to waste the opportunity, they bombarded the child with questions for discussion. "What did you and Daddy do this morning? What would you like for dinner? What's your favorite toy?" But each question was met with silence. Brandon just looked outside the car, apparently oblivious to all discussion. Exasperated, Grandpa asked, "Brandon, what are you thinking?" Again he was met with total silence for an extended period. Finally, Brandon said, "I am thinking . . . I am thinking about the birds." Again, a pause. "I am thinking about how the birds fly."

We as parents, teachers, and caregivers become so determined to communicate with and help children grow that we sometimes forget that we need to, at times, get out of the way and let children internalize, explore, and think through their ideas.

Observe, from a distance, a child at play. From his actions, identify questions that you think are going on in his mind. Later, talk with the child and have him tell you what he was thinking. How often do the child's thoughts involve questions?

If Grandpa had not asked Brandon what he was thinking and had not given Brandon the time to respond, one could have interpreted that, being a 2-year-old child, Brandon had not readily developed the ability to understand and communicate at a basic conversational level. In reality, at this time, the basic conversation was getting in the way of Brandon's framing and developing a complex concept. It was important to Brandon to think about this idea, and it was not an easy inquiry for Brandon to verbalize into a clear question. He needed to exclude external forces and the time to think and phrase his question.

Questions involving "when" tend to be verbalized a little later in the development of a child, because "when" incorporates the concept of time, which requires more abstract development. For example, child wakes up at sunrise and says, "It's morning." Later in the day after a nap, he wakes up and says, "It's morning!"

Raths et al. (1986) identify specific thinking and reasoning operations that are basic to the development of young children. These include observing, imagining, problem solving, and collecting and organizing data.

By identifying, understanding, and appreciating these specific operations, we can monitor each child's development in thinking and reasoning. We can also monitor our skills as teachers in supplying classroom activities that promote the development of the child's skills in thinking.

Observing

Observing is the skill of using the five senses to take in information, organize it, and respond to it. We take in thousands of observations each second. Our mind records these observations and makes decisions based on what we observe; for example, we observe that it is snowing and we put on a coat to stay warm. To become efficient, we develop skills in selective observation, and thus ignore much of what we see. Indeed, this becomes a matter of survival. We learn to filter out disruptive noise when reading. When we look at a photograph, we focus on details of the photograph and ignore the hand holding the photo.

Developing skills in observation involves deciding and recording what observations are important (see Figure 1.3). With children, when we promote being good observers, we usually are referring to the amount of detail that the children observe. "What do you see when you look at the tree? What type of bird do you think built this nest in the tree? What do you think the bird is doing on the branch above the

FIGURE 1.3 Observing children.

It is critical for us as teachers to develop good observation skills when observing students. Can a teacher spot a child who is having difficulty with a task? Which manipulative does each student gravitate to during free time? How do children communicate with each other?

nest? Do you hear the baby robins?" Good observations identify detail that gives us information and contributes to our learning.

We can conclude that observing real things in our world is quite important in the development of logical thinking and reasoning in the mathematical and scientific minds of young children. It is also important for children to use their thinking processes within their own imaginations and thinking.

Imagining

Imagining is forming ideas about something that does not exist, dreaming in the mind ideas that have not occurred. Imagining tends to be a pleasant exploration of the mind. While imagining, we are not prohibited from ideas because of practicality or reality. We can design an intricate machine without worrying about how the gears will mesh. We can be an astronaut, hit home runs, and build cities. Imagining is personal. The ideas remain private in each person's own little world.

As teachers we sometimes have concerns about our children daydreaming. We desire for them to be involved in the classroom tasks at hand and paying attention. Their daydreaming is prohibiting them from learning whatever we want them to learn. Obviously we have little idea what they are daydreaming about. The ideas that they may be formulating could be far more complex than those we are trying to get them to learn. Perhaps, at times, our classroom is getting in the way of children using their highest levels of thinking.

Creativity is a form of imagining. When we use the term *creativity*, we are inferring that the creative thoughts go beyond the internal ideas to an expression of those thoughts. Creativity infers that the ideas are communicated to others through symbols, written words, story problems, drawings and diagrams, graphs, models, or illustrations.

Our greater goal as teachers is to help students learn to expand their daydreams beyond the mental images to hard-copy ideas that they share with their classmates, teachers, and families. Our classroom activities need to be created to encourage new and different ideas. We need to design our children's projects so that each child can express individuality. Can our classroom displays express different ideas rather than 25 similar drawings of a sunrise?

Observing and imagining are rich ways of being present in the world. Young children should be nurtured and encouraged to use these wonderful skills to solve problems.

Problem Solving

Problem solving has been defined as "what you do when you don't know what to do." If you know what to do, it is not a problem, it is an exercise (Keller, 1993). We often

A Child's World   17

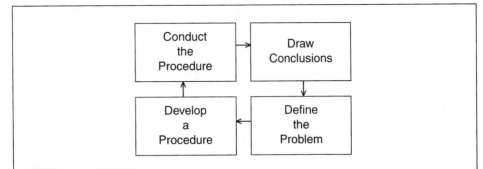

1. Define the problem.   Defining the problem is simply asking questions. Each time we ask a question we are defining a problem that we would like to study "How do seeds germinate?" "Why do kites fly?" "What causes the wind?" Questions of this nature indicate a need to know. The questions define problems that need to be answered.

2. Develop a procedure.   Once the problem is defined, a process or procedure must be developed that will collect the information needed to form an acceptable answer. Usually, more than one process can be used to give an acceptable answer. For example, ask children how high they can build a tower with straws or design a way to make a light work using batteries, wire, and a lightbulb.

3. Conduct the procedure.   Once the process has been established, the procedure needs to be conducted to collect the pertinent information or data. Processes might include taking measurements, completing mathematics calculations, and organizing data.

4. Draw conclusions.   Ideally, the data collected give the problem solver the information needed to answer the problem. Obviously, at times, the conclusion is that the answer is not obvious and that the problem-solving process must continue.

FIGURE 1.4   The four stages of problem solving.

give to our students tasks that we present as problems; however, we often explain to them how they should complete the task. When we outline the process for students, we take away the opportunity for them to use their actual skills in problem solving.

> Problem solving is a hallmark of mathematical activity and a major means of developing mathematical knowledge. It is finding a way to reach a goal that is not immediately attainable. Problem solving is natural to young children because the world is new to them, and they exhibit curiosity, intelligence, and flexibility as they face new situations. (NCTM, 2000, p. 116)

Kolb (1984) and Polya (1971) both identify four stages of problem solving as follows (see Figure 1.4):

1. Define the problem.
2. Develop a procedure for solving the problem.
3. Conduct the procedure.
4. Draw conclusions.

One can enter and exit this cycle at any area depending on the task at hand. Problem solving is a necessary part of life. We are constantly put into predicaments in which we need to develop a solution. Why won't my car start? How can

I find enough money to buy a new car? Why won't the rolls that I am baking rise like mother's rolls? In each of these situations, the answer is not obvious. We have to make decisions about how we will solve the problem.

Traditional classrooms tend to approach student learning through predesigned procedures. Teachers explain to the students how they should answer each problem. In mathematics we explain the "correct" process for adding two numbers together. In science, we give students a step-by-step procedure that they need to follow if they are to develop the correct results. These practices cause children to feel uncomfortable when they are put in actual problem-solving situations. Having been taught specific processes that they are required to follow in classroom situations, students become unsure when they have to make decisions about how to go about solving this new problem. An example of this is the insecurity that many children feel when asked to do a science fair project. They are concerned that regardless of how they do their project, it will not be done in a way that the judge or teacher would consider correct. They have been "taught" that there is only one correct way to do it.

During early development, children are highly responsive to direction by any authority figure. If they are constantly directed on how they should do things, they will look for additional direction from an authority figure rather than try to go it on their own. If they are encouraged to explore and try doing things their own way, they will feel comfortable experimenting. This attitude is critical for their developing confidence in handling daily responsibilities. Even in adulthood, we see people who have little confidence. They feel uncomfortable being put in decision-making situations because they might not do it the "accepted" way.

Children look at problems differently when they are able to self-define them. The difference is ownership. The question that they are examining is *their* question. They thought of the question and they want to answer it. Questions raised by other people such as teachers tend to not be as interesting or as important. An important skill for teachers to develop is to encourage students to ask questions and to use students' questions in leading classroom activities and projects. The Concept Explorations presented in this book give examples of activities in which children are encouraged to explore questions that they design and want to study.

Collecting and Organizing Data

Collecting and organizing data are basic thinking skills that relate directly to problem solving. In basic problem solving, the procedures that are developed often require the collection of information or data: "How high can the water rocket go?" "How many of the seeds germinate?" "How long does it take to run around the track?" These types of activities are important to the development of children because they require the students to collect and organize data.

NATIONAL STANDARDS IN MATHEMATICS AND SCIENCE

National standards have been developed for science and mathematics. The *National Science Education Standards* has been developed by the National Research Council (1996) through the cooperation of the National Science Teachers Association. The

Principles and Standards for School Mathematics has been developed by the National Council of Teachers Mathematics (2000). These standards identify specific **contents and** Processes that students should develop during their formal education. In science, content standards have been developed for Kindergarten to Grade 12. In mathematics, specific content **and process standards** are developed for Pre-kindergarten through Grade 12. This text focuses on the K–4 science standards and the Pre-K–2 math **content** standards. A complete list of the mathematics **Pre-K–12** process standards (problem solving, reasoning and proof, communication, connections, and representation) can be found in the Appendix. Charts showing the correlation of the chapter topics with the science and mathematics content standards are provided at the beginning and end of the text.

Identification and analysis of specific standards in science and mathematics underlie the processes and explorations presented throughout this book. The national standards for science and mathematics will be cited at length for each of the Concept Explorations in Part II of this book.

In the next chapter, we will present a sound theoretical foundation of teaching and learning at the preschool and primary level. Understanding how children think, learn, and feel is an important part of preparing for early childhood education. As we develop a philosophy and belief system for educating young children, we are challenged with providing inviting environments for children to explore. We must ask these questions: How do we invite inquiry and curiosity about a child's natural world and address the mathematical and scientific thinking that is essential for young learners? How do we engage in interactions that support children's curiosities and intentions for learning?

Review and Discussion Questions

1. How does understanding child development help us construct classroom environments that encourage children's natural curiosities and interests?

2. Give examples of resources, materials, and activities you would include in your preschool or primary-grade classroom that would promote problem solving and critical thinking.

3. Describe a scenario in which a young child might demonstrate an understanding of basic mathematics concepts such as patterns, sorting, classifying, and rational counting.

CHAPTER 2

Nurturing Child Development—
Environments That Promote Learning

Childhood has its own way of seeing, thinking, and feeling, and nothing is more foolish than to try to substitute ours for theirs.—J. J. Rousseau

Jean-Jacques Rousseau (1712–1778) was an 18th-century philosopher born in Geneva, Switzerland. As part of the intellectual movement called the Enlightenment, he theorized about teaching, learning, and childhood. Rousseau placed a great deal of emphasis on learning by experience, thus minimizing the importance of "book" learning. Rousseau also believed that children learn best when they are given opportunities to discover knowledge for themselves. He captured childhood as a time of exploration, invention, and discovery.

Throughout his life, Rousseau had a great interest in the natural sciences. When troubled, he would take refuge on the isolated island of St. Pierre in the canton of Bern, Switzerland. There, he would leave behind all his worldly concerns and immerse himself in the complete enjoyment of nature.

Rousseau's philosophy embraces children's curiosity, wondering, inquiry, and nature. During the Enlightenment period, Rousseau and other philosophers and educators advanced the thesis that learning should be centered on authentic experiences. Rousseau's philosophical ideas profoundly influenced educational leaders such as John Dewey, who advanced the ideas and ideals of experiential education during the first half of the 20th century, and Jean Piaget, a most influential leader in cognitive science.

> "Put questions within reach and let him solve them himself. Let him know nothing because you have told him, but because he has learned it for himself."
>
> J. J. Rousseau

Rousseau's philosophy is echoed in the reform movements of today that champion constructivist approaches to teaching and learning. Having children engage in authentic, naturalistic experiences involving science and mathematics supports Rousseau's ideas of meaning-making at its best. His idea about using concrete rather than abstract materials for young children also reflects current thinking about appropriate practice (Gordon &

Brilliant flowers, enameled meadows, fresh shades, streams, woods, verdure, come, purify my imagination . . . My soul, dead to all strong emotions, can be affected now only by sensory objects, and it is only through them that pleasure and pain can reach me. (J. J. Rousseau, 7th promenade)

Williams Browne, 2004). As we invite children into a world of exciting ideas and phenomena, we invite them to be curious, to wonder, to ask questions, and to explore. Whether it be gazing at clouds, measuring and mixing paints, wondering how seeds turn into trees, or simply chasing a shadow, these are the experiences that put learning within a child's reach.

We also hear Rousseau's wisdom echoed in the visions and philosophies of the present-day learned societies in mathematics and science—the National Council of Teachers of Mathematical (NCTM) and the National Science Teachers Association (NSTA). They encourage creative scientific and mathematical involvements for young children that are based on children's curiosity and approaches to inquiry that lead to sense-making about the world. This philosophy is at the core of current reform movements. If children are to truly become deep thinkers, problem solvers, and theory builders, they need to experience their world firsthand; they need to experience the many things and phenomena in their surroundings.

Note that the term *theory* as used in this book refers to the conjectures that children make about what they observe and think.

"A key factor to keep in mind is that the term 'theory' is used by scientists in a manner different from common usage. For most contexts, a theory is just a vague and fuzzy idea about how things work—in fact, one which has a low probability of being true. This is where we get the complaint that something in science is 'only a theory' and hence shouldn't be given a great deal of credibility. For scientists, however, a theory is a conceptual structure which is used to explain existing facts and predict new ones" (Science FAQ: Scientific Theories—Microsoft Internet Explorer, 2005).

In this chapter, we will investigate what it means to respect and nurture children so that they can develop personal confidence and competence in themselves as scientists and mathematicians. Specifically, we will present ideas for creating a culture of caring in which children are secure enough to explore, contribute, follow their natural ways of experiencing the world through play, and in the process begin to build theories about how things work. We will also discuss how to create a physical classroom environment that values curiosity and creativity and provides motivation for independent thinking that evidences autonomy and critical thinking.

CREATING A CULTURE OF CARING:
THE TEACHER'S ROLE

We are mainly concerned for our students as carers and cared-fors. We have to show in our own behavior what it means to care. Thus we do not merely tell them to care and give them texts to read on the subject; we demonstrate our caring in our relations with them.—Nel Noddings (1995, p. 190)

If we are to work constructively with young children so that they are engaged in creative exploration, discovery, and invention, then we need to provide environments in which all children feel safe expressing their ideas and feel secure that their ideas are valued. Relationships should cultivate mutual respect, understanding, and support between a teacher and a student, and among all students.

We can support children's naturalistic learning with a sound understanding about how children learn and how they seek meaning for scientific and mathematical ideas and concepts that they deal with in their lives. We need to create classroom environments that support creativity, inquiry, and wondering with interesting materials to explore and examine. In this type of environment, teachers exercise patience as they allow children to explore, experiment, and discover interesting phenomena. Teachers also become co-inquirers with the children as they investigate together the many questions posed and theories promoted by the children. Allowing children to explore and investigate at their own pace suggests to the children that their involvements are important and interesting. When children are engaged in learning that is meaningful to them, their learning is naturalistic and authentic. In such environments, we see motivation and ownership in their engagement and discovery.

Newmann and Wehlage (1993) examined five standards of authentic learning in the classroom. It is when children are engaged in authentic, naturalistic exploration, based on their curiosities, that they can begin to build theories and make sense of their world. Such freedom to explore is embraced in a culture where the ethic of caring is modeled.

Valuing Children and Childhood

As a teacher, it is important to recognize the meaning of childhood and what it means for each child. Most children embrace newness with curiosity and excitement. Children find joy in making sense of new experiences. Building relationships can be delightful and enriching as well. Such relationship building is facilitated when children spend time in environments that are caring, nurturing and supportive. When children have opportunities to explore their immediate environment, such as a meadow, a window-box garden; rain and a puddle; trees and seeds; sunshine and shadows; or rocks and sea shells, they develop strong, long-lasting bonds with their environment. The people, places, and experiences become a store-house of knowledge. Children will venture and explore their environment more confidently when they feel valued. When children work together with adults and other children to develop these environments, they also develop important long-lasting relationships.

Building relationships is an essential part of a child's growth. As adults, we need to respect and value children's natural development and their unique approaches to exploration and investigation. When we provide safe and inviting environments in a culture of caring, wondrous events can happen and lifelong relationships can build. To be a child is to be an explorer, a discoverer, and a wonderer of natural phenomena.

> Part of becoming an effective teacher in early childhood is to be able to differentiate between *childlike* and *childish*. Adults whose ideas we value most may exhibit childlike openness, curiosity, and interests.

Safety Within a Caring Culture

Childhood involves exploration and wonder, play and pretend. In these contexts, children are joyful in their approaches to figuring things out about their world. They revel in discovery and are curious about everything. As children explore, however, adults must ensure the children's safety at all times. Safety is important when children delve into dangerous activities. Limits need to be given gently but firmly so that children understand how to act in safe ways to avoid injury to themselves and others.

Besides safe ways to explore, safe environments are also a must. When gathering materials, be aware of how safe they are for children to explore. It is a good idea to discuss appropriate and safe ways to investigate materials. Tools for exploration should be easy to use and free of sharp or pointy parts. A safe environment also takes into account children's allergies to certain materials or foods, and the minimization of germs.

It is a good idea to consult local and national safety councils such as the Consumer Product Safety Commission and the National Safety Council for important guidelines. It is our role as teachers and caregivers to make learning fun and safe.

Play

A child's play is equivalent to an adult's work. As adults, we need to encourage children's curiosity and wonder. Play is an important part of this process. Even such great thinkers as Albert Schweitzer and Ralph Waldo Emerson espoused the value of play in their writing.

I know of no other manner of dealing with great tasks, than as play.—Albert Schweitzer

It is a happy talent to know how to play.—Ralph Waldo Emerson

As children develop, their play becomes more organized and predetermined. They plan ahead and make goals about what they want to accomplish through their play. Early experiences with blocks, for example, tend to be a general manipulation of the blocks into piles or towers. In this exploration, children are noticing the characteristics of the shapes and which ones stack and which ones roll. Later experiences with blocks are preplanned with specific goals such as building a bridge, road, or a whole community. In these types of experiences that include geometric exploration and construction, the NCTM explains, "Students should use their notions of geometric ideas to become more proficient in describing, representing, and navigating their environment" (2004, p. 97). Social contexts are interwoven in children's play as they relive and take on many different roles from their own life experiences.

Providing Emotional Security

Children feel secure and safe when they are among people who treat them with respectful care. When young children begin schooling in their preschool years, they encounter many new and interesting people and things. They will feel emotionally safe if their basic needs are met and they can "settle in" to their new environment without parents or the primary teacher. As teachers interact with young learners, they must listen and offer clear reflections to the children that each is an important person and contributor to the classroom culture.

In their book *Beginnings and Beyond*, Gordon and Browne (2004, p. 561) share statements (shown in Figure 2.1) about creative growth in young children. Modeling these beliefs and validating children's various approaches to learning and investigations lets children know that they are valued and that their unique ways of learning are acceptable.

Being Responsive

Young learners will gain a sense of competence and confidence when they contribute in class among their peers and with adults. For example, when children talk about the characteristics of a leaf, they use content-specific vocabulary such as *veins, symmetry, lobes, toothed* or *serrated edges,* or *pigments.* These conversations help children to gain confidence in their ability to verbalize about facts and ideas that they are exploring.

When we model acceptance, listen closely, and are responsive to children, we communicate to them that we are interested in them and value them for their ideas, questions, and approaches to thinking and problem solving.

The feelings young children experience in the early years can last a lifetime. It is important, then, to be sure these experiences validate young learners' competence and value. As children interact with each other, we need to be sure to help them validate their ideas to the group and to help them communicate and justify their thinking.

#2 my role during lessons

Constructing Meaning Through Misconceptions

At times, children will construct incorrect explanations and theories. When we help them to probe and ask additional questions related to the concept and provide

---

- It's OK to try something you don't know.
- It's OK to make mistakes.
- It's OK to take your time.
- It's OK to find your own pace.
- It's OK to bungle—so next time you are free to succeed.
- It's OK to risk looking foolish.
- It's OK to be original and different.
- It's OK to experiment (safely).
- It is special to be you. You are unique.
- It is necessary to make a mess (which you need to be willing to clean up!).

FIGURE 2.1 Statements that foster creative growth in young children. *Source:* Gordon and Browne, 2004.

meaningful and exciting provocations for more exploration and investigation, they begin to see the inconsistencies in their thoughts and revise their ideas, explanations, and theories. This process fosters the construction of logic and truth for mathematical and scientific ideas. Piaget likens this development of children's construction of logic to adults' construction of science. He explains that just as children go through levels of being wrong, scientists have developed theories in a similar manner. One example he cites is that scientists conceptualized the heliocentric theory, which is the theory that the Earth revolves around the Sun, after the establishment of the geocentric theory, which states that the Earth is the center of the universe. Once scientists had accepted the heliocentric theory, some 2,000 years later, they nullified the geocentric theory (Kuhn, 1962; Piaget & Garcia, 1983/1989). Piaget suggests that scientific truth is verified by empirical proof and rigorous logic. Likewise, once children establish more sound theories, they will not support their previous "immature" ideas. The suggestion is that children need opportunities and support to construct their own knowledge, ideas, and theories through exploration, debate, and critical thinking. Such actions support children and lead to their building autonomy and personal confidence. Teachers can support this developmental process by providing interesting environments for children to explore, asking provocative questions that spark thought and imagination; encouraging students to challenge others' ideas, modeling thought-provoking debate, and providing resources and ideas for experimentation.

Children are more apt to take a risk and share their ideas if they are in an environment or culture that views them as competent learners and contributors. Children's self-concept in a group impacts how they will react to new problems and ideas. Confident students develop a positive self-image that allows them to feel valued and important.

Building a Sense of Community

As teachers of young children, it is our responsibility to create, in the classroom, a caring community of learners. Having the children get to know each other and work together is an important part of engaging them in productive inquiry. To accomplish this important goal, teachers must encourage children to display mutual care, listening, and respect for each other. Teachers should also model ways to collaborate in problem solving and provide validation for children when they collaborate. The classroom design can contribute to children communicating and sharing ideas. Creating physical space that encourages communication and socialization is important. For example, having a carpeted area for gathering as a group, having cozy areas with a small couch or pillows for individual or small group gatherings, or putting desks into face-to-face groupings helps those in a classroom to develop a sense of community.

As we communicate with young learners, listening to their ideas and approaches to problem solving is important. Careful listening helps us to know what a child is thinking. When appropriate, reflect back to children what you think they are saying. We can be most responsive to children when we understand their thinking. We can then carefully ask questions, interact with them, and provide appropriate tools to support further exploration.

When we work alongside our students, we learn about them and how they engage in problem solving. We learn what they are curious about and what they feel is important to learn. Careful observation, including watching and listening, helps us to know children's interests and guides our instruction.

Keep in mind that teachers are the critical persons who determine and define how the children in the classroom function together. For children, teachers are critical in defining success and failure. As we engage in daily routines involving social and academic practices and experiences, we begin to define a way of learning and living together—we define our *classroom culture*. The ways we respond to children and engage them in daily activities determine the type of culture that will form in our classroom. This means that we must be good listeners when children talk and we must show them that we value what they say. We should reflect back to them what we understand about their ideas. We should be careful not to dismiss children's ideas or say things that will deter or stop their thinking. To build a strong sense of community, we need to model and value respectful communications and engaging collaborations. What the teacher does and what he says becomes a model for how children speak to each other and how they relate to each other and to the teacher. Establishing a community of learners requires a teacher who engages in learning himself. Establishing a community of kindness requires a teacher who treats children kindly.

FAMILIES AND SCHOOLS TOGETHER

An important part of the classroom and school community includes a child's family unit and culture. As teachers, we can gain a great deal by involving parents and families in their child's schooling. We need to regularly share information with parents about what the children are studying and discovering. The more we communicate with a child's family, the more the learning experiences that occur in the classroom will be continued through family activities and experiences.

We can accomplish home–school communication in a number of ways. We can invite families into the school to participate in daily activities alongside the children, write classroom newsletters with the children, hold family meetings in which children's work is observed and studied, display children's work that is carefully documented, and have parents and families engage in home inquiry.

Providing these types of communication and ideas for home exploration and inquiry, as well as providing books to read at home, demonstrates to the child that school and home are two connected cultures that value both the learner and the learning. When we send home narratives such as newsletters, explanations of projects being explored, or descriptions of units of study, we provide a window into our philosophy and practices. Oftentimes, parents' own experiences in school have been different from what their children are experiencing. Parents are appreciative of learning about the current philosophy of teaching and learning as it relates to their child's well-being and education.

CHILDREN'S QUESTIONS AND CURIOSITIES

If we value children as thinkers, it is important to design the classroom culture as one in which children are encouraged to make their thinking visible and evident. The world of science and mathematics should be one that is inviting and accessible to all children. Traditionally, these disciplines have not always been connected to the real lives of children. In her book *Talking Their Way into Science*, Gallas (1995) tells us, "I haven't met a child (or an adult) who was unable to think and talk like a scientist. I have met people who couldn't use the appropriate terminology or factual references about a scientific phenomenon, but they were all in full possession of a natural ability to question, wonder, and theorize about every aspect of the natural and physical world" (p. 3). When children are encouraged to ask questions and feed their curiosities, they are given opportunities to construct meaning about their world.

> "Almost all young children in almost all environments 'do science' most of the time; they experience the world around them and develop theories about how that world works"
>
> Conezio & French, 2002, p. 13.

Experiencing Newness

When children enter the classroom, they are met with newness in people, things, routines, and environment. Think about what children see when they enter your classroom. Do they see interesting things to explore? Are they allowed to touch them? Do you provide familiar and novel items to investigate? Can they reach the objects without disturbing other objects? How we fashion such an environment is critical to what will happen and unfold before our eyes.

You never get a second chance at a first impression. What will be your children's first impression of your classroom?

If we want to encourage children in natural exploration, we must provide interesting things for them to explore. We must also model the joy of wondering, being curious, posing questions, and exploring. Our classrooms should have an assortment of familiar and unfamiliar items from nature. If your classroom has a collection of pinecones and seashells on a sensory table or in a touch center, children see that these are valuable parts of their classroom. They should be encouraged to contribute other natural items that are of interest to them. As children bring in natural items, allow them time for show and share, because the social contexts of these items are important. Perhaps an item is from a family outing or something discovered while taking a walk in the park. The item may even be a family

FIGURE 2.2 Experience chart.

Seashells—What We See, Smell, Hear, and Feel
• **I see shapes** that are round, wavy, oval, straight, and jagged.
• **I see colors** that are white, brown, black, silvery, tan, beige, and orange.
• **I see shells** that are big, little, tiny, and humongous.
• **I smell the ocean and the beach**—it smells fishy and salty.
• **I hear the ocean** when I put the shell to my ear.
• **I feel the textures** bumpy, smooth, jagged, and rough.

treasure. Sharing these contexts tells children that their lives outside school are important and valued. Mathematical ideas of sorting, counting, measuring, and graphing also can be introduced as children observe the collections.

As children bring items in to school, sorting these items can be a worthwhile experience. Children can construct their own classification schemes with the shared items. For example, looking at an interesting collection of seashells, we can observe them with our senses and use rich language to describe what we see, feel, hear, and smell. Children's descriptions can be recorded on an experience chart (see Figure 2.2). Then children can be encouraged to group the seashells in ways that make sense to them. For example, shells can be grouped or classified as clamshell shapes or cone shapes, smooth or ridged, big or small, long or short, wide or narrow, and pink or brown. Sometimes, children can develop three or even four classification schemes. It is important for children to explain their classification scheme to you and to the class. At this point, a new shell can be introduced to the class to be placed in one of the groups. Such experiences utilize observation and logical thinking. These classification schemes can be recorded on the experience chart with the sensory descriptions. For support, you may want to read books about seashells, such as Pluckrose's (1994) *Walkabout Seashore*. The book displays beautiful photographs of seashells of different shapes, sizes, and textures. Using this book will spark the adventurous spirit of children to find shells like those featured.

As children see their ideas about seashells growing on the experience chart, other conversations about seashells can occur. We can move their thinking from *observation*, which is what they can actually see, feel, and smell, to *inference* about seashells, or what they do not actually experience. This movement from observation to inference is an important step for young learners, because it relies on experience, social and cultural contexts, and knowledge passed along from other sources such as parents, books, nature videos, or an oceanographer. An experience chart like the one shown in Figure 2.3 can be constructed.

Such discussion and conversation can lead the children to ask questions about seashells—a beginning step for scientific investigation and research. The *National Science Education Standards* (NRC, 1996) explains that "inquiry . . . includes the

FIGURE 2.3 Experience chart with inferences.

What We Know about Seashells

- They are from the water.
- They are in the ocean.
- We find them on the beach.
- We collect them.
- They had real animals living in them.
- They are pretty.
- We eat the things that are inside them.
- Clamshells are flat.
- Seashells are made of calcium.
- The shell protects the animal inside.
- They are in fish tanks.
- They are on jewelry.
- We use them for decoration.
- Newly found seashells are salty.

'process of science' and requires that students combine processes and scientific knowledge as they use scientific reasoning and critical thinking to develop their understanding of science" (p. 105).

Encouraging Wonder and Discovery

Having conversations, nurturing children's questions, and listening to their theories contribute to defining what is valued in the classroom. As we interact with the children in our class, we need to find ways to encourage their sense of wonder, curiosity, and discovery. As you introduce children to new experiences and new things, set aside time for them to ask questions and share their theories. When thinking about what they observed and what they know about seashells, for example, they can develop generalizations or theories about seashells as well as questions or curiosities (see Figure 2.4). Such processes of discovery can lead to a wonderful study of virtually anything. Try this process with a topic that children find interesting in their immediate environment, perhaps a collection of leaves, seeds, rocks, pinecones, fabrics, or plants. Watch, listen, and enjoy what happens.

Our Theories about Seashells	Our Questions about Seashells
• They come from the water.	• What lives in them?
• They grow living things.	• How big can they be?
• We eat things in them.	• How do they grow?
• They are homes for our hermit crab.	• What are they made of?
• They are in museums.	• Do they have eyes?

FIGURE 2.4 Theory and question chart.

Likewise, when gazing at the clouds, what are children thinking about? How can you build awareness for the clouds? What newness can be experienced about clouds? What do children see, hear, and feel when gazing at the clouds? What questions do they have about clouds? What do they think clouds are made of? As children share these rich contexts of their thinking, we can begin to provide opportunities for them to observe and study clouds. This process will help the children to refine their developing conceptualizations, theories, and knowledge about clouds.

With similar approaches to building awareness of the clouds, we can help children ponder about mathematics. For example, focus children's attention to things with patterns such as butterfly wings or an assortment of seashells, or things that show numbers or collections such as flower petals or a kitten's legs. Focusing on descriptions that involve numbers will model for children that mathematics is an important part of communicating about things in their world.

Teachers' Roles in Creating a Curious Classroom

Teachers have important roles when they allow children to construct curriculum and pose interesting questions to investigate and explore. Harlan and Rivkin, in their book *Science Experiences for the Early Childhood Years—An Integrated Affective Approach* (2004), delineate teaching roles for effective guidance of discovery science.

The *facilitator* creates a learning environment in which each child has a chance to grow. Planning, gathering needed cast-off materials, and actually trying experiments are science facilitator tasks. In this role, there is a tolerance for messiness as children work, a willingness to risk new ventures, and an ability to profit from mistakes.

The *catalyst* turns on children's intellectual power by helping them become aware of themselves as thinkers and problem solvers. This role contrasts with the "teacher" image so many of us carry from our own school days in which the teacher seemed to be the ultimate source of all knowledge. A teacher like this can dim children's intellectual power by somehow magnifying the distance between the teacher's knowledge and that of the students. Catalysts, on the other hand, set a positive, encouraging tone by staying in touch with their own excitement in discovery.

The *consultant* observes carefully, listens closely, and answers questions simply, while children engage in their explorations. In this role, the consultant offers small bits of information as learning cues, then asks students questions to help them focus on relevant parts of a problem. The consultant allows each child time to reflect on the new idea and tackle the solution independently. This role often intimidates beginning teachers until they can accept themselves as learners, too. The consultant role is a supportive coaching role rather than a directive one.

The *model* deliberately demonstrates to children the important traits of successful learners, such as curiosity, appreciation, persistence, and creativity. (pp. 22–23)

These conceptualizations of the teaching roles we model help us to examine our self-perceptions as teachers. We need to continually be mindful of how children learn. By engaging in the Concept Explorations presented later in this book, you will take on the supportive role of one who respects and encourages child-initiated inquiry and problem solving. Teachers who model interest, wonder, curiosity, and inventiveness are likely to have students who exhibit these characteristics or dispositions. The Concept Explorations provide numerous ideas for exploration of the natural world of the child. The invitation to be curious and explore awaits each of you.

WIGGLE ROOM AND OPPORTUNITIES FOR MOVEMENT

Wondrous opportunities await young learners both outside and inside the classroom. Classroom environments should have ample materials for exploration such as puzzles, mosaics, blocks, ramps, toys, books, art, and items from nature. Such materials help children to represent their ideas and theories about their world through individual and collective investigation, exploration, expression, and play.

Consideration should be given to the size of the manipulative materials that are available for the children in your classroom. For young children, because gross motor skills are developed earlier than their fine motor skills, they have difficulty in handling small objects. Large objects give more flexibility for young children's competencies. Having an assortment of items to manipulate can promote gross and fine motor experiences.

Classrooms should be equipped with many materials and tools to maximize approaches to problem solving. Multirepresentational explorations contribute to the processes of problem solving, theory building, and exploration, as well as to the development of reasoning and logic. As children test their ideas with a variety of materials, they are able to consolidate their understanding. Communicating and sharing their discoveries is a natural part of this type of classroom culture.

Classroom materials and resources should be accessible to all children. Care should be given to accommodate children with special needs. Talk to parents and caregivers of children with special needs about specific needs so that you can construct play spaces that are inviting, safe, and engaging for every child. Individual Educational Programs that have been developed for students with special needs should be reviewed and updated by teachers and collaborating professionals. Such accommodations are important if we are to model ways for all children to be inclusive and accepting of others' special needs.

Creating an Environment

A child's living space is wherever he is at the moment. It could be his backyard jungle, his pirate ship bed, his fort under the dining room table, or his home away from home—his classroom. In any of these environments, imagination and reality come together to spark imaginative play, exploration, discovery, and learning. What we choose to put in these living spaces is most important. A child's living space should be filled with interest to promote knowledge. Items found in nature are just as important as commercial items. Try to think about how you feel in different environments and what it takes to spark your interest, curiosity, and imagination. Then create your classroom around specific interests that students demonstrate, so they gain ownership in the learning experience. "Look closely to see what children are curious about—then look for opportunities to help them choose their pleasures!" (Honig, 2003, p. 29).

Cooperative Culture for Independent Thinking

Respecting children as capable learners and contributors of knowledge is an important part of creating motivation and independent thinking. Children have great potential and can be encouraged to put forth their ideas when they feel that their ideas will be embraced as important and enlightening. An environment that supports children as important contributors is one in which cooperation is valued over competition. Children should not feel that they are vying for recognition and "right" answers. When children experience cooperative approaches to problem posing and problem solving, they feel valued to take risks in advancing their thoughts, questions, and ideas.

As we work with children, we need to be actively observing and listening to what they do and what they communicate. Oftentimes children discover a concept in science without saying a word; their actions define their exploration and discovery. It is important to make note of these discoveries and reflect the discovered concept or idea to the child as an acknowledgment of that discovery. When children hear language attached to what they do, they learn ways to express themselves. In this way, children have a model to follow and then they learn ways to communicate their ideas and discoveries to others. This communication models the importance of group discussion and the exchange of ideas. Listening and verbal discourse are both important parts of a community of learners. Through active listening, adults demonstrate interest in what children are expressing. Active listening requires adults to put aside their own thoughts to connect deeply to the child's thoughts. This important practice cues adults in to children's interests and curiosities.

Classrooms need to be fashioned is such a way as to provide ample opportunities for play, imagination, magic, and make-believe. Ample time blocks are required for children to become involved in exploration. If children are interested in a particular investigation, then they can attend to it for long periods of time. Oftentimes, the attention span displayed is connected to the level of interest and engagement. The more interesting an investigation is, the longer students can stick with it. Within reason, then, it is important to allow children to pursue their interests without interruption.

CONCEPT EXPLORATIONS

The Concept Explorations in this book are catalysts for inventive and creative exploration and learning. Each one is designed to excite children's natural ability to wonder and to ask questions. As discussed in Chapter 6, children should "own" the curriculum and guide its development and inquiry. As children wonder, ask questions, and explore interesting environments and phenomena, curriculum unfolds. It is the responsibility of the teachers, then, to provide children with the appropriate structure, resources, tools, and stimulating provocations to advance the concept explorations to fit the interests, emerging ideas, and theories of the children.

Concept Explorations can be considered as either long-term projects or short-term investigations. It is in the spirit of these studies that we take cues from children and their curiosities to advance their approaches to learning and theory building. In this sense, concept explorations are different from units and thematic-based teaching. They are more child centered and less prescribed than traditional curricular unit-based or theme-based approaches to teaching. Teachers involved in Concept Explorations with their children make fewer decisions about the path the explorations take and instead support the children's line of inquiry and investigation. Children pose their own questions and design their own approaches to investigation. Teachers support the design and the carrying out of experiments and projects. In this way, children have a greater stake in their learning and gain confidence in their abilities to be seekers of knowledge rather than absorbers of knowledge that is transmitted to them through direct teaching and prescribed lessons.

The philosophy of the Concept Explorations described in this book are in concert with the principles espoused in Dewey's theory of experience. Dewey advanced the theory that children learn best when they plan their own activities and carry out their own plans for learning. He believed that children learn through experience and that children and teachers need to have real-world investigations with real things in order to gain deep conceptual knowledge. He believed that education is a social process, education is growth, and education is not preparation for life—education is life itself (Dewey, 1938; Dewey & Dewey, 1915).

Since Dewey's time, others have provided contemporary support for the "project approach," a cornerstone of these concept explorations. Katz and Chard, for example, in *Engaging Children's Minds: The Project Approach* (2000), advanced the idea of children engaged in inquiry that is child centered and question focused. Projects evolve around questions that children ask so naturally about their world. These questions capture what children wonder about and are interested in learning. Projects are ways of organizing collective approaches to problem solving. The project approach is also exemplified in the Italian early-childhood programs of the Reggio Emilia schools as cited in *The Hundred Languages of Children: The Reggio Emilia Approach to Early Childhood Education* (Edwards, Gandini, & Forman, 1998).

DOCUMENTING EXPERIENCES

Documenting children's work is a wonderful way of capturing the history and development of their thinking and ideas. As children begin to define what they are interested in investigating, as they begin to put their curiosities and interests in the form of questions, and as they begin to define problems they want to solve, their ideas need to be recorded. When these ideas are documented, children can reflect upon and sort them. Teachers can support children to examine their questions and thus construct and implement approaches to problem solving. The first step is for children to define problems to explore. A thorough explanation of the four stages of problem solving will be addressed in Chapter 3.

Documenting Through Concept Exploration

- *Classroom journaling* can be done to record children's evolution of thinking and approaches to problem solving. Each day, the children and teacher can assemble to discuss the day's accomplishments. Perhaps initial experiences or observations of materials set out in the room (e.g., a collection of seeds or shells, geometric shapes, pictures of patterns in nature, or a session gazing at clouds) can be recorded. As children hear themselves sharing their ideas, questions and curiosities can emerge; and approaches to getting answers can be formulated. Each stage of problem solving can be recorded in this ongoing journal.

- *Pictures and video clips* can be taken throughout the concept exploration process to enhance the text of the journal. Photographs of children engaged in exploration, observation, experimentation, and investigation capture the process for later reflection and analysis. Video clips can capture children's verbal and physical engagement.

- *Poster or panel construction* can be done at each step of the way to represent aspects of the concept exploration. These will tell a wonderful story of how a concept exploration was initiated, developed, and explored. The posters or panels can be displayed in the classroom or the hallways in order to share the development and process involved in the concept exploration with others. Having photographs with captions adds richness to these types of displays.

- *Parent newsletters* can be constructed on a regular basis to provide a window into classroom activity. Parents and families are part of a child's world. Sharing school work with a child's family enhances a child's sense of importance and accomplishment.

- *Web sites* can be designed and updated with children's activities to provide parents and other friends and relatives from around the world visual and auditory observations of classroom experiences.

Documentation is a collaborative process initiated by teachers and children. As children begin to see how their ideas and work can be documented, they become excited to see the story of their work unfold. In this way, students experience a great sense of accomplishment.

Review and Discussion Questions

1. Describe a classroom environment, including outdoor play spaces, that reflects the ideas and philosophy advanced by theorists such as Rousseau (nature), Dewey (experience), and Piaget (thinking).

2. Describe the teacher's role in a classroom that embodies and promotes the ideas espoused in this chapter—creating a culture of caring, building confidence in children, modeling critical thinking, and encouraging joy in learning.

3. Share ways to include families in your explorations in mathematics and science so that children see how their experiences in school are extensions of their daily life.

CHAPTER 3

The Process of Problem Solving for Children

Problem solving is what we do when we don't know what to do.

Problem solving is decision making. Throughout our lives, every day, we are constantly making decisions, big and small. Should I feed my cat now? Should I wear my green shirt? Should I have oatmeal for breakfast? Should I purchase a particular car? Should I study for the math test, or write my English composition?

We make each of these decisions based on information that we gather. Is my cat meowing for food and is her food dish empty? Is my green shirt clean? Is there oatmeal in the cupboard? Did Mom or Dad volunteer to make pancakes? Have I saved enough money to buy a car? How much time do I have before I need to leave for school? Developing good skills for examining and solving problems is critical for being successful and confident and enjoying life.

In Chapter 1, an overview of the four stages of problem solving was presented. This chapter stresses the design and nature of experiences that we offer our children to help them develop good problem-solving skills.

THE NATURE OF PROBLEM SOLVING

Problem solving is an immediate part of everyone's world. We are constantly put into predicaments in which we need to develop a solution to a particular problem. Why won't my car start? How can I find enough money to by a new car? Why won't the bread that I am baking rise like my grandmother's bread? In each of these situations, the answer is not always obvious, so we have to make decisions about how we will solve the problem.

The National Council of Teachers of Mathematics (NCTM), in their *Principles and Standards for School Mathematics* (2000), states that for students in preschool through grade 12,

> [p]roblem solving means engaging in a task for which the solution method is not known in advance. In order to find a solution, students must draw on their knowledge and through this process, they will often develop new mathematics understandings. (p. 52)

For preschool through grade 2, NCTM (2000) states the following in the *Problem Solving Process Standard*:

> Problem solving is natural to young children because the world is new to them, and they exhibit curiosity, intelligence, and flexibility as they face new situations. The challenge at this level is to build on children's innate problem-solving inclinations and to preserve and encourage a disposition that values problem solving. (p. 116)

Kolb, Rubin, and McIntyre (1984) and Polya (1971) identify four basic stages of the problem-solving cycle: (1) define the problem, (2) develop a procedure for solving the problem, (3) conduct the procedure, and (4) draw conclusions (Figure 3.1). These four stages lead from one process to the next. Often during the fourth stage, new problems are defined and the cycle starts over again.

1. *Define the problem.*   Defining the problem is accomplished by asking questions. Each time we ask a question, we are defining a problem that we would like to explore, study, and solve. Why do leaves fall off trees? Why are some rocks smooth? What are stars? How do seeds germinate? Why do kites fly? What causes the wind? Why does my shadow follow me? Questions of this nature indicate children's curiosity and wonder about a particular phenomenon. They also provide a personal need to know, to find out, to understand. The questions define problems that we want to ponder and answer. When we pose our own questions, there is a high level of motivation to explore and discover.

2. *Develop a procedure.*   Once the problem is defined, we need to develop a procedure that will define a way to collect the information needed to form an acceptable answer. Usually, more than one procedure can be used to give an acceptable answer, and more than one resource can be identified. Time to think and share ideas during this stage is very important. Developing a plan or procedure to find something out will help children focus on the defined problem.

3. *Conduct the procedure.*   Once the procedure has been established, it is conducted to collect the pertinent information or data. Procedures include observations,

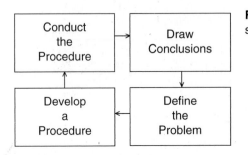

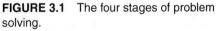

FIGURE 3.1   The four stages of problem solving.

reflections, discussions, thinking, taking measurements, completing mathematics calculations, and organizing data. These procedures should be documented so that they can be evaluated as useful or not useful in answering their questions posed in the "defining the problem" stage of problem solving.

4. *Draw conclusions.* Ideally, the data collected give the problem solver the information needed to answer the defined problem. Obviously, there are times when the conclusion is not obvious and the problem-solving process must continue or start over. So we ask new related questions and start the problem-solving process over. Stress to children that this process is the same one used by scientists to solve their defined problems.

PROBLEM-SOLVING STYLES

Kolb et al. (1984) have examined the nature of how people solve problems. With respect to the four stages of problem solving just discussed, they have learned that each of us has our own strengths in solving problems and that we feel more comfortable with one or some particular stages than others. This does not infer that one stage of problem solving is more important or more critical than another. It merely means that people approach problem solving in different ways.

If people's strengths in problem solving tend to be at the third and fourth stages of the problem-solving model, conducting the procedure and drawing conclusions, then they tend to be much more structured in the way they approach problems. These people are called **concrete sequentials** (Figure 3.2). They are people who function well when they follow standard routines that are set up by others. They are more comfortable if they are given thorough guidelines and procedures to follow or carry out. Concrete sequentials feel more comfortable if they and other people all follow the same standard procedure. The questions that they ask tend to be aimed at clarifying their tasks. This strength in organization helps them be more efficient in completing the tasks at hand.

People who are more comfortable at stage 1 of problem solving, defining the problem, and stage 2, developing the procedure, are said to be **random abstracts** (Figure 3.3). Sometimes they are casually referred to as *random romantics* because they tend to look at problems somewhat differently and enjoy the creative bent. Random abstracts prefer to have flexibility when examining problem-solving situations. They like to consider different options and try different approaches to problems.

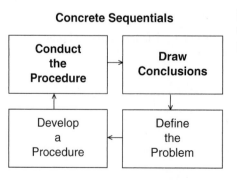

Concrete Sequentials

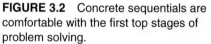

FIGURE 3.2 Concrete sequentials are comfortable with the first top stages of problem solving.

They are not tied to routines. Their questions tend to be of the tangential nature: "What are some related situations that might affect the task of phenomenon?" This flexibility can sometimes divert their attention from specific aspects of the problem, but their creativity often expands the options for problem solving.

To a concrete sequential person, a random abstract person seems to be disorganized and somewhat "off-task." On the other hand, a random abstract person might view a concrete sequential as inflexible. In either case, the two types of problem solvers can complement each other and model useful techniques as they work together to solve defined problems.

Active Versus Reflective Styles

In addition to looking at whether people have strengths at the random abstract or concrete sequential stages, it is important to examine their strengths as **active** or **reflective** participants. People who have strengths at the developing the procedure and conducting the procedure stages are termed, in this model, *active people* (Figure 3.4). They tend to see a task and want to initiate the problem-solving process as quickly as possible. Hence, they might start a project without complete concern for details that might arise later.

People who have strengths at the defining the problem and drawing conclusions stages tend to be more reflective (Figure 3.5). Whereas others might see a problem as complete, they want to linger and reflect on whether they completed the problem correctly or completely to their satisfaction. When presented with a situation, they tend to want to sit back, reflect, and think about the task before they initiate the

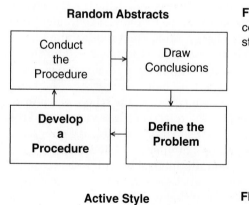

Random Abstracts

FIGURE 3.3 Random abstracts are comfortable working with the bottom two stages of the problem-solving model.

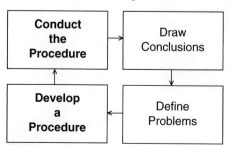

Active Style

FIGURE 3.4 Active participants want to "get right to work."

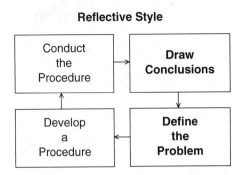

Reflective Style

Conduct the Procedure → Draw Conclusions → Define the Problem → Develop a Procedure → (Conduct the Procedure)

FIGURE 3.5 Reflective participants want to "sit back and think about" the situation.

process. They might say "Let's not jump into this until we think about what we have to do and what we want to find out."

HOW PROBLEM-SOLVING STYLES AFFECT CLASSROOM PRACTICES AND STUDENT EXPERIENCES

Teacher Tendencies

As teachers, our classrooms tend to accentuate the areas of problem solving that relate to our particular problem-solving styles. Teachers who are concrete sequentials tend to introduce more structure into their classrooms. The class routine tends to be more consistent and predictable. Each period of the day is well defined and each day consistently follows that schedule. Students are expected to follow specific identified guidelines for completing their assignments. Having a consistent routine often helps students identify the pattern of the day and the goals and expectations set for them.

Teachers who are random abstracts tend to be more open to alterations in the daily routine. They alter their activities and schedules based on what they perceive as the needs of the students or events that are taking place in the school or community. The classroom often appears to be "busy" with projects and materials around the room. The schedule may change based on current situations or students' questions.

These explanations of teacher tendencies do not infer that one type of teacher is superior to the other—they are just different. Both of these groups demonstrate particular strengths as teachers. Having a consistent classroom structure is an important tool for classroom management. When students know that there is a regular routine, they know what is expected of them, and this structure can promote the development of better organizational skills. Having a flexible classroom, however, is also valuable. This helps students learn to adapt to changes and explore alternative opportunities. For example, if students become very interested in an event, such as a raccoon that visited the school yard, a random abstract teacher is comfortable changing lesson plans and learning about raccoons.

It is important for us to recognize our strengths and approaches to problem solving so that we can expand ourselves in ways that support children in their unique approaches to problem solving and learning.

Student Tendencies

The nature of each student's problem-solving style is also critical in ensuring class-room successes. Concrete sequential students tend to need and want more structure. When given assignments, they want to know the details and requirements. How should I sort the rocks? How can we make a kite? Should I use a pencil or a pen? How many pages? What do I need to do to earn an A? Being given a wide variety of options can be frustrating to them because they are determined to please the teacher and do the project correctly. In pleasing the teacher, they often feel rewarded and successful.

Random abstract students, on the other hand, are often more open to options. When told that they may use a variety of options when studying a topic, they are comfortable. In fact, they tend to find the most unusual option for tackling the problem. When given detailed guidelines for their class work, they often feel limited or confined. For them, structure can be a barrier instead of a support.

TEACHER AND STUDENT INTERACTIONS

Recognizing our problem-solving styles as teachers and recognizing the nature of our students' styles are critical aspects of our classroom successes. When we understand the nature of our students better, we can give them better individualized support. Our open-mindedness is important. Deciding how to encourage and support students in their creativity is important. Deciding how much structure to provide in an exploration is also an important consideration as we think of realistic expectations and safety issues.

Random Abstract Teachers and Concrete Sequential Students

A teacher who fits into the random abstract style tends to answer students' questions in a way that gives the students freedom. When given an assignment, a student with concrete sequential tendencies might ask, "How long should the paper be?" A random abstract teacher might answer this by saying, "Long enough to tell us what you think is important." This can cause the student to feel frustrated because she wants to meet the teacher's guidelines for success, but may be unable to determine what those guidelines are. If the teacher instead responded by saying, "I find it difficult to do a good job in less than X pages," the student now has structure, but is not limited in how far she can go. This response also does not seem to be as confining to the random abstract students, because they have not been given a concrete number.

Concrete Sequential Teachers and Random Abstract Students

Let's look at the reverse situation of a concrete sequential teacher and a random abstract student.

A teacher once gave an assignment to his class to write a paragraph beginning with the sentence "I looked into the mirror and saw. . . ."

One student responded with "I looked into the mirror and saw nothing! I could not find my mirror. I had so much junk on my dresser, that I could not see my mirror." The student then went on to describe how he cleaned his room for the first time in three years and (in the last sentence) wrote "Yes, I had a mirror."

Because all of the other students in the class responded by describing their facial features, hair, eyes, teeth, freckles, and so on, the teacher tended to feel that the one student was being sarcastic toward the assignment and the instruction. From the student's perspective, however, he had completed the assignment to the letter, and enjoyed the opportunity to be creative.

Students who tend to be random abstracts are sometimes considered to be "difficult" by teachers who fit into the concrete sequential category because they are not as concerned with structure and prefer not to have a structure imposed on them. They answer questions in ways that might be considered sarcastic or confronting, because they are not similar to the responses that the teacher expected. Thinking outside the box fits these random abstract students. This independent thinking should be supported and encouraged.

CLASSROOM EXPERIENCES WITH PROBLEM SOLVING

Our goal, as teachers, is not to change our students' problem-solving styles. We should value and encourage them to grow in their own image. Likewise, our goal is not to discount our own teaching strengths. Our goal is to help each student develop strong skills in *each* of the four areas of problem solving. In addition, our goal is to strengthen our skills as teachers by having numerous activities representing *each* of the four stages of problem solving.

As discussed earlier, concrete sequential students have stronger skills in the areas of conducting procedures and drawing conclusions. They tend not to have strong skills in defining problems and developing procedures. Thus, our activities should expand on and encourage experiences for these students that strengthen those skills.

Random abstract students have strong skills in defining problems and developing procedures. They often need assistance in developing organizational skills. Thus, we need to incorporate activities that given them experience in recognizing the value of good organizational skills.

Active students have strong skills in developing and conducting procedures. Students in this classification usually become very involved in the classroom activities. They like to be physically involved; hands-on activities are their forte.

Reflective students have strong skills in defining problems and drawing conclusions. Students in this classification at times appear to be daydreaming because they are taking observations and information and thinking about them. They are often thinking about further questions that they have formed in answer to the original one.

Typical classrooms and textbooks tend to approach student learning through activities at the third stage of problem solving, conducting the procedure. Predesigned procedures and activities are presented to the class. Students are told what they need to accomplish and how they should go about the carrying out the assignment. Students are encouraged to follow particular step-by-step, well-defined procedures. It is suggested that in traditional classrooms, the majority of instruction is at the conduct the procedure stage. Students are told specifically what to do and how to do assignments.

In mathematics, teachers often explain to the students how they should solve and answer each problem. We explain the "correct" process for adding two numbers, for measuring something, or for defining geometric shapes. In science, we give students step-by-step "cookbook" procedures to follow in an exploration or an experiment if they are to get the correct results. We explain a specific process that the students should follow. We tell them that "If you do not follow the proper procedure, you will not get good results."

We often give our students tasks that we present as problems. However, we immediately explain to the students how they should complete the task. When we outline the process for the student, we have taken away the opportunity for them to use the reasoning skills critical for problem solving. Being aware of this practice can help us be more accepting of student-directed learning. Encouraging students to become critical thinkers is an important goal. Developing autonomy for learning is a lifelong benefit.

Experiences in "figuring out your own way" to solve problems are critical for giving students the confidence to explore. Having been trained to "follow the procedure!" students feel uncomfortable when they are put in problem-solving situations where they actually need to develop their own ideas about how to proceed. Having been taught specific processes that they were required to follow in classroom situations, they become unsure when they have to make decisions about how to go about solving this new problem. "Perhaps this is not the way the teacher expects and wants us to do this!" An example of this is the insecurity that many children feel when asked to do a science fair project. They are concerned that, regardless of how they do their project, it will not be done in a way that the judge or teacher would consider correct. They have been "taught" that there is only one correct way to do it. We can help children to become more autonomous by examining the way we think about the four stages of problem solving.

AUTHENTIC LEARNING—PROBLEM SOLVING IN THE REAL WORLD

We design our classrooms to be bright, attractive, pleasant, and inviting. We include many items to stimulate and entice the students to explore and examine. We want them to look forward to entering the classroom and being involved. But teachers often use commercial materials when "decorating" their rooms. Prefabricated cutouts, bulletin board borders, posters, and stickers are available. Use of these commercial materials can result in classrooms and classroom activities that become artificial. We ask our children to learn things that are not part of their everyday lives. We ask them to memorize facts and information that at some future time might be useful or valuable for them to know, but at this stage of their lives is not important to them.

Such experiences are frequently very scripted and artificial. These experiences cause students at all ages to lose interest in the task at hand and to divert their attention to other things. Thus, it is important for teachers to design students' experiences to relate to their daily lives and environment as much as possible. Opt for student-designed bulletin boards and borders, student-made posters and displays, student-generated collections, and see the excitement that this involvement generates.

During early development, children are very responsive to direction by an authority figure—parent, teacher, bus driver, and so forth. If they are constantly directed on how they should do things, they will look for additional direction from that authority figure, rather than try to "go it on their own." If they are encouraged to explore and try doing things their own way, they will feel more comfortable and confident when experimenting and exploring. This attitude is critical if they are to develop confidence in handling daily responsibilities. Even in adulthood, we see people who have little confidence and are very insecure when given tasks to solve or execute on their own. They feel very uncomfortable being put in decision-making situations because they might not do it the "accepted" way. They continually seek guidelines and expectations.

An analysis of most classroom texts, across the grade levels for mathematics and science education, will show that a majority of the activities tend to dictate to the students the content and procedures that they are to follow. This process in itself makes many of the experiences artificial. These are not typical of our daily real-life or "authentic" experiences. In typical situations, we do not have a standard, set plan that needs to be followed. We have to decide what we need to do to accomplish our goals and we need to decide how to do it. Many different activities are available that could be used with success to reflect these daily, real-life experiences. We will discuss some of these activities in the following section.

DESIGN OF CLASSROOM ACTIVITIES THAT ENCOURAGE PROBLEM SOLVING

Classrooms can be made to model real life in a process that is very natural both for the students and for the teacher. The basis for this curriculum design is a process called **inquiry**. *Inquiry* means many things to many people. The *National Science Education Standards* publication (1996) defines inquiry as:

> Inquiry is a multifaceted activity that involves making observations; posing questions; examining books and other sources of information to see what is already known; planning investigation; reviewing what is already known in light of experimental evidence; using tools to gather, analyze, and interpret data; proposing answers, explanations, and predictions; and communicating the results. (p. 23)

Particularly at an early age, it is important that we give our children continuous experiences that cause them to inquire.

Another definition for *inquire* is "to question." Questioning is a very natural process as anyone talking with a 3-year-old knows. Young children include in any conversation the terms "Why does . . . ?" "How come . . . ?" "When will . . . ?" "Where is . . . ?" "What . . . ?" These questions are very helpful to us as teachers and caregivers because they let us know what the child is thinking and the magnitude of his thought. At times the questions come so rapidly that we feel that they "get in the way" of our teaching. It is important to "sit back" and listen, because these questions could lead to the best explorations.

We can often see the results of children internalizing their own questions. We can observe them at play creating situations to observe cause and effect. They might run with a piece of crepe paper to see how it waves in the air. They might jump up and down to watch what their shadow does. They might change the position of a barrier before rolling a toy car into it to see how it affects the crash. No verbal question was asked. However, the child's actions verified the inquiry. We need to take note of these expressions of inquiry if we are to support children as thinkers and problem solvers.

Children's questions accomplish two major things. First, these questions transfer the ownership of learning to the child. They are learning about things important to them. In addition, these questions are the vehicles for helping teachers contribute to the child's learning because these questions help us understand how completely she has developed her ideas. In addition, these questions give us guidance in knowing how far along developmentally the child is in her stages of learning as related to how young children develop.

Consider one teacher's experience: While in an elementary school in India, a visiting instructor gave a group of fourth-grade children a bean and asked, "What questions do you have about this bean?" A boy responded with "Is this bean a monocotyledon or a dycotyledon?" The other students in the class all agreed that this was important to know. This information gained from the question told the visiting instructor that he needed to revise his learning activity. He needed to expand the scientific development so that it was at the level of the students.

TEACHING AT EACH OF THE FOUR STAGES OF PROBLEM SOLVING

We can initiate our classroom learning activities at any of the four stages of problem solving. Depending on the nature of the activities, there usually is a natural starting point and a process continuing through the different stages.

To help students *define problems* we can invite them to ask questions about things that are part of their daily world. What questions do you have about clouds? What do you wonder about when you think of birds? What are you curious about when you think about the wind? The questions that the students share with the class then serve as a nucleus for study. In addition, these questions inform us about the background knowledge that the students have. We can determine if the children have a much greater background in a certain subject than we thought, and when they have a very limited background. It also informs us about the ideas children have related to their own experiences as well as their involvements with books and multimedia.

To give our students an opportunity to develop skills at the *developing procedures* stage, we set up situations for the students to explore. For example, we might ask children to design a bridge made out of Popsicle sticks or plastic straws. We have defined the problem for them. We have not said how they should make the bridge. Their task is to develop a procedure for making the bridge.

Young children, often on their own, create activities at the developing procedures stage. From a distance, they might be considered to be just "fooling around." For example, a child putting together a train track of her own design is actually making many decisions about where the train will go and what the train might do when it arrives at a specific location. A child may try many ways to shake off his shadow or make it bigger or smaller. In each case, she or he is deciding on a procedure to answer a curiosity or specific question.

Experiences at the *conduct the procedure* stage are typically presented by the teacher, who explains to the students the process that they are expected to follow. An example of this includes having students complete a science experiment in which a step-by-step process is given. Students are to follow the procedure carefully and make observations. For instance, in science, we might give students a detailed procedure for measuring their temperatures. We might give them a procedure for collecting rain or building a bird's nest. The detailed procedure helps the children get more consistent results and can ensure their safety. As children come up with questions to explore, we can support their ideas about how they think they can develop the procedure and conduct the activities. We can provide ideas that ensure safety and are realistic.

Activities at the *drawing conclusions* stage typically give students some background information and then ask the children to summarize what the information tells us. Teachers might say, "So what does this tell us?" During the defining problems stage, we are encouraging the children to ask their own questions. At the drawing conclusions stage, we as teachers ask the questions that cause our students to use their experiences and observations to mentally organize the information. The questions that we select should be based on the experiences that the children are having. Ideally, many of the questions should actually come from the children as a result of an activity that they conducted in the class. Children are capable of drawing their own conclusions and we, as teachers, need to support this process. For example, in Figure 3.6, we see questions that could be asked at the end of an exploration.

Newman and Wehlage (1993) have identified five standards of authentic learning (Figure 3.7). For learning to be authentic, it needs to cause children to question and reason why things happen. It is not enough to just be told something. Authentic

---

Why does a kite fly better on some days than others?
Why do some balls bounce more than others?
Why do some types of seeds take longer to germinate than others?
Why do leaves drop in the fall?
What makes a yo-yo come back up to your hand?
Why does a wooden spoon make more noise than a plastic spoon when banged on a metal pan?

FIGURE 3.6 Sample activities at the drawing conclusions stage.

1. Higher order thinking
2. Depth of knowledge
3. Connectedness to the world beyond the classroom
4. Substantive conversation
5. Social support for student achievement

FIGURE 3.7 Five standards of authentic learning. *Source:* From Newman & Wehlage (1993).

learning encourages going beyond basic information and knowledge. When children follow their own ideas and curiosities about a topic, their studies on that topic tend to involve a longer time period. They are not a one-time event but extend indefinitely based on children's curiosities and ideas.

Authentic learning activities involve the student's immediate community as well as the world around them. They give students opportunities to talk about their interests and share their ideas. In addition, authentic learning acknowledges students' ideas as important and valuable to others. Authentic learning also helps to build a child's self-confidence and self-worth as a learner.

Children look at problems differently when they are able to define their own problems. The difference is ownership. The questions they are examining are their questions and they want answers to them. There is a built-in motivation in this process. Questions raised by other people such as teachers may not be as interesting or as important to the child. We often discuss how teachers need to develop their questioning skills. However, perhaps a more important skill for teachers to develop is to encourage students to ask questions and to use the students' questions in leading classroom activities and projects. We can model good questioning techniques and encourage children to ask questions alongside us.

COLLECTING AND ORGANIZING DATA

Collecting and organizing data are important tasks that encourage thinking processes that are valuable for solving problems. In basic problem solving, the procedures that are developed often require the collection of information or data. When do shadows disappear? How tall is my bean sprout? How high can the water rocket go? How many of the seeds germinate? How long does it take to run around the track? Data collection activities are important to the development of children because they require the students to observe, take measurements, collect and organize data, and use data in authentic experiences. Chapters 4 and 5 will examine designs and techniques for collecting and organizing data in detail.

The Concept Explorations included in Part II of this book are designed to promote student-centered, problem-solving experiences. Note that each of the concept Explorations of Chapters 7 through 18 has characteristics that support the Concepts presented in authentic learning. Each theme can be explored anywhere there are curious children.

Review and Discussion Questions

1. Discuss how you would apply the problem-solving cycle as identified by Kolb et al. (1984) and Polya (1971) as you conceptualize and develop one of the Concept Explorations (see Part II).

2. Choose science content from one of the Concept Explorations in Part II such as rocks, seeds, clouds, leaves, or water. Discuss how you would set up an investigation that promotes the problem-solving cycle.

3. Explain how you would encourage children to pose their own questions about a topic of interest so that they are actively engaged and allowed to experience learning.

CHAPTER 4

Measurement—*A Way to Capture Observations in Mathematics and Science*

How wide is the ocean?
How high is the sky?
How big is your heart?
How far can birds fly?

Measure my flower.
How long will it bloom?
Measure my sneaker
Somewhere in my room.

How do I know how far
is too far?
When will we get there?
How far is a star?

How much do I weigh?
How big is your cat?
How do you measure
all this and all that?

Genevieve A. Davis

We have included this chapter on measurement because we have found it to be a critical part of each Concept Exploration (see Part II). Measurement provides the mathematical framework and language necessary to describe the events and investigations in the Concept Explorations. Our experiences in the schools show that teachers and preservice students benefit from grounded work in measurement as they scaffold their children's understanding about how to document and preserve observations.

Mathematics is an unending search for patterns and a quest to find out how much or how many. Young children are constantly observing their world and seeking ways to find answers to the many curiosities they have about what they observe. As they experience and perceive their multifaceted and intriguing world, young children's observations become important in many ways:

- They are using their senses to notice and experience things in their world.
- They are observing how things change and grow.
- They are learning ways to share and communicate what they observe and perceive.
- They are seeking inventive ways to capture change and growth.
- They are learning about the tools to help them measure change and growth in their world.

It is important for us to remember to provide safe, interesting, and inviting environments both indoors and outdoors for children to explore. Equally important is providing young children with ample opportunities not only to explore their world but also to share their ideas, discoveries, and theories about their world. We also need to give children mathematical, scientific, and linguistic tools to describe the fascinating world around them. As children become immersed in their environment and culture, the importance of awareness, observation, exploration, inquiry, and discovery cannot be overemphasized.

The many phenomena in our world are rich with mathematical and scientific connections. These connections are important for us to understand if we are to help children see how mathematics and science describes the world they sense, explore, and discover. The famed astronomer Galileo expressed the importance and impact of the connections between mathematics and science:

> . . . that vast book which stands forever open before our eyes, I mean the universe, cannot be read until we have learned the language. It is written in mathematical language without which it is humanly impossible to comprehend a single word.

All aspects of observation and sensory experiences can be captured with children's inventive and intuitive sense of taking in, describing, keeping track, recording, and measuring. As children become more experienced with informal approaches of describing what they observe, more formal approaches and techniques of measurement can be explored and employed.

Measurement is a very important and broadly used application of mathematics. Not only does measurement help us to describe and compare things; it helps us to record and keep track of information and allows us to capture and make predictions of how things may grow and change (Figure 4.1).

As children experience their world through their senses, they are, unknowingly, developing intuitive notions about measurement. As they see and touch things in their surroundings, they are experiencing firsthand the attributes of measurement. That is, children sense the many attributes of size including mass, volume, and length. It is these very first sensory experiences that will lay the foundation for the more formalized and sophisticated process of measurement that they will use in later years.

FIGURE 4.1   What do we measure?

We constantly use measurement to quantify values such as length, area, volume, and weight. At other times, however, quantifying measurements is more difficult. Below are some examples:

- How do you measure temperature?
- How do you measure how much humidity is in air?
- How do you measure the opaqueness of milk?
- How do you measure the hotness of jalapeno peppers?
- How do you measure the squeezeability of chewing gum?
- How do you measure the grindability of sand paper?
- What other measurements can you think of?

USING SENSES TO EXPERIENCE THE WORLD

As children use their senses to observe, explore, and experience their world, they become aware of their surroundings and begin to recognize and differentiate among the many phenomena they sense. They sense lightness and darkness; they hear different sounds; they feel different textures in their food, toys, and surroundings; they feel different temperatures and different currents of air; they experience various smells; and they taste a variety of foods. These sensory experiences are forms of observation.

From birth, children begin to differentiate among the sounds, sights, smells, feelings and tastes as they explore their world. As children acquire language to describe their world, they begin to differentiate among what they are sensing and observing. With this awareness comes the ability to begin to classify what they sense and observe. Words can be attached to and used to describe sights, sounds, temperatures, tastes, textures, and smells. Language of description is readily heard when children say *big, little, loud, soft, hot, cold,* and so forth. These first words are purely descriptive and lead to notions of comparison.

Later, at about age 5 or so, the language of *seriation* (arranging in a series) begins to help children describe relationships they perceive involving multiple comparisons. For example, they use words such as *big, bigger,* and *biggest* instead of simply using the words *big* and *small* or *big* and *little.*

HOW THINGS CHANGE AND GROW

One important aspect of observing is noticing how things in the world change and grow. As children become immersed in their world, they experience many new and wonderful phenomena. They experience the daily changes of light and darkness, the various temperature they feel against their skin, the soft breezes and strong winds blowing their hair, the rain tickling their heads and toes. Over a longer period of time, they experience the sequence of a day, a week, and the changing of the seasons.

They see their environment change as flowers bloom, trees bud, grass grows, leaves change color, leaves fall, the sun sets, snow melts, and rain pours.

Other changes that children witness is their own growth or the growth of their pets as they get bigger and bigger. They begin to see evidence that they themselves change and grow. Not only do children know that they grow taller and stronger, that their feet get bigger and that their hair gets longer, but they also see how other living things change and grow. Baby brothers and sisters grow, seemingly, right before their eyes; their pets grow very quickly. As children focus on these changes, they recognize the excitement of documenting, recording, and keeping track of such changes and growth. Photographs of them at different times in their lives, growth charts documenting their height, and the simple act of reaching things that used to be out of reach are concrete ways children learn about change. They experience the documentation of these changes at home, in the doctor's office, and in their world. They begin to see the value of the tools and process of measurement as they realize that change is an interesting and inevitable part of life.

Children also constantly observe changes in nonliving things. Colorful magic markers transform a piece of white paper into a rainbow. Toy cars roll down an incline and knock down a barrier of blocks. On a more abstract level, sugar will dissolve in a glass of lemonade. On a warm afternoon, ice cubes will melt on the sidewalk and the water will evaporate. Children can observe clouds grow or dissipate. Sand can be observed rolling along a stream bed after a storm. Ocean waves knock down sand castles and deposit shells on the beach.

Seeking Inventive Ways to Capture Change and Growth

A good way to begin engaging children in capturing their observations is through language and communication. Having conversations with children about what they see, feel, smell, hear, and taste is a good starting point. Using descriptive language helps children to express their developing conceptualizations of their observations with words and gestures. A common scene comes to mind when a baby, with outstretched arms, tells everyone that she is "Soooo big!" The language of comparison helps children to attach words to the phenomena and the sequences of change that they observe.

As children use words such as *big, bigger,* and *biggest* or *tall, taller,* and *tallest,* they are learning how to organize their conceptualizations of comparison, gradation, and seriation. Later, these captured descriptors can lead to creative and meaningful graphing and charting.

An inventive way to keep track of observed changes and growth is through photography. Taking photographs of real things, as children see and observe them change and grow, is a very powerful way to have children think about and reflect on these interesting processes in their world. We can assist young children in taking pictures of pets or plants or themselves, over time, so that they can examine the photographs and talk about how to order them in sequence. For example, when viewing these two pictures of the growth of a puppy to an adult dog (Figure 4.2), children may explain that a certain picture is first because the puppy in it is smaller. They can say that another picture is next because the puppy grew. When taking these types of pictures, be sure to keep the camera at the same distance from the animal so that the

Virginia Keller

Virginia Keller

FIGURE 4.2   Serial photographs can help children give voice to their observations of change and growth.

comparisons are not confounded by distance and perspective. It is also recommended to have a child in the photograph so that there is a basis for comparison.

This kind of reflection and analysis leads to children being able to suggest generalizations, build theories, and make predictions about what happens in their world. The availability of economical digital cameras permits the instant printing of children's photographs and eliminates the costs of processing film. In addition, these photographic sequences can be included in classroom Web pages.

Also, photographs of many serial events can be accessed on the Internet. Many live Web cams show nature sites. For example, a live camera of a bald eagle nest (*http://www.wa.gov/wdfw/wildwatch/eaglecam*) shows the changes that take place in the growth of an eaglet. These photographs can be downloaded and printed for use in your classroom.

Change is constant in the lives of small children. They observe changes daily as the sun appears to move through the sky. They observe changes as a rain shower develops or snow falls. They observe leaves falling from trees or a bird carrying dried grass to build a nest.

They observe changes over longer periods of time as they watch their seeds germinate into flowers, witness tadpoles transform into frogs, see caterpillars blossom into butterflies, and experience the changes in temperature as the months progress across the seasons.

Taking pictures or drawing pictures of a sequence of events is helpful for children to experience change. For example, children can take pictures of planting beans. Then every third day or so take another picture until the bean sprouts and becomes a plant. Examining these pictures helps children to re-create the growth that they witnessed. Keeping track of the number of sprouts adds quantification to this exploration.

Cooking with children can also help with sequencing and is an activity children enjoy. Use recipe cards that show the various steps for making play-doh, muffins, or fruit salad. Teachers may want to access children's cookbooks to support these activities.

Another good activity is to gather three to six cartoons depicting change and have the children put them in order. Cartoons like *Peanuts* with several squares depicting a sequence of events such as building a snowman can be glued to cardboard and cut out so that the children can put the squares in the correct order. Such an activity can be enhanced by having the children tell the story of change or growth. Prompting children with questions such as "How do you know?" "What would do you think comes next?" "What would the next picture show?" "Why did the picture change?" can help children organize their thinking and enhance their ability to reason and predict. Captions or text can be added to the seriated sequence of photographs. Appropriate language of description, comparison, ordination, gradation, and seriation should be emphasized.

A good example of a gradation would be to put in order shades of a color, say, green, from the lightest to the darkest shade. Have the children carefully drop green food coloring into clear plastic, water-filled bottles. Put one drop of green food coloring in the first bottle, two drops in the second bottle, three drops in the third bottle, and so forth, up to five or six bottles. Cap the bottles for extended use. Then, mix up the order of the bottles. After the bottles are mixed up, the children can put them in order from the lightest or least dense shade of color to the darkest or most dense shade of the color. Paint chips from your local hardware store can also become a good classroom resource for comparisons of brightness. Again, asking children questions about what they see and what they predict helps them to develop logical thinking and reasoning skills.

Another activity for children to experience that demonstrates gradation would be volume of sound. Children could begin a hand-clapping or tapping sequence. First, they would clap only their pointer fingers together or tap them on the edge of a table or desk. They would then add their middle fingers, then their ring fingers, their little fingers, and finally their thumbs. As a whole class does this experiment, they can hear the increase of sound. Reversing this sequence allows the children to hear the gradation of sound reverse from loudest to softest. When using this experience with children, you might relate the sounds to the sequence of a rain shower. Other contexts for gradation besides shades of color and volumes of sound include textures of softness, speed of the wind, bounciness of balls, and brightness of light.

Keeping track of, recording, and measuring change can also be done in informal, inventive ways. For example, when children are observing seeds and bulbs grow into plants, they can be assisted in measuring the growth of the plant with a variety of tools, such as strips of paper or yarn or a tall stick. The tall strip of paper or stick can be placed next to the plant at dirt level and marked off and labeled with the height of the plant at that time. These markings can be labeled with the date and attached to a chart. Another way this can be done is by measuring the height of the plant with individual strips of paper, or yarn, cut to the height of the plant. In a week's interval, the plant can be measured with a different strip of paper or piece of yarn. Cut to match the plant's current height. Then place the new strip next to the first strip along the same baseline. This process can continue so that the seriated sequence of growth is recorded with strips of paper or yarn, forming a visual representation of the growth of the plant. This representation makes a pleasant visual display. To enhance this activity, photos can be taken to support the graphic display of growth.

Children can use a variety of familiar, nonstandard materials such as blocks or counters, crayons or markers, stickers or ink stampers to keep track of growth or to capture how big something is. It is the process of measuring with nonstandard tools that lays the foundation for using standardized units of measure to capture the "how much-ness" of things. As they become more experienced with using manipulatives for nonstandard measuring, they will begin to see the importance of lining up the units end to end and of becoming more precise in their measuring.

A similar measurement process can be constructed by using stickers or ink-pad images to capture the height of the growth, thus generating a visual, iconic display of growth. As with manipulative nonstandard units of measurement, using stickers and water-soluble ink-pad stampers also allows the children to count actual units, that is, the stickers or stamped images, to tell how many stickers or stamped images tall the plant is. Attaching numbers to this type of process helps children to understand, at a rational and logical level, that the markings on standardized rulers refer to how many units of length something is rather than just focusing on the end points or lines on the ruler.

FORMAL APPROACHES AND TECHNIQUES OF MEASUREMENT

As children utilize and experience how to measure with nonstandard units of measure, they begin to build meaning of *measurement* as a way of capturing or recording the measurable attributes of things. "My leaf is six beans long" or "My shoe is fifteen blocks long" or "My book is eight stickers long" become good mathematical descriptions of measured items. Learning the notion that units of measure can be as arbitrary as a block or a paper clip is a major milestone in a child's development. The informal process of measuring can then be related to more precise, standardized units and tools of measurement. Children as early as preschool age can be supported in their use of both nonstandardized and standardized tools for measuring things.

As children try to communicate the measurements they make to others, the value of having standard measurements becomes important. If different children use different measuring units, they cannot make meaningful comparisons. When children are provided with rich opportunities to explore the different types of measurement of linear distance, weight, and capacity, they will begin to understand and know which type of measuring tool or device best measures the item to be measured. For example, they will know that to see how long something is, they would use discrete units or a ruler of some type. Measuring volume requires containers that can be filled. Finding out how much something weighs requires a scale of some sort, whether a

Weight and *mass* are two terms that have become interwoven into our common language and used interchangeably.

Weight is a measurement of the force of gravity on an object. We commonly use the unit of pound for measuring weight. If a person weights 100 pounds, that means the Earth is pulling the person toward the Earth with a force of 100 pounds.

Mass is a measurement of the amount of matter in an object. We commonly use grams or kilograms (1,000 grams) to measure mass.

The terminology of weight and mass become critical when we travel to space. On the moon the gravitational force on an object changes. Thus a person who weighs 100 pounds on the Earth, would only weigh about 17 pounds on the moon.

Kilograms is the unit of measurement of the amount of matter. A person would have the same amount of matter, whether on the Earth or moon, so that same person would have a mass of about 45 kilograms on the Earth and on the moon.

With young children, it is not recommended that the differentiation between weight and mass be stressed. Because these differences are very abstract, young children (even some adults) have difficulty making transitions between weight and mass.

FIGURE 4.3 Weight and mass.

homemade pan balance or scientific spring scale. Figure 4.3 discusses the standard terms of *weight* and *mass*.

As young children become aware of and observe their world, their observations draw them to many different attributes of objects. They experiment with and explore containers at a water or sand table and notice how much different-sized containers will hold. Pouring water or sand from one container to another helps children to see and experience how the size of a container relates to what it can hold. They can explore how many scoops of sand can fill a bucket or how many quarter cup measures it takes to fill the cup measure. In this type of exploration, children are learning about the relationship between attributes to be measured and the tools to measure them.

Children also experience differing of objects as they hold them in their hands, feeling the different amount of gravitational force the different items exert on their hands. Indeed that is how we sense or perceive weight. What they are experiencing in all of this exploration are attributes of length, volume, and weight. As they use cups to scoop water, rice, or sand, they are learning about volume being the "how much-ness" something will hold. As they feel the masses of different objects, they are learning that things have different masses. As they lay blocks end to end across a linear space, they are seeing that things have length. In order for these discoveries to be made, we need to be sure that our classrooms and outdoor spaces are filled with interesting objects and living things for our children to observe, examine, and sense. Recognizing that these objects and living things have measurable attributes of length, volume, and weight is a very important discovery for children to make. As children are given these opportunities to explore the attributes of length, mass, and capacity, they become familiar with the tools that measure them. At this point the tools of

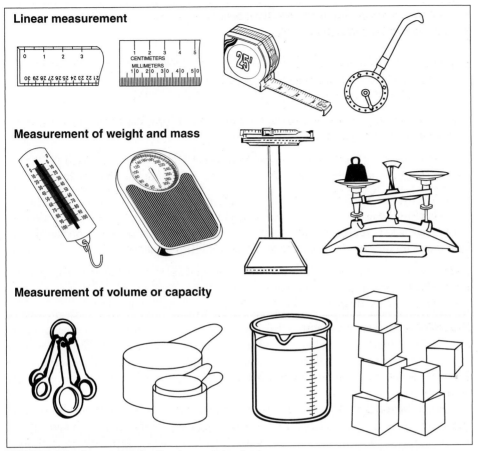

Linear measurement

Measurement of weight and mass

Measurement of volume or capacity

FIGURE 4.4 Some standardized measuring tools.

measurement are exciting to explore, become familiar with, and use. Figure 4.4 illustrates some of these common standardized tools.

National Standards Concerning Measurement

It is important for us to note that measurement is an essential tool to both the mathematician and the scientist. Being able to document the "how much-ness" of things helps mathematicians and scientists understand how the world is put together and how things relate to each other. Understanding relationship helps mathematicians and scientists make predictions about events and growth and changes in the world. Theory building and the development of conceptual knowledge are dependent on systems of measurement.

As we work with young children, we can gain a great deal of information and insight if we look to the National Mathematics and Science Standards for guidance in our efforts to supply the appropriate mathematics and science contexts for meaningful learning regarding measurement.

National Science Education Standards: Content Standards K–12

The National Science Education Standards (NSES) recognize that as children develop, their observations move from qualitative observations to more quantitative values. By measuring characteristics, they can better organize data and make comparisons of properties and changes that take place.

There are two commonly used standard systems of measurement: the international system of measurement, often referred to as the metric system, and the U.S. customary system of measurement, formerly referred to as the British system of measurement.

The NSES recognizes that the different systems are used in different situations. Scientists usually use the metric system. An important part of measurement is knowing when to use which system. For example, a meteorologist might use degrees Fahrenheit when reporting the weather to the public, but in writing scientific reports, the meteorologist would use degrees Celsius (National Science Education Standards, NSES, 1996, p. 118).

As children develop facility with language, their descriptions become richer and include more detail. Initially no tools need to be used, but children eventually learn that they can add to their descriptions by measuring objects, first with measuring devices that they create and then by using conventional standardized measuring instruments such as rulers, balances, and thermometers. By recording data and making graphs and charts, older children can search for patterns and order in their work and that of their peers (NSES, 1996, p. 126).

Science Education Program Standards

The science program should be coordinated with the mathematics program to enhance student use and understanding of mathematics in the study of science and to improve student understanding of mathematics.

Science requires the use of mathematics in the collection and treatment of data and in the reasoning used to develop concepts, law, and theories. School science and mathematics programs should be coordinated so that students learn the necessary mathematical skills and concepts before and during their use in the science program.

Coordination of science and mathematics programs provides an opportunity to advance instruction in science beyond the purely descriptive. Students gathering data in a science investigation should use tools of data analysis to organize these data to formulate hypothesis for further testing (NSES, 1996, p. 214).

NCTM Principles and Standards for School Mathematics

The National Council of Teachers of Mathematics (NCTM) helps us put the standard of measurement within the larger context of mathematical learning. The *Principles and Standards for School Mathematics* states the following:

> Measurement is one of the most widely used applications of mathematics. It bridges two main areas of school mathematics—geometry and number. Measurement activities can simultaneously teach important everyday skills, strengthen students' knowledge of

NCTM Measurement Standard 1 for Grades Pre-K–2

Instructional programs from prekindergarten through grade 12 should enable all students to—

Understand measurable attributes of objects and the units, systems, and processes of measurement.

In prekindergarten through grade 2 all students should—

- Recognize the attributes of length, volume, weight, area, and time;
- Compare and order objects according to these attributes;
- Understand how to measure using nonstandard and standard units;
- Select an appropriate unit and tool for the attribute being measured.

NCTM Measurement Standard 2 for Grades Pre-K–2

Instructional programs from prekindergarten through grade 12 should enable all students to—

Apply appropriate techniques, tools, and formulas to determine measurements.

In prekindergarten through grade 2 all students should—

- Measure with multiple copies of units of the same size, such as paper clips laid end to end;
- Use repetition of a single unit to measure something larger than the unit, for instance, measuring the length of a room with a single meter stick;
- Use tools to measure;
- Develop common referents for measures to make comparisons and estimates.

FIGURE 4.5 NCTM sample measurement standards. *Source: Measurement Standard for Grades Pre-K–2* (NCTM, 2000, p. 102).

> other important topics in mathematics, and develop measurement concepts and processes that will be formalized and expanded in later years. Teaching that builds on students' intuitive understandings and informal experiences with measurement helps them to understand the attributes to be measured as well as what it means to measure. A foundation in measurement concepts that enables students to use measurement systems, tools, and techniques should be established through direct experiences with comparing objects, counting units, and making connections between spatial concepts and number. (NCTM, 2000, p. 103)

More specifically, the NCTM (2000) identifies major expectations for children in preschool through grade 2 in the content of measurement. Figure 4.5 outlines the NCTM measurement standard and includes the two major overarching standards for preschool through grade 12 as well as the specific expectations for each standard as they apply to children in preschool through grade 2.

Instructional Psychology for Teaching Measurement

In this section we discuss the instructional psychology of exploring and learning about the process of measurement. As teachers, we need to remember that young children need to be engaged in hands-on and minds-on learning experiences. Children should be given the opportunity to form mathematical concepts for measurement through many varying experiences with a variety of inviting, real objects. Their first experiences with measurement should be manipulative, hands-on, tactile, and active. They must be engaged in *doing* the measuring, in touching the things to be measured, and feeling the measurable attributes of things. Next, children can use and create pictorial, iconic representations of what they measured. Such representations can include photographs, pictures, graphs, images, and visualizations of the things measured. Last, the use of symbolic representation can be used to record and label the measurements with words, signs, and symbols. Symbolic representation can be as simple as "My teddy bear is nine sticks tall" or "My teddy bear weighs sixteen blocks." Later, as they become more experienced with the process of measuring and the tools of measurement, children can determine that "My foot is six inches long" or "My cup holds 200 milliliters of juice."

Some Ideas for Teaching Children to Measure

As children begin to explore the process of measuring as a means of describing data and recording data, change, and growth, they are developing important foundations for more advanced and precise processes of measurement. As teachers of primary children, we need to be able to bridge theory and practice about how young children form mathematical concepts and construct generalizations relative to the concepts and processes of measurement. In constructivist settings, developing logic is essential. As we take a journey together through Part II's Concept Explorations, and as we co-inquire with young children, many activities will utilize concepts and processes of measurement that help develop a broad understanding and application of measurement skills.

WAYS TO HELP CHILDREN COMMUNICATE AND SHARE MATHEMATICAL IDEAS

As we provide children with rich experiences and environments to explore and observe, we also need to provide opportunities for them to communicate and share their discoveries with others. As children explain their observations and the ways they capture these observations, they are making their own thinking more clear and visible to themselves. There are many ways to accomplish the important task of sharing.

Group Sharing and Discussion Format

As children come together as a group during the course of the day, they should be encouraged to express the discoveries and observations they have made. Figure 4.6 lists some sample prompts that teachers can use to assist students with collecting their thoughts and expressing their ideas.

What did you see?
What happened first?
Tell us what you think about. . . .
How do you know?
What do you think will happen next?
How tall is your plant?
How did your shadow change?
How much does your rock weigh?

FIGURE 4.6 Questions that encourage children to organize and express comparisons and measurements.

Journaling

As children become more skilled at writing their thoughts, they can keep daily journals of their observations. They can keep track of the changes that they are observing and the phenomena that are occurring in their world. For example, if they are exploring their shadows, they may journal about how their shadow changes length at different times during the day. When children make such deliberate attempts at making their observations and their thinking visible, like scientists, they are able to make predictions and develop conceptual schemes about scientific phenomena.

Making a Book

As children have opportunities to observe, explore, and experiment with many phenomena of change and growth, they will be able to build theories about their world. As these theories become evident, a book of "Amazing Discoveries" can be created. For example, when children explore and examine what happens to shadows at different times of the day, they can begin to make claims about the position of the sun in the sky as it relates to the length of a shadow. Class statements can be made such as "When the Sun is high in the sky above, our shadows are shorter than they are late in the evening when the Sun is low." This concept is certainly an "Amazing Discovery."

These experiences are valuable for young children because they are the basis for much more complex and abstract concepts. The concrete experiences such as comparing the length of their shadows to the position of the Sun will, over time, expand to an understanding of the very abstract concepts related to the movements of the Earth and sun.

With each Concept Exploration, children's theories and discoveries should be celebrated and recorded. At the end of the year, you will have constructed a wonderful book that captures the rich problem-solving experiences of the children across many topics of interest. They will have, in fact, written their own textbook, chapter by chapter, of each Concept Exploration.

Modeling Appropriate Mathematical and Scientific Language

As children observe and measure change and growth, it is important for teachers and collaborating adults to model appropriate mathematical and scientific language. As children describe phenomena of change and growth in their own language, we can

- Use all modes of instruction—concrete, iconic, and symbolic—and supply language.
- Pose questions and get children to explore and wonder.
- Dialogue with children about what they are measuring, how they are measuring, and what tools they could use to measure.
- Discover and invent together and independently at school and at home.
- Share and see other viewpoints and expressions.
- Make sense out of a lesson.
- Model standard mathematics.
- Have fun!

FIGURE 4.7 Measurement problem-solving strategies for young children.

supply different levels of description reflecting a more specific vocabulary. For example, "Our bean grew six centimeters in ten days," "Our shadows were the shortest at noon," "The wind was blowing thirty miles an hour," "The water in the rain gauge was more than three inches high," and "The oak tree was more than one hundred feet high." Examples of measurement problem-solving strategies for young children are shown in Figure 4.7.

Relating Rational Counting of Units to the Process of Measurement

In order for young children to solve problems in mathematics, they need to be able to count with meaning. Young children solve mathematical problems with rational counting. As children count how many building blocks long a plant is, it is important for them to count rationally and in a stable order, knowing the appropriate sequence of numbers. Using one-to-one correspondence (that is, touching one object at a time when counting objects in a set and keeping track are important aspects of rational counting. When a child can consistently keep track of which object he touches and which sequences of numbers is used, he will be counting with meaning. When children count with meaning, they know that the last number named in a counting sequence tells how many in the set, that is, it tells the cardinal property of the set.

Rational counting is not simply naming a sequence of numbers. Children who do not count rationally use numbers as they would name people's names in a group. That is, the counting sequence of "one, two, three, four" is done with the same purpose and understanding as naming "Carlos, Ben, Judy, and Nicole." When children know that "one, two, three, four" tells how many are in the set, they are rationally counting.

Providing Discrete Items to Count When Measuring

Children need real objects to use when measuring things. If they are measuring how tall their teddy bear is, they need to lay objects end to end so that they can count how many of them fit the distance from the top of the teddy bear to the bottom, or from head to toe. Objects such as blocks, large paper clips, plastic ants or bugs, craft sticks, pom-poms, small toy cars, or tracings of children's feet can all be used to measure linear distances.

Links or blocks that snap together in a straight line or flexibly linked blocks can be used to measure straight or curved linear distances. The important thing to remember is that linear distances are made of discrete, countable units, whether they are inches, centimeters, blocks, clips, or cutout tracings of feet. Units of measure are the emphasis in this process.

Likewise, for mass or weight, objects such as blocks, metric weights, marbles, or any other fairly dense material can be used to fill a pan balance. Like linear distance, mass is measured with discrete units of measure. An item weighs so many grams, blocks, or marbles. So, counting units of weight is an important part of the process of learning the underlying concept of how much something weighs.

For capacity, any pourable substances such as water, sand, rice, or small beans can be used to

Stacking cup toys are designed so that a child can fill the number 3 cup with rice and pour it in the number 6 cup, which will be filled only halfway.

fill and refill containers. Ample exploration with toys and tools that are volumetrically related is essential. Toys or tools are volumetrically related if they are designed to be iterations of each other. For example, measuring cups and measuring spoons are good examples of how containers are volumetrically related. That is, if you fill the quarter cup container four times, it will fill the cup measure. If stacking cup toys are volumetrically related, they will be designed to be iterations of each other. In the photograph, you can see the stacking cups with numbers on them. In this set, if you fill the number 3 cup with rice and pour it in the number 6 cup, the rice will fill it halfway. Another filling of the number 3 cup will fill the number 6 cup. When buying stacking toys, this is an important feature to determine. Playing with water, sand, or rice and such containers helps young children to conceptualize about size and proportion. Making these discoveries in a natural, inviting, and interesting setting builds a strong conceptual base for units of measure and eventually for standardization of measurement.

A good way to transition children from measuring with manipulatives to measuring with rulers is to have them construct their own iconic, pictorial rulers. This idea was developed by a group of first graders who were not quite ready for rulers. On strips of stiff poster board cut out in a shape similar to a ruler (that is, a rectangle approximately 2 inches by 12 inches), the children used a large ink-pad stamper to continually stamp an image of a rainbow, in a line across the poster board. With the images in a line next to each other, the children knew that to measure something, they could simply count how many rainbow images long it was. The children were not merely looking at an end point on a centimeter or inch ruler; they were counting discrete units of measure, in this case, rainbows.

As another example, the ink-stamped frogs in a row on the iconic ruler shown in Figure 4.8 can be used for measurement.

FIGURE 4.8 An iconic "frog" ruler.

With this particular frog ruler, the child can count how many frogs long an item is. This closely mimics the process they used when they measured with manipulative nonstandard units. The only difference is that the units are icons stamped on a strip of paper, the iconic ruler. This process can also be done by using large stickers on the poster board strips. Other resources for constructing the iconic rulers are Ellison cutouts, potato prints, large erasers used as stampers, sponge prints, and so forth. The important concept here is that whatever stamp or sticker is used has to be identical across the poster board. For measurement, iteration of identical units is the concept that underlies the process of measurement.

As children continue to measure by counting units—first manipulative, then iconic—they begin to have a logical, clear understanding about what the lines on a ruler represent: discrete units. The first graders who invented the iconic rulers helped themselves keep track of the measuring process with clothespins to mark the beginning and ending points of the item they were measuring. If you use an iconic ruler, children measure items at different starting points to show the static nature of an item's length. For example, measuring a toy car will yield the same length whether you place it at the beginning of the ruler or somewhere else on the ruler. This is an important concept for young children to discover and learn.

Developing Referents for Measurement

When children are ready to use formal tools to measure, such as rulers, they should begin to develop **referents** for the units they will be using. For example, knowing that a centimeter is about the distance of the width across a child's little finger at the first crease helps that child to "know" how big or how long a centimeter is. Putting the child's finger across a centimeter ruler to check to see how close her finger's width is to a centimeter helps the child to conceptualize the distance more precisely.

Next, you could ask the children to try to draw a line segment 1 centimeter long. They will look at their little fingers and try to replicate the distance on paper. Then take the centimeter ruler and check to see how close the drawn estimate of that length is. Next, ask the children to draw a line segment 5 centimeters long. Follow the same procedure of checking and reflecting on the results. Use many different lengths. Find other similar referents for 10 centimeters and so forth.

After some experience in constructing line segments of different lengths, you can engage the children in estimation activities. Place a few items in front of the children and ask them to estimate how many centimeters long each item is. They can use their fingers to help with this process. Placing their fingers across the length of an item can help them to see the concreteness of the linear distance.

After children have clearly developed a referent for a centimeter, another approach to estimation can be taken. You can ask the children questions such as "I found a bug on the sidewalk today. Do you think it was one centimeter long, 50 centimeters long, or one hundred centimeters long?" Such questions get at conceptualization of what a centimeter is. Of course, fun stories can be told when they choose a "silly" answer. After all, silliness occurs when there is a break in what they understand at a logical level. A 100-centimeter-long bug, oh my! What fun stories and art could be constructed about such a creature?

A similar approach could be taken with a milliliter. If children could hold a cubic centimeter (a base-10 unit) in their hands and imagine it filled with water, they would have a referent for how much a milliliter is, because they are the same thing (Figure 4.9). Another referent for milliliter is how much water a scooped-out jelly bean will hold. Using a very small container, say, 10-milliliter capacity, children could estimate how many times they would have to fill the centimeter cube or the jelly bean, and pour it into the container to fill it up. After they estimate how many milliliters will fill it, they should actually fill it up and measure it with a milliliter measure. This small container could be labeled and used as a referent itself.

After more of this type of experimentation, you could ask questions that get at conceptualization of the amount of a milliliter. For example, "Today I washed my hair. Do you think that I used eight milliliters of shampoo, 60 milliliters of shampoo, or five hundred milliliters of shampoo?" Again the logical answer is 8 milliliters, but we could conjure up interesting scenarios about what would happen if we used 500 milliliters of shampoo in our bathtubs. Imaginations can take charge when answering these types of measurement questions.

It is a good practice to apply a child's understanding of referent to estimation and problem solving. For example, if we have a referent developed for millimeter, centimeter, and meter, we can ask children fun questions such as these:

- I found a bug on my driveway this morning. It was about 8 _____ long! (mm, cm, m)

- If I wanted to measure how tall my pencil is, I would use _____. (cm, m)

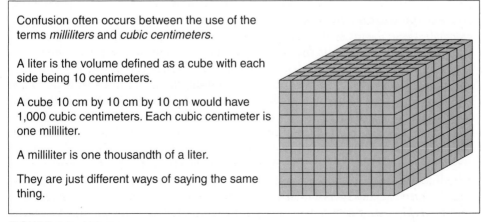

Confusion often occurs between the use of the terms *milliliters* and *cubic centimeters*.

A liter is the volume defined as a cube with each side being 10 centimeters.

A cube 10 cm by 10 cm by 10 cm would have 1,000 cubic centimeters. Each cubic centimeter is one milliliter.

A milliliter is one thousandth of a liter.

They are just different ways of saying the same thing.

FIGURE 4.9 Volume.

- I want to know how much water my aquarium holds. I would measure the water with a _____ measure. (l, ml)

Figure 4.10 lists some useful referents for commonly used metric measurements. For young children, it is recommended that you use only common metric measurements—measurements that are often referred to in their conversations, activities, or their listening or speaking vocabulary. Solid experience with commonly used metric measurements will build a solid foundation for using other, less common increments of metric measurements in later experiences.

It is important to make your own referents based on your own situations and environment. When possible and appropriate, measure out these amounts and construct a "Referent Chart" with the children.

Temperature

Temperature is a measurement of the warmth or coldness of air, water, or any substance or item. It is usually measured with some type of standard value, such as degrees Fahrenheit or degrees Celsius. What is the meaning, notion, or concept of temperature to a young child? Perhaps one of the first temperature-related words a toddler learns is "Hot!" When motivated by safety issues, careful caregivers are quick to help toddlers learn what is hot and why it is important not to touch or eat something too hot. Other contexts of temperature for young children include climate, cooking, a weather person, an indoor thermostat or thermometer, an outdoor thermometer, or a people thermometer.

As children experience temperature daily, they begin to have a sense of what happens to the temperature at different times of the day, season, or year. They may notice that in the morning when they go to school, they wear a sweater or a jacket. Then, during outside play later in the day, they are too warm to wear outer garments. Then at night they feel the temperature drop again. Observing these temperature changes helps children to suggest theories about what happens to the temperature across their day.

Likewise, as children experience changes in seasons, they begin to generalize what happens across the seasons. What types of activities or events happen in the summer and what activities or events happen in the winter? Children can begin to associate these events with climate and temperature. Broad ideas of temperature measurement can be made in these contexts. When it is in the 80s (degrees Fahrenheit), we want to go swimming and drink cold lemonade. When it is in the teens (degrees Fahrenheit), we want to bundle up, go ice skating, and drink hot chocolate. These broad generalizations help children to develop concepts for units of measure of temperature.

Children begin to understand that it snows when it is very cold outside, below 32 degrees Fahrenheit or 0 degrees Celsius. Similarly, they want to wear shorts when it is very hot outside, say, in the 80s (degrees Fahrenheit) or in the 30s (degrees Celsius). Children also begin to notice what happens in their environment during different temperatures. A cold snap will cause leaves to change color; very hot temperatures without rain cause plants to wilt; an early frost will destroy some plants and vegetables; or certain temperatures will cause hail or sleet to precipitate from the sky.

As children are engaged in the many Concept Explorations of Part II, being aware of using temperature as a measurement is important. Recording the temperatures of the air indoors and out or taking soil or water temperatures can help children make generalizations about the effects of temperature on their experiments. Children can pose questions relative to measurement. For example, when exploring wind, they may ask, "Is it colder when it is windy?" or "Why is my breath cooler when I purse my lips and blow out air and warmer when I open my mouth and 'huff' out the air?" Similarly, when children are exploring growing seeds, they may wonder about how the soil temperature may affect growth or what would happen if you watered the plants with ice water instead of tepid water. Such inquiries and curiosities should be encouraged and modeled.

On a daily basis, children can be involved in finding out and recording the daily temperature and the weather conditions. In recording the daily temperature, whether you use degrees Fahrenheit or degrees Celsius does not matter (although Figure 4.11 offers an easy way to convert between them and Figure 4.12 lists some comparisons). What you are accomplishing is conceptual understanding of what that particular standard value means to a child on a personal level. What did the children wear to school today and what did the air feel like? These are the important connections that children can make between temperature and what it means to them. Comparing the temperature from day to day, from week to week, and then from month to month helps children see the trends and changes in temperature across time. Such observations can help children develop theories about what happens to the temperature across the school year. In a similar fashion, keeping track of the weather can support their developing ideas about what weather accompanies certain temperatures. Understanding about seasons and changes across time are important observations and perceptions for young children to experience.

Linear Measurement

- *Centimeter:* the width across a child's little finger at the first joint, or the width of a standard paper clip
- *Millimeter:* the thickness of a dime, or the diameter of the wire on a standard paper clip
- *Meter:* height of a door knob from the floor
- *Kilometer:* distance you could walk comfortably in 15 minutes; or six-tenths of a mile

Mass

- *Gram:* a regular jelly bean, a standard paper clip
- *Milligram:* one thousandth of a regular jelly bean
- *Kilogram:* two footballs, a little more than 2 pounds (2.2 pounds)

Volume

- *Milliliter:* the liquid you could fit in a regular-sized jelly bean or in a base-10 unit cube
- *Liter:* a "1-liter" bottle, a little more than a quart (1.06 quarts)

FIGURE 4.10 Useful referents for common metric measurements.

FIGURE 4.11 Celsius.
Source: Genevieve A. Davis.

From Celsius to Fahrenheit is easy to do
You double the number—then what do you do?
Take the sum to which you add 30.
So 2 degrees C doubled add thirty
Is 34 Fahrenheit—with snow it's a flurry.

With this easy way you can readily see
That 10 degrees C is as pleasant as can be.
30 degrees C is as a very hot day
With scorching heat—I'd honestly say (90° F).

Now you try one—from 20 degrees C
When doubled it's 40 as plain as can be.
So then you add 30 to get the degrees
It's 70 Fahrenheit—as warm as a breeze.

	Degrees C	Degrees F
Temperature at which water freezes	0	32
Temperature at which water boils	100	212
Normal body temperature	37	98.6
Comfortable room temperature	20–25	68–77

FIGURE 4.12 Comparison of the Celsius and Fahrenheit temperature scales.

As children become aware of temperature in their immediate world, it is interesting to "see" what is happening in other parts of the world. Perhaps children have relatives or friends living in another part of the country or in another country. Having the opportunity to chart the temperature and weather in another geographic region can help children become aware of the differences and similarities in climate across the globe.

Conversations can be centered on where people like to go in the winter time. If they live in a cold wintertime climate, do they like to stay in this cold climate to enjoy the snow or do they want to find sunshine somewhere because they do not enjoy being outside in very cold temperatures? Developing awareness of different climates and regions in other parts of the world helps children feel connected to others in faraway places. If you can, have a pen-pal exchange or an e-mail exchange with a child's relative or friend or with a whole class. With this arrangement, you could share information about climate and what people do in their part of the world. Charting similarities and differences can be fun.

Review and Discussion Questions

1. Describe a scenario in which children are encouraged to use their own approaches to keep track of observed changes in nature, such as snow melting, a seed growing, a cloud moving, a shadow shrinking, or a season changing. Explain how measurement can be a useful tool to help us capture, record, and preserve these changes.

2. Explain the developmental sequence young children may use to experience the process of measurement—from informal, nonstandard approaches to formal, standard approaches.

3. Discuss the importance of children learning to use referents in measurement to develop conceptual understanding of standard units.

Resources for Teachers

Books

Rohrig, B. (2004). *Pure slime—50 incredible ways to make slime using household substances.* Plain City, OH: Fizbang Science.

CHAPTER 5

Organizing Data in Science and Mathematics

Problem solving is a combination of many important and interrelated processes. In Chapter 3, we identified the four stages of problem solving: defining the problem, developing a procedure, conducting the procedure, and drawing conclusions.

Defining the problem is the process of wondering and asking questions. Our curiosity causes us to want to learn more about the natural events and phenomena that surround us. We wonder: "How many times does my heart beat in one minute?" "How many of my bean seeds will germinate?" "How many different types of birds will come to our feeder?" "How hot does the air in the car get on a sunny summer day?" "Why does my shadow follow me?" Each of these questions causes the need for us to observe, collect information or data, reflect upon our data, determine answers and form theories about our world.

Developing procedures is the process of making decisions about what information (data) we need for examining our questions and how we can best plan and collect the necessary information. In Chapter 4 we looked at the processes for taking and collecting measurements. This is the active process of conducting the procedure.

We know, however, that collecting the data is only one important part of the process. Once we have collected the data, we need to organize it and our measurements to find patterns, trends, and relationships that help us make sense about what we are investigating and hence begin to develop theories about our world. This organization of data is critical for the drawing conclusions phase of problem solving.

This chapter examines various techniques for organizing data. We will look at how the developmental level of children will determine what types of charts and graphs are best suited for examining the data that they have collected.

Young children should be introduced to charting early in their education so that they come to think of it as a model and tool for capturing and displaying information that is important to them. As children start to collect data of their own, encourage them to design their own charts.

DO YOU LIKE RAIN?

Yes, I like rain.	No, I do not like rain.

FIGURE 5.1   A tally mark is used to easily record children's responses in this chart.

USEFULNESS OF CHARTS AND GRAPHS

Charts are valuable tools for organizing data. By definition charts are graphic representations exhibiting information. They are one of the first forms of data display that we use with young children. We simply "chart" ideas, information, preferences, or facts on paper or a similar medium. Charting captures information and preserves it for us to examine. We begin with a very simple idea to explore, such as "Do you like rain?" Children can simply vote yes or no to this question with a tally mark (Figure 5.1), vote with a sticker or pertinent object, or add their name to the desired column in a two-column chart (Figure 5.2).

DO YOU LIKE RAIN?

YES	NO

FIGURE 5.2   Children record votes (data) by writing their names in the appropriate columns.

A way to make this type of chart more concrete is to develop a template for voting by clipping clothespins directly onto a chart. Across the edge of each clothespin, front and back, you can write each child's name or glue on a small class photo of each child. Then the children simply clip their vote along the edge of the chart. True to the definition of a chart, information captured and preserved in this way can be viewed and analyzed.

We often use charts to keep track of and record data on a variety of information. As children become skilled with charting simple, two-column investigations, we can help them to collect and record multiple forms of data. Charts can display the answers to many questions all at once, as we see in Figure 5.3.

Charts of this nature can also be designed so that the information is presented in a more concrete way. Instead of representing data with words, stickers, or tallies, a chart can be made with real objects. For example, children can create a "living" chart with actual objects. If children are finding out about the class's favorite colors, children can be presented with a collection of different-colored square pieces of paper. They would pick the color square that represents their favorite color. Then, each paper square selection can be charted; that is, the color squares can be taped or glued directly onto the chart. This type of chart is visual.

The construction of this color square chart can take two forms, a *random* placement of squares or an *organized* charting in rows, columns, or sections of the chart. In the random placement of color squares, the teacher can allow the children to secure their square anywhere on a big chart. Then, the teacher counts how many there are of each color. This is done with the children, modeling one-to-one touch counting and keeping track with checkmarks. The teacher records how many squares there are of each color. Then the teacher can ask the children to look at the chart and ask if there is another way the color squares could be displayed. Sorting of the colors first, before gluing them down, would be a typical response that leads to an

"Our Favorites"				
Name	**Color**	**Number**	**Food**	**Sport**
Alice	Blue	3	Ice cream	Swimming
Juan	Orange	5	Pizza	Baseball
Celeste	Green	3	Chocolate	Soccer
Donald	Red	7	Pizza	Soccer
Edward	Blue	3	Ice cream	Basketball
Natalia	Blue	4	Pizza	Soccer

Charts are valuable tools for putting data into a format that can be easily examined. When the data are related to the students in your class, the children will have a natural interest because they are involved in the data; that is, the data represent their thoughts, likes, or interests.

FIGURE 5.3 Sample multiple-column chart.

organized charting experience. Repeating the activity with an organized chart where the children could place the squares in a section of the chart, or line them up forming columns of same-colored squares, would show them the importance of such organization. This organized representation provides a visual that is easy to use for making comparisons. In this linear form, keeping track of the squares one by one is easier to do. However, both of these types of charts are visual. Analysis of these types of charts is easy and appropriate for young children.

Replacing words with visual information, such as the paper squares or color tiles, enables young children to focus on examining the data rather than struggling to understand the words in the chart. Other iconic representations, such as different-colored paper cutouts of flowers, serve the same purpose.

TYPES OF CHARTS

We commonly think of **charts** in the form of a table with rows and columns, but they can also be constructed in other ways, as we discussed in the earlier example of charting children's favorite colors. There are many other forms of charts that are easy for young children to construct and are useful for our classrooms. Two examples are discussed next.

Webs

Webs are another wonderful way to capture and organize what we think and wonder about. They are used to organize ideas about specific themes or topics, and to generate a collective body of information that can serve as a springboard for analysis and investigation. For instance, as children experience different events in their day, they notice and observe many things. Perhaps when they are outside they notice some squirrels and birds. They wonder what other animals come to their school yard. Ideas for observation can be shared and as children observe the animals in the school yard, they can share their information in a class meeting. A teacher may help the children construct a web to capture their many wonderful observations. Such a web could be called "Animals That Come to School" (Figure 5.4). Beginning with this idea or concept, children can think about what they observe, what they infer, and what they know to construct the web.

Venn Diagrams

As children become experienced in observation, they will notice that some things share common characteristics with other things. For example, in the fall, many fruits and vegetables are harvested. Children will see these foods in the supermarkets, on farms along the road, in their own backyards, in their kitchens, or in books about the fall season. Being aware of this bounty is the first step to careful observation, analysis, and study. Children learn that some foods are called fruits and some are called vegetables. What makes something a fruit and what makes something a vegetable? Such a distinction could be researched, but to be more exciting and engaging, this distinction can be made through careful observation and analysis and then by forming conclusions and generalizations.

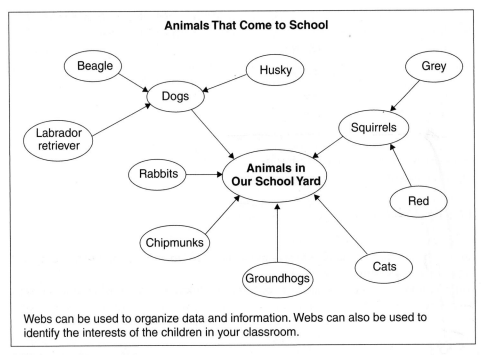

FIGURE 5.4 Sample web chart.

First, children should notice the similarities and differences among the produce. Color is something children will focus on in their first observations of the food. They will also notice shape. Some fruits and vegetables are round like apples, oranges, beets, tomatoes, and pumpkins; whereas others are long like zucchini, string beans, carrots, corn, and bananas. How can we help children focus on these similarities and differences and hence increase their abilities for observing, analyzing, classifying, logical reasoning, and critical thinking?

Actually, botanists define a fruit as the part of the plant that contains the seed. Using this definition, many of the "vegetables" that we eat such as corn, squash, beans, and tomatoes are fruits. True vegetables are from the root or leaf part of the plant. Thus, carrots, beets, spinach, potatoes, cabbage, and rhubarb are vegetables.

Here is a good example for this type of investigation. Choose two different pieces of produce to explore, such as apples and pumpkins. These are typical foods that are harvested in the fall and are abundant in many places. Bring some apples and pumpkins into the classroom. The ideal way to do this is to visit an apple orchard and a pumpkin farm. There are also many wonderful books available from public libraries that can be shared about apples and pumpkins. The information learned from these sources, as well as from the real apples and pumpkins, can be used as a part of your students' investigation.

Using the apples, pumpkins, and information resources, children can be given opportunities to explore and investigate apples and pumpkins with simple observational prompts. What do we see, smell, and feel when we explore the apple? How do we

Apple	Pumpkin
Red	Orange
Smooth	Bumpy
Small	Big
Round	Round
Used to bake pies	Used to bake pies
Has seeds	Has seeds
Grows on trees	Grows on vines
Cannot eat the seeds	Can eat the seeds

FIGURE 5.5 Sample chart for gathering data.

describe the apple? What do we see, smell, and feel when we explore the pumpkin? How do we describe the pumpkin?

A simple chart can be used to capture the children's observations. Each observation can be recorded on an index card, perhaps using pink cards for the apples and yellow cards for the pumpkin. The cards can be placed onto a chart; one column for the apple and one column for the pumpkin (Figure 5.5). During this time of exploration, teachers can invite children to describe exactly what they directly observe about the apple and the pumpkin. So, if a child says, "A pumpkin has a lot of seeds," we would have to develop a way to find out if that is true. Finding out can be done by cutting the pumpkin or by finding pictures in books or other available resources. Once these observations and investigations are made and the chart is somewhat complete, invite the children to study their observations and investigations. Again, we see that a chart is a wonderful way to capture and preserve our thoughts, observations, inferences, and knowledge. Wow, how much we know!

An important distinction can be made about observation versus inference versus social knowledge. Some things we can see directly; some things we can infer from our observations; and some things we know because of our experiences. Children can see the color of the apple, feel the texture of the pumpkin, and smell the aroma of each. They might eat a muffin that has small chunks of apple in it. They would infer that the muffin was made with apples, but that the recipe did not call for pumpkin. In reality, the muffin might have had some pumpkin in the mix, however it was blended into the batter.

Likewise, children may know that they have had apple cider or an apple pie even though they may not be able to see the process of turning apples into cider or baking the pie. This is an example of social context "knowing." Similarly, children may know that pumpkins grow in a patch, but may never have been to a pumpkin patch. We can validate their knowledge with a field trip or with an appropriate book, DVD, or video.

Once the charts are made (see Figure 5.5), we can ask the children if the apple and pumpkin have any characteristics that are the same. Then we can ask the children how to reorganize the index cards to show how the apple and pumpkin are different and the same all on one chart. Figure 5.6 is a **Venn diagram** that helps children sort their data according to similarities and differences.

Organizing Data in Science and Mathematics

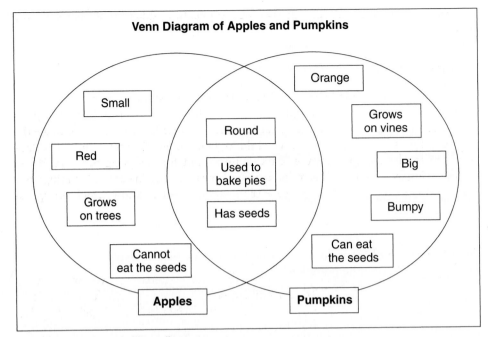

Venn Diagram of Apples and Pumpkins

Small

Red

Grows on trees

Cannot eat the seeds

Round

Used to bake pies

Has seeds

Orange

Grows on vines

Big

Bumpy

Can eat the seeds

Apples

Pumpkins

FIGURE 5.6 Sample Venn diagram.

Dogs and cats

Turtles and snakes

T-rex and stegosaurus

Soccer and basketball

Leaves and seeds

FIGURE 5.7 Venn diagrams can be constructed for a wide variety of subjects.

Based on children's interests, experiences, and curiosities, Venn diagrams can be constructed for a wide variety of subjects (Figure 5.7).

TYPES OF GRAPHS

The word **graph** comes from the Greek language and means "drawn" or "written." Graphs are representations or diagrams that represent a connection or interrelationship among two or more things. Graphs are as individualistic as the data that are used to construct them. Graphs allow us to organize relationships among data. The purpose of graphs is to make comparisons and identify changes and trends that occur. The way that the data are organized in a graph assists us in answering the questions that we are trying to answer.

Some forms of graphs are very simplistic. Others can be very complex, requiring advanced mathematics and abstract reasoning. We next examine a variety of graphs and discuss their values. We also discuss their application and appropriateness for use with young children.

People Graphs

People graphs can be made by grouping or lining up the students by particular characteristics or interests. For example, you could ask your children to form groups or lines based on what they're going to eat for lunch or their favorite sport. To make the comparisons more complete, ask each child to stand on one tile on the floor. The children can see how displaying the "data" is important for analyzing the data. When children simply form lines, it is difficult to see how many are in each line. Lining up— that is, organizing the data more carefully—helps them to know which group has more or less.

Concrete Graphs

Concrete graphs can be made by organizing the actual materials that you are studying. For example, one teacher invited each child to bring in a piece of their favorite fruit. (If you try this, for germ control, each piece of fruit should be placed in a baggie.) The class viewed the different types of fruit brought in and made a list so that the graph could be organized. The teacher then helped the children construct a graph by putting each type of fruit in a column labeled with the name and picture of the fruit on the top of the column. (It is important for a concrete graph to have cells or boxes to keep the one-to-one comparison of the columns equal.) After this concrete graph was constructed, the students counted and compared the number of each type of fruit.

Children can make other concrete graphs with other materials. For example, they can separate different colors of M&Ms or Skittles and line them up to make comparisons.

Pictographs

Pictographs are graphs that use drawings or photographs as the entries in the graph. For example, a graph showing the types of birds that come to the classroom feeder would have photographs of the different types of birds (Figure 5.8).

Pictographs are iconic representations of data. They are easier than other types of graphs for children to understand because they can visualize the items that they are comparing.

Bar Graphs

Bar graphs are used in similar situations as pictographs. The difference is that bar graphs are more abstract. The reader of the graph has to understand what each of the bars represents. Thus, bar graphs are not the first choice for use with young children. As children develop, both forms of graphs should be used side by side so that children can see the relationships between the different forms of graphs and also develop more abstract skills of observation (see Figure 5.8).

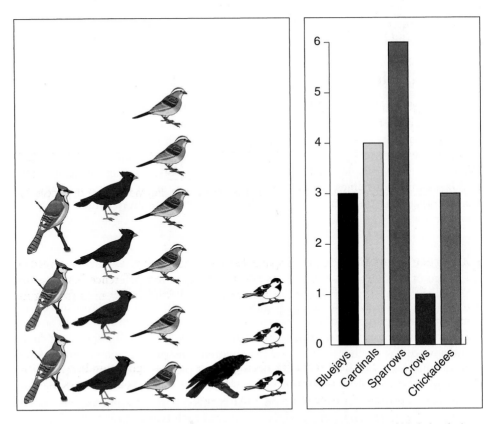

In the pictograph on the left, the reader can quickly differentiate types of birds by their visual chracterization. To gain a similiar understanding with the bar graph on the right, the reader has to be able to read the words for the different birds and then visualize what each of the birds look like.

FIGURE 5.8 Sample comparison of a pictograph and bar graph using the same data.

Histograms

Histograms are very useful forms of graphs for examining numerical data that the children contribute. For example, you might ask your students how many pencils they have in their desk. On the chalkboard, you could draw a horizontal line marked from zero to the highest number of pencils that any student has. Students could mark a yellow sticky note with the number of pencils they have (Figure 5.9).

Histograms are valuable tools for examining basic statistical values including range, mean, median, and mode. We examine each of these values next and discuss their usefulness with young children.

Range

The **range** is the spread of the data, from the most to the least amount. To calculate the range, you can count the spaces between the lowest number and the highest

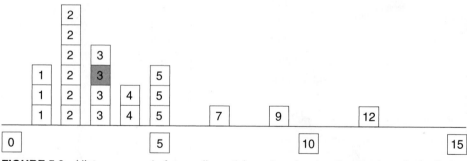

FIGURE 5.9 Histogram made from yellow sticky notes showing the number of pencils for students in a class.

number, one by one. The number of spaces between the numbers will be the spread or the range of the numbers. Mathematically, the range is the difference between the lowest and the highest value. For the histogram of the students' pencils (see Figure 5.9), the range would be 12 minus 1, or 11.

Mean

The **mean** is the statistical term for *average*. Because averaging numbers requires division, it should not be used in primary classrooms unless you are working with ideas related to multiplicative thinking and division.

Median

The **median** is the middle value, or the data point that divides the data set in half. For the pencil histogram, there are 21 participants. Often this is referred to as the N value. With an N of 21, the middle value would be the 11th value since there are 10 values below and 10 values above. Thus, if we count from either end to 11, we will locate the median. For our histogram the median is 3 pencils and is marked by the shaded square.

Mode

The **mode** is the most common value or, as more commonly thought of by young children, the most popular answer or item. For this pencil histogram, there are more students that have two pencils than any other value. Thus, the mode is 2. It is possible to have more than one mode if different values have equal numbers of respondents. If there are two most common values or two most popular answers, we say that the distribution is *bimodal*. It is possible to have a trimodal distribution and even a multimodal distribution, depending on the data.

Histograms can be used for a wide variety of information. Some examples are listed in Figure 5.10. You could also make a histogram of your children guessing how many M&Ms are in their closed bags. After they open their bags and count the M&Ms, a second histogram could be constructed and the children could make comparisons of their guesses to the actual values.

Guess how many trees are in the school yard.
Guess how many babies the class gerbil will have.
How many books have you read this month?
How many flowers are on the plant that you are growing?
How high did your toy rocket go?
How many chicken nuggets can you eat?

FIGURE 5.10 A variety of histograms could be constructed for your class.

Care must be taken to make sure that histograms are only used for quantitative data, not categorical data. For example, if the children are asked what their favorite pet is, a pictogram or bar graph could be constructed. However, a histogram for this information would not be appropriate because it is impossible to find the range, mean, or median of categorical or qualitative data.

One of the values of using children's own data is that it increases each child's attention to the histogram because they are part of the data. Each child will tend to look carefully at the chart to find his or her contribution to the data.

Circle Graphs

Circle graphs are sometimes called *pie graphs* because they are circular or round, like a pie. Also, pie pieces are cut in wedges from the center to the outside rim, forming sectors of the circle. In this sense, they are graphic representations that show a part-to-whole relationship or ratio among data. The data displayed in the circle graph can be information gathered on a topic, student preferences for something, or a representation of a sorting or classification activity.

A circle or pie graph captures information and preserves it in an interesting, visual way. Although the idea of ratios is complex for young children, we can construct circle graphs with young children in a way that is meaningful mathematically and visually descriptive. Instead of focusing on degrees in a circle and the ratios of the constructed wedges to the whole circle, we can focus on the construction of a circle graph through sorting and classifying. This process of sorting is appropriate because young children's early experiences with mathematical ideas begin with sorting. Children can also use counting in this process to find out how many, but counting is not a necessary condition when constructing a circle graph. We next consider an example of this process.

Children are exploring a collection of bean bags in four colors: red, yellow, blue, and green. If the goal of this activity is to construct a circle graph, it is recommended that at least one-half of the bean bags be of one color. Let's see why! Each child takes a bean bag. They look around and notice the colors of the bean bags around the room. The teacher asks the children to sort themselves into groups according to the color of the bean bag each child is holding. At this point, clusters of children begin to form. We can do many things with these same-color bean bag clusters of children. We can count off to find the number of children in each group. This idea is appropriate because young children count to solve problems quite naturally. We can also line up to create a people graph of bean bag colors. In this way, we can compare the length of the lines.

Or, we can create a circle graph. Once the children are clustered, we can have them form a circle with all the same-color bean bag holders forming an arc one by one next to each other. The circle will then be constructed with each color forming the circumference of the circle. You may want to construct a circle on the floor with tape or string to help the children form the circle. At this point, we can look to see the "length" of the arc formed by the red bean bags, the yellow bean bags, the blue bean bags, and the green bean bags. We can then take lengths of yarn into the center of the circle. Anchor the yarn in the center of the circle with tape and then trail the yarn to the places on the circumference of the circle where the colors of bean bags meet. This action constructs the wedges of the pie. Children can look at the sectors to see the relative amount of each color of bean bag. Such a graph can be analyzed without actual counting. The analysis is visual. Ideas and concepts for *half* can be developed at an intuitive level.

Once this living circle graph is constructed, the children can place their bean bags on the circumference of the circle and step away. The yarn will then display a discernable circle graph where the ratio of bean bags can be seen.

Line Graphs

Line graphs are extremely useful graphs for examining changes and trends. Line graphs tend to be abstract and therefore very difficult for young children to utilize. As the teacher, however, your being able to read and interpret line graphs is critical, because line graphs are often used to examine data about student and school test scores. Being able to interpret this information is valuable for discussions with parents, teachers, and administrators.

Line graphs are reserved for examining data where numerical changes occur. Their value is for situations where measurements are collected over a period of time, or for specific variables such as length, weight, temperature, or air pressure.

Line graphs give us information about how two variables are related to each other. Let's suppose that we take measurements of the air temperature for a day, as shown in Figure 5.11. Although the temperatures were recorded each hour, we can estimate the temperature for the intervals of time between each point. The result is that the lines tend to be curved to indicate the temperature that is constantly changing. From the graph, we can make inferences. For instance the high temperature was at approximately 3 PM. We could also infer that a rain shower occurred in the midafternoon that cooled things off.

A distinct value of line graphs is that they indicate to us trends that occur between two variables. These trends are given by examining the slope of the line.

Let's look at a few graphs that demonstrate a variety of slopes. Assume that we collect a number of round objects. For each object, we find the diameter and the circumference. By wrapping a piece of string around the object and measuring the string we can get fairly accurate measurements. The measurements are recorded in the chart shown in Figure 5.12. These data can be recorded on a line graph. In Figure 5.13, we have recorded the diameter on the vertical axis and the circumference on the horizontal axis.

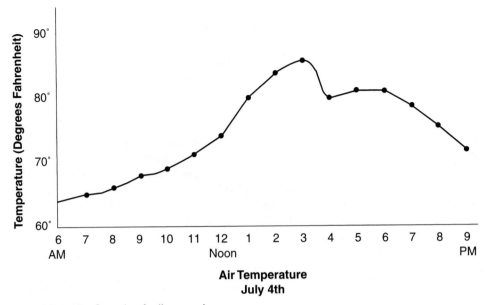

FIGURE 5.11 Sample of a line graph.

Diameter (inches)	Circumferences (inches)
0.5	1.5
1.0	3.2
1.5	4.75
1.75	5.5
2.0	6.5
2.5	8.0
3.0	9.5
3.9	11.0
4.4	13.5
5.0	15.75
5.5	17.5

FIGURE 5.12 Chart giving the measurement of diameter and circumference for a variety of round objects.

Notice in Figure 5.13 that all of the points on the graph line up in a straight line (allowing for small errors in measurement). This shows us that there is a constant relationship between diameter and circumference. As the diameter increases, the circumference also increases. In addition, we can compare the relationship between the values for the diameter and the circumference. This is sometimes

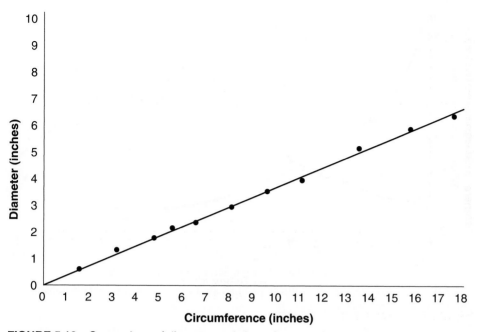

FIGURE 5.13 Comparison of diameter and circumference of round objects.

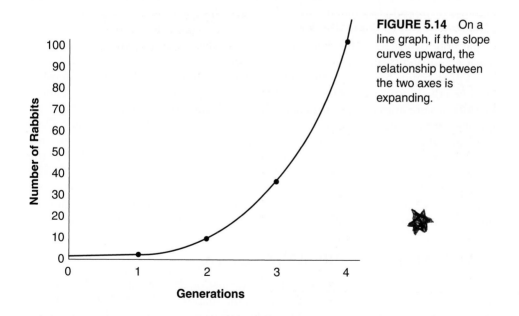

FIGURE 5.14 On a line graph, if the slope curves upward, the relationship between the two axes is expanding.

called the **slope** of the line. For this graph, the slope is approximately 3.14 (the approximate value of pi).

Other graphs will have slopes that are constantly changing. If the slope of the line curves upward, then the relationship between the two axes is expanding, as shown in Figure 5.14. For example, a graph that shows the number of offspring that

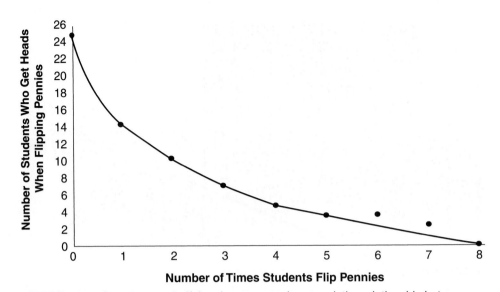

FIGURE 5.15 On a line graph, if the slope curves downward, the relationship between the two axes is decreasing.

can come from one pair of rabbits would increase for each generation. Because the number of reproducing rabbits expands with each generation, the total number of rabbits increases dramatically. A graph of a family tree can also demonstrate the expansion: two parents, four grandparents, eight great-grandparents, sixteen great-great-grandparents, and so forth.

Other graphs have slopes that curve downward, indicating that the relationship between the two axes decreases over time. For example, look at Figure 5.15, a graph of student outcomes of flipping pennies. Each time the students in the class flip their pennies, approximately one-half will have heads and one-half will have tails. Only students who flip heads can continue. The result is that after the first flip you only have about one-half of the class remaining. After the second flip, only one-half of the remaining students (or about one-fourth of the total) will be able to continue. The downword-sloping line that results can be seen in Figure 5.15. This graph is sometimes referred to as a **half-life graph** because the value decreases to one-half for each unit of time. Graphs showing decreases in radioactivity always form a half-life graph.

USING MAPS TO ORGANIZE DATA

Maps can be effective tools for organizing information. For example, students could make a map of the school yard and mark on the map the location of any trash they find (Figure 5.16). They could then use this information to make inferences about wind direction, which may have moved the trash around, and traffic patterns of people walking through the school yard.

As you explore the Concept Explorations delineated in the second part of this book, keep in mind the many tools that are available for organizing and displaying data charts and graphs.

FIGURE 5.16 Locations of trash found in our school.

Review and Discussion Questions

1. Discuss the importance of children learning to use different types of charting and graphing early in their education so that they can use them as models for capturing and displaying information that is important to them.

2. Describe a scenario in which children are encouraged to use a variety of charts and graphs to display gathered data. Think of a specific Concept Exploration such as rocks, birds, light and color, insects, clouds, toys and tools, or seeds for your ideas.

3. Share ways to have children use mathematical language and concepts to interpret charts and graphs. For this question, you may choose any Concept Exploration for content (see Part II).

Resources for Teachers

Books

Kolb, D. A., Rubin, I. M., & McIntyre, J. M. (1984). *Organizational psychology* (4th ed.). Englewood Cliffs, NJ: Prentice Hall.

Polya, G. (1971). *How to solve it: A new aspect of mathematics method* (2nd ed.). Princeton, NJ: Princeton University Press.

Journals

Newmann, F. M., & Wehlage, G. G. (1993, April). Five standards of authentic instruction, *Educational Leadership*, pp. 8–12.

CHAPTER 6

Criteria for Developing Concept Explorations

Concept explorations are catalysts to help children focus their interests on the experiences of daily life and to learn from these experiences. Concept explorations help children take notice of common experiences that sometimes become so "natural" that they lose curiosity value. The purpose of concept explorations is for children to actually take part in exploring their world. Children's curiosity and sense of wonder are boundless. The concept explorations in Part II of this text capitalize on this sense of wonder and engage children in creative and interesting investigations designed to help them make sense of their world and enjoy learning.

A quality concept exploration has several criteria that cause it to be a productive experience for children:

- Provides solid science and mathematics content.
- Considers the appropriate level of child development.
- Integrates mathematics and science.
- Is guided by the child's world.
- Incorporates children's literature.
- Actively involves children as they investigate basic materials. —hands on
- Is founded on a safe environment. how your room is organized

Each of these criteria is examined in detail next.

PROVIDES SOLID SCIENCE AND MATHEMATICS CONTENT

The content related to the concepts of science and mathematics that are presented need to be accurate and consistent with present knowledge. On the surface this would appear to be obvious. However, many inaccuracies have become common "wives' tales" that show up in science and mathematics textbooks. Just as your grandmother incorrectly put butter on burns, many resources include activities that we now know to be incorrect and, in many circumstances, unsafe.

Solid Science Content

A very common activity that is presented to children is to make a volcano out of papier-mâché with a baby food jar at the top. Baking soda is put in the jar with food coloring added. Vinegar is dropped into the jar using an eye dropper. A foaming reaction occurs that supposedly duplicates a volcano's action. Actually, this activity demonstrates the reaction of acids and bases. Volcanic eruptions are caused by heat and pressure deep within the earth—a totally different process. We do not want our children to infer that volcanoes are formed by raining vinegar on baking soda. A better alternative activity would be to put a pastry bag filled with whipped cream underneath a layer cake and as you squeeze the bag, the pressure will force the cream through the cake, forming a volcano. This much more closely represents the process of a volcano.

Figure 6.1 illustrates another common science activity for which an incorrect explanation of the science involved is often given. A common activity in science textbooks is to place a burning candle in a tray of water and to place a glass jar on top. The candle goes out when the oxygen is used up and water rises in the jar. The explanation given that as the oxygen is used up in the burning process, the water replaces the oxygen.

In reality, the oxygen combines with the carbon in the candle wax to produce carbon dioxide. The carbon dioxide has the same volume as the oxygen. The water actually rises because the heat from the burning candle causes the air to expand. The expanding air will bubble out of the bottom of the jar. As the air cools, it contracts causing the water to be drawn into the jar.

The inaccuracies that exist in many experiments can be decreased by reading the current literature. Journals for teaching science, such as *Science for Children*, often have updates of research on basic science processes. These articles are reviewed by professionals and specialists for accuracy. Another excellent resource is your

FIGURE 6.1 An example of incorrect science.

colleagues. If you have concerns regarding an activity, contact your local biology, earth science, chemistry, and physics teachers to confirm you are teaching "good science." If they have concerns, often they can recommend alternative demonstrations and activities.

Solid Mathematics Content

We have available to us wonderful references in mathematics that are specifically related to working with and teaching young children. Publications from the National Council of Teachers of Mathematics (NCTM), including *Principles and Standards for School Mathematics* and their journal *Teaching Children Mathematics*, offer wonderful information, ideas, and suggestions for appropriately and effectively applying mathematics content to young children's explorations and learning. More detailed information on these resources is presented later in this chapter.

The mathematics used with young children is often used in wrong contexts. These inconsistencies can cause long-term difficulties when they are presented to children. One common error, related to graphing, is found in many books about transferring information for bar graphs to line graphs. Each form of graph has characteristics that make it ideal for specific types of data. Let's look at some examples.

In the two graphs shown in Figure 6.2, students of Mrs. Mertz's class each identified their favorite color. The bar graph would be a proper form of graph to indicate the popularity of the different colors with her students. It would be improper to use a line graph because there are no relationships between the different colors. There is actually no value for each point on the line between the different colors. Line graphs must be used only when there is a numerical relationship between the different values.

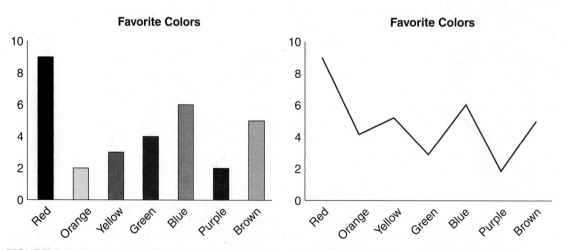

FIGURE 6.2   An example of the correct use of a bar graph, but the incorrect use of a line graph.

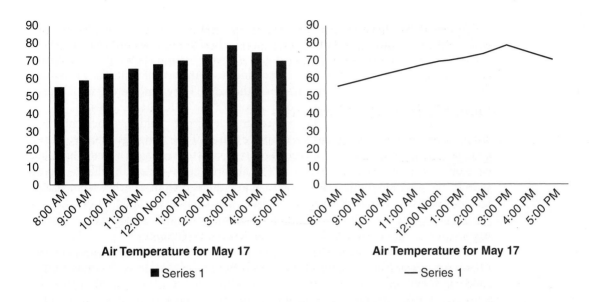

FIGURE 6.3 An example of the correct use of a bar graph and a line graph.

An example of the proper use of a line graph is given in Figure 6.3. In this figure, the line graph of data the students collected on temperature would be a proper form of graph because a temperature can be recorded for each point along the graph. This line graph would, however, be more difficult for children to understand than the bar graph because it is more abstract.

CONSIDERS THE APPROPRIATE LEVEL OF CHILD DEVELOPMENT

In Chapter 2 we discussed the sequences of child development that take place as children grow. The work of Rousseau, Piaget, Dewey, Vygotsky, and others gives us good guidance in designing appropriate activities for our students.

This book is designed for use with preschool and primary school children, ages 3 through grade 3. The Concept Explorations described in Part II have been tested in early childhood settings as part of the field experience connected with a college-level Early Childhood Preschool Mathematics and Science course. As the college students in the course have begun to work in primary classrooms, they have reported that many of these Concept Explorations work just as effectively with primary children. It is the intention of this book to stress the inquiry process at all levels of primary education. The level of description and understanding of concepts are the variables. The mathematics and science grids provided for each Concept Exploration indicate which standards are addressed in each of the activities.

As children develop, their thinking related to specific concepts in mathematics and science goes through four distinct stages of representation: concrete, semi-concrete, semi-abstract, and abstract.

For an experience to be concrete it must be part of a child's immediate world—and it must be real. For example, let's say each child in our class brings in a piece of fruit. We place each piece of fruit on a grid forming a graph showing the fruit preferences for the children in the class. The children see the actual fruit. They can touch and manipulate the fruit to organize their thoughts. They can use the visualization and manipulations to make direct comparisons of the different varieties.

To have a similar activity at the semi-concrete level, one could have each child draw the piece of fruit or select a picture of the piece of fruit. Their drawings of the fruit could be taped on a grid on a chart. This type of chart is often referred to as a **pictograph** since each object is represented by a picture. The children can visualize the different types of fruit that are represented. However, they lose the benefit of the three-dimensional tactile experience. This requires more complex reasoning by the children.

At the semi-abstract level, the drawing of the fruit would be replaced by an abstract form such as a square. The children can see that certain columns in the graph have more squares than others. However, they must translate in their minds that each square represents a piece of fruit. And they must reason to themselves that each column represents a different type of fruit. A productive way to produce a graph of this nature is to use sticky notes with the name of the fruit on them. This form of graph should be reserved for later experiences after children have had opportunities to develop their ability to visualize graph structures. Bar graphs would fit into this category (Figure 6.4).

At the abstract level, the chart would not give any visual support to the commonality of the different fruits. The only way that the children would be able to understand which fruits are most common is to understand the abstract symbols for each number and to know the amount that each symbol represents. For more detailed information about data, charting, and graphing, see Chapter 4.

For complete understanding, children's experiences must be initiated at the concrete level. Then, over an expanded period of time, they work toward the abstract level. Many experiences must be given at each level before moving toward more abstract experiences.

Let's say that you want to learn the Russian language. You find that the alphabet that you have used all your life is no longer applicable. Suddenly, you need to learn the Cyrillic alphabet which has 33 characters, each with its own sound. To be able to recognize, internalize, and verbalize each character would take many hundred

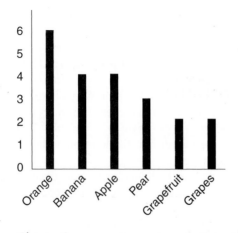

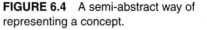
FIGURE 6.4 A semi-abstract way of representing a concept.

experiences for each character. In addition, each character, by itself or in combination with other letters, has particular meanings. How many times would you have to visualize these different combinations before you develop the necessary understanding to communicate? This is the exact process that children need to process before they understand the representations for each number in the number system. When they see the number 4, they see a triangle on a stick. They need hundreds of visualizations before that abstract figure instantly represents four balls, four apples, or four objects of any type. This development comes only after numerous experiences at the concrete, semi-concrete, and semi-abstract levels (Figure 6.5).

Young children have a very difficult time understanding concepts that they cannot visualize. When water on the chalkboard evaporates, from the child's perspective, it disappears. It does not exist anymore. It requires more abstract reasoning to believe that the water is still around in our air; we just cannot see it. Discussions of the basic particles of matter, of atoms and molecules, are difficult because children cannot visualize them. As children's minds develop, the ability to create mental vision develops. However, the visualization patterns that each child develops are not identical to those of peers. The development is a slow and complex process.

When algebra is investigated, the need for the child to be able to understand abstract ideas increases dramatically. In science, presenting topics such as atoms and

Concrete activities are activities that use real objects to examine characteristics. For example, one could show four pens. The children can actually see and hold the four pens.

Semi-concrete activities include visual representations of objects. For example, one could draw four pens. The children can visualize the pens, but they cannot manipulate the pens as though they are real.

Semi-abstract representations are ones that the child cannot visualize. They must visualize from a simplistic form. For example, one could make four dots. The child would be told that each dot represents a pen. The dots on dice are good examples of semi-abstract representations.

● ● ● ●

Abstract representations have form that is nonfigurative. The shape of an abstract representation does not relate to the shape of the object represented. Instead it has a theoretical representation.

4

FIGURE 6.5 Four stages of development of understanding.

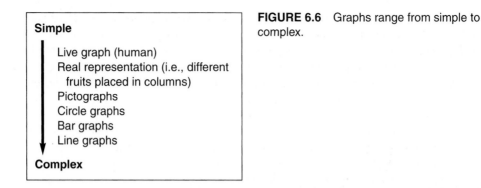

FIGURE 6.6 Graphs range from simple to complex.

molecules at too young an age often causes much frustration for young children. It is best to begin with concrete experiences and allow children to construct the abstractions from within.

When selecting which type of graph to use for an activity, you must be aware that graphs range in complexity, as illustrated in Figure 6.6. Consider your children's level of development—concrete, semi-concrete, semi-abstract, abstract—before choosing a particular type of graph. (Graphs were discussed in detail in Chapter 5.)

TRULY INTEGRATES SCIENCE AND MATHEMATICS

For organizational convenience, schools traditionally separate curricular areas such as mathematics, science, language arts, and social studies. This separation permits us to concentrate on particular skill areas of the curriculum. But as we utilize this knowledge in life situations, we find that we need to incorporate and integrate all of these subject areas into accomplishing our goals. These curriculum divisions that we have set up are in reality nothing but a classification of knowledge developed by our predecessors. If we are going to design our classrooms to represent children's lives in as realistic a way as possible, we need to break down these artificial curricular barriers. The thematic nature of concept explorations makes them natural and ideal for integrating all areas of the curriculum.

> In the late 1940s and early 1950s, schools taught geography, history, and government. Now, educators have regrouped these subjects and developed the term *social studies*.

A quality concept exploration includes a wide variety of activities that integrate all discipline areas. They encourage more detailed observations and inquiry through music, prose, poetry, dance, and art. They incorporate all of the children's senses. They elicit children's questions. They encourage each child to share ideas and interests with other children and adults. They help children develop learning and organizational patterns through the activities of collecting and classifying information. They help children take ownership of their learning by involving them in the process of inquiry. They are catalysts for children's continuous exploration for the rest of their lives.

> "Mathematics is the language of science."
> Galileo Galilei

Science and Mathematics in particular become integrated in a natural process. The recognizing and understanding of trends and relationships that occur in scientific processes require organization and analysis of data. This is true with Einstein's theory of relativity. This is also true with comparing how high a variety of balls can bounce. This is true when we collect data on how many birds come to the classroom bird feeder. We utilize the relationships of mathematics and science every day throughout our lives when we count the calories we eat, analyze our gas mileage for our car, and fertilize our garden.

Science activities utilize skills in mathematics to reason out scientific relationships. Many characteristics such as height, weight, temperature, and pressure must be measured. Thus, utilizing basic skills of mathematics throughout experiences in science is imperative in that it ensures that the science taught utilizes a process approach. In addition, the mathematics taught through science activities is presented in authentic situations, which increases the retention of mathematics skills.

IS GUIDED BY THE CHILD'S WORLD

The world of a child is much more limited than an adult's world. Their world encompasses their immediate environment. Their world is based on their home, school, and neighborhood. Their real world is limited to places that they have actually been.

What they view on TV may be faraway places captured on a nature special or imaginary places such as *Sesame Street* or Barney's world. For a young child, the Care Bears or Barney may be as real as Mr. Rogers.

For children to be mentally and physically involved in learning experiences, the experiences must be part of their actual world. They must explore their world. Activities need to explore the tree in the school yard, the rocks in the stream, or the melting snow on the hill. Unless your class lives near a rain forest, the children will have great difficulty understanding what a rain forest is about.

Children have a natural curiosity about their world. At a very young age, they realize that they can manipulate and control some aspects of the world around them. A rock causes waves when it is thrown in a pond. A slice of bread attracts ducks. Shadows follow me wherever I go, unless clouds come.

Being able to control their immediate world is the beginning part of the process of developing personal responsibility. It is through these experiences that children learn that the fish need to be fed daily. They understand that if they do not water the plants, the plants will die.

As teachers, we can quickly find the interests of our children through our conversations. Their interests and questions are shared with us constantly. It is imperative that we listen carefully to these questions and that we share our enthusiasm about these interests with the children. We must also support children as they seek ways to find answers to their questions and make sense of their world.

Our responses to children's discussions must indicate that we are also interested in the same things in which they are interested. We need to help them feel that their comments are valued; that what they say is a contribution to the learning process for us as well as them.

INCORPORATES CHILDREN'S LITERATURE

An appropriate environment for young children is always print rich. An assortment of books invites young children to think, imagine, learn, and enjoy many worlds. Picture books, information books, storybooks, and books of every genre stimulate theory building, creative thinking, and imaginative play. When children settle in with a good book in their laps, they are transported to another place and time. They see things that they may not have in "their own backyard." They can identify with a character's adventures or imagine themselves in the character's world.

When adults model the enjoyment of reading, it becomes more valuable to children. Also, when children and adults read together, habits of book reading and book sharing abound. Books indeed are an essential component of literacy development. As we structure our classroom environments, we need to be very careful to include a variety of books that reflect the interests and curiosities of children. Trips to the library are also wonderful ways to model lifelong habits of joyful reading and information seeking.

Children should also be encouraged to bring special books from home to share at school. Oftentimes, even before children can "read," they can recite their favorite books verbatim. This repetition and pattern awareness are important parts of the development of literacy and critical thinking. As children learn to treat books as special parts of their world, they begin to value books' presence in their world and are more likely to continue to treasure the powerful act of reading. What a wonderful gift to give to your students.

As children become involved in the many exciting Concept Explorations provided in this book, it is important to review the list of suggested resources included for each one. The resources included are varied in content. There are storybooks of fiction and fantasy; trade books written for children; and information books for adult reading. As we model using books for gaining and gathering information, children see that books are one exciting way to learn. Using books to support the concept explorations can also spark creative pursuits. Children can be encouraged to write and publish their own books that display the learning and theory building they are developing for each topic. Having children become authors is a wonderful way to celebrate their creativity and their individual accomplishments. Such child-authored books can be shared with other children in other classes as well as with families.

Indeed, creating a literacy-rich environment as children develop their abilities to seek knowledge and information is an important part of our role as early childhood educators. Creating a classroom culture that values books will increase children's enjoyment of books and help to promote lifelong interest and joy in reading.

Invite your children to visit their library and find books related to each Concept Exploration in Part II that include mathematics and/or science concepts appropriate for young children. Incorporate the information and resources in these books into the classroom studies. Children's contributions to the information gathered are valuable tools for increasing children's ownership of the learning process. This ownership is critical for developing positive attitudes about learning in general. A list of excellent children's resources is included in the bibliography of children's books at the end of each chapter in Part II.

ACTIVELY INVOLVES CHILDREN AS THEY INVESTIGATE COMMON BASIC MATERIALS

The more that materials basic to the child's world are involved in the learning process, the more authentic the learning experience becomes. This authenticity motivates children to more actively involve their minds in causing changes to occur.

Toys become interesting to children because they can manipulate and control the actions of the toys. Children want to explore how to make the toy make noise, light up, or move. When they find the on/off switch for a TV, they continue to keep pushing the button until an adult takes action. Children like to cause things in their environment to be active. It gives them a feeling of power. This is critical for their development. When they understand that they can control basic objects around them, this power becomes a catalyst for their curiosity.

The materials found to be the most useful when used with young children are the most simplistic. For instance, blocks and balls can hold a child's interest for extended periods. The child can explore and experiment. How high can I stack the blocks? How high does the ball bounce? These materials also encourage imagination. The blocks become a road, a house, a barn for their animals.

Many basic games and puzzles expand children's understanding of basic numerical concepts. Games that encourage sorting, sequencing, seriating, patterning, counting, color identification, and geometric shapes should be available. Experiences that encourage children to manipulate basic objects such as rocks into different groups are valuable for developing basic mathematical ideas and concepts.

Preferably, activities that promote children's personal accomplishments cooperation and collaboration should be used. Competitive experiences should be kept to a minimum.

IS FOUNDED ON A SAFE ENVIRONMENT

Safety should always be a primary consideration when planning activities with children. For many children, fear is not a factor in basic learning experiences. They have no concept of danger. Many toddlers have no concern about climbing on furniture, up walls, or over barriers. Also, some children tend to put many objects into their mouths. Always consider safety.

As teachers, we must be responsible for providing safe environments for our students. Doors to cabinets containing questionable cleansers or chemicals and materials should be locked or have childproof safety features. Sharp objects and heavy objects should likewise be monitored and kept secure.

Early in each child's school experience, routines need to be established that set safe practices and guidelines. Children need to know the proper and safe use of the materials available to them. They need to know—and should be given boundaries for—where, when, and how they can try particular activities.

Particular activities that might be beneficial learning experiences, but also have features that could be hazardous, should be presented with adult supervision and should model safe practices. For example, if you are exploring the nature of how particular chemicals react, you could invite a few parents into class to conduct the activity with each group. Be sure you have enough supervision for the number of children.

Field trips provide excellent opportunities for children to explore the world around them. However, it is critical that the children understand basic rules before the field trip is initiated. Once a field trip has started, it is difficult to set new ground rules and to change your students' behavior to the new guidelines.

When conducting a walking field trip, set a guideline that you as teacher are always in the front of the class and that students are to never be in front of you. In addition, a second adult should remain at the back of the group. All students should be between the two adults. With particularly young children, it is wise to have a rope that all children hold onto as you travel.

CONCEPT EXPLORATIONS

This book includes 12 prepared concept explorations that are designed to help teachers and children direct their interests. These concept explorations have many more activities for study than time will permit. They include alternative approaches for observing and studying particular themes. We suggest that you select from the "menu" the opportunities that best suit your school environment and the developmental level of your students.

Countless other concept explorations can be developed on topics of interest to the children in your setting or to topics of local interest in your communities. You are encouraged to take the design attributes and activities format presented here and design your own concept explorations based on themes of local interest. If a pond is located close to your school, then a concept exploration on ponds could be an exciting experience. Often, student interests identified in your classroom will "develop themselves" and cause the children to make an in-depth study related to the events. For example, a pair of robins might build a nest outside a classroom window. A camcorder could be aimed at the nest so that the children can observe these life processes.

Students at a school adjacent to a cemetery developed a concept exploration that included a comparison of rocks used for the tombstones and how they weathered. Tombstone rubbings were developed as part of the art class. Family trees were developed. A timeline showing the number of deaths each year was developed by the children. A peak year in 1915 was found to have been caused by a smallpox epidemic. The date on one tombstone led students to realize the young man had died during the Civil War.

Another example comes from a kindergarten class experience. At the beginning of the school year, the children were drawn to and intrigued by the sunflowers growing outside their school. At recess times, they observed and explored the sunflowers carefully and began to develop theories about how they got there, how they grew, and who ate the seeds. The teacher was quite taken with the interesting theories the children were developing and decided to develop a concept exploration about sunflowers. Curiosities were shared, books were read, experts were consulted, drawings and stories were "published," and sunflower seeds were planted and eaten. This exploration was then expanded to a concept exploration about seeds.

This chapter explains the format for the concept explorations presented in this book. It includes discussions on identifying the levels of development of your children and selecting activities that utilize learning skills that are appropriate for meeting your students' needs. It focuses on utilizing all the children's senses. You are encouraged to incorporate this format into concept explorations that you construct on your own for your specific learning community.

In the following subsections, each aspect of concept explorations is examined with examples of classroom experiences that support good learning practices.

Concept Exploration Introduction

The purpose of the introduction of a concept exploration is to develop children's interest and curiosity. It is important to involve the children physically, cognitively, and emotionally in their learning. It is critical that children's early learning experiences relate to their immediate real lives. These experiences validate the process of learning. They help children understand the value of learning because these experiences determine how they function in their own environment.

Nothing can be as frustrating and exasperating as being asked to learn things that appear to have no purpose or value. "When will I ever need to know this?" Having these "removed from life" experiences too often causes children of all ages to lose interest in learning. Thus, our first task is to focus on how the concept exploration relates to the children's everyday lives.

As a way to initially engage children in the topic of a concept exploration, many formats for initial exploration are encouraged. As children show interest in a topic or theme, conversations can be conducted to determine the children's curiosity and wonder about the topic. Webs of information can be generated with ideas and theories the children may have about the topic as well as some of their questions and ideas for inquiry. Building ownership for learning is a good way to help children become confident in their learning skills and feel appreciated for their contributions.

Songs, stories, and poems involving hand and body movements are encouraged. Trade books can be read while the children play the roles of the characters. In books that incorporate mathematics, the children can manipulate related materials to involve themselves in the story. When science concepts are included in the stories, poems, or songs, children can duplicate these processes in the classroom or the school yard.

These introductory activities serve to focus the children's attention. Having had conversations, sung the song, read the story or poem, or other introductory experiences, the subsequent activities and investigations will take on greater meaning and purpose. Their attention is directed toward expanding the information gained from the introductory activities and engaging in meaningful learning.

The introductory activities also contribute to developing students' understanding of the consistency of natural processes. The processes they observe in their community are the same processes that occur in different regions of the world, and the same processes that have occurred throughout history. Having selected a theme that is part of the children's everyday world, we demonstrate that this topic is part of the larger natural framework that children all over the world experience. The topics for the concept explorations presented in this book are relevant to children everywhere. They were selected on the basis of what children everywhere wonder about, such as sunshine and shadows, clouds, water, wind, and seeds. The contexts may be different in different geographic regions, but the exploration and richness of the experiences and learning are the same.

Concept Exploration Activities for Your Classroom

Concept exploration activities are the vehicles for children's learning experiences. They are the actual activities that direct the students through their inquiries.

In Chapter 3, the nature of problem solving was discussed. Concept exploration activities should provide opportunities for children to develop their skills in all four stages of problem solving. By basing the exploration activities on students' own experiences and questions, you greatly expand the skill development for the *defining problems* and *developing procedures* stages.

Because they are designed to be authentic learning experiences, concept explorations should cover a variety of curriculum topics. Concept explorations should incorporate literature, poetry, history, geography, music, dance, and many other areas.

Conceptual Framework for Science and Mathematics

When developing a concept exploration, teachers must have a strong background in the exploration's topic. This is one of the difficult aspects of teaching because teachers need to be "experts" in all fields. Even though the children will not be at the stage of development or have the background experiences to understand many of the scientific aspects of a topic, it is important that you as their teacher have this basic understanding and knowledge. This understanding will help direct you to recognize opportunities for students' observations. For example, when taking classes on nature walks, teachers who can identify a milkweed plant might look at the bottom of a leaf and find the eggs of a monarch butterfly. Or, they might find the beautiful caterpillar of the monarch. Teachers who do not recognize the plant might walk by, losing a good opportunity for a learning experience. As teachers, you will spend your entire career expanding your knowledge related to all the various fields of education. Indeed, we are lifelong learners!

Identifying Resources

Many resources are available to assist you in improving your background knowledge on all topics. The professional journals of the different teacher associations, such as *Science and Children*, published by the National Science Teachers Association (NSTA); *Teaching Children Mathematics*, published by the NCTM; *Young Children*, published by the National Association for the Education of Young Children (NAEYC); and *Childhood Education*, published by the Association for Childhood Education International (ACEI), are excellent resources. All of these journals publish articles each month that are related to numerous topics. Typically, these articles include both background information and classroom activities conducted by the authors. Often resource material sources are included.

Many teachers, curriculum and research-oriented organizations such as NSTA, NCTM, NAEYC, and ACEI also conduct national, state, and local affiliate conferences and workshops that include many sessions related to classroom practice and projects.

Internet searches can be excellent quick resources for classroom teachers and children. Because Internet sites change continually, it is not practical to list particular sources. Fortunately, many search engines are available that will identify numerous valuable sites by just typing in the key words. Some particularly useful search engines for teachers and classrooms include Ask Jeeves (*http://www.ask.com*), Ask Jeeves for Kids (*http://www.ajkids.com/*), Kids Click! (*http://www.kidsclick.org/*) Education World (*http://www.educationworld.com*), and Google (*http://www.google.com*).

Care must be taken to ensure that children are supervised when they are using the Internet. Unfortunately, at times very innocent words can have double meanings that will select sites totally inappropriate for children. Filters to decrease the accessing of inappropriate sites are available. Kid-Safe directories can be found by googling Kids Search Engines.

Local and school libraries also have valuable resources including numerous trade books, educational journals, books, audiotapes, videotapes, CDs, and DVDs.

People resources are also important. Local experts on the topic of the concept exploration are wonderful resources. Perhaps a parent, grandparent, aunt, uncle, sibling, neighbor, colleague, friend, or community member has an expertise related to a hobby, profession, or interest. For example, someone in the community may be an avid bird watcher or gardener. This person could be an interesting guest to have in class or on a field trip. Perhaps a local science or mathematics teacher or university professor could come to school and work with the children as they investigate their topics of inquiry.

Community resources are a wonderful source of support and information. Local businesses, nurseries, orchards, museums, centers, nature preserves, and national, state, or local recreation areas and parks are also wonderful resources. Organizing a field trip to a place that is related to the concept exploration is enriching. For example, visiting a pumpkin farm or an apple orchard could be related to children's investigations of seeds, leaves, or trees.

Using the Five Senses

In Chapter 1, we said that everything a child learns is through her or his senses. We receive our information through the five major senses: touch, smell, taste, sound, and sight. Other forms of sense also exist; however, they are related more to body functions. For example, the sense of balance is centered in the inner ear. This is why persons who have an inner ear infection have a difficult time standing up.

Pleasurable sensory experiences exist in many contexts. The smell of a favorite food cooking or baking, the sound of a familiar voice, the wind rustling through the trees or the sound of water lapping on a shore, the sight of a beautiful sunrise or sunset, the feel of a soft pet or stuffed animal, or the taste of a delicious orange or favorite sweet all contribute to our sensory pleasures.

We value the development of sensual experiences. We listen critically to music from our stereo and study the quality of different types of speakers and systems. We enjoy movies that have special visual effects. We prepare foods that have specific tastes and aromas, often reminding us of wonderful experiences in the past. We create for ourselves an environment that is rich in experiences that we find pleasurable.

Helen Keller's story is spectacular in that she had no sight or hearing. The only means by which she could receive information was through touch, taste, and smell. Her teacher, Anne Sullivan, taught her to spell words by touching Helen's hand at varying positions. Helen Keller was able to learn to talk, and she became a prolific author.

Interestingly, these experiences that we create are very individualistic. Particular foods that we grew up enjoying and consider a special treat can be unattractive to others. This implies that the development of sensory appreciation of specific experiences, particularly odors and tastes, is a learned experience that is unique to each of us.

Experiences for children must be designed to be inviting to the senses. The learning environment that we create for our students tends to concentrate on visual and auditory senses. We want our classroom to be bright and colorful. We have our students watch demonstrations that we arrange. We invite them to watch videotapes. We have pictures on the wall. We have aquariums, terrariums, and other "learning stations" arranged around the room.

We engage in conversations with our students, read stories with them, have them listen to tapes, and have electronic toys that make all types of sounds. As we become more aware of how all the senses contribute to a child's engagement in learning, we will be able to maximize children's learning environments to include many multi-sensory experiences.

There are many simple observation stations that can be designed and constructed for your classroom. Several simple designs are presented in the following subsections for each of the senses. These observation stations are designed to be flexible tools that you can alter to fit the needs of your students and vary according to the nature of your concept exploration. Different stations can be developed to concentrate on particular senses.

Stations for the Sense of Touch

Children are very tactile. They love to touch everything that they can reach. They like to feel different textures. They have a favorite blanket or sweater that gives them a feeling of ownership or comfort. They like to feel the soft fur of a pet or stuffed animal.

J. David Keller

Sand, mud, water, cotton, shells, and stones all provide rich sensations that are inviting to young children.

Some young children want to put everything in their mouths to get a better sense of feel. The tongue is the most sensitive organ for touch. A small hole or chip in a tooth sometimes feels like a cavern to us. This is because the touch nerve endings are very close together on the tongue.

When we have children who want to feel with their tongue, we need to be selective about the materials that we make available. We can give our students opportunities to observe the textures of different foods. The feeling of touch sometimes contributes to our enjoyment

Seeds can be used for a valuable learning station. The texture of the seed coat gives us information about how the plant reproduces. Some seeds have a type of Velcro surface so that they will stick to animals and be transported to different areas. Other seeds have a smooth, hard coat that protects the seed.

of "tasting" as much as the actual taste. Children's allergies must be considered and care must be taken to wash hands and prepare clean areas for handling and tasting food.

Sensory touch tables or learning tables are very valuable because they give children opportunities to handle a variety of items. These sensory stations encourage students to touch natural materials such as seeds, rocks, twigs, pinecones, and plants. Manufactured items such as a collection of beads, buttons, metals, or polymers can also be valuable. Learning stations should include questions that encourage the children to observe, explore, and compare the different textures presented. Encouraging children to talk about their ideas provides wonderful opportunities for them to use expressive language. Being able to classify the way things feel provides rich opportunities for comparing, classifying, and graphing discoveries.

Shake Containers   Shake containers can be made using safe food canisters. Put different materials in each of the canisters. For instance put some sand in one. In another, put a rock. Pour some water in a third. Secure the lids with strong tape. Let the children shake the different canisters and compare the feel and sound. Some materials, such as water, will feel cold because they absorb heat from the hand. The canisters will create different sounds and rhythms when shaken. It is interesting to make at least two of each canister so that the children can try to match the sounds and feel of each type.

Feely Cans   Feely cans (Figure 6.7) are valuable tools for encouraging children to use their sense of touch. Children can explore and investigate a variety of different textures and items and then try to identify them. Expressing the feel of the items is a wonderful process for developing interesting and inventive vocabulary.

Different items can be placed in the feely cans when different themes are presented. For example, when children are exploring trees, different types of seeds such as acorns, maple "propellers," or sycamore "buttons" could be used. A variety of geometric shapes could also be used to help students develop a sense of various shapes.

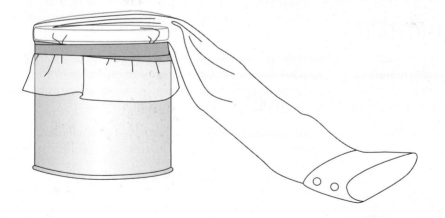

Feely cans, made from a one-gallon fruit container and a shirt sleeve, serve as excellent touch stations. Tape an old shirt sleeve to the side of the can. Be sure the can you use has no sharp or rough edges. Place a variety of natural items with varying textures in the can and have the children reach in to feel the objects.

FIGURE 6.7   A feely can example.

Stations for the Sense of Smell

The sense of smell is called *olfaction*. Smell is one of two chemical senses along with taste. When we breathe, particular chemicals are absorbed in the mucus of the nose. Nerves in our sensory system detect these chemicals and send messages to the brain. We can recognize very specific odors. For example, babies can distinguish their mother's odor from any other person. Smells can also make us remember events or places and awaken our emotions. The smell of something cooking or baking can make us think of a certain time or place or person. Smells invoke strong associations for past experiences and events. Familiar smells can be comforting or stimulate the imagination.

Smell is a very useful sense. Many animals rely on the sense of smell for safety. For example, deer can detect the smell of a hunter. This is why a good hunter tries to approach from downwind. Dogs' sense of smell is said to be many thousands times more sensitive than that of humans. This ability makes them valuable for detecting drugs and explosives.

Our sense of smell is also valuable for our safety. We can smell smoke, warning us about a fire. Because natural gas has no odor, mercaptin, which has a sharp pungent odor, is added to it so that when there is a gas leak, we can smell it and become aware of the problem.

Describing the different types of odors that we smell is a valuable language development activity that strengthens children's vocabularies. We need to select words to differentiate and classify the odors. This is often not easy for us even as adults. As children decide on words to describe the smells, a chart or graph can be made to organize and keep track of them.

A 35-mm film canister can be used to make a "smell box" (Figure 6.8). Put a couple of cotton swabs in the film container and add a spice from your kitchen. Common spices available include vanilla, lemon extract, cinnamon, clove, dill, garlic, bay leaves, pepper, and brown sugar.

Make up numerous smell boxes, duplicating each at least once. Then give each child a container and have them find other members of their "family" by sniffing each person's container.

Smell Gardens Plants can be grown that have strong aromas (Figure 6.9). A garden in the school yard or container gardens in the classroom can be grown by the students. Many herbs can be grown from seeds. Others can be obtained as plants from neighborhood gardeners or purchased at local nurseries.

Nature Walks Short walks in nature provide opportunities to smell many basic natural materials. For example, crushing the leaf of sassafras can release a strong "root

FIGURE 6.8 A spice "smell box."

Basil	Marigolds
Catnip	Onions
Dill	Radishes
Eucalyptus	Rosemary
Fennel	Sage
Garlic	Sweet marjoram
Lavender	Tarragon
Lemon basil	Thyme

FIGURE 6.9 Common plants with strong odors.

beer" odor. Scraping a tender shoot from a wild cherry tree can give a "Dr. Pepper" odor. Rubbing peppermint leaves gives off a strong aroma of mint. If you collect and wash peppermint leaves, you can put them in hot water and make peppermint tea to sample. Similarly, crushing flower petals can emit the flower's aroma more dramatically than by just smelling the bloom. Obviously, many flowers have pleasant (and sometimes unpleasant) odors.

Stations for the Sense of Taste

Taste can be a complex and difficult sense to understand. In reality, the sense of taste and smell are interrelated. To truly taste an item, you need to hold your fingers over your nose so that the sense of smell does not interfere or mask the sense of taste.

Taste, like smell, is also a chemical sense. Nerve sensors on the tongue detect different chemicals. There are four primary taste sensations: salty, sour, sweet, and bitter.

Many textbooks refer to a map of the tongue showing regions of the tongue that concentrate on each of the primary taste sensations. These maps have been found to be in error. All taste sensations can be elicited from all regions of the tongue (Smith & Margolskee, 2001).

Identifying different tastes can be difficult. It is often challenging for children and adults alike to describe the taste of foods. In reality, not all meat tastes like chicken. It is just difficult to find descriptive words to differentiate between the many flavors.

Children can taste samples of food such as a lemon slice, bittersweet chocolate, sugar, pretzel, or cookie and attempt to describe the taste or what the taste reminds them of. This sharing provides a wonderful opportunity for constructing a chart or a graph of their perceptions.

A talented and creative kindergartner teacher came up with a simple way to explore these primary taste sensations. She placed four different food items representing the four tastes on a paper plate: pretzel, sour gummy worm, sugar, and bitter dark chocolate. The paper plate was marked into four sections with a nontoxic marker. Each section was numbered 1, 2, 3, or 4. The children were asked to taste the food in each part of the plate. Children then shared their perceptions, which were recorded on a chart.

Caution is important when children have certain food allergies. Be sure that the foods you choose are safe for all children involved.

Activities that give children opportunities to taste different foods are valuable. Most children enjoy tasting their favorite foods. However, some children have few experiences in tasting different foods and consider it unpleasant. Tasting activities gives children a chance to explore and expand their tasting experiences. You should start with foods that most children enjoy and feel safe tasting. One such food may be sugar-free lifesavers. Several white lifesavers have different flavors (i.e., wintergreen and peppermint). Mix the different flavor lifesavers in a plastic bag and have your students describe the flavors to each other.

Tasting activities also provide experiences with the multicultural aspects of food. When you are exploring different nationalities and cultures, include activities to taste the different traditional foods. Opportunities for children to share the foods of their culture with their classmates can be done in relation to the senses of smell and taste. Cookbooks with ethnic foods and recipes are good resources for this exploration.

Again, caution must be taken in terms of children's allergies and when washing hands and preparing clean areas for tasting food.

Stations for Sound

Hearing is an important basic sense. We can detect sounds even when we are asleep. If we couldn't, alarm clocks would be of little value!

Sounds become important security signals to us. We are concerned when we are alone in a house and hear strange sounds. A mother can hear her baby crying even though she is surrounded by other noises. We listen for sirens to indicate fire, ambulances, or police. We have tornado sirens to warn us of oncoming danger.

Sounds help create attitudes and emotions and fuel our imaginations. Sounds can indicate feelings of happiness and sadness, laughter and anger. Before a sporting event we listen to loud marches. When we want a quiet evening, we may listen to soft music. The sound of waves on a beach, a soft rain on a metal roof, or the crackling of a campfire seems to slow the pace of our lives. Invite children to share sounds that make them think of something comforting, fun, or happy.

Teachers can engage in conversations with children about sound. Asking children to describe sounds they are familiar with provides a wonderful opportunity to examine the contexts in which sounds are made. An interesting activity involves asking children to be very quiet for a short period of time, perhaps 5 minutes. After the time is up, the children can share what sounds they have heard. Charting these sounds can be saved and contrasted with sounds heard on the playground, in the classroom, in a kitchen, or other interesting places.

Anthony Magnacca/Merrill

Take your children to a natural setting and have a "quiet period." See how many natural sounds they can identify. How many different types of life do they recognize? What are the different sources of the sounds? Do the sounds emanate from the ground, trees, or sky? What sounds do they hear at different times of the day?

We need to provide numerous experiences for exploring the different natures of sound. Sound stations should include natural sounds such as the sounds of insects, birds, wind, rustling leaves, or water. Others stations can be designed to help children recognize a variety of interesting sounds from common devices such as a motor, machine, or a tool. Having natural items at a listening center that make interesting and distinctive sounds, such as gourds and seed pods, add to this exploration. Activities can be developed using tape recorders to see if children can recognize voices of familiar people in their school, such as a teacher or a student, or familiar make-believe characters, such as Mickey Mouse, Big Bird, Scooby Doo, Dora, or Barney.

Stations can be set up at which musical instruments are made. Children can tape each other's voices or create sounds and play recognition games.

Making Musical Instruments   Making musical instruments can be a productive and enjoyable classroom project. Musical instruments are grouped into categories including string (piano, violin, guitar), woodwind (flute, clarinet, saxophone), horns (trumpet, trombone, tuba), and percussion (drums, cymbals, maracas). As illustrated in Figures 6.10, 6.11, and 6.12, simple instruments can be made from household materials that the children will enjoy using. With a variety of instruments, they will be able to differentiate and identify the different types of sounds produced.

Drums can be constructed easily by stretching some stretchy material across a wide canister such as an oatmeal container. Secure with a rubber band and use sticks as the percussion tool.

Musical instruments provide an excellent opportunity to share with children the different cultures and traditions. Each culture has particular styles of music and instruments that give characteristic sounds for the different cultures. When we hear a guitar and castanets, we may think of Spanish dancing. When hear the sound of steel drums, we may think of the Caribbean Islands. Music recordings from various cultures can be shared and enjoyed. Perhaps multinational guests can come in and talk with the children about music and instruments from their cultures.

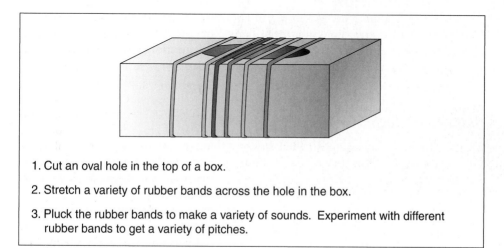

1. Cut an oval hole in the top of a box.

2. Stretch a variety of rubber bands across the hole in the box.

3. Pluck the rubber bands to make a variety of sounds. Experiment with different rubber bands to get a variety of pitches.

FIGURE 6.10 Making a simple guitar.

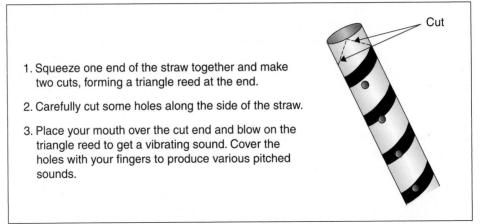

1. Squeeze one end of the straw together and make two cuts, forming a triangle reed at the end.

2. Carefully cut some holes along the side of the straw.

3. Place your mouth over the cut end and blow on the triangle reed to get a vibrating sound. Cover the holes with your fingers to produce various pitched sounds.

FIGURE 6.11 Making a simple clarinet.

1. Add some dried beans or rice to a small treat can to make a maraca.

2. Children can shake the can to their music to develop rhythm skills.

Variations: Maracas can also be made by putting beans, rice, or small pebbles between two paper plates and then taping the paper plates together along the outside circumference. Dried gourds and seed pods make excellent natural maracas.

FIGURE 6.12 Maracas can be made with everyday objects.

The flute is an excellent example of a cultural instrument. The history of the flute goes back several thousand years. Early flutes were made of bones, hooves, horns, and reeds. A flute was found in an archaeological dig at a Neanderthal site. Early flutes were used as signaling devices. Flutes are found in many different cultures, including Celtic, Native American, Chinese, Indian, and African.

Stations for Sight

Vision is the most consistently relied on sense that we use. We use vision to explore our environment. We use vision to direct our motions whether we are crawling, walking, riding a bicycle, or driving a car. We use our vision to read books. We use vision to "read" people's reactions to us and to events and experiences.

It is not by chance that our eyes are located close to our brain. In fact, scientists often consider our eyes to be an extension of the brain.

The eye is approximately 1 inch in diameter. Light enters our eye through an opening in the front called the pupil. The diameter of the pupil is controlled by the iris, which can expand and contract depending on the amount of light available. If a room is dark, the pupil will enlarge, permitting additional light to enter the eye. If we are in a bright location, the pupil contracts, decreasing the light rays entering the eye.

Inside the eye is a coating called the retina. The retina has nerve cells that sense light. These nerve cells are called rods (approximately 100 million), which detect low vision light, and cones (approximately 7 million) that give us color vision and detail. These cells are coated with a photosensitive chemical called rhodopsin. When light activates the rhodopsin, an electrical impulse is transmitted through the optic nerve to the brain.

The cones are concentrated at the back of the eye in an area call the fovea. That permits us to see the detail of objects at the center of our vision. The rods give us black and white vision. Because the rods concentrate on the perimeter of the retina, we can detect dim light better when we see it off to the side of our view. Interestingly, when we are viewing the nighttime sky, we can often see dim stars better if we don't look directly at them. That is because light from the side strikes more rods (detecting white light) and fewer cones (detecting color).

We need to provide children with continuous activities that cause them to explore their vision skills. The vision skills and techniques that they develop will be critical for the rest of their lives. Discussions about how to protect our eyes can be helpful. Wearing sunglasses and being cautious not to stare directly at the sun are helpful suggestions. Perhaps an eye health care professional can come in and talk to the children about taking care of their eyes.

Part of the process of developing skills of observing through vision encourages the use of optical devices such as lenses. When light is transmitted through a prism, its speed is altered, causing the light to bend (Figure 6.13).

A lens is actually a combination of many prisms with varying angles. The combination of all the prisms makes a lens that collects the light from the object. This causes the image to be enlarged or magnified (Figure 6.14). The bending of light is called refraction. The greater the angle of the two sides of a prism through which light travels, the greater the angle of refraction.

Single lenses, often called hand lenses, are valuable tools for young children. They are valuable in that they enlarge the object to be viewed, and they help children focus on the particular item being observed. Hand lenses should be constantly available to all children. Children should develop the custom of using the hand lenses as part of everyday observing.

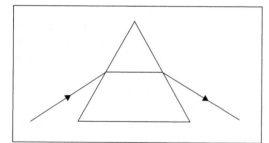

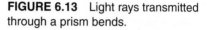

FIGURE 6.13 Light rays transmitted through a prism bends.

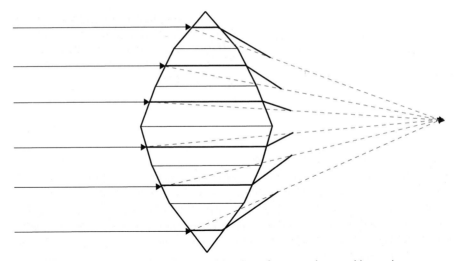

FIGURE 6.14 A lens is actually a combination of many prisms, with varying angles causing changes in the angle of refraction.

Lenses used in combinations are called microscopes and telescopes, depending on whether we want to enlarge small objects or make distant objects appear closer. Standard microscopes should be used only sparingly with young children. When used, the teacher needs to prepare the slide and focus the instrument for the children. Many students lose interest in using microscopes because they have trouble focusing and seeing the objects under the microscope. Having had a few negative experiences, they may believe that they are not capable of using the instrument and never return for future enjoyment.

Economical microscopes designed for children are available. Select microscopes that have magnifications from approximately 10 to no more than 30 power. When higher magnifications are used, the object appears dim and difficult to see. In addition, because the viewing area is very small, it is difficult to find the object to be viewed.

Simple microscope slides that are safe for children to use can be made using construction paper. These slides function well for viewing basic compounds such as salt, sand, and seeds.

Cut two squares approximately 2 inches in length. Use a hole punch to put a hole in the middle of one sheet. Use white glue to glue the two squares together and deposit the item to be viewed on the hole.

When the glue dries, it will be clear so you can observe the item. You can write the name of the item being observed on the paper.

Hand lenses should be a permanent fixture at science tables for viewing natural items such as leaves, insects, and rocks.

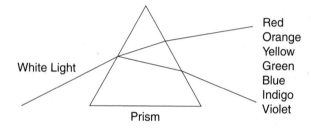

Red
Orange
Yellow
Green
Blue
Indigo
Violet

White Light

Prism

FIGURE 6.15 White light is "bent" as it passes through a prism, and is separated into the different colors of the color spectrum.

Children enjoy seeing celestial objects in telescopes. However, the same rule applies as for standard microscopes: The teacher needs to sight and focus the objects for the children. Many economical telescopes have very flimsy tripods, which make it difficult to locate and to keep in view the object being observed. Because the image is being magnified, a small vibration of the telescope can make viewing extremely difficult. In addition, each person's eye is different, which means the telescope has to be focused for each person.

Constellation viewers can be easily constructed. Using large cardboard canisters, such as oatmeal or hot chocolate containers, take off the plastic lids and paint them black. Cut off the bottom end of the canister. At this point, you have an open cylinder with a reattachable plastic lid. Punch holes in the blackened lid to represent a constellation. Then place the lid back on the open cylinder. When viewed upward, toward a light, the constellation can be seen. A dramatic effect can be achieved by placing a small flashlight inside the canister and aiming the light at the lid. In a relatively darkened room, the constellation is projected on the ceiling or wall. Try it! You can find diagrams of common constellations in resource books. A note of caution: An adult should do the hole punching.

Light and Colors   The color of light is dependent of the wavelength of the light waves. When all visible wavelengths are combined, the light appears to be white. When white light travels through a prism, however, the different colors (each of which is a different wavelength) are separated by refraction. **Refraction** is the bending of the light waves. Each color is "bent" different amounts, which causes the white light to be separated into the colors of the spectrum. This somewhat complex process can be illustrated for children by means of a prism (Figure 6.15) or, better yet, by nature: A rainbow is created when sunlight is refracted through raindrops.

CHILDREN'S EXPLORATIONS

Children's experiences need to involve a variety of their senses. Obviously, when multiple senses are used, the realism of the experience is compounded. We can maximize opportunities for all children to make sense of their world if we take a multisensory approach to learning. The more senses that are involved, the greater the students will be involved.

Many research studies document that children have different learning styles. Some children tend to be better visual learners. Others tend to be more auditory. Still others tend to be tactile. This is why some toddlers never put things in their mouths, whereas others are constantly putting items into their mouths. We need to be sure, however, children are always safe in their explorations.

NATIONAL SCIENCE EDUCATION STANDARDS

The *National Science Education Standards* were developed in 1996 by the National Research Council with the support of the National Science Teachers Association. Specific details on the national science standards were addressed in Chapter 4.

> A critical concern of the national standards is to "ensure a safe working environment." Care needs to be given to apply the necessary safety regulations in the storage, use, and care of the materials used by students.

The philosophy of the *National Science Education Standards* strongly supports the nature of inquiry that is encouraged through concept explorations. A comment often made about the science and mathematics curriculum in the United States is that our curriculum is "a mile wide and an inch deep" (Raloff, 1996). The standards encourage teachers of students at all levels to "teach more about less." By presenting fewer topics, but teaching more about each topic, students can raise more questions and experience more inquiry than if they are presented with lots of basic facts about different topics.

NATIONAL COUNCIL OF TEACHERS OF MATHEMATICS STANDARDS

The NCTM standards, *Principles and Standards for School Mathematics* (NCTM, 2000), emphasize the importance of mathematics for the youngest learners. NCTM suggests that appropriate mathematical experiences should challenge young children to explore their world and make discoveries that invite them to see patterns, shapes, and space with increasing sophistication:

> "Adults support young children's diligence and mathematical development when they direct attention to the mathematics children use in their play, challenge them to solve problems, and encourage their persistence"
>
> NCTM, 2000, p. 77.

Young students are active, resourceful individuals who construct, modify, and integrate ideas by interacting with the physical world and with peers and adults. They make connections that clarify and extend their knowledge, thus adding new meaning to past experiences. (NCTM, 2000, pp. 74–75)

Because many mathematics concepts develop intuitively before children come to school, it is our charge to extend these conceptualizations and provide environments where thinking is encouraged and exploration is supported.

The Pre-K–2 Content Standards

The pre-K–2 content standards for number and operations, algebra, geometry, measurement, and data analysis and probability are not meant to be separate topics of study. Mathematics for young learners should be very integrated, very interwoven. The standards are designed to help teachers see how the integrated nature of mathematics relates to the world of young children. These content standards will be referred to in each Concept Exploration in Part II of this text.

The Pre-K-2 Process Standards

The pre-K–2 process standards of problem solving, reasoning and proof, communication, connections, and representation are designed to help teachers maximize the ways in which children can approach and make sense of mathematical content. They are intended to support the learning of and are developed through the content standards. These process standards will be applied to each of the Concept Explorations in Part II of this text. Please refer to the Appendix for a complete list of the NCTM process standards.

RESOURCES

Resource Books

With every concept exploration, books are essential. A variety of books are available for children and teachers to use as they explore and learn about a specific topic. Information or trade books are useful for gathering facts and interesting information. Teachers can use information books that are written for adult readers. Seeking detailed information about a topic enables teachers to gain enough information about a topic to conduct meaningful conversations with children. Ample information can also help a teacher guide children with their inquiry and approaches to learning. Information books that are written for children are valuable resources and provide children with facts.

Storybooks

Storybooks related to concept explorations are motivating and appealing to children. Information can be gained from these books in the context of a story. Children relate to storybooks through characters and interesting contexts and situations. Some storybooks have fantasy ideas that are quite appealing to young children. Magic and exaggeration are sometimes contained in fantasy books, such as Eric Carle's *The Tiny Seed*, in which a seed travels a long distance to finally plant itself and grow bigger than a house. Even though this book uses exaggeration, it is very engaging and appealing. Children love to read Eric Carle books.

Picture Books

Picture books are wonderful resources for young children. Pictures can impart a lot of meaning and information that help teach a child about a topic. Young children can interact with pictures and relate them to their own everyday experiences.

Multicultural Books

Multicultural books are a wonderful way to bring other parts of the world to your classroom. Finding books depicting life in other cultures is appealing and enlightening. Perhaps children from other cultures have books at home that they can bring in to share in the classroom.

Writing Your Own Book

As concept explorations unfold, wonderful opportunities will arise for capturing children's theories, discoveries, and ideas. Sharing these theories, discoveries, and ideas in a book form makes their work lasting. Sharing these books with other children and with families extends learning beyond your classroom.

Review and Discussion Questions

1. Design a concept exploration that captures the curiosity and interest of young children. Come up with ways to find out the children's interests and discuss how you would design and develop engaging explorations.

2. Find three to five resources in your community that would support your classroom study of one or two of the Concept Explorations described in this book.

3. Discuss how you can create an environment for young children that promotes using the five senses. You may choose any of the Concept Explorations in this text for content as you answer this question.

Correlation of NSES Standards and NCTM Principles and Standards to Astronomy Concept Exploration Activities

	1. Solar System Models	2. Solar Dances	3. Golf Ball Lunology	4. Moon Watching	5. Binocular Beauties	6. Observing the Sun	7. Collecting Micro-Meteorites	8. Balloon Rockets	9. Flim Canister Rockets	10. Water Rockets	11. Air Rockets	12. Chemical Rockets	13. How High Did It Go?
SCIENCE													
Inquiry	X	X		X	X	X		X	X	X	X	X	X
Physical Science			X		X	X	X	X	X	X	X	X	
Life Science													
Earth and Space Science	X	X	X	X	X	X	X	X	X	X	X	X	X
Science and Technology			X		X	X	X	X	X	X	X	X	X
Personal and Social Perspectives		X				X	X						
History and Nature of Science	X			X		X	X						
MATHEMATICS													
Number and Operations	X	X	X	X		X		X	X	X	X	X	X
Algebra			X		X			X	X	X	X	X	X
Geometry	X	X		X									
Measurement	X	X	X	X				X	X	X	X	X	X
Data Analysis and Probability	X	X	X	X	X	X	X	X	X	X	X	X	X
Problem Solving	X							X	X	X	X	X	
Reasoning and Proof	X	X										X	
Communication		X	X	X		X		X	X	X	X	X	X
Connections	X	X						X	X	X	X	X	X
Representation	X	X	X	X				X					X

CHAPTER 7

Astronomy and Space Science

The Man in the Moon

Staring up high at the Man in the Moon
Wondering about craters and flying there soon.
Where are its mountains, craters, and rocks?
And how can we get there in our spaceship box?
I wonder about how the moon shrinks and grows.
Where is the rest of it when the thin crescent glows?
So many mysteries yet to explore
Learning and thinking forever more . . .
So, Man in the Moon, please help me to see
the wonders and beauty of our galaxy.

Genevieve A. Davis

As soon as children begin to observe their surroundings, they look toward the heavens with wonder and awe. They see the sun, moon, and stars and notice their presence and motion through the sky. As they start to talk, they begin to ask questions about space. The nighttime sky seems mysterious. "Is there really a man in the moon?" "Where does the sun go at night?" "Why do stars twinkle?" "How far away is the moon?" "Will I ever get to go to Mars?"

With the heightened awareness of scientific study of the universe, and with such visible organizations as NASA, children are made aware of the phenomena of astronomy at an early age. Space travel, planets, satellites, astronauts, and stars are popular subjects for trade books and the media. Such exposure creates curiosity.

In our classroom we want to take advantage of this curiosity. We try to help children observe the sky and notice the wide variety of objects that are visible to our naked eye and with telescopes. We want to nurture their curiosity by exploring the heavens, and encourage them to ask many questions. At a young age, the questions that children contemplate range from factual to fantasy, from wondering how hot the sun is to wondering if you could ride on the rings of Saturn or if the creatures in *Star Wars* are real.

At a young age, children do not possess the ability to understand the very abstract and complex nature of our universe. Even adults have some difficulty understanding the immensity of space. Even the best minds in the world have not yet been able to understand the basics of matter and energy that form our universe. Hopefully, this immensity contributes to our interest in learning about space. We can accept that there are things beyond our understanding but not beyond our interests and curiosity. It is this curiosity that we must nurture with our children.

The nature of space is such that astronomy activities that are tactile and concrete are most difficult to find. We cannot touch the planets. We cannot visualize how stars are born. What we can do, however, is help children develop an interest in space. The activities in this Concept Exploration are designed to make their experiences related to space more concrete.

One area of space science that can be used to excite children about space is rocketry. Fortunately, there are several very basic and safe forms of rockets that we can use with children. The rocketry activities presented in this chapter are not only valuable for creating interest in space but also for developing a strong basic understanding of the physics of motion.

SCIENCE CONCEPTS FOR TEACHERS

The conceptual framework included here is intended to provide instructors with background information. It is not intended as instructional material for the children, but as basic supporting information for you, their teachers. The concepts and information presented here could, however, be presented to the children at an introductory level. For example, while your class is outside they might see the moon in the daylight sky. You might point out that the moon can be seen at different times of the day and night and that we can see the different phases of the moon. However, young children do not have the abstract framework to understand details about how and why the different phases occur.

Newton's Three Laws of Motion and Basic Rocketry

Sir Isaac Newton was the first scientist to explain the basic principles of motion of matter. He did this through three natural laws that he defined.

It is not recommended that you try to teach the nature of Newton's laws in the primary grades; however, as teachers, we must have a basic understanding of these principles. Understanding them is essential if you are going to help your children make good observations and formulate good "experiments" as they probe the techniques of basic rocketry. These concrete experiences form the groundwork for later development of their understandings.

> ***Newton's First Law of Motion:*** *When an object is at rest, it tends to stay at rest. When an object is in motion, it tends to stay in motion.*

We often refer to this as the **principle of inertia**. The principle of inertia was originally defined by Galileo.

This basic principle tells us that if we have an object on a table that it will tend to stay there unless an external force acts on it. It will not move unless a force such as a wind acts on it, or if the table is not level and gravity takes it toll.

Likewise, if an object is in motion, it tends to stay in motion. Thus, when our car is traveling at 60 miles an hour, it tends to keep traveling at 60 miles an hour unless we apply an external force by putting on our brakes or stepping on the gas pedal.

> ***Newton's Second Law of Motion:*** *The relationship between an object's mass and how quickly it is accelerated depends on the force that acted on it. This relationship is usually shown as a mathematical relationship: force = mass of the object times the object's acceleration (F = M × A or, simply, F = MA).*

Unfortunately, mathematical formulas tend to turn off laymen from basic physics. Stephen Hawking, the theoretical physicist, was told that for every equation he used in a book, he would halve the sales (Hawking, 1993). This is unfortunate because basic relationships such as $F = MA$ help us understand some very basic concepts.

What $F = MA$ tells us is that if I have an object such as a golf ball and I act on it with a force such as a golf club, the ball will be accelerated. If I apply a greater force the next time I hit it, the ball will have greater acceleration and travel even farther than it did the first time. (Interestingly, if we didn't have friction, in this case the air and gravity, our golf ball would continue forever because of its inertia.)

The mass of the object also plays a role. If instead of hitting a golf ball, we placed a baseball on our tee, the baseball would not be accelerated as much and travel as far because the mass of the baseball is greater than the mass of the golf ball.

> ***Newton's Third Law of Motion:*** *For every action, there is an opposite and equal reaction.*

We see the effect of Newton's third law when we watch a hamster on an exercise wheel. The hamster is trying to run forward, but the wheel under him travels backward.

We normally relate Newton's third law to projectiles such as bullets, cannons, and rockets. When a cannon is fired, the cannon ball is projected forward, but there is an opposite and equal reaction of the cannon itself rolling backward. Because the cannon has a much greater mass than the cannon ball, it does not travel as far as the cannon ball. When we shoot a rifle, we refer to the opposite and equal reaction as kickback.

Star Formation

Many excellent sources are available that explain the nature of stars in laymen's terms. Several are listed at the end of this chapter. We recommend that you look through some of these resources. In addition you might want to examine the concept exploration in Chapter 15, Sun and Shadows, which has a brief description about the nature of our sun, which is a typical star.

We present in Figure 7.1 brief descriptions of basic astronomical terms.

Star   A star is a celestial body with a sufficient mass of gas (predominantly hydrogen) that it is held together by its own gravity. The mass must be great enough to create the heat necessary to produce atomic fusion. Our Sun is a star.

Planet   A planet is a celestial body that revolves around a star. A planet gives off no light and is illuminated by its star.

Galaxy   Stars are always found in large groups called galaxies. Galaxies have between 1 billion and 1 trillion stars. Our Sun is part of the Milky Way Galaxy. Estimates for the number of stars in the Milky Way Galaxy range from 100 billion to 200 billion stars. Astronomers are constantly increasing their estimates of the number of galaxies; however, present estimates are around 200 billion.

Nebula   A nebula is a general term for clouds of gas and dust in space. Dark clouds indicate that the nebula is blocking light from more distant, brighter objects. Some nebulas also emit light by being excited by nearby stars.

Open star clusters   Within a galaxy, there are areas where stars concentrate in groups. Open star clusters can have a few dozen to several thousand stars.

Globular cluster   Within a galaxy, there are many locations that have a concentration of gas from which many stars develop. Globular clusters can have from a few hundred thousand to several million stars.

Binary stars   Binary stars are two or more stars that orbit around a common center of gravity. More than half of all stars are binary stars.

Variable stars   Variable stars are stars that change in their brightness over periods of time. Variable stars are classified into various types, including the following: nova, supernova, Cepheid variable, and eclipsing variable.

Red giant   Red giant stars are stars that greatly expand during their declining years. When our Sun begins to die, it will expand to become a red giant and its diameter will encompass Earth's orbit.

White dwarf   White dwarf stars occur in the last stage of stellar evolution. After the star has exhausted its nuclear fuel, the star collapses under its own gravity.

Neutron star   A neutron star is a remnant of a star that collapses because of gravitational force. It is thought that supernovas result in the formation of neutron stars.

Black holes   Black holes are regions in space where the gravitational force is so great that even photons of light cannot escape. It is thought that black holes occur when massive stars collapse. There is no hard evidence that black holes exist.

FIGURE 7.1   Basic definitions in astronomy.

Telescopes and Children

Telescopes are exciting tools. Just the thought of looking through a telescope and seeing the rings of Saturn or the moons of Jupiter might cause children to want to use a telescope.

However, some of us experienced frustration and intimidation the first time we used a telescope. This often occurs because the telescopes that we used had design defects or were inexpensively constructed.

Much care should be given when selecting a telescope and designing activities for children using telescopes. The purpose of this section is to help you as a teacher recognize the critical characteristics and qualities of telescopes that should be considered. In addition, we examine some of the procedures that will help you plan observing sessions for your students.

Principles of Telescopes

All telescopes are designed to do one thing: collect light. By using a telescope, you are condensing the light from a larger area through a system of mirrors and or lenses to a small area that can be seen through the pupil of your eye. For instance, using a 6-inch optical telescope will increase the amount of light that reaches your pupil by approximately 200 times. Thus, a very dim object that typically cannot be seen with the naked eye in the nighttime sky will appear much brighter through a telescope.

Except for close objects, such as the moon and planets, and for viewing nebular objects such as galaxies, the magnification of a telescope is of little value. Even with the world's largest telescope, all stars appear as just a pinpoint of light. But through the telescope, the pinpoint will be much brighter. Thus, when purchasing a telescope you should be much more concerned about how much light a telescope collects than its magnification.

Optical telescopes are divided into two basic categories: refracting telescopes and reflecting telescopes.

Refracting Telescopes   Refracting telescopes utilize a system of lenses that collect and refract light to magnify the image (Figure 7.2). They have a larger diameter lens called the *objective lens* and a small lens called an *eyepiece*. Good refracting telescopes utilize multiple lens systems to correct for color aberrations. Chapter 6 discusses lenses in the section on "Stations for Sight".

Reflecting Telescopes   Reflecting telescopes utilize one or more concave mirrors for the objective lens to condense the light and a small lens called an eyepiece (Figure 7.3).

FIGURE 7.2   A refracting telescope.

FIGURE 7.3   A reflecting telescope.

Criteria to Consider When Selecting Telescopes for Use with Children

Unfortunately, small inexpensive telescopes are difficult even for adults to use. The result is that the initial excitement of viewing objects through a telescope disappears with the frustration of trying to sight a particular object, focusing the lens, and keeping the image in the field of view.

These exasperating experiences can often dim the excitement of viewing the sky and children's curiosity about astronomy in general. Children's first experience with telescopes must be a positive and rewarding one.

Let's look at some basics to consider when selecting a telescope.

Mount or Tripod   The support for the telescope is very critical. Quality telescopes require at least as much money for the mount as they do for the telescope itself. The mount must be sufficiently heavy and sturdy enough to support the telescope without movement.

Because telescopes typically magnify an object from 50 times to several hundred, the vibration of a mount is also magnified. For example, a vibration of 1/50 of an inch will be viewed through a telescope as a vibration of a full inch, making the image impossible to view.

In addition, unstable mounts make the aligning and focusing of the object to be viewed very difficult. The first time a tripod is bumped by a foot or arm, you will lose the object and focus and will have to start all over.

Field of View   The field of view is the angular diameter of the viewing area of the telescope. Inexpensive telescopes have a small field of view, which makes it much more difficult to find the objects that you are looking for.

In addition, the lower the power of the telescope, the greater the field of view. Therefore, when viewing an object through a telescope, view first in the lowest power and then change eyepieces to work your way up to the higher powers.

Size of Objective Lens   The diameter of the objective lens or mirror determines the amount of light that you collect. Obviously, the larger the objective lens, the more light you collect and, unfortunately, the higher the cost of the telescope. A quality telescope requires a significant investment.

When selecting a telescope, it is critical that you do not sacrifice the quality of the mount and the size of the field of view for the size of the objective. In, general, avoid telescopes that advertise the magnification as their greatest quality.

With young children, you might find that viewing the moon with a good pair of binoculars is a more rewarding experience than using a telescope. With a good-quality pair of binoculars, other beautiful objects, such as star clusters and galaxies, can also be seen. A good basic suggestion for using binoculars for looking at celestial objects is to focus your eyes on the object you want to see and then bring the binoculars up to your eyes, rather than trying to locate the object with the binoculars. A tripod to steady the binoculars can be a valuable asset.

Is Pluto a Planet?

In August 2006, the International Astronomical Union downgraded what was considered our ninth planet, Pluto, to a dwarf planet. Their reasoning is that the orbit of Pluto is more elliptical than the other planets and that it is made up of mainly ice. An additional factor is that Pluto does not have a spherical shape. It is interesting that Pluto does have a named moon, Charon.

Perhaps the critical factor in this decision was the discovery of Eris, in 2003. Eris has an orbit outside Neptune, and is slightly larger than that of Pluto. Eris also has a moon.

Other similar objects have been found outside of the orbit of Neptune. These ojects have become referred to as Trans-Neptunian objects (TNO).

MATHEMATICS: ADDRESSING THE NCTM STANDARDS THROUGH CONCEPT EXPLORATIONS

Stargazing and moon watching are age-old events in which everyone, at one time or another, has been engaged. We can all remember back to our childhoods when we were outside at night looking up at the sky and being filled with a great sense of wonder and awe. What's up there? How far away is a star? Why does the moon change shape? Does everyone in the world see the Big Dipper? The fascination of the heavens has been a mystery since the beginning of time. Capturing this fascination in children can yield a rich and interesting study. Many mathematical ideas and concepts come into play as we live, sing, and dance in the sunshine and the moonshine of our planet Earth.

Numbers and Operations

Anytime children are given opportunities to use numbers to describe something, they are getting authentic experiences with one-to-one correspondence and stable order in counting. As they describe the Moon at first quarter, they are seeing that fractions can be used to describe a phase of the moon as it makes its trip around the Earth. When they are seeing how the Moon changes and how the sun appears to move across the sky, they are getting real-life experiences with sequencing and seriation.

Another example of authentic use of numbers is evident in the rocketry part of the Concept Explorations in this chapter. As children keep track of the distance a rocket flies, they are using numbers to represent an event. Numbers can be used in meaningful ways to help children share what they are finding out and seeing.

Algebra and Patterns

Repetitive observation of the heavens can help children develop and enhance their abilities in discovering the many patterns around and above them. They can see the patterns of constellations, the waxing and waning of the moon, the apparent movement of the Sun across the sky, and the navigation and trajectory of a rocket.

These different patterns can be documented in many creative ways. For example, when viewing the night sky at the same time each night, you can ask the children to draw a picture of what the Moon looks like. As children watch the Moon change from evening to evening, they can capture their observations in a variety of ways with a variety of representations: sketches, descriptions, paper cutouts, or paintings. As time passes, the child will see the progression of the Moon's changing phases. The pattern will continue to repeat itself across the month. As they capture their observations, they will be able to document the seriated sequence of growth of the visible parts of the moon. Notions such as crescent, first quarter and full can be applied to what they are seeing. If children go outside at the same time each evening with a parent or other adult and look at the moon, many wonderful experiences will be shared.

Another pattern that can be documented is that of the apparent movement of the Sun across the sky. Being careful not to look directly into the Sun, you can document where the Sun appears in the sky at different times of the day. This movement is indeed a repetitive pattern. Generalizations and theories can be generated with the collective data. How long does it take for the Moon to be full? Or, how long does it take the Moon to seemingly disappear? These questions about the phases of the moon can be raised and then studied.

Geometry

Geometric concepts are explored when children watch the changing phases of the Moon. They see a full moon and a quarter Moon—a seemingly two-dimensional image of the spherical Moon.

As children watch the apparent movement of the Sun across the sky, they are using ideas about relative position of the Sun to the Earth. Such navigational concepts help children with directionality and sequence.

Stargazing can be enhanced with maps of the night sky. Locating certain constellations on a map can assist children in locating them in the sky. Making a connection to maps and the real sky helps children understand how scientists use geometry to plan out and construct maps.

Measurement

The activities in this Concept Exploration involving the planets provide many opportunities for children to explore, in very fundamental ways, the relative size of the planets. With such abstract concepts of proportion and huge magnitudes, which cannot be made concrete, we can only begin to help children understand the vastness of the universe.

In this Concept Exploration, many experiences with measurement exist. Specifically related to the models of the solar system, relative size, proportion, and distance are important concepts. As children measure distances to place planets in their modes, they gain practice using measuring tools.

Similarly, with the help of an adult, children can contribute to the process of measuring a rocket's launch distance.

Data Analysis

Children can construct simple charts to show the observed phases of the Moon. They can chart the date and the image of the Moon on that date. Similarly, children can construct a simple chart to show the time of day and the apparent position of the Sun in the sky. As the Sun appears to go across the sky, its movement can be documented alongside different times of day.

OBSERVING WITH ALL THE SENSES

Giving children opportunities to use multiple senses in their explorations increases their retention of these experiences.

Sight

The eye is the principal tool for observing astronomy. The eye can detect much detail. We often enjoy the challenge of observing the first star in the evening sky. This expands in the nighttime sky to observing particular objects.

Our eyes take awhile to adjust to dark vision. This is true for two reasons. First, the pupils in our eyes need time to expand to accept more light. Second, a chemical in the eye called rhodopsin assists the eye's sensors as they collect light. A certain period of time is required for rhodopsin to become active. Thus, the longer we are in a dark environment, the better our night vision becomes.

Sound

Static sounds can be heard on the radio (and sometimes on cellular phones) during sunspot activity. Typically, about 3 days after a solar flare eruption, the charged particles from the Sun enter Earth's atmosphere, causing static radio waves. These charged particles are also the cause of the northern lights, or aurora borealis.

SAFETY

Safety should be a constant concern when studying astronomy. No person should ever look directly at the Sun. Doing so can cause permanent damage to the eyes. Design your activities to ensure that children cannot look at the Sun even accidentally. Observing the Sun requires special techniques and equipment.

CONCEPT EXPLORATIONS ON ASTRONOMY AND SPACE SCIENCE FOR YOUR CLASSROOM

In Chapter 3, the importance of engaging children in all four stages of problem solving was discussed. Assisting children to pursue their own questions is the key to developing a positive and interested attitude in learning, particularly as it relates to mathematics and science.

The following Concept Explorations use children's experiences involving rockets and space to examine several basic science processes and utilize basic math skills. The following explorations provide a wide variety of activities that are appropriate for young children. They are designed to assist you in identifying, designing, and teaching authentic concrete activities with your children. Throughout Part II's chapters, remember that it will not be possible to complete all of the activities provided. Each exploration gives an alternative process that you can use. Particular suggestions and opportunities are given to direct you in the explorations. Which ones you select for your class can be determined by the interests and developmental level of your students. However, you are strongly encouraged to use these suggestions as entry points from which your children will explore their universe.

As often as possible, help the students explore their own questions. It is important to record children's initial questions and theories about rockets and space to guide the investigation and learning. As children investigate and research, their theories will reflect what they have learned and what they still are curious about learning.

One of the most valuable techniques of evaluating the understanding of children is to examine the questions that children ask. Asking pertinent questions requires a level of knowledge and reasoning. Utilize your children's questions as a tool for selecting the complexity and nature of activities that you conduct with your children.

Watching things move is exciting for people of all ages. The faster they move and the farther they travel, the better it is. Children enjoy being able to make, control, and observe basic projectiles. Fortunately, several different types of safe basic rockets can be made by young children. Interest in rocketry can be a catalyst for learning and discovering the nature of space. The small rockets children will make based on these Concept Explorations use the same principles that NASA's rockets use to travel in space.

1. Solar System Models

Children need opportunities to visualize and make comparisons of the planets in our solar system. Looking at a variety of photographs of the planets in our solar system can give misleading concepts about the size of planets to children because the different photographs are taken at varying scales.

Inviting children to make models of the solar system can be a valuable experience. However, teachers must be careful to clarify the purpose of the model and what the model's comparisons are. Models can be made for three different properties of the planets: size, distance to the Sun, and planet density.

Each of these models must be made independently using separate scales. If you tried to make a model using the same scale for size of the planets and for distance to the Sun, the model would become impractical. For instance, if Jupiter were 12 inches in diameter in our model, we would have to place Neptune 5.95 miles away.

Your decisions on how much student involvement to encourage should be based on students' level of skill development. The complexity of the classroom models should be determined by the age and development of the students. For example, younger classes might have a classroom model that would only include the eight planets. Intermediate classes might also include the prominent moons for the planets. These children might also search the Web for photographs of the planets so that they can depict their model with greater detail.

TABLE 7.1 Basic data on the Sun's planets.

Planets	Mean Distance to Sun (million miles)	Equatorial Diameter (miles)	Number of Observed Moons	Length of Day (Earth days)	Length of Year (Earth Year)	Density of Planet (grams/ centimeter^3)
Mercury	36	3,031	0	58.6	.24	5.43
Venus	67	7,521	0	243.0	.62	5.25
Earth	93	7,927	1	1.0	1.0	5.52
Mars	141	4,222	2	1.03	1.88	3.95
Jupiter	483	88,848	> 28	0.41	11.86	1.33
Saturn	886	74,901	30	0.44	29.46	0.69
Uranus	1,782	31,816	24	0.72	84.0	1.29
Neptune	2,793	31,404	8	0.67	164.8	1.64

TABLE 7.2 Comparative sizes for constructing models of planets.

Sun and Planets	Actual Size	Proportional Size Related to Mercury	Relative Size of Models in Inches
Sun	864,000	286.0	110.3
Mercury	3,031	1.0	0.4
Venus	7,521	2.5	0.9
Earth	7,927	2.6	1.0
Mars	4,222	1.4	0.5
Jupiter	88,848	29.5	11.3
Saturn	74,901	24.8	9.5
	(Rings = 155,000)	(Rings = 51.4)	(Rings = 19.7)
Uranus	31,816	10.6	4.1
Neptune	31,404	10.4	4.0

For younger classes, Table 7.1 can be used to determine the size of the models. For children who have the mathematical skills, you might have them calculate the relative sizes of the planets. These experiences give children practical experiences in developing proportions.

Teachers can utilize books to find ways to entice children to be curious about the planets. Laura Driscoll's book *Let's Look at the Planets* gives teachers and primary-aged children a good look at the planets.

Size of the Planets

The most common models representing the planets are designed to show the relative sizes of the planets. Table 7.2 gives us the necessary data for constructing such a model. Often, models are constructed based on making the Earth 1 inch in diameter, as is done in Table 7.2. This works well for classroom models in that the smaller planets can be constructed from small balls that are available, and the largest planet, Jupiter, is still at a workable size of less than a foot in diameter.

You might want to include a model representing the Sun to indicate its immense size related to the planets. For a model based on the numbers given in Table 7.2, the

TABLE 7.3 Distance of the planets from the Sun.

Planet	Distance to Sun (million miles)	Proportional Distance Related to Mercury	Relative Distance from Sun for Model Based on 1 Inch/Million Miles
Mercury	36	1	3 feet
Venus	67	1.86	5 feet 7 inches
Earth	93	2.58	7 feet 9 inches
Mars	141	3.91	11 feet 9 inches
Jupiter	483	13.42	40 feet 3 inches
Saturn	886	24.61	73 feet 10 inches
Uranus	1,782	49.50	148 feet 6 inches
Neptune	2,793	77.57	232 feet 9 inches

Sun will be 9 feet 1 inch tall. To represent this in a classroom, we could produce an arc representing a portion of the Sun to show comparative size.

Models of any other proportional size can be made using the "Proportional Size Related to Mercury" column in Table 7.2. (Mercury is used because it is the smallest planet.) Let's say that you wanted Mercury to be 1 inch in diameter. Then the diameters of the other planets could be calculated by multiplying 1 inch times the proportional size given for each planet (see Table 7.2). Earth would now be 2.6 inches in diameter and Jupiter would be 29.3 inches in diameter.

Distance of the Planets to the Sun

Students can construct a model to show the comparative distances of the planets from the Sun (Table 7.3). This model might gain additional reality if the scale is large. For instance, the students might make their model the length of the main hallway in the school. Or they could use a sidewalk or the school's property line.

Models can be predicted using the scale of 1 inch equals 1 million miles. This model would be as long as a football field. Or, your class can develop models for any size using the Proportional Distance Related to Mercury column in Table 7.3. (Mercury is used as the base because it is closest to the Sun.) It is suggested that you consider the position of the Sun and Neptune first so that your model will fit into the required space.

Let's assume that we place a model in your community's mall and that the length of the mall from one end to the other is 1,000 feet. If we place the Sun at one entrance to the mall, Neptune could be placed at the opposite entrance 1,000 feet away. By dividing 1,000 feet by the Proportional Distance Related to Mercury column's entry for Neptune (77.57, we determine a constant that we can use for all the planets). In this case the constant is 12.9.

By multiplying this constant times the proportional distance for each of the planets, we will get the distance to place the planet from the Sun. That is, Mercury = 1 ft × 12.9 = 12.9 feet from the Sun at the entrance to the mall. Venus = 1.86 ft × 12.9 = 24 feet from the Sun. Earth = 2.58 ft × 12.9 = 33.3 feet from the Sun. The distance to the remaining planets can be calculated using the same constant (12.9).

The location that you select for constructing your model can expand the students' experiences. An obvious choice is your classroom. However, if a central location in the school or school yard is available, this increases the visibility of the students' project. This contributes to the learning of other students and adults in the school setting, and expands the pride that your students develop toward their work.

Densities of the Planets

Making models of the planets that compare their densities can be a simple but rewarding experience. The densities of each planet can be represented by a container such as that used for snacks. Add sand or other suitable material to each container in the proportional amounts given in the "Density of Planet" column in Table 7.1. Children can make comparisons of the densities by picking up and shaking the different containers.

2. Solar Dances

Models of the solar system in which the children play the roles of the planets can add clarity to the manner in which the planets travel around the Sun. These experiences help the children visualize the patterns and processes that take place in our solar system. Your model can be very simple or complex, depending on the age and development of your students.

Select an open area, such as the school yard, or a multipurpose area with enough room for the children to move around. In the center of the area place an object such as a large beach ball to represent the Sun. Ask each child to play the role of Earth and walk around the Sun.

Each trip around the Sun represents 1 year. After they have had an opportunity to understand the annual motion of Earth, suggest that they spin around as they travel around the Sun. This would demonstrate the daily motion of Earth. As they face the Sun, they would have day. As they face away from the Sun, they would have night. They would spin many times (365 1/4) during one trip around the Sun.

The model can be expanded by having two children hold hands and spin around each other as they travel around the Sun. One child would represent Earth and the second child would represent the Moon. This model can also demonstrate the different planets. Children can stand at different distances from the Sun and travel in a circle around the Sun. Point out to the children that the farther they are from the Sun, the longer it takes for them to make a complete circle, as charted in Table 7.4. This demonstrates why a year on the planets farther from the Sun is longer than a year on planets closer to the Sun.

TABLE 7.4   Planets and the time required to circle the Sun.

Planet	Length of Trip Around the Sun
Mercury	88 days
Venus	225 days
Earth	1 year
Mars	687 days
Jupiter	11.9 years
Saturn	29.5 years
Uranus	84.0 years
Neptune	164.8 years

As your children are participating in the model of the solar system, key in on their questions behavior. Their questions might suggest that you expand your model. Their behavior will give you clues about their understanding. Their behavior can also suggest to you when they have reached the limit of their comprehension.

3. Golf Ball Lunology

Students and adults often have difficulty explaining the causes of the phases of the-Moon. The cause of the phases of the moon is an abstract and difficult idea. For young children, it is not critical that they be able to explain in detail all the factors that cause the phases. Our primary objective should be for students to observe and enjoy seeing the apparent changes of the Moon in their sky.

Children can better experience the phases of the Moon when they become part of a model that is created. An effective demonstration can be produced by using a bright light source, such as an overhead projector, and a golf ball. The light source represents the Sun. The child's head represents Earth, and the golf ball represents the Moon. For children to visualize this relationship, each child must have the opportunity to do this activity independently.

The children can hold the golf ball (representing the Moon) in front of the overhead, casting a shadow on their head. As they hold the ball they can slowly move it toward the left. As they move the ball, point out to them that the portion of the golf ball toward the light source (the Sun) is illuminated and the opposite side is dark. The farther the ball is rotated around the child, the greater the visible area that is illuminated. This duplicates the phases of the moon. One-quarter of the way around their head (representing Earth), the right half of the ball is illuminated. This would duplicate the first quarter phase of the moon. When the ball is on the opposite side of their heads from the light source, the entire visible ball is illuminated. This represents the full moon.

Your students might notice other details while conducting this demonstration. For instance, the dimples in the golf ball are more visible along the terminator, or the border between the light and dark areas. This effect is often noticeable when you look through a telescope at the Moon and can see many more craters along the terminator. This is caused by the Sun's light not reaching the bottom of the crater, hence producing dark shadows.

In addition, the concept of eclipses can be modeled when the light from the light source to the golf ball is blocked by the child's head. This would represent a lunar eclipse. When the golf ball is between the light source and the child's eye and, hence, is blocking the light, a solar eclipse would be produced.

4. Moon Watching

Encourage your children to watch for the Moon in the sky. The Moon is the brightest object in the sky other than the Sun. This makes it easily observable in the sky during days and nights.

Because the phases of the Moon are determined by its relative position to the Sun and Earth as it revolves around the Earth, the position of the Moon in our sky changes each day, as illustrated in Figure 7.4.

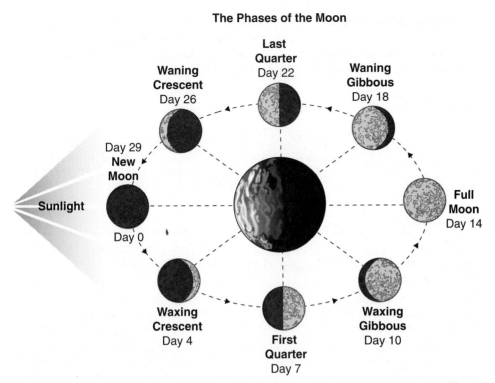

The Phases of the Moon

FIGURE 7.4 As the Moon circles Earth, the shape of the moon appears to change. The shape varies from a full moon (when Earth is between the Sun and the Moon) to a new moon (when the Moon is between the Sun and Earth).

As the Moon is going from the new moon phase through first quarter to a full moon, it is observable in the evening sky. During this period the Moon is said to be *waxing*. This means that the visible portion of the Moon (illuminated by the Sun) is increasing.

Each night the Moon moves a greater angle from the Sun, so it is higher in the sky and sets later each evening. When the Moon is full, it will rise in the eastern sky about the time that the Sun sets in the western sky.

When the moon is going from the full moon to new moon phase, it is observable in the morning sky. During this period the Moon is said to be *waning*. This means that the visible portion of the Moon is decreasing. As the Sun rises in the eastern sky, the Moon will be visible. Each day, as the moon is waning, it will be closer in the sky to the Sun.

An interesting time to observe the Moon is when it is a thin crescent. The illuminated crescent is the side of the Moon illuminated by the Sun. It is interesting to note that the "back side" of the Moon, although much dimmer, is still visible. This is because of light from the Sun that is reflected from Earth to the Moon. If we were on the Moon during the night, this would be called *earthshine*.

The more often children observe the Moon in the sky during the different phases, the easier it will be for them to understand how the phases of the Moon are caused. However, young children do not have the abstract development to understand the relationship of all of the factors that cause the different phases of the Moon.

Astronomy and Space Science

Once in a Blue Moon!

Did you ever wonder what a blue Moon is?

The more recent definition is that a blue Moon is when you have two full Moons during the same month. Since full Moons occur approximately every 29 1/2 days, the first full Moon must occur on one of the first two days of the month and the second occurring on the last two days. February can not have a blue Moon because at most it has only 29 days.

Older definitions of a blue Moon are based on having four full Moons during a season, or having 13 full Moons during one year. These events caused difficulty in developing the Christian calendar particularly in determining the date for Easter which is based on the first Sunday after the first full Moon in spring.

5. Binocular Beauties

Binoculars can be valuable tools for observing the nighttime sky with children. Their wide-screen view makes successful observing much easier than with a telescope. Binoculars gather 20 to 40 times as much light as the human eye. They can bring into view dramatic features on the Moon such as mountains and craters. The four Galilean moons on Jupiter, double stars, star clusters, and nebula can be easily seen.

Figure 7.5 lists some prominent celestial objects that are visible in the evening sky using binoculars. Economical sky charts that are adjustable for the different days of the year and the time of night include many of the objects listed in the figure. These charts make locating the objects possible.

Plan your observing sessions to ensure successful experiences. Many resources, such as the sky charts mentioned earlier, are available that will identify objects that are visible through binoculars. Recognize that, particularly with deep sky objects, the visibility varies with each evening. The air temperature, humidity, and pollution are all factors that affect visibility. Cold winter nights tend to produce the best observing.

All observing sessions with young children should be designed to develop interest and wonder. Without getting into detail, share with your children the immensity

Spring	Fall
Beehive cluster (M44)	Cygnus open cluster (M39)
Messier 47 open cluster	Wild Duck globular cluster (M11)
Hercules globular cluster (M13)	Mizar double star (Ursa Major)
Coma Berenicis (M53) globular cluster	
Summer	**Winter**
Epsilon Lyra double star	Great Orion nebula (M42)
Ring nebula (M57)	Pleiades (M45) (open cluster)
Globular cluster (M22)	Andromeda Galaxy (M31)
	Crab nebula (M1)

FIGURE 7.5 Binocular beauties.

of space. Use statements like "If Earth were the size of a BB, the Sun would be the size of a basketball."

6. Observing the Sun

The Sun is a fascinating object to observe when proper care and procedures are followed. Sunspots are fascinating objects to view and are visible on most days. Although rare, solar eclipses are easily monitored with observing equipment that can be made using very basic materials.

An apparatus for observing the Sun that is similar to a pinhole camera can be constructed using a cardboard box. Figure 7.6 illustrates such a piece of equipment. Attach a cloth to one side so that the observer can look under the cloth to see the darkened box. Place a piece of white paper to serve as a screen on the side interior wall. On the opposite side of the box cut out a small hole and cover the hole with aluminum foil. Prick a small hole in the aluminum foil. Align the box so that the light from the Sun shines through the pinhole onto the white paper. The inverted image of the Sun will be visible on the paper. The longer the box, the larger the image will be.

Alterations can be made to your apparatus to expand your observing opportunities. The pinhole can be replaced by a small lens. This will make the image much brighter. The distance from the lens to the paper must be adjusted to focus the Sun. You can also use one side of a pair of binoculars or a small telescope to project the image. Current solar images can be obtained from the Internet. By checking the

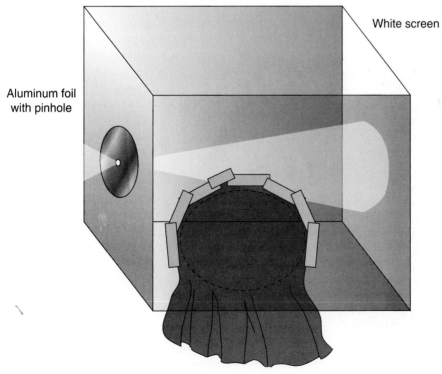

FIGURE 7.6 Solar-observing box.

images each day over a period of a week or two, your students can observe the changes that occur, including the development and demise of sunspots and related solar flares. The rotation of the Sun around its axis can also be observed.

7. Collecting Micro-Meteorites

Meteors are constantly entering Earth's atmosphere from space. A few are of significant size and can survive the trip through Earth's atmosphere, but most are far too small. These small particles become part of our atmosphere. Meteorites are formed from iron-nickel compounds. This makes them magnetic.

Children can collect these micro-meteorites using very simple means. Because the micro-meteorites are part of the atmosphere, they become particles around which water droplets form. By collecting rainwater your class can actually collect micro-meteorites. A convenient way to do this is to place a couple of clean rubber garbage can lids in an open area before a rainstorm. After the water is collected, "stir" the water with a strong magnet. The micro-meteorites will become attached to the magnet. If you cover the magnet with a plastic wrap, it will be easier to detach the particles.

Children will enjoy observing the micro-meteorites with a hand lens or a binocular microscope. The micro-meteorites usually appear to be somewhat like a bubble because they became extremely hot when they entered the atmosphere.

8. Balloon Rockets

Children love to watch things fly around. Anytime something moves it can be exciting. The faster it moves the better. Balloon rockets can provide this excitement and at the same time demonstrate the basic nature of rockets.

When you release a balloon, its propulsion demonstrates Newton's basic laws of physics, which were discussed earlier in this chapter. Balloons are ideal for introducing rocketry to young children. They are economical, safe, and large enough for children to observe easily. Children should be told not to put balloons in their mouth or near their face.

You might introduce balloon rockets by just blowing up a balloon and releasing it to travel randomly around the classroom. This experience can be expanded by having the children construct their own rockets using balloons, drinking straws, and string (Figure 7.7). Thread a string though a drinking straw and tie one end of the string to an elevated object at one end of the classroom. Tie the other end to a chair or other convenient object across the room.

Blow up a balloon and hold the opening shut. Tape the balloon to the drinking straw with the opening directed toward the chair. When you release the balloon, the balloon will travel up the string to the far end of the room. Children might want to have rocket races to see which balloon travels the farthest.

9. Film Canister Rockets

Simple rockets can also be made using film canisters from 35-millimeter camera film. (Photo shops are usually glad to give you large quantities of canisters since they have no need for them after they develop the film.) Some film canisters seal more

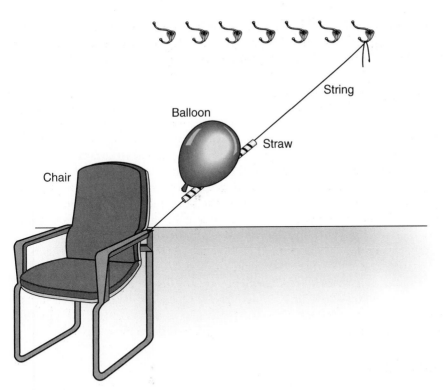

FIGURE 7.7 Balloon rocket.

tightly than others. We have found that the semi-clear plastic canisters function much better than the black canisters with the gray caps.

Place half of an effervescent tablet such as an Alka-Seltzer® into a film canister and add sufficient tap water to fill the container approximately half full. If you quickly seal the container and step back, in a few seconds the carbon dioxide formed by the water acting on the tablet will create sufficient pressure to pop the cap off with sufficient force to hit the classroom ceiling. If you place the canister upside-down, the canister will be propelled rather than the cap. It is advisable for students to wear goggles while conducting this activity.

Your students can construct simple rockets by taping construction paper around the canister and adding a cone and fins. A template is provided in Figure 7.8. Tape the rectangle around the canister with the overhang at the bottom of the canister so that the rocket can be placed on the ground upside-down. Add the cone and fins. These rockets will lift 10 to 15 feet.

10. Water Rockets

Water rockets offer a simple and safe way for children to experience rockets. These rockets work on the same principle as the balloon and film canister rockets: pressure. By filling the rocket approximately half full with water and pumping in air under pressure, the water will be forced out of the container, pushing the rocket to the sky. Toy stores often have economical and simple rockets that include a small hand pump.

Construction Paper

Cone

Fin

Fin

FIGURE 7.8 Template for film canister rockets.

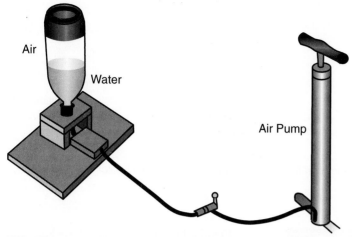

FIGURE 7.9   A 2-liter water bottle rocket.

You can also construct your own very effective water rockets using 2-liter beverage bottles. (These common recyclable bottles are designed to hold up to 300 pounds of air pressure.) A launch system can be built with a wood base, plastic tubing, a one-hole rubber stopper, and a tire pump, as shown in Figure 7.9.

Fill the 2-liter bottle approximately one-half full with water and invert it on the rubber stopper mounted to the wooden base. Pump the air into the bottle until the air pressure is greater than the friction holding the stopper to the bottle. When this occurs, the bottle will launch. These bottle rockets can rise up to 70 feet. Care needs to be taken to use this apparatus in an open area, and under strict supervision. Your 2-liter water rockets can be improved and decorated by adding a cone (made from a party hat or other simple material) and fins.

11. Air Rockets

Recently, simple and safe rockets that work only on air pressure have been marketed. These rockets are economical and will lift several hundred feet.

12. Chemical Rockets

Chemical rockets are the high end of amateur rocketry. Used properly, they offer a safe and dynamic experience for children. With young children they should only be used as a demonstration by a person who has used these rockets sufficiently to develop skills and basic safety practices.

13. How High Did It Go?

Observing any rockets can be an exciting and motivating experience. Your children will naturally want to know how high the rocket travels. Depending on the age and development of your students, you can use these experiences to help them develop simple processes to determine the height the rocket reaches.

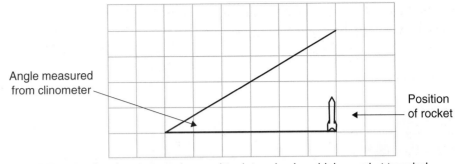

FIGURE 7.10 Graph paper can be used to determine how high a rocket traveled.

Clinometer for determining how high a rocket traveled.

Depending on the type of rockets and the height that they travel, different processes can be explored. For the more simple rockets, such as the film canister rockets, measurement might be calculated by observing the rocket against the background wall of a building and counting how many blocks high it traveled.

For more advanced students, a clinometer can be used. The person with the clinometer stands back a determined distance from the rocket. When the rocket lifts off, the person will observe the angle or inclination the rocket reaches. Knowing the distance the observer is from the rocket and the angle, the height can be obtained. While the calculations for this process are too advanced for younger children, the results can be obtained by means of a simple graph. As shown in Figure 7.10, using graph paper, the height that your rocket travels can be determined. Set up a scale such as "each square equals 10 feet." If the person is standing 100 feet from the rocket, draw a line 10 squares long along the bottom of the paper. Using a protractor, draw a second line at the angle measured using the clinometer. By counting the number of squares above where the rocket was shot, the height of the rocket can be estimated. (Each square equals 10 feet.)

The altitude of a rocket's flight can also be tracked by sight. Tracking uses math to calculate how high the rocket went. This process is called *triangulation*. This principle of triangulation (determining height or some location by the use of angles and degrees, that is, trigonometry) is important to astronomers and other scientists.

While somewhat complex and abstract for young children, noticing the flight patterns of rockets gives children experience in predicting, estimating, measuring, graphing, and interpreting data.

Activities in Other Explorations That Relate to Astronomy and Space Science

Light and Color (Chapter 12)

1. Pinhole Projects

Sun and Shadows (Chapter 15)

1. Here Comes the Sun
2. I Saw the Sun Move
8. The Warmth of the Sun

Resources for Teachers

Books

Caduto, M. J., & Bruchac, J. (1989). *Keepers of the Earth: Native American stories and environmental activities for children.* Golden, CO: Fulcrum.

Driscoll, L. (1996). *Let's look at the planets.* New York: Grosset & Dunlap.

Friedman, H. (1975). *The amazing universe.* Washington, DC: National Geographic Society.

Hawking, S. (1993). *Black holes and baby universes and other essays.* New York: Bantam Books.

Raymo, C. (1982). *365 starry nights: An introduction to astronomy for every night of the year.* New York: Simon & Schuster.

Ridpath, I. (2003). *Norton's star atlas and reference handbook* (20th ed.). Upper Saddle River, NJ: Prentice Hall.

Trefil, J. (1992). *1001 things everyone should know about science.* New York: Doubleday.

Article

Keller, J. D. (1971). Golf ball lunology. *Texas Science Teacher,* p. 18.

Web Sites

http://www.adlerplanetarium.org/learn/planets/planetary_geology/density.ssi
Information on the density of the planets.

http://www.ameritech.net/users/paulcarlisle/MoonCalendar.html
Gives Moon phases and times for moonrise and moonset for any time and any location.

http://www.enchantedlearning.com/subjects/astronomy/moon/Phases.shtml
Information on the Moon.

http://www.grc.nasa.gov/WWW/K-12/airplane/newton.html
Basic information on Newton's three laws of motion.

http://pds.jpl.nasa.gov/planets/special/planets.htm
A variety of information on the planets.

http://www.lightandmatter.com/binosky/binosky.html
Excellent resource for using binoculars for observing.

http://www.nasm.si.edu/research/ceps/etp/ss/ss_planetdata.html
Physical data about planets.

http://www.pubquizhelp.34sp.com/sci/planets.html
Excellent source for current information on the number of identified moons for each of the planets.

http://umbra.gsfc.nasa.gov/images/latest.html
Excellent source for current solar images using a variety of solar filters.

http://tycho.usno.navy.mil/vphase.html
Gives phases of the Moon for any day.

Children's Books on Astronomy and Space Science

Bennet, J. (2003). *Max goes to the moon.* Boulder, CO: Big Kid Science.
Bond, P. (1999). *Dorling Kindersley guide to space.* New York: DK Publishing Eyewitness Books.
Branley, F. M. (1998). *The planets in our solar system.* New York: HarperCollins Publishers.
Davis, K. (2001). *Don't know much about space.* New York: Harper Trophy.
Dickinson, T. (1987). *Exploring the night sky: The equinox astronomy guide for young astronomers.* New York: John Wiley & Sons.
Douglass, J. (2003). *My big busy space activity book.* New York: Priddy Bicknell.
Florian, D. (2007). *Comets, stars, the moon, and Mars.* New York: Harcourt.
Gibbons, G. (1997). *The moon book.* New York: Holiday House.
Gibbons, G. (1995). *The planets.* New York: Holiday House.
Hatchett, C. (1988). *The glow-in-the-dark night sky book.* New York: Random House Trade.
Hollan, S. (2001). *Space.* New York: DK Publishing.
Leedy, L. (1996). *Postcards from Pluto.* New York: Holiday House.
Levy, D. (1997). *Sharing the sky: A parent and teacher's guide to astronomy.* New York: Plenum Press.
Love, A. & Drake, J. (2004). *The kids' book of the night sky.* Toronto, Ont.: Kids Can Press Ltd.
Malloy, C. (2003). *The solar system (pull-out-book).* San Francisco, CA: Chronicle Books.
Matloff, G. L. (1993). *Telescope power: Fantastic activities and easy projects for young astronomers.* New York: John Wiley & Sons.
Mitton, J. (1998). *Zoo in the sky.* Washington, DC: National Geographic Society.
Peddicord, J. A. (2005). *Night wonders.* Watertown, MA: Charlesbridge.
Rabe, T., & Dr. Seuss. (1998). *There's no place like sky.* New York: Random House.
Ripley, C. (1996). *Why do starts twinkle?* Toronto, ON: Greey de Pencier Book Inc.
Silver, D. (1998). *One small square, the night sky.* New York: McGraw-Hill.
Simon, S. (2002). *Destination: Space.* New York: HarperCollins Publishers.
Simon, S. (2003). *The moon.* New York: Simon & Schuster.
Simon, S. (2004). *Destination: Mars.* New York: Harper Trophy.
Simon, S. (1994). *Comets, meteors, and asteroids.* New York: HarperCollins Publishers.
Stott, C. (1997). *Night sky (DK Eyewitness Explorers).* New York: DK Publishing.
Stott, C. (2002). *I wonder why stars twinkle.* New York: Kingfisher Books. Larousse Kingfisher Chambers.
Thompson, C. E. E. (1999). *Glow-in-the-dark constellations: A field guide for young stargazers.* New York: Grosset & Dunlap.
Tomecek, S. (2003). *Jump into science: Stars.* Washington, DC: National Geographic Society.
Tomecek, S. (2005). *Moon.* Washington, DC: National Geographic Society.
Vogt, G. L. (1996). *Mars.* Brookfield, CT: Millbrook Press.

Correlation of NSES Standards and NCTM Principles and Standards to Birds Concept Exploration Activities

	1. Adopt a Bird	2. Feed the Birds	3. Chart the Birds	4. Food Preferences of Birds	5. Constructing Bird Hotels	6. What's a Bird Have to Say?	7. Construction Time	8. Fright Distance	9. How Do Birds Interact?	10. How High Do Birds Fly?	11. Where Do Birds Go for the Winter?	12. Feathers of Fine Friends	13. Egg Incubators	14. How Much Does a Bird Weigh?	15. Birds in Different Cultures
SCIENCE															
Inquiry	X	X	X	X	X	X	X	X	X	X	X	X	X	X	X
Physical Science				X	X		X			X			X	X	
Life Science	S	X	X	X	X	X	X	X	X	X	X	X	X		X
Earth and Space Science	X		X	X							X				X
Science and Technology					X	X				X	X	X	X		
Personal and Social Perspectives	X	X	X	X	X	X	X	X	X		X		X		X
History and Nature of Science			X	X					X		X				X
MATHEMATICS															
Number and Operations	X	X	X	X	X	X			X	X	X		X	X	
Algebra	X	X	X	X					X			X			
Geometry		X			X		X				X				
Measurement		X		X	X		X	X		X		X		X	
Data Analysis and Probability	X	X	X	X		X		X	X	X	X		X	X	
Problem Solving					X		X			X			X	X	
Reasoning and Proof									X	X					
Communication	X	X	X	X	X	X		X	X	X	X	X		X	X
Connections		X	X	X	X		X	X	X	X				X	
Representation		X	X	X	X		X	X	X	X	X		X	X	

CHAPTER 8

Birds

Birds Soar

Birds soar and dance across the sky,
It is a wonder how they fly.
Graceful and soft they seem to be
with their flight being a mystery.
A bird's bones are hollow, don't you know?
It keeps her light and set to go.
Her feathers are light but keep her warm
So she can fly against the storm.
If I could fly I'd like to see
how the world would look to me!

Genevieve A. Davis

Birds defy gravity. We watch as a sparrow flies effortlessly up to a tree and lands with grace. On a hot summer day a hawk soars high above us. We watch and wonder about what it must be like to see our neighborhood from above, almost like a map, from this different perspective. We question how a hummingbird, weighing just a few ounces, can hover at one moment and then dart almost more quickly than the eye can follow. How can they fly thousands of miles to winter in a warmer climate?

We chuckle as we see a line of ducklings following their mother. Make way! We see a loon on the water disappear as it dips below the surface only to reappear at a different location on the lake. We watch a robin on the grass of our yard "listening" to find its next worm. We watch the mother birds feeding their young. Birds are excellent vehicles for exploring the world around us. They are a catalyst for our curiosity. Indeed, birds make our imaginations soar high above the clouds!

This concept exploration utilizes our curiosity of birds to examine many basic principles in science and mathematics. It is designed to guide and assist you in developing a variety of experiences for your students. Particular suggestions and opportunities are given to direct you in these explorations. Use these suggestions to initiate divergent experiences based on your children's questions, interests, and curiosities.

SCIENCE CONCEPTS FOR TEACHERS

The science conceptual framework is included here to give you, the teachers, background information. It is not intended as instructional material for the children, but instead as supplying basic supporting information. Having a basic knowledge of science is critical for guiding you in developing classroom activities.

Bird Basics

Although other forms of life, such as bats (mammals) and insects (arthropods), can fly, birds are the only animals that have feathers. It is the feathers that biologists use to classify animals as birds, phylum Aves. Some birds such as penguins, and the dodo bird, now extinct, cannot fly.

Birds have been around for approximately 150 million years. Fossil evidence of the *Archaeopteryx* birds from the Jurassic age shows well-developed feathers that indicate that *Archaeopteryx* was probably able to fly like modern birds.

There are approximately 10,000 different species of birds in the world (Richmond et al., 1992). They range from the world's smallest bird, the 2.5-inch-long bee hummingbird native to Cuba, to the largest bird, the ostrich of Africa, which can reach up to 9 feet.

All birds lay eggs. The incubation period for an egg ranges from 13 to 42 days. The larger the bird, the longer the incubation period. The eggs tend to be oval with one end more pointed than the other. This keeps the eggs from rolling far from the nest. They are many different colors and often speckled, which helps camouflage the eggs.

Feather Structure and Types

Feathers are made from the protein keratin. Their structure is designed to be extremely strong, waterproof, and as light as possible.

Feathers consist of the quill, the center shaft of the feather, and barbs, which extend from both sides of the quill. The barbs have interlocking hooklets, which give stiffness and flexibility to the feather. The barbs also contribute to the feathers lining up with each other. One feather has approximately 300 million barbs. Feathers that lack interlocking barbs are soft and downy.

Birds' wings have a curved shape. This shape causes the air to flow over and under the wing, as shown in Figure 8.1. The air flows more quickly over the top of the wing. This causes the air pressure to be greater on the underside of the wings. This gives the bird lift, which permits the bird to fly. Physicists call this airflow pattern the Bernoulli principle.

Migratory Patterns

Many types of birds migrate during the different seasons. Shore and water birds, along with insect-eating birds, tend to migrate more than birds that eat seeds. Some

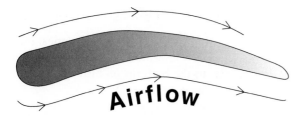

FIGURE 8.1 How birds fly.

Airflow

birds migrate just a few hundred miles. Others travel a much greater distance. The champion for migration is the arctic tern, which breeds in the Arctic and winters in the Antarctic.

Birds tend to migrate through several different *flyways*, or routes. These flyways are controlled by geographic factors such as mountains, which limit travel, and water, which supports food sources.

The migratory flyways are a controlling factor for determining which birds live in what areas. Mainly because of the barrier caused by the height of the western mountains, many of the birds found in the western United States are different from those in the eastern United States.

MATHEMATICS: ADDRESSING THE NCTM STANDARDS THROUGH CONCEPT EXPLORATIONS

Many of the activities in these concept explorations that are designed to help children become aware of birds and their habits involve counting, patterns, sequencing, geometry, measurement, data collection, organization, and analysis. As you engage in these fun explorations with your students, be aware of the many opportunities in mathematics that present themselves. Following are examples of ways to use mathematics in your explorations about birds. Infuse creative and thoughtful observation, thinking, and communication about our fines-feathered friends and the feelings they inspire.

Number and Operations

Counting birds that come to the bird feeder gives children experience with rational counting. Using one-to-one correspondence and stable order in counting is important for young children. Within the context of counting birds, this experience comes with great motivation and enthusiasm.

Counting will also be important when gathering information for constructing simple charts and graphs. Children's ability to count with meaning will help them to describe data sets with their cardinal property. When comparing the numbers of birds, they will gain experience with the concepts of more and less, of comparison and seriation. Which birds are the most frequent at our bird feeder? Which birds are least frequent? These types of questions give children experiences hearing the mathematical vocabulary of comparison and seriation.

You can construct a picture number book with each page showing one, two, three, four, five, and so on, birds on each successive page. This experience can support bird identification, counting, and sequencing and children are very proud of creating their own books!

Algebra and Patterns

Patterns are abundant in bird study. Looking for patterns in physical appearance, birdcalls, flight, and behavior provides many opportunities for children to recognize patterns in nature. Constructing designs similar to the patterns on bird feathers can help children to appreciate the loveliness of patterns in nature.

Many different types of sorting and classifying come to mind in this exciting concept exploration. Sorting types of sounds, physical characteristics, bird food, feeders, nests, and types of eggs can be quite engaging. For example, children can order bird eggs by size. This gives them experience with seriation. Other attributes for seriating data from the bird observations could be size of birds, beaks, or feathers or volume of their bird calls.

Geometry

Geometric ideas are inherent to these activities: navigating and mapping the location of bird nests and flight patterns; fitting pieces together to build a birdhouse; determining relative position in space of birds nesting and in flight, that is, high flying or low flying, high nesting or on-the-ground nesting; and recognizing geometric shapes and structures in the environment.

Measurement

Building nests and birdhouses can provide opportunities for children to use measurement and organize their approaches to an activity by planning a sequence of steps to follow. For example, ordering actions for making a bird feeder could begin with determining what type of food to use, then selecting something to put the food on, then gathering the necessary ingredients, and so forth. It is important for children to think and plan events if they are to enhance their reasoning ability. Using multiple forms of representation should be encouraged: written and spoken words, gestures, pictures, sketches, or the laying out of the materials in a sequential order.

The building of birdhouses provides ample opportunities for utilizing measurement skills. Using appropriate tools, reading scales, and recording measurements are required to complete this type of activity.

Data Analysis

Studying birds requires many mathematical ideas and concepts. Starting with simple observations, children begin to experience collecting certain types of data. As they see, hear, smell, and feel, they are gathering information through their senses. Children should be encouraged to record, in some way, the information they perceive. This is an important part of learning how to communicate ideas and information to others. Collecting data and recording data lead naturally to organizing and charting data in a comprehensible way. Children should be given opportunities to construct panels, charts, picture graphs, bar graphs, circle graphs, and other simple organized and creative displays. In this sense, they are learning to organize, classify, and sort.

Part of data collection can be accomplished by frequency counts. For example, when watching birds at a bird feeder, a large, simple chart can be made with equal size columns. A picture of each type of bird that frequents the feeder can be glued to the top of each column. As children observe the birds coming to feed, they can place a tally or a counter (perhaps a seed) in the appropriate column. After a designated amount of time, the tallies or counters can be counted to see how many of each bird came to eat. Comparisons can be made according to magnitude of the numbers.

Similar frequency counts can be taken for preferred time of feeding, type of food enjoyed most, ways birds fly, where nests are found, and fright distances. It is important for children to generate the criteria for collecting the data.

OBSERVING WITH ALL THE SENSES

Birds are valuable resources for exploring the senses. Giving children opportunities to use multiple senses in their explorations increases their retention of these experiences.

Sight

Birds have ideal characteristics for encouraging critical observations. Each type of bird has specific characteristics that aid in making comparisons and classification.

The observation of birds provides an interesting opportunity to recognize a characteristic of vision related to movement. Often, a bird in a tree is difficult to see. However, when the bird moves, we can see the bird more easily. This characteristic is also very valuable for many birds of prey. A hawk will see a mouse in a field when it moves. But, when the mouse is stationary, it is much more difficult for the hawk to see. This is why some animals will "freeze" in their path.

The observation of birds also gives children excellent opportunities for learning to use binoculars. Children should use binoculars with a wide field of view and lower magnification. This will make the object easier to find and to see.

Binoculars usually come rated with two numbers such as 7×35. The first number indicates the magnification power of the binoculars. The second number indicates the diameter of the main lens in millimeters. The greater the diameter of the lens, the more light the lens collects.

Touch

Children might have an occasional opportunity to touch birds in nature. They can feel the different textures for different types of feathers. Flight feathers have a structural body that gives strength for flight. Body feathers are designed for insulation and feel very soft. Children enjoy these close examinations of the different types of feathers. Care must be given to wash hands throughly after such an investigation.

Sound

Birdcalls provide great listening experiences for children. Each bird has its own call. Listening to the different birds helps children differentiate between sounds. Some calls such as that of the Eastern wood pewee are very high pitched. Others such as the call of a mourning dove are very low sounds. Birdcalls also provide opportunities for comparing the attitudes that are expressed. Some are soft and musical; others are shrill and aggressive.

SAFETY

Care should be taken when studying birds. Some children have allergies to birds. Before you bring a bird such as a parakeet or other small bird into the classroom, you should check to see if any of your students are allergic to birds.

Birds' nests should be handled carefully. Once a nest is abandoned, bird mites tend to leave a nest. But it is more prudent to observe birds' nests in nature rather than bringing them into the classroom.

Areas around bird feeders need to be cleaned. Moist seed and bird droppings can cause diseases for birds and humans. Periodically, clean out old seed from your bird feeder and clean up the seed that collects on the ground below the feeder. You can also use weak vinegar or bleach solutions to clean your feeders. Exercise caution with these solutions—wear gloves and protect your eyes.

CONCEPT EXPLORATIONS ON BIRDS FOR YOUR CLASSROOM

In Chapter 3, the importance of engaging children in all four stages of problem solving was discussed. Assisting children to pursue their own questions is the key to developing a positive and interested attitude in learning, particularly as it relates to mathematics and science. Exploring the world of birds gives children many opportunities to examine their own interests and questions. It is important to record children's initial questions and theories about birds to guide their investigations.

You may want to begin your exploration of birds with some shared reading. Ron Hirsch's book *What Is a Bird?* presents beautiful photographs of birds accompanied by simple text. This book shows close-up photos of birds that children may not have access to in their own neighborhoods. Another great beginning resource is Dean Morris's book *Read About Birds*. This book introduces various kinds of birds with a focus on migration, food gathering, and nest building—the focus of three of the following concept explorations. As children investigate and research about birds, their theories will reflect what they have learned. Children are curious and full of wonder. Remember, wisdom comes from wondering!

The following explorations provide a wide variety of activities that are appropriate for young children. Note that through these studies about birds, much information and details about birds will be gained. On completing any of these studies, even adults would feel that they have learned much. Also note that the nature of these activities and the basic skills required do not prohibit young children from participating in these explorations.

The species of birds that live in your geographic area will vary from season to season, but all areas have certain species that are more common than others. So choose activities that involve the common birds in your own community to assist your children in learning more about their particular environment and its inhabitants.

1. Adopt a Bird

Identify and select a variety of birds common in your community. Each child or group of children can "adopt" one of the birds. Observe the physical characteristics of the bird. Watch its behavior. Look for, but don't be limited to, the following tasks and questions:

- Describe the physical characteristics of your bird.
- How does its coloring relate to its environment? Are males and females colored differently?
- Where does it tend to stay? Does it spend time on the ground, in fields, or in woods?
- What does it eat?
- What birdcalls does it make?
- How does it move, both in the air and on the ground?
- What time of day is it active?
- Do your birds tend to be alone or do they congregate?

Keep a written log of the activities that your students have observed. Planning and organizing the log should be a collaborative venture between you and the children. Describe each of your observations and what you have learned from it. Collect and share the class's findings in an organized and creative way. For instance, your findings could be published on a panel in your school hall or displayed in the school paper or PTA newsletter. A Web site could be developed to highlight your class's findings. For an extension, use a videocam to make live observations of a bird's nest outside your classroom.

2. Feed the Birds

You can easily make any of a wide variety of bird feeders with your students or purchase one for a reasonable price. Birds are not particular about the aesthetics of the feeders—they are hungry. Remember to have conversations about this fact with the children so they can try to construct a feeder that is made for eating!

To attract a variety of birds, you need to have a variety of feeders. There are three main variables to consider. The first is the type of food that you put into your feeders. The second is the shape and materials used to make the feeder. The third is the location of the feeder. Let's look at each of these variables.

Food for birds varies from many types of seeds to fruits and suet. Suet is raw beef fat. Most of the seeds used for feeding birds are from plants common in nature. Each type of food attracts particular birds. Figure 8.2 lists a variety of different foods and the types of birds attracted to them.

The shape and materials used are important considerations when selecting and/or constructing your feeders. Birds will feel more comfortable if bird feeders

Corn	**Nectar**
Grackles	Hummingbirds
Crows	Orioles
Starlings	**Sunflower Seed**
	Blue Jays
	Cardinals
Fruit	**Suet**
Orioles	Woodpeckers
Mockingbirds	Nuthatch
Cedar waxwings	Tufted titmice
Woodpeckers	
	Peanuts/Peanut Butter
Insects	Bluejays
Woodpeckers	Chickadees
Robins	House finches
	Sparrows
Millet	Titmice
Doves	
Sparrows	**Thistle**
Juncos	Goldfinches
Blackbirds	Purple finches
Cow birds	

FIGURE 8.2 Common types of bird feed and the birds that are attracted to them.

Post feeders attract a variety of birds.

J. David Keller

are made with natural materials. Wood such as cedar and redwood weather well in nature and are attractive to birds. Glass and plastic tubes can make good feeders because it is easy to see how much food is left. Feeders usually have several perches so they can accompany several birds at one time. You should never use a bird feeder with metal perches because in cold weather, birds can actually get their feet frozen to the perch. Wood perches are good but squirrels and other rodents tend to gnaw on them; however, they are easy to replace with dowel rods available at local hardware stores.

You need to consider several criteria when locating your bird feeders. The height of the feeder from the ground should be considered. Some birds, for example, mourning doves, prefer to feed on the ground. Other birds prefer to feed several feet off the ground.

Having landing areas close to a bird feeder will help birds feel safer. Children can try to take the perspective of the bird by imagining what it means for a bird to feel safe when it feeds. Being able to fly to a small tree, brush, or shrub helps protect them from predators such as hawks and cats.

Ground feeders can be formed by placing a shallow container on the ground in an open area. A small log or flat stone might serve this purpose. Select a ground feeder that drains well to keep snow and rain from collecting in it. Children should be encouraged to discuss the best way to place a ground feeder. This type of activity helps children develop critical thinking and problem-solving skills. Ground-feeding birds prefer open areas to keep themselves away from predators. Fortunately, or unfortunately as the case may be, often squirrels visiting post feeders will scratch away seeds. This action forms a ground feeder on the ground below.

Suet feeders are not as common as post and ground feeders. However, they are well worth the minimal effort needed to keep them because they attract different species of birds, including several types of woodpeckers. You can purchase suet cakes with various seeds added that can be placed in a wire cage. These feeders are relatively inexpensive and can be found in many multipurpose stores. A more natural approach is to purchase some beef fat from your butcher and place in an onion net bag. Hang the bag from a tree. The birds will feed through the netting.

Hairy woodpecker at suet feeder.

J. David Keller

3. Chart the Birds

Bird feeders provide excellent opportunities for your children to learn to observe, collect, and analyze data. Ask your children "What questions do you have about the birds coming to your feeder?" Typically their questions will relate to what types of birds come to the feeder, what types of food particular birds like, and what time of day the birds tend to come to the feeder. Use these questions to develop charts that the children can study. An example is shown in Figure 8.3. These charts can become excellent displays for bulletin boards.

4. Food Preferences of Birds

After much observation of birds, children will begin to have an idea of what birds like to eat. They can then suggest a variety of food for the birds to eat. Gather the food and set out as many different types of bird food as you can in separate containers. For instance, different foods could be placed on small paper plates on the ground or on a picnic table. Consider some of the following foods: sunflower seeds, thistle, millet, peanuts, suet, bread, grapes, apples, and oranges. What types of birds go to each food? Using measuring cups will give children experiences with tools of measurement.

Observe how the birds eat their food. Compare the shape of their beaks to their food preferences. Are their beaks designed for breaking seed coats or for probing?

How many birds came to our feeder between 9:00 and 10:00 in the morning?

Blue Jays   Cardinals   Sparrows   Chickadees   Titmice

FIGURE 8.3 Pictographs are excellent graphs because the children can visualize the data to make comparisons.

5. Constructing Bird Hotels

Encourage your children to construct simple birdhouses from natural and man-made materials. Birdhouses can be a simple as a hole drilled into the side of a dried gourd. The design of bird houses can become very intricate in that particular species of birds demand specific characteristics. For example, swallows prefer nest boxes that have an entry on the bottom, whereas sparrows will reject these types of homes.

Constructing simple birdhouses gives children opportunities to use measurement and to utilize many geometric shapes. Birdhouses often demonstrate basic geometric shapes such as circles, triangles, squares, and trapezoids.

Observing birdhouses also provides excellent opportunities to collect and examine basic data. When your students have constructed and installed birdhouses in their school neighborhood, encourage them to ask questions related to their birdhouses. Some questions that may come up are listed in Figure 8.4.

Questions About Our Birdhouses

1. What kind of bird will move into my birdhouse?
2. How long will the birds live there?
3. How many babies will live in the birdhouse?
4. How long will it take for the birds to move in?
5. How long will it take for the eggs to hatch?

D. McNeal's book *The Original Birdhouse Book* can be used as a resource about structures in which birds live. Students can then extend their ideas about where birds live as they construct homes for their feathered friends. Perhaps situating the constructed birdhouse near a classroom window will allow students to watch birds "move in."

6. What's a Bird Have to Say?

Birds have intricate methods of communicating with each other. Each species of bird has its own call. Some birds have one distinct call. Others have several different calls. For instance, blue jays have the distinctive shrill "jay" call and they also have the distinctive call that sounds like a "pump handle." Other birds, like the mockingbird, will mimic the calls of other birds that they hear. Some birds, like the hawk, have piercing calls, whereas others such as robins and orioles have a very musical call.

With today's improved technology, many sources are available for hearing birdcalls. CDs are available that include the voices of birds along with information about each bird's range and so forth. Numerous Web sites also include birdcalls.

Your student can record birdcalls with tape recorders. In addition, there are remote microphone devices that you can hang next to a bird feeder so that you can hear the birds while in the classroom.

Do not concentrate on identifying the different species of birds and their calls. Emphasize that the birdcalls are a tool for communicating. Help your children enjoy the diversity of sounds created.

7. Construction Time: Can You Build as Well as a Bird?

Birds construct intricate nests so that they can raise their young. How difficult is it to produce one of these beautiful nests? Supply some nesting materials to your children. Small twigs, grasses, string, and dog hair are common materials that birds use. Let your students see if they can reproduce a nest.

This birdhouse demonstrates a classic circle shape.

J. David Keller

You will need an example of a nest for the children to look at. There are laws, however, against taking nests from nature while there are eggs or young in the nests, except for some nonnative species such as starlings. If you know of a nest close by, after you have observed the babies develop and leave the nest, it is reasonable to remove the nest. Most birds never use the same nest more than once. Also, be aware that, although the chance of getting disease from a nest is small, birds' nests often are inhabited by mites that can bite. A better idea than using a real nest is to photograph different nests for your students to use as models.

Your class can also take a nature walk around the community in the spring to locate birds' nests. Often, you can see birds collecting nesting materials, which will give you an opportunity to follow them to their nests. The class could develop a classification system based on the variations in the materials and construction of the nests.

Your children might make a map of the community indicating the location of the nests that they find (Figure 8.5). Digital photographs could be taken and the students' photo collection of birds' nests could be put on a Web page.

8. Fright Distance

Fright distance is defined as how close a person can come to a bird or other animal before the animal will fly off or hop away. Select a bird and collect data on the fright distance for that species of bird.

A common way to do this is to observe a bird, such as a robin, that is in the schoolyard. Slowly walk toward the bird until the bird takes notice of your presence. Visually note the location and take a few steps toward the bird. When the bird moves away from you, measure the distance to the bird's location.

9. How Do Birds Interact with Each Other and with Other Animals?

Feeding stations attract a wide variety of birds and other animals and allow us to observe the interrelationships of the animals. If their preferences for particular types of food are similar, they might compete with one another. This can be observed through a form of "pecking order" at the feeder. When a particular bird flies to a feeder, do other birds of the same species or of other species fly away? How do birds exhibit this aggressive behavior?

Bird feeding stations attract other forms of wildlife along with the birds. How do the birds react to other visitors such as squirrels and chipmunks?

Observations of this type can be charted by your students. For example, children can make drawings of the different types of birds and other animals and use them on a vertical chart by moving the order of the different animals up and down to represent the pecking order.

10. How High Do Birds Fly?

Flight patterns of different types of birds vary. Some birds fly close to the ground. Others can be seen soaring high in the sky. The flight patterns of birds tell us a lot about the nature of the birds. For instance, in the evening we might see purple martins

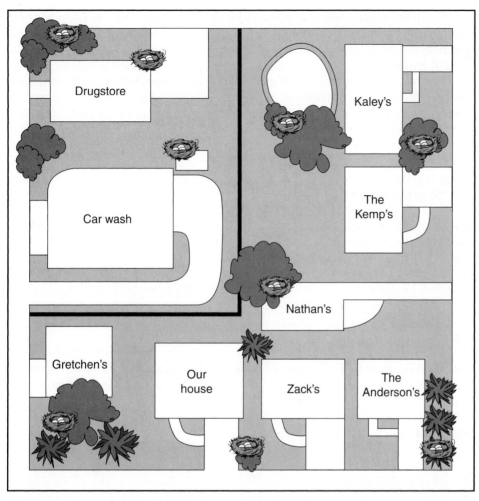

FIGURE 8.5 Birds' nests located in our community

flying high in the sky as they feed on insects. A hawk or a vulture can be seen soaring with wings spread wide to catch updrafts of air currents.

As children observe birds and their flight patterns, encourage them to record the patterns in creative ways. For example, they might make a drawing showing a hummingbird flying around a hummingbird feeder.

11. Where Do Birds Go for the Winter?

The migratory patterns of birds can be a source of wonderment for children. That some birds will fly thousands of miles for the winter is truly amazing. The range of migratory patterns is extremely wide. In the northern states, we look forward to the first robin or red-winged blackbird in the spring. Some species of birds, for example, the slate-colored junco, spend summers in Alaska and northern Canada and then winter throughout the United States.

Some basic activities can help children understand this phenomenon. For example, children could mark on their class calendar the first sighting in spring for the different birds. (It seems to be a little more difficult to mark the last sightings in the fall for birds.)

Several Web sites such as Signals of Spring (*http://www.signalsofspring.net*) monitor the migration of several species of birds including bald eagles. Signals of Spring has attached GPS (Global Positioning System) monitors to the birds so that satellites can monitor their daily movements. The positions are indicated on maps on the Web site. As your children monitor these changes, they can also develop better map skills.

12. Feathers of Fine Friends

Feathers of birds provide opportunities for comparisons and classifications. Children enjoy looking at feathers they find on the ground. Closer examination with a hand lens or small microscope can add to this interest.

Children can make comparisons on how different feathers "fly" when they are dropped. Do they spiral or arc back and forth? Which feathers travel the farthest? Which feathers take the longest time to land?

13. Egg Incubators

It is not difficult to hatch the eggs of ducks, chicken, quail, and pheasants. If you decide to hatch eggs, before you initiate the activity, you should make arrangements for the care of the hatchlings. Chicken and ducks often find homes on small farms. Under supervision to select proper areas and stage of development, quail and pheasants can be introduced into nature.

Small egg incubators can be purchased or constructed with basic materials. All incubators need to have a controlled heat source that keeps the temperature at approximately 102 degrees Fahrenheit (39 degrees Celsius). A source of moisture is also important to keep the humidity elevated. It is important that the eggs be turned over each day. This will keep the hatchlings from being deformed. Some incubators have an automatic turning device that turns the eggs periodically each day.

14. How Much Does a Bird Weigh?

Birds are very light, which makes it possible for them to fly. Unlike other animals, the bones of birds are hollow, which permits strength without adding a large amount of weight.

Children can have fun exploring ways to estimate or measure how much a bird weighs. For example, birdseed could be placed on a postage scale. When the bird lands on the scale, you can measure the weight of the bird.

When birds land on a thin branch, how much does the branch bend? How much weight do you need to attach at that point of the branch to deflect the branch the same amount? The accuracy of the measurements is not critical. The value of these experiences is that the children have an opportunity to explore ways to observe and take measurements.

15. Birds in Different Cultures

Birds are viewed differently in many cultures. In many parts of the world, birds have religious meanings. That birds can fly toward the heavens gives significance to their role in religion.

Many tribes of Native Americans greatly respect the eagle. The eagle would take their prayers to the Great Sprit for them. Eagle feathers have great significance and are still used today for traditional costumes.

Birds also have significance in the cuisines of different cultures. One example is in Asia where the white-nest swift uses its saliva to string together a tiny gauze-like nest. Gathered at great risk, these nests form the chief ingredient of the wildly popular Chinese delicacy, bird's nest soup.

Bedrock, soil conditions, and climate all have major influence in what vegetation and animals live in a geographic area. These are all critical factors in developing the culture of an area because they control what foods are available and they also affect the nature of economics and the type of occupations available.

The study of birds provides many opportunities to explore how geography, climate, and the species of wildlife contribute to the different cultures. A simple example is to make comparisons of the variations of the state birds for each U.S. state.

A good companion book to read for this exploration is Mark J. Rauzon's *Seabirds*. In this book, children can see actual photographs of penguins, puffins and other auks, pelicans, tropical birds, and frigate birds. This book will expand the world of birds from our backyards to afar.

Activities in Other Explorations That Relate to Birds

Seeds (Chapter 14)

3. What Do Our Animal Neighbors Eat?

Toys and Tools (Chapter 16)

5. The Toy Factory (Bird in the Cage)

Wind (Chapter 18)

6. Animals Using the Wind

Resources for Teachers

Books

Alsop, F. J. (2001). *Birds of North America—Eastern region*. Washington, DC: Smithsonian Handbooks.

Breining, G. (1994). *Return of the eagle—How America saved its national symbol*. Helena, MT: Falcon Press.

Brenner, B., & Takaya, J. (1996). *Chibi: A true story from Japan*. New York: Clarion Books.

Bull, J., & Farrand, J. (1997). *National Audubon Society field guide to North American bird—Eastern region*. New York: Alfred A. Knopf.

Burton, P. (1989). *Birds of prey*. New York: Gallery Books.

Crook, B. C. (1978). *Invite a bird to dinner: Simple feeders you can make*. New York: Lothrop, Lee & Shepard.

Fowler, A. (1993). *Quack and honk.* Chicago: Children's Press.

Hawkins, C. (1907). *Tenants of the trees.* Boston, MA: L. C. Page & Co.

Latimer, J., & Nolting, B. S. (1999). *Peterson field guide for young naturalists—Backyard birds.* Boston, MA: Houghton Mifflin Company.

Macbean, J. C., Stecher, A., Wentworth, D. F., & Couchman, J. K. (1977). *Birds: Examining your environment.* Toronto ON: Holt, Rinehart and Winston of Canada.

Macdonald, J. D., Goodwin, D., & Adler, H. E. (1962). *Bird behavior.* New York: Sterling Publishing Co.

McNeal, D. (2002). *The original birdhouse book.* Bird Watcher's Digest Press.

Peterson, R. T. (1980). *A field guide to the birds.* Boston, MA. Houghton Mifflin Co.

Richmond, C. W., et al. (1992). *The Richmond index to the genera and species of birds.* Boston, MA: G. K. Hall Micropublications.

Rockwell, A. (1992) *Our yard is full of birds.* New York: Macmillan.

Trost, L. W. (1975). *The amazing world of American birds.* New York: G. P. Putnam's Sons.

Udvardy, M. D. F., & Farrand, J. (1997). *National Audubon Society field guide to North America birds—Western region.* New York: Alfred A. Knopf.

Webb, S. (2004). *Looking for seabirds. Journal from an Alaskan voyage.* Boston, MA: Houghton Mifflin Company.

Zimm, H. S., & Gabrielson, I.N. (1956). *Birds, a guide to the most familiar American birds.* New York: Golden Press.

Journal

Birds & Blooms. Greendale, WI: Reiman Publications.
A journal with many ideas for feeding and watching birds.

Computer Disk

North America Birds. Peterson Multimedia Guides.
Includes birdcalls for all birds of North America.

Web Sites

http://www.audubon.org

http://www.birdwatchers.com/index.html

http://www.conservation.state.mo.us/nathis/birds/birdfeed

http://cm27personal.fal.buffalo.edu/birds/index.html

http://www.geocities.com/felicitax
A wonderful site all about feathers and activities with feathers.

http://www.signalsofspring.com

http://www.urbanbirds.org/celebration

http://www.wildbirds.com/Feeding.htm

Children's Books on Birds

Arnold, K. (1997). *Duck, duck, goose?* New York: Holiday House.

Arnosky, J. (1992). *Crinkleroot's guide to knowing the birds.* New York: Bradbury Press.

Raffi. (1999). *Five little ducks.* New York: Crown.

Asch, F. (1999). *Baby bird's first nest.* San Diego: Harcourt Brace & Company.

Atkins, J. (2001). *Bobin's home.* New York: Farrar, Straus, & Giroux.

Brawn, T. (1998). *My goose Betsy*. Cambridge, MA: Candlewick Press.

Brown, W. M. (2004). *The golden egg book*. Racine, WI: Golden Books.

Burnie, D. (1988). *Eyewitness books: Birds*. New York: DK Publishing.

Cannon, J. (1993). *Stella luna*. San Diego, CA: Harcourt Brace & Company.

Chermayeff, I. (1995). *Feathery facts*. Singapore: Harcourt Brace & Company.

Cherry, L. (1997). *Flute's journey*. New York: Harcourt Brace & Company.

Demuth, B. P. (1994). *Cradles in the trees: The story of bird nests*. New York: Macmillan.

Downing, J. (1989). *White snow, blue feather*. New York: Bradbury Press.

Eastman, P. D. (1968). *The best nest*. New York: Random Press.

Ehlert, L. (1990). *Feathers for lunch*. San Diego CA: Harcourt Brace & Company.

Flanagan, A. (1996). *Night birds*. New York: Grolier Publishing.

Florian, D. (2000). *On the wing*. New York: Voyager Books Harcourt.

Fowler, A. (1990). *It could be a bird*. Danbury, CT: Children's Press.

Fox, M. (1998). *Boo to a goose*. New York: Dial Books.

Freschet, B. (1985). *Owl in the garden*. New York: Lothrop, Lee & Shepard.

Frost, H. (1999). *Baby birds*. Mankato, MN: Pebble Books.

Hirschi, R. (1987). *What is a bird?* New York: Walker and Company.

Holub, J. (2004). *Why do birds sing?* New York: Dial Books for Young Readers.

Jenkins, B. P. (1995). *A nest full of eggs*. New York: HarperCollins Publishers.

Jonas, A. (1999). *Bird talk*. New York: Greenwillow Books.

Kittinger, J. S. (2001). *Birds of North America*. New York: DK Publishing Inc. & Smith Senior Institute.

Kottke, J. (2000). *From egg to robin*. Danbury, CT: Children's Press.

Le Tord, B. (1985). *Good wood bear*. New York: Bradbury Press.

Lerner, C. (1994). *Backyard birds of winter*. New York: Morrow.

Lewin, B. (1995). *Booby hatch*. New York: Clarion Books.

Lyon, D. (1985). *The runaway duck*. New York: Lothrop, Lee & Shepard.

Morris, D. (1977). *Birds*. Milwaukee, WI: Raintree Children's Books.

Pomerantz, C. (1989). *Flap Your wings and trip*. New York: Greenwillow Books.

Rabe, T. (1988). *Fine feathered friends*. New York: Random House.

Rauzon, M. J. (1996). *Seabirds*. New York: Franklin Watts, Grolier Publishing.

Richardson, J. (1993). *Birds*. New York: Franklin Watts.

Rockwell, A. (1992). *Our yard is full of birds*. New York: Macmillan.

Royston, A. (1992). *Birds*. New York: Alladin.

Seuss, D. (1940, 1968). *Horton hatches the egg*. New York: Random House.

Simon, M. (1997). *The goose that almost got cooked*. New York: Scholastic Press.

Stewart, M. (2001). *A true book: Birds*. New York: Grolier Publishing.

Stocke, J. M. (1988). *Minewa Louise: The mixed-up hen*. New York: Penguin Books.

Wood, A. (1997). *Bird song*. Singapore: Harcourt Brace & Company.

Correlation of NSES Standards and NCTM Principles and Standards to Clouds Concept Exploration Activities

	1. Head in the Clouds	2. Capture the Clouds	3. Catch Your Breath	4. How High Is a Cloud?	5. What to Do with the Weather	6. Cloudy Sky Stories	7. I've Looked at Clouds from Both Sides Now	8. Which Way Are You Going?	9. As the Saying Goes
SCIENCE									
Inquiry	X	X	X	X	X	X	X	X	X
Physical Science	X	X	X	X	X	X	X	X	X
Life Science				X	X				X
Earth and Space Science	X	X	X	X	X	X	X	X	X
Science and Technology		X		X			X		X
Personal and Social Perspectives	X	X	X		X	X			
History and Nature of Science		X					X		
MATHEMATICS									
Number and Operations					X				X
Algebra					X				X
Geometry		X	X	X			X		
Measurement	X			X			X		
Data Analysis and Probability					X				X
Problem Solving		X	X	X		X	X	X	X
Reasoning and Proof				X					
Communication	X	X	X		X	X			X
Connections	X		X						
Representation	X						X	X	

158

CHAPTER 9

Clouds

Clouds

Clouds float and change across the sky
Some are billowy, I do not know why.
They can be white and pink and gray
They change with the weather everyday.
Are they the pillows in the sky?
Or are they blankets for planes that fly by?
I like to sit and spend the day
Watching the clouds drift away.

Genevieve A. Davis

Clouds are part of our daily experiences. At one time or another, we have been awestruck and mesmerized as we gazed up at the clouds. Children and adults can watch them move and see them create wonderful art forms right before our eyes. They affect us in many ways. They can be a determining factor in planning our outdoor events. "Why is it always cloudy on weekends?" "Will clouds cover the eclipse of the moon or a coming meteor shower?" Baseball players often like to play when it's cloudy because clouds keep the sun out of their eyes.

Clouds contribute to our demeanor. Some clouds cause us to dream, to slow down the pace of life. At times clouds, which provide the steady rain that we can hear on the roof, cause us to be somber or pensive. Other times, in strong winds, storm clouds seem to be musical or perhaps frightening. Leah Polacco's book *Thunder Cake* is a story about how Patricia Polacco conquered her childhood fear of Michigan thunderstorms with the help of her caring grandmother. This book can be a great story starter for young children who may have experienced similar emotions during a loud thunderstorm.

Often we can see wind patterns by looking at clouds. This photograph shows a strong wind current traveling over a cumulus cloud.

J. David Keller

Other emotions are also tapped when weather-watching. It is a wonderful experience to see the sun peak in and out of clouds, especially if we are trying to keep warm with the sun's rays. Watching the moon dance in and out of the clouds can give special significance to tall stories around an autumn campfire or other outdoor experiences.

Clouds are great communicators. They tell us many things. Clouds give us an indication about what the weather is going to be like. When we see fluffy cumulus clouds that look like small pillows in the sky, we expect a beautiful day. Seeing the high cirrus "mares' tails" often indicates that it might rain a day or two in the future. Many sayings have been developed over the centuries relating weather predictions to the clouds, such as "Red sky at night, sailor's delight. Red sky in the morn, sailor be warned!"

Clouds are the basis for the Concept Explorations in this chapter for many reasons. First, they are a major factor in our daily lives. Clouds are everywhere in the whole wide world and provide endless fascination to all who observe them. We interact with clouds in one way or another each day. This factor gives reality to your children's learning. Having a basic knowledge about the nature of clouds also is critical for comprehending many other natural scientific processes. The interconnectedness we have with nature provides wondrous phenomena to ponder and explore.

Clouds are the basis for the nature of our environment. Without clouds we would have no precipitation. Without precipitation there could be no lakes, no rivers, no streams no erosion and no weathering of rocks. Without precipitation, vegetation as we know it would not exist. Animals would have no food. In this sense, looking at the nature of clouds gives us a basis for looking at all of nature.

Clouds give us opportunities to observe change. Developing skills in observing changes is an important part of science and mathematics. Documenting changes helps to develop the concept of order and sequence. Documenting changes is also valuable for developing skills in organizing, analyzing, and displaying data through basic charts and graphs. Obviously, these skills are also paramount in developing other basic mathematics skills such as determining length, volume, mass, temperature, and speed.

As you look at the development and understandings of your students, you can select and plan activities from the explorations presented in this chapter that present opportunities for your children to apply specific skill areas.

SCIENCE CONCEPTS FOR TEACHERS

The science conceptual framework included here is designed to give background information about clouds, their formation, and their effect on climate and the environment. Its purpose is to give you background knowledge to assist you in your teaching. It is not intended as instructional material for the children, but instead to give you a framework to ensure that what you teach is indeed accurate and factual in nature. Having a basic knowledge of how clouds form and change is valuable for you as a teacher. This knowledge will help you recognize opportunities to share with your students about the roles clouds play in many natural processes. Throughout your life, your knowledge will continue to grow. In addition, as scientists uncover new ideas and knowledge, you will be able to better understand these processes and patterns of nature. These developments assist us in communicating ideas to our students.

The concepts and information provided here should only be presented to the children at an introductory level. For example, when a thunderstorm occurs, you might ease the distress of some of the students by pointing out characteristics of the storm clouds. As you and your class observe the development of the storm, you might encourage your children to predict what will happen. However, it would not be appropriate to expect your children to understand the specifics of lightning and thunder.

What Causes Clouds?

Clouds form when there is more water vapor in the air than the air can hold. When this occurs, water molecules will form around hygroscopic particles, forming water droplets or, if it is very cold, ice crystals. Hygroscopic particles are extremely small particles of matter that are suspended in air. Many hygroscopic particles are minute particles of salt that are formed by the evaporation of water sprayed by ocean waves.

The greater the amount of water in the air, the larger the water droplets become. At some stage, the water droplets can no longer be suspended by the air and precipitation occurs.

The larger the cloud, the greater the amount of moisture in the air. It is difficult to imagine how much water is in a cloud until that cloud emits a heavy rain. For example, during a 24-hour period, 43 inches of rain fell over a portion of Texas. If you have ever seen a flash flood caused by the action of a downburst, you can start to visualize the amount of water that is in a cloud.

Clouds often indicate an upward movement of air. As air rises, it becomes less dense and the air

Clouds often indicate the upward movement of air. The cloud in this photo was formed by a cold front forcing the lighter, warm, moist air to rise. As the warm, moist air rises, it cools and the cloud forms and grows.

temperature lowers from 2 to 5 degrees Fahrenheit (1 to 3 degrees Celsius) for each 1,000 feet of height. This lowering of the air temperature increases the humidity. At 100% humidity, the air cannot hold any additional water vapor. At that point, water droplets (or if the air temperature is below 32 degrees F, or 0 degrees C, ice crystals) are produced, forming clouds. Fog is simply a cloud that is at the surface of the earth.

Types of Clouds

Each cloud has unique properties that meteorologists use to classify clouds. They have identified three basic types of clouds: cumulus, stratus, and cirrus.

Cumulus clouds are low-altitude, billowy clouds that are usually dark on the bottom while the top resembles a giant white cotton ball. Small cumulus clouds can indicate "fair skies." A cumulus cloud may be relatively tall, extending from a base at around 2,000 feet to a top near 10,000 feet above the ground. Large cumulus clouds cast dark shadows and may be a source of moisture, but generally produce no more than a summer shower.

Stratus clouds are wispy foglike clouds that hover a few hundred feet above the ground, sometimes obscuring hills or tall buildings. They may begin as ground fog and can be a source of drizzle. They tend to cover most, if not all, of the sky.

Cirrus clouds are generally the highest clouds, forming "mares' tails" at altitudes between 20,000 and 40,000 feet. The clouds may appear as delicate white filaments, feather-like tufts, or fibrous bands of ice crystals. Cirrus clouds are not a source of precipitation.

Because clouds actually are much more diverse than just the three basic types discussed above, meteorologists also classify clouds by identifying characteristics that include properties of two of the basic forms of clouds. For example, cirrocumulus clouds have properties of both cirrus and cumulus clouds. They have the loosely packed sheets of small white cloud segments often associated with cumulus clouds, but these segments can dominate and cover the sky, as is typically seen with stratus clouds. Cirrostratus clouds show the characteristics of both cirrus and stratus clouds.

Clouds that are delivering rain are often given the suffix *-nimbus*. For instance, a cumulonimbus cloud is a large cumulus cloud associated with thunderstorm clouds. These clouds can vary considerably in altitude from ominously dark lower portions below 5,000 feet to white anvil-shaped tops that may reach upward to 50,000 feet. They contain large amounts of moisture, some of which may be in the form of hail. The cumulonimbus cloud may appear alone or as part of a wall of advancing storm clouds.

MATHEMATICS: ADDRESSING THE NCTM STANDARDS THROUGH CONCEPT EXPLORATIONS

Many of the activities in these Concept Explorations in which children observe clouds, involve patterns, sequencing, geometry, measurement, data collection, organization, and analysis. As you engage in these creative inquiries and explorations with your students, be aware of the wonderful opportunities that present themselves to infuse creative and thoughtful observation, thinking, and communication about clouds and the feelings they inspire.

Algebra and Patterns

Children use mathematical ideas to observe, classify, and sort clouds. Children also observe patterns of growth as they watch how clouds change across a time span. They are continually demonstrating that they can ". . . recognize and apply mathematics in contexts outside of mathematics" (NCTM, 2000, p. 132).

As children spend time cloud gazing, they will continue to see different shapes and configurations of clouds. These observations will help children experience the dynamic and aesthetic characteristics in nature. Opportunities for describing the similarities and differences among the clouds should be given. Looking for these similarities and differences among the clouds is also important for sound development in building and understanding classification schemes. Children can use their own language to describe what they see and feel. Using language that describes magnitude as well as shape helps children organize their observations and thinking. Using words such as *tall, short, wide, long, thin, big*, and *bigger* can help a child communicate observations with more detail.

Children can also create artistic representations of cloud shapes with a variety of art media. Children can be asked what materials they think would be best to use to make their own clouds.

Geometry

Cloud exploration with young children will provide many rich opportunities to explore geometric concepts. As children explore ideas such as shape, position in space, symmetry, and congruence, they begin to appreciate the aesthetic nature of geometry. Children can use geometric language to describe the interesting shapes that they see, and they can create artistic representations of cloud shapes. The use of multiple forms of representation, ranging from art supplies to gestures to language, broadens children's opportunities to share their ideas and theories.

Clouds can be described as they move and change, highlighting a sequence of events. Using the language of space and shape also helps children to expand their level of descriptions as they cloud gaze. For example, using words such as *curve, straight, oval*, and *round* makes children aware of the many ways they can describe things in nature. You can go on a "Cloud Shape Hunt" with your students. Bring large cutout geometric shapes outside with you, such as an oval, circle, rectangle, triangle, rhombus, and pentagon. Gaze at the clouds to see if you can find any that resemble these shapes. Children will be counting "edges" of the clouds to find a particular shape. Sometimes children will see a cloud change from one shape to another in a matter of seconds or minutes. Such observations and awareness can be engaging and fun.

As children observe the clouds and how they move, they should be encouraged to apply concepts of relative position in space using specific language and vocabulary such as *over, under, on, in, above, below, up, down, together, near, far, top, bottom, next to, in front of, behind*, and *in between*. As they attach descriptive language to their observations, they will be expanding their power to communicate in creative ways. These concepts should be extended through conversations and story construction. Using the language of sequence, navigation and movement in natural ways strengthen a child's ability to make sense of our fascinating and dynamic world.

Measurement

Measurement will be an important tool for documenting the evidence of clouds. Children can explore creative ways of measuring the cloud's movement and engage in interesting activities and experiments to determine how high the cloud is and how quickly or slowly the cloud moving. Children can pose interesting questions about measuring size, height, and movement of the clouds. Support for this exploration can be provided with stopwatches and standard and nonstandard measuring tools. Children should be given many opportunities to use the tools and to examine carefully the attributes they are measuring. Inherent in this comparison are opportunities for language development and record keeping. Modeling and validating appropriate language—utilizing words that relate to comparison and seriation—should be encouraged. Having children become fully engaged in their explorations helps them to generate theories about clouds.

Data Analysis

Much of the exploration involved in observing clouds can be documented through creative graphing. As children make observations, they can begin to classify the types of clouds they see. They can attach their own language to the classification scheme. For example, the terms *fluffy clouds* and *long, stringy clouds* can be used in addition to the scientific classification. Coupling their own scheme with the scientific one helps them to make concrete connections to a more scientific level of description and classification.

As the children continue to observe clouds, they may decide how they are going to keep track of the types of clouds that they see and how they are going to represent the clouds. Exploring multiple representations of the clouds through pictures, cotton replicas, finger painting, sponge paintings, language, or photographs will be important.

Organizing these data will be a creative collaboration as the children determine how to represent the clouds. It is important for children to design ways of collecting, representing, and displaying their data. Teachers can provide a variety of media for the children to explore in the construction of the tables and graphs.

OBSERVING WITH ALL THE SENSES

Clouds are excellent tools for exploring with different senses. Involve your children in as many of the following experiences as possible.

Sight

Clouds are particularly interesting for us to observe. That we can see clouds that are miles above us is interesting to think about. At times, clouds that we see low in the sky, can be as much as 100 miles from us.

Sight is also a great tool for detecting change. As clouds move and also change shapes, we can see the variations. These variations give us much information about the movement of air. Clouds are great tools for developing inquiry in children.

Sound

Thunder is a sound that gets our attention. Thunder is caused by the buildup of static electricity in a cloud. When the electrical charge becomes too great, it is discharged between the cloud and the ground or another cloud. This electrical flow through the air heats the air so rapidly that the expanding air causes thunder, similar to an explosion by the expanding air of a firecracker.

Sound travels approximately 1 mile in 5 seconds. You can estimate the distance a lightning strike is from your location by counting the seconds: one thousand one, one thousand two, one thousand three, and so forth. Count the time from when you see the lightning to when you hear the thunder. Divide the seconds by 5 and you will know the distance in miles.

SAFETY

As children gaze at the clouds it is important to remind them not to look directly at the sun. They should be aware that the sun can peak out from behind the clouds at any time and they need to be sure that their eyes stay healthy.

CONCEPT EXPLORATIONS ON CLOUDS FOR YOUR CLASSROOM

These concept explorations direct children's interests toward the clouds. Through these experiences, several basic science processes and math concepts can be defined and developed. These explorations are designed to assist you in identifying, designing, and teaching authentic concrete activities with your children. Particular suggestions and opportunities are given to direct you in these explorations. Use these suggestions to initiate your study of clouds along with your students. Take advantage of the children's curiosities, interests, and questions about clouds to direct your inquiries. We encourage you to expand and redirect the concepts presented below.

As in all learning processes, your aspiration as teacher is to encourage your children to ask their own questions and to have them take part in choosing the direction and nature of the exploration. Their participation in these processes helps them feel they have ownership in their learning, and contributes to their development of basic learning skills and positive attitudes about learning. These processes also become valuable to you as a teacher in assessing the children's prior knowledge.

As the explorations of clouds are completed, a summation of the knowledge, attitudes, and learning processes gained by examining the questions identified can serve as a valuable tool for assessing the development that has taken place. Such evaluations are the real basis for authentic assessment because they have developed from authentic learning experiences.

The following explorations give a wide variety of activities that are appropriate for young children. Obviously, it is not possible to complete all these activities with your students. Each exploration gives an alternative process that you can select. Which ones you choose for your class can be determined by the interests and developmental level of your children.

The nature of your weather on particular days might redirect your activities each day. Whichever explorations you select, engage your children in a way that encourages them to express their creativity, thoughts, theories, and questions about clouds.

1. Head in the Clouds

Discuss how each cloud is unique. Its characteristics are determined by the temperature of the air, the nature of the wind, and the moisture in the air. Clouds are ever changing. As we watch a cloud for even a few minutes, dramatic changes take place. These changes can evoke thoughts and feelings. Describing these observations causes our children to purvey how the clouds affect their feelings. This becomes an excellent exercise in developing expressive language and vocabulary. It may be interesting to begin this study of clouds by reading some of the books listed at the end of this chapter. For example, you may want to look through Maryellen Gregoire's book *Clouds* as an introduction to the different types of clouds. The photographs give children an accurate look at the various ways cloud formations present themselves across the skies.

For this exploration, each day the children should, at approximately the same time, go outside and gaze at the clouds. Have the children observe what the weather is like at that time and describe the clouds. Encourage them to think of three different adjectives or phrases as descriptors of the clouds for each day of observation and record them (Figure 9.1). In addition, each day, invite the children to describe how they feel while they are gazing at the clouds. Ask them what the clouds are "saying" to them (Figure 9.2). Encourage the children to develop creative ways to organize and display the "data" they have collected.

The most important questions that are asked in your classroom are the questions that children ask. Children's questions are critical in your classroom for two reasons. First, children's questions transfer ownership of learning to the children who are asking the questions. When children are asked "What questions do you have about clouds?" they are examining ideas that they are curious about and deem important. Having opportunities to contribute to defining what will be studied in their classroom is a great motivator. Second, children ask questions because they are curious. Children who have opportunities to ask and study their own questions tend to have a much more positive attitude toward science and mathematics and toward learning in general. This type of involvement and personal investment in learning promotes what Rosengrant and Bredekamp (1992) call *focused participation*.

Clouds Affect My Feelings

Monday: high, feathery, thin

Tuesday: fluffy, light, floating

Wednesday: low, dark, wet

Thursday: small, lonely, still

Friday: cottony, racing, pleasant

FIGURE 9.1 Encourage students to describe clouds in various ways.

"Coo-koo"
"Be good."
"SHHHHHHH."
"Be quiet and go to sleep."
"They say to talk."
"I love you, Maria."
"They say how does it feel for everyone to be good."
"Boom, boom, ka-boom."
"I think the clouds will like me."
"They say, they love leaves."
"Come visit in the sky, and they talk about what they do."
"They like trees."
"They are talking about the green, green ground."
"They are sad because it is gray."

FIGURE 9.2 What preschoolers think clouds are "saying."

This phrase is used to describe engagement in learning. They explain that focused participation is an important predictor of children's achievement and highly correlates with children experiencing success in learning and developing a sense of competence.

Second, children's questions give you, the teacher, much insight into the level of background and knowledge that the students have. Figures 9.3, 9.4, and 9.5 list some questions and comments that preschoolers have made about clouds. Gathering this type of information provides the teacher with valuable input about student knowledge. This knowledge can be related to the specific concept, such as clouds, or it can reveal misunderstanding about general concepts in science and mathematics. For instance, a question such as "Do cumulus clouds produce the most rain?" reveals that the child has a developed vocabulary and knowledge related to clouds. Children's comments also can indicate a basic knowledge of facts and concepts. For example, a child might say, "Snow comes from cold clouds."

A question such as "Can a cloud be more than fifty feet above our school?" reveals that the child has a limited understanding of distances. This developmental information is critical to the teacher in determining the nature and the complexity of the unit. It is the teacher's responsibility to support learning by providing resources and materials that promote appropriate exploration, investigation, and learning.

2. Capture the Clouds

Inviting your children to develop expressive language and vocabulary and to identify their feelings, as demonstrated in Concept Exploration 1, can lead to an experience in which the children capture the image of a cloud and describe what they believe the cloud

"Why are clouds up in the sky?"

"Why are they always in the sky?"

"Why are clouds always white?"

"What are clouds made of?"

"Do scientists make clouds?"

"How many clouds are there?"

"Where do clouds come from?"

"Are clouds made of air?"

"Are clouds made of rain?"

"Can we touch clouds?"

"Can I walk on clouds?"

"Can you touch clouds?"

"How do clouds get in the sky?"

"Can there be clouds below the trees?"

"Can clouds be up above the sky?"

"What are clouds, anyway?"

"Where do clouds come from?"

"Why are clouds so big?"

"Can airplanes touch clouds?"

"Do clouds have friends?"

"Why do clouds always change?"

"How high are the clouds? One hundred feet tall?"

"Why do clouds move?"

FIGURE 9.3   Questions preschoolers have about clouds can provide teachers with valuable input about student learning.

"Snow comes from clouds! You dont flo at on them!"

"I think about clouds when they turn into animals."

"I like clouds when they get snow."

"It's far away."

"Clouds change into animals."

"A cloud is made from smoke and the sun."

"Storms, thunder."

"Clouds are made of the sky."

"Clouds rain on my head."

"When a cloud gets too full it drips."

"Rain turns into snow."

"Rain melts the snow."

"I see clouds shaped like fish or turtles. There are snow clouds and wind clouds."

"The rain comes from the clouds, and it helps the flowers."

FIGURE 9.4   Preschoolers' comments about clouds and what they know about clouds.

"Snow, rain, storm, tornado, and lightning."

"White stuff."

"I don't know."

"Cotton, snow, stuffing, stuff that's in pillows, and feathers."

FIGURE 9.5 Preschoolers' thoughts about what clouds are made of.

is feeling and thinking. This may be done through a story, poem, song, or perhaps a cartoon. Young children relate to activities that deal with personification. **Personification** is a figure of speech in which inanimate objects or abstractions are endowed with human qualities or possess human form. Children's imagination helps them develop images of objects like clouds having feelings and purpose. Children often believe that inanimate objects wonder, feel, and think just as they themselves wonder, feel, and think.

3. Catch Your Breath

Clouds are formed by condensing water vapor. Because water vapor is colorless, tasteless, and odorless, children have a difficult time believing that there is really water in the air. Activities that can collect water vapor from the air help children understand this concept so they can relate to how clouds are formed.

When warm moist air is cooled, the air can no longer hold all the water vapor. The water vapor condenses. We can see this in many forms. A curious one for children is when they can see their breath. When their breath contacts cold air, the moisture instantly condenses, forming a miniature cloud. The "visible" breath disappears very quickly as their breath is mixed with the surrounding air and evaporates.

On a cold day or evening, document evidence of your breath. The experience can become more dramatic by shining a light on the children's breath. Children can explore ways to make their breath do different things. For example, have the children experiment with changing the shape of their lips and mouth, simply moving around, or changing breathing patterns.

Another example of water condensation is the common experience of seeing water condense on the side of a cold drink. The sides of cold, dry glasses and beverage cans quickly become wet when in the presence of warm, moist air. When the warm, moist air contacts the side of the glass, it is cooled. The cooler air can no longer hold all of its water vapor and the water condenses on the side of the glass.

4. How High Is a Cloud?

Clouds vary in height. Clouds have been detected above the North and South Poles at a height of 50 miles (80 kilometers). More common clouds such as those we often refer to as thunderhead clouds can reach upward of 10 miles (16 kilometers). Cirrus clouds, commonly called "mares' tails," typically reach to a height of about 8 miles (13 kilometers).

Children can develop broad estimates of the heights of clouds by several techniques. For instance, does a plane fly above or below a cloud? Actually, the purpose of this activity is to demonstrate that clouds exist at many different heights. Some clouds are extremely high. Others, such as when we have fog, reach the ground. The movement of a cloud can be a valuable tool for estimating height. The apparent rate at which a billowing cloud moves across the sky can be a good indication of the height. The higher the cloud, the slower it will appear to move. Likewise, when traveling in a car or perhaps on a school bus, how quickly you pass a cloud in the sky can be a good indication of its height.

5. What to Do with the Weather

Many of the activities that we plan are based on clouds and weather conditions. Children can be quickly disappointed by a rain cloud spoiling a ball game or other outdoor event. Such experiences, however, can become a catalyst for a long-term learning experience. Rethinking plans and turning a cloudy outdoor day into a sunny indoor day is a good problem-solving activity.

Invite your students to make a chart, like that shown in Figure 9.6, of activities they can do under different weather conditions. As you watch the weather predictions, let the children plan when they will try the different activities. A nice companion book for teachers to read in preparation for this exploration is Dean Galiano's *Clouds, Rain, and Snow.* It gives ample information about the science of weather.

6. Cloudy Sky Stories

Invite your children to take photographs of many clouds using a digital camera. Once they have collected several photos, suggest that they write a story based on the cloud

Cloudy Sky Activities	
Snow clouds	Ride a sled
	Build a snowman
	Make snow angels
	Make a fort
	Catch a snowflake on your tongue
Rain clouds	Test umbrellas
	Watch water form miniature streams in the playground
	Observe how birds and small animals react to the rain
Partly cloudy skies	Race a cloud's shadow across the playground
	Fly a kite to a cloud
	Write stories about the sun and the clouds

FIGURE 9.6 Help your students make charts of activities appropriate for certain weather conditions.

FIGURE 9.7 Your students can create stories that relate to their experiences with clouds.

images they have collected. They might want to cut out the cloud from the photograph and paste it on the paper. Or they can re-create the photograph with other media such as cotton or paint. They can write their text to go along with their photographs or other graphic images (Figure 9.7). For primary-grade students, provide some basic resources on clouds that identify types of clouds. Encourage students to incorporate basic information in their stories.

7. I've Looked at Clouds from Both Sides Now

Clouds are ever changing. Cumulus clouds—the fluffy, pillow-shaped clouds—are excellent for observing changes. Their formation and dissipation are caused by air currents and temperature. By watching a cloud for a short period of time, you can observe these changes in a cloud's structure. Even in a period of 10 to 20 minutes, you can see dramatic changes in the shape of a cloud.

These changes indicate movement of air currents in which air is moving upward and downward as well as west to east, north to south. As you watch the clouds in transition, these air currents are observable. Ask "From which direction are the clouds coming?" "How do you know?" "Which way are they traveling?" "How do you know?" Clouds will tend to grow on one side, and diminish on the other.

Having children observe these changes is valuable for helping them understand that clouds are dynamic systems. Observing these changes gives the children a more concrete visualization of the process of cloud formation and the related precipitation. Concentrate your observations on the edges of the cloud to highlight the changes that take place. For example, during a very short period you can see a small peak of a cloud disappear.

If you live in a location where there is a mountain ridge, you can often see a band of clouds over the ridge. As the air moves up over the ridge, clouds form. As the air travels down the other side of the ridge, the clouds dissipate. The result is that the clouds, although seeming to be stagnant, are in reality growing on one side and diminishing on the other.

8. Which Way Are You Going?

Clouds travel at whims of the wind. By observing the direction that clouds move for many days, you can develop general patterns of wind for your locality. Keep track of such patterns on graphs or tables. In addition, the direction of the wind can influence

Day	Cloud Description	Wind Direction	Weather
Monday	pillow	west	cool, nice
Tuesday	low, solid overcast	east	sprinkles, humid
Wednesday	clear	west	sunny, warm
Thursday	thunderstorm cloud	southwest (strong)	rain
Friday	mares' tails	west	warm, nice
(These descriptions could be drawings rather than words.)			

FIGURE 9.8 One example of how to record one week of cloud observations.

the nature of the weather. For example, in many areas, westerly winds bring mild weather. Winds from the northeast can bring storms; hence, the term *nor'easter*. In the eastern United States, hurricanes tend to come from the southeast. Encouraging children to watch the movement of clouds can become a valuable long-term experience. Forming the habit of observing weather patterns causes people to be much more in tune with nature in general.

Invite children to watch the clouds, feel the atmosphere, and record in a creative way the movement of clouds each day for a period of time. If possible, do this at the same time each day. You could also make it part of the morning routine and assign it to one child for a week. For each recording, describe the cloud, the direction of the wind, and indicate the type of weather that you have (Figure 9.8). It may take a little practice to develop this type of observation and awareness of the atmosphere. But you are developing independent observers of the clouds and wonderers about nature.

9. As the Saying Goes

Weather has been a major contributor to folklore since man first started to communicate. Weather folklore has been a tool for sharing observations of nature and inferring the type of weather that is associated with these observations. Some of these sayings have no real scientific significance such as the sayings "If a groundhog sees its shadow on February 2, you will have six more weeks of winter" and "Lightning never strikes twice in the same place."

Other sayings have developed after many years of observation, such as "When bees stay close to the hive, rain is close by" and "Rain is on the way if people with curly hair find their hair curlier and people with straight hair find their hair straighter." Some other examples are shown in Figure 9.9.

Many of these sayings have to do with clouds. Inviting your children to collect sayings about clouds and weather in general can be an effective way for them to look at cause-and-effect relationships. For example, when the air temperature cools because of a cold front coming through the area, you tend to have clouds and perhaps rain. It also helps children develop mathematical relationships by comparing two characteristics such as air temperature and amount of rain.

Ring around the sun, time for fun. Ring around the moon, storm is coming soon. When the fog goes up the mountain hoppin', then the rain comes down the mountain dropping.	Evening red and morning gray set the traveler on his way. Evening gray and morning red bring down rain upon his head. If the clouds be bright, t'will clear tonight. If the clouds be dark, t'will rain, will you hark.	

FIGURE 9.9 Old folklore weather sayings.

These activities are also valuable for developing language skills. Because these sayings have been around for many years, they often reveal colloquial phrases and terms. Sayings from different geographical regions can be interesting to study. Perhaps linking to a class in another part of the world can provide interesting sharing of weather-related sayings.

A valuable resource for weather sayings is senior citizens. Your students could interview their grandparents to collect different sayings. Or they could visit a senior citizens' center to interview the people about their favorite sayings and whether the people believed these sayings or could give instances in their life when the sayings held true. Studying these sayings can become a wonderful intergenerational activity.

The sayings the children collect could be developed into a bulletin board, a book, or a Web page on the Internet. As the Internet becomes more common and economical, classrooms need to take advantage of its value for communication. By developing Internet sites for your classroom, your children's work can be viewed by family and friends around the world. They can share and compare weather on certain dates with other classrooms in different countries and climates. In addition, it gives the children a feeling of more significance and reality to their projects. A wonderful book to read together is Marilyn Singer's book, *On the Same Day in March*—a tour of the world's weather. You can also link studies about weather to recent events, such as the tsunami that hit Southeast Asia in late 2004 and the hurricanes in 2004 and 2005 that devastated the southern U.S. states. Children hear about these events in the media and in family discussions and are curious about them.

Activities in Other Explorations That Relate to Clouds

Leaves (Chapter 11)
7. A Tribute to Transpiration

Wind (Chapter 18)
1. See the Wind
8. Water Evaporation

Resources for Teachers

Books

Caduto, M. J., & Bruchac, J. (1989). *Keepers of the Earth: Native American stories and environmental activities for children.* Golden, CO: Fulcrum.

Couchman, J. K., MacBean, J. C., Stecher, A., & Wentworth, D. F. (1977). *Mini-climates.* Canada: Holt, Rinehart and Winston.

DePaola, T. (1975). *The cloud book.* New York: Holiday House.

Galiano, D. (2000). *Clouds, rain and snow.* New York: Rosen Central Publishing.

Rosegrant, T., & Bredekamp, S. (1992). Planning and implementing transformational curriculum. In S. Bredekamp, & T. Rosegrant (Eds.), *Reaching potentials: Appropriate curriculum and assessment for young children* (Vol. I). Washington, DC: National Asscociation for the Education of Young Children.

Web Sites

http://dcrafts.com/weathersayings.htm
Weather sayings.

www.ea.pvt.k12.pa.us/html/Units/IsDevon/DFormSS/weathersayings.html
More weather sayings.

http://www.noaa.gov/
Home page for the National Oceanic and Atmospheric Administration.

http://www.nssl.noaa.gov/
Home page for the National Severe Storms Laboratory links.

http://www.nssl.noaa.gov/edu/storm
Questions and answers about thunderstorms.

http://www.nssl.noaa.gov/resources/
Weather and climate resources.

http://vortex.plymouth.edu/clouds.html
A description of the different classification of clouds.

Children's Books on Clouds

Alexander, M. (1992). *Where does the sky end, Grandpa?* Orlando, FL: Harcourt, Brace Jovanovich.

Barrett, J. (1978). *Cloudy with a chance of meatballs.* New York: Simon & Schuster.

Branley, F. (1983). *Rain and hail.* New York: Thomas Y. Crowell.

Branley, F. (1985). *Flash, crash, rumble, and roll.* New York: HarperCollins.

Branley, F. (1988). *Tornado alert.* New York: Thomas Y. Crowell.

Brenner, B. (1984). *The snow parade.* New York: Crown Publishers.

Burningham, J. (1996). *Cloud land.* New York: Crown Publishers.

Bush, P. (1989). *Wind and weather.* Alexandria, VA: Time-Life Books.

Carle, E. (1996). *Little cloud.* New York: Philomel Books.

Carroll, C. (1996). *How artists see the weather.* New York: Abbeville Kids, a division of Abbeville Publishing Group.

Cole, J. (1996). *The magic school bus: Wet all over.* New York: Scholastic.

Cole, J. (2000). *The magic school bus kicks up a story.* New York: Scholastic.

Crews, D. (1999). *Cloudy day, sunny day.* San Diego, CA: Harcourt.

de Paola, T. (1975). *The cloud book*. New York: Library of Congress.

Dickinson, T. (1998). *Exploring the Night Sky:* Buffalo, NY: Firefly Books.

Ford, M. (1997). *What color was the sky today?* New York: Greenwillow Books.

Fowler, A. (1992). *It could still be water*. Canada: Children's Press.

Fowler, A. (1995). *When a storm comes up*. Chicago: Children's Press.

Fowler, A. (1996). *What do you see in a cloud?* New York: Children's Press.

Greene, C. (1983). *Hi, clouds*. Chicago: Regensteiner Publishing Enterprises.

Gregoire, M. (2005). *Clouds*. Mankato, MN: Capstone Press.

Harper, S. (1997). *Clouds form mare's tails to thunderheads*. New York: Franklin Watts.

Hopkins, B. (1994). *Weather*. New York: HarperCollins.

Johnson, A. (1990). *Do you like Kyla?* New York: Orchard Books.

Kahl, J. (1996). *Weather watch: Forecasting the weather*. Minneapolis: Verner Publications, Co.

Locker, T. (2000). *Cloud dance*. San Diego, CA: Harcourt.

Macmillan, B. (1991). *The weather sky*. New York: HarperCollins.

Markert, J. (1992). *Clouds*. Mankato, MN: Creative Education & Britannica.

Parent, N. (1994). *Disney: the hunchback of Notre Dame: I see the clouds*. Singapore: Disney Enterprises.

Peters, W. L. (1995). *Water's way*. New York: Arcade Publishing.

Polacco, L. (1997). *Thunder cake*. New York: Philomen Books.

Renberg, H. D. (1985). *Hello, clouds!* Canada: Harper & Row.

Sanfield, S., & Winter, J. (1995). *Snow*. New York: Philomel.

Saunders-Smith, G. (1998). *Clouds*. Mankato, MN: Capstone Press.

Shaw, C. (1947). *It looked like spilt milk*. New York: Scholastic.

Silver, N. (1995). *Cloud nine*. New York: Clarion Books.

Singer, M. (2000). *On the same day in March—A tour of the world's weather*. New York: Harper Collins.

Spier, P. (1986). *Dreams*. Garden City, New York: Doubleday & Company.

Correlation of NSES Standards and NCTM Principles and Standards to Insect Concept Exploration Activities

	1. Let's Build an Insect Zoo	2. Create an Insect and Design Its Habitat	3. Bedtime Bonanza	4. Plant Hotels	5. My Life Story by Billy Beetle	6. Insect Galls	7. Butterfly Detectives	8. Interviewing Insects	9. Ant Investigations	10. Insect Picnic	11. Air Explorations	12. Insect Songs	13. Underground Activities	14. Chromo Pubescents
SCIENCE														
Inquiry	X	X	X	X	X	X	X	X	X	X	X	X	X	X
Physical Science	X										X	X		X
Life Science	X	X	X	X	X	X	X	X	X	X	X	X	X	X
Earth and Space Science	X	X	X	X									X	X
Science and Technology	X	X										X		
Personal and Social Perspectives	X	X	X	X	X	X	X	X	X	X	X	X	X	X
History and Nature of Science					X				X				X	
MATHEMATICS														
Number and Operations	X		X	X	X	X	X		X	X		X	X	X
Algebra	X		X	X	X	X			X	X			X	X
Geometry	X	X					X		X		X			
Measurement	X	X					X		X		X			
Data Analysis and Probability			X	X		X	X		X	X		X	X	X
Reasoning and Proof														
Problem Solving		X	X							X		X		
Communication			X		X			X						
Connections		X												
Representation							X				X			X

CHAPTER 10

Insects

Butterfly Wonderland

Butterfly, Butterfly, come sit by me
Display your colors for me to see.
Flutter as the wind blows you near
The gust lifts you high, you show no fear.

Flowers you visit along the way
Present such a colorful bouquet.
Not a whisper is heard when on petals you land
The nectar you collect must taste really grand.

Butterfly, Butterfly, come sit by me
Display your colors for me to see.

J. David Keller
With assistance by Jackson and Parker Keller

Remember when Danny Kaye sang *Inchworm* in the movie *Hans Christian Andersen?* The inchworm is actually the caterpillar stage of the Looper moth. Inchworms like to feed on the green leaves of plants such as cabbage. Time seems to slow down when we watch an inchworm.

Many insects are interesting to observe. What joy, to pick up a grasshopper or cricket and observe it looking at us. How fascinating to observe a delicate butterfly as it travels through the garden or to collect fireflies in a jar for a temporary night-light. We watch as an army of ants travels along its selected route collecting its bounty.

Insects are a real part of our everyday world. We could not live as we do with-out their support. They pollinate our vegetables and fruit. They produce the silk for our clothes. On the other hand, they can cause extensive damage beyond belief. Ter-mites can eat the wood in our homes causing major structural damage. Locusts have eaten entire crops, causing famines killing millions. The boll weevil can destroy cotton fields worth millions of dollars.

SCIENCE CONCEPTS FOR TEACHERS

The science conceptual framework is included here to provide background information for instructors. It is not intended as instructional material for the children, but instead is intended to supply basic support information.

Insect Basics

Insects are the most common animals on our planet. In fact there are more types of insects than all other animals combined—well over 1 million different known species of insects have been identified. Some experts estimate that there might be as many as 10 million.

Insects have existed for more than 300 million years, During the Pennsylvanian period in the Paleozoic Era, insects were so common that some scientists have called that era the "Age of Insects." The rocks formed during this period were formed in a warm, humid environment with many swamps and forests, a perfect habitat for many forms of insects.

Insects have a wide range of sizes. Some stick insects have been found that are 36 centimeters (14 inches) long. Butterflies have been found with wing spans of 32 centimeters, or more than a foot across. Most insects are incredibly small. Many are less that 1 millimeter in length.

Insects are part of the phylum Arthropoda. Arthropods include crustaceans, arachnids (spiders, ticks, and others), millipedes, and centipedes. The arthropods are segmented animals with a chitinous exoskeleton. Chitin is a natural material similar to cellulose. When we see beetles and roaches, we can recognize their chitinous exoskeleton.

All insects have three body regions: the head, thorax, and abdomen. Insects have three pairs of legs, one on each segment of the thorax. Insects usually have two pairs of wings at the adult stage, however, some only have one pair. A few, such as springtails, lice, and flees, have no wings.

Insects are classified into different orders based mainly on wing structure, mouth parts, and type of metamorphosis (Table 10.1). Most entomologists recognize around 32 different orders of insects, some of which are not very common.

Metamorphosis

Metamorphosis is one of the more fascinating aspects of insects. Most insects go through distinct stages of life. These stages of development are so different that one might think that the animals during the different stages are not even related, even though they are actually the same animal. For example, the yellow mealworm is the larval stage of the darkling beetle. Caterpillars are the larval stage for butterflies and moths.

The metamorphis of moths and butterflies is one of the most interesting and well observed. The adult lays eggs that hatch into larvae. The larvae grow and go into a resting stage called pupae. From the pupae stage, they molt into adult butterflies. This metamorphis is termed *complete metamorphosis* (Figure 10.1A).

TABLE 10.1 Insect classifications

Common Name	Taxonomic Name	Example
Ants, bees, and wasps	Hymenoptera	Honeybee
Aphids, white flies, and cicadas	Homoptera	Cicada
Butterflies and moths	Lepidoptera	Monarch
Caddisflies	Trichoptera	Caddisflies
Dragons and damsels	Odonata	Dragonfly
Earwigs	Dermaptera	Earwigs
Fleas	Siphonaptera	Dog flea
True flies	Diptera	Housefly
Grasshoppers	Orthoptera	Common grasshopper
Lacewings, etc.	Neuroptera	Green lacewings
Mantids	Ephemeroptera	Praying mantis
Mayflies	Mantidae	Stream mayflies
Roaches	Blattodea	Cockroach
Scorpionflies	Mecoptera	Scorpionflies
Stick insects	Phasmida	Walking stick
Stoneflies	Plecoptera	Common stonefly
Termites	Isoptera	Powder-post termite
True bugs	Hemiptera	Milkweed bug

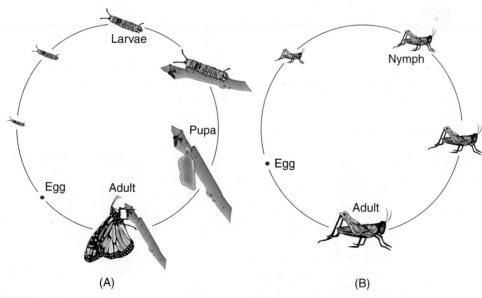

FIGURE 10.1 (A) Complete metamorphosis and (B) simple metamorphosis.

Simple metamorphosis (Figure 10.1B) has three stages: the egg, nymph (if aquatic, often called naiads), and adult. Bees, cicadas, dragonflies, and houseflies are common insects that undergo simple metamorphoses.

MATHEMATICS: ADDRESSING THE NCTM STANDARDS THROUGH CONCEPT EXPLORATIONS

Mathematics for young learners should be integrated and interwoven into their world. The NCTM standards are designed to help teachers see how the integrated nature of mathematics relates to the world of young children. Many of the mathematics standards can be used as children enter the fascinating and intriguing world of insects.

Numbers and Operations

In prekindergarten through grade 2, all students should count with understanding and recognize "how many" in sets of objects. Counting insects and their body parts helps children understand what cardinal numbers are used for. Cardinal numbers name the number of items in a set of wings, legs, body segments, or the number of insects. Teachers can use number words or numerals to represent the sets the children are counting and keeping track of. When looking at insects, children can also relate fractions to what they observe. For example, children can see segments and name them with fractional words.

Children can be engaged in addition, subtraction, multiplication, and division when they keep track of how many legs are on two insects, or three insects—or how many wings are on four butterflies. Similarly, they can try to figure out how many insects there would be if we observe a total of 12 legs—or six pairs of wings. Children can construct word problems for each other as they share their discoveries about insects. For example, they could pose interesting questions such as "How many wings are on three butterflies?" "How far can an ant travel in five seconds?" "How wide do the butterfly's wings spread?"

Algebra, Patterns, and Sorting

Young children are surrounded by fascinating patterns in nature. Insects provide an exciting context for children to explore patterns. Individual designs on insects are interesting. Butterfly and moth wings have beautiful patterns. Likewise, growth patterns of insects, as they change from stage to stage, are remarkable. Such seriation of growth is wonderful to chart with photographs or drawings.

Children should observe patterns of how insects live, eat, and grow; observe patterns on insects' bodies; and count and measure insects and their habitats. They are showing that they can "... *recognize and apply mathematics in contexts outside of mathematics*" (NCTM, 2000, p. 132).

Children can also be engaged in sorting insects and comparing insects. As we observe and inquire about insect habits, we can record how different insects move, eat, and behave. Venn diagrams, like that shown in Figure 10.2, can be made comparing two different insects.

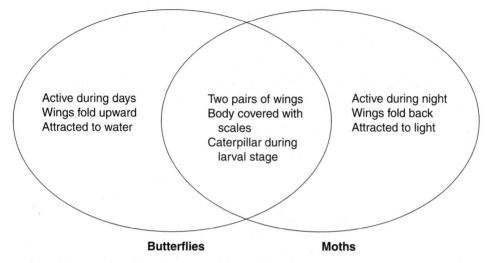

Active during days
Wings fold upward
Attracted to water

Two pairs of wings
Body covered with
scales
Caterpillar during
larval stage

Active during night
Wings fold back
Attracted to light

Butterflies

Moths

FIGURE 10.2   Venn diagrams are useful for making comparisons.

Geometry

Geometric ideas including symmetry and relative position can be explored as children are investigating and discovering wonderful facts about insects. As children observe a variety of insects, they can see the design of their bodies and investigate which insects have symmetry in their wings or bodies. Replicating these designs and patterns can produce enjoyable and expressive art.

As children observe insects in their natural habitats, they can use the language of navigation and space to describe the insects' movements and habits.

Measurement

As young children learn about insects and spend time exploring them, measurement can be a useful tool. Children can use the language of measurement to describe the insects they are observing. Some insects are very small and some are large. More precise measurements can be done depending on the age and experience of the children. Standard and nonstandard tools can be used. For example, rulers or small strips of paper can be used to mark lengths or widths of insects.

Children can compare and seriate insects by size. Charts of these comparisons and seriations are good ways to represent children's observations.

Data Analysis

As children explore insects and begin to classify and sort them by different schemes, they can engage in simple graphing. Graphs can take the form of a simple frequency graph of how many of each insect we have or can reflect discovered facts about insects, such as which insects fly and which ones do not fly. Gathering data and organizing it according to some agreed-on criteria are important as children develop and strengthen their abilities to reason and to think critically.

OBSERVING WITH ALL THE SENSES

Insects provide many opportunities to explore using our five senses.

Sight

The bright colors of many insects give children opportunities to observe and identify colors. Butterflies, damselflies, and beetles all have varieties that are bright and colorful.

Sound

Some types of insects make interesting "chirps," whereas others give off a buzzing sound made by the flapping of their wings. Cicadas, related to aphids and whiteflies, are considered one of the world's loudest animals and can be heard a half mile away. They make a loud, continuous riveting sound by vibrating ribbed plates on their abdomen. Their body resonates, amplifying the sound.

Sound can even be used to measure temperature, as explained in Figure 10.3.

Touch

We can feel some insects as they walk or rest on our hands. Butterflies and ladybug beetles are light and delicate. Grasshoppers seem to pinch. Children can compare the different sensations they feel by holding different insects. Care must be taken to be gentle with insects and to wash hands after these touchy explorations.

Smell and Taste

It is not common for one to eat insects; however, in some cultures insects are considered a delicacy. Students can smell and taste products of insects by eating the honey produced by honeybees.

FIGURE 10.3 Measuring temperature with cricket chirps.

You can estimate the temperature of the air by counting cricket chirps.

Count the number of chirps in 15 seconds and add 40. That is the air temperature.

For example, if you count 20 chirps in 15 seconds, the air temperature, would be 60 degrees Fahrenheit.

SAFETY

It is estimated that 1 to 2 million people are allergic to insect stings. Approximately 100 people die from insect stings each year. Offenders include bees, wasps, hornets, yellow jackets, and fire ants.

Honeybees do not tend to sting unless provoked. When a honeybee stings a person, the stinger is pulled from the abdomen, causing the bee to die. If stung by a honeybee, scrape off the stinger with a credit card or finger nail. Do not try to remove the stinger with your thumb and forefinger, because this tends to inject more of the venom into the skin.

More commonly, the stings we receive are from wasps, hornets, and yellow jackets. Wasps, hornets, yellow jackets, and other stinging insects can sting multiple times and live to another day. Usually insects sting when they are aggravated. If you are aware of an insect nest, keep your students back a safe distance. Be aware of any students that have allergies to insect stings.

CONCEPT EXPLORATIONS ON INSECTS FOR YOUR CLASSROOM

In Chapter 4, The Process of Problem Solving Development for Children and the importance of engaging children in all four stages of problem solving was discussed. Particular emphasis on assisting children to pursue their own questions is the key to developing a positive and interested attitude in learning, particularly as it relates to mathematics and science. The nature of insects is such that children, very early in their lives, develop strong attitudes about them. Being creepy and crawly can be considered a very good thing or a very bad thing. Giving children opportunities to explore their own interests and questions about insects can give them an understanding that develops curiosity and diminishes fear.

As children investigate and research, their theories will reflect what they have learned. Children are curious and full of wonder. We as teachers support the natural curiosities of children by supplying our classrooms with appropriate resources and materials for use in exploration, investigation, and information gathering. As we partner with children's families, they become strong supporters with their own materials, resources, and knowledge. Learning alongside each other enhances the experience.

The following Concept Explorations provide a wide variety of activities that are appropriate for young children. Although these activities focus on exploring the world of many types of insects, the processes of science that are incorporated are universal. Also note that the nature of these activities and the basic skills required do not prohibit even young children from participating in these explorations. As you proceed, help the students pose and explore their own questions. It is important to record children's initial questions and theories about insects to guide their investigations.

The specific species of insects that live in your geographic areas will vary. However, all areas do have insects that can be observed. Your local climate will direct you on selecting a time of year that is best for observing insects. For most temperate areas, the largest variety of insects can be found in summer and fall. Thus, the study of insects is an ideal unit to introduce to your children at the beginning of the school year or near the end.

Consider the nature of the common insects that your children see in their local environment. Select activities for your children from the following concept explorations. The development of these experiences for your children will assist them in learning more about their local environment and the common insects in your area.

1. Let's Build an Insect Zoo

Children love to explore the variety of life and the habits of animals, including what they eat and drink. Children love to compare types of animals and observe animals' reactions to each other and to themselves. Zoos provide opportunities for teachers to develop vocabulary and to develop comparisons of ideas such as large and small; striped, spotted, and one color; and herbivore and carnivore.

Children also love to develop their own projects. They love to design and construct their own materials and environments. They feel valued when their parents, other adults, and other children visit and learn from their accomplishments and productions. Developing an insect zoo in or near their classroom gives children an excellent opportunity for taking ownership of their learning. All environments have numerous varieties of insects that can be collected for study. Preparing a safe and accommodating home for each type of insect can give the children much knowledge about the nature and needs of insects. Having insects in a confined area also promotes much more detailed and extended observations of the insects.

The nature of your classroom insect zoo can be developed through a variety of processes. As a class you could select one species of insect, such as monarch butterflies, and raise them in your classroom. After the children have researched and developed this habitat, additional species could be added one by one. A second approach would be to have each child or perhaps two or three children develop a section for the zoo for their type of insect.

It is best to select insects common to your area. This way, children will be able to extend their learning and observations to their community. Some common insects that are good for classroom activities are listed in Figure 10.4. Care must be given to the safety of the children and of the insects.

FIGURE 10.4 Common insects for classroom activities.

Ants
Crickets
Ladybugs
Grasshoppers
Madagascar hissing cockroaches
Milkweed bugs
Monarch butterflies
Painted lady butterflies
Praying mantis
Wax worms
Wollybears
Yellow mealworm beetles

Particular types of insects are considered valuable for our environment. For instance, honeybees not only supply honey but also are very important for pollination of fruit trees and vegetables. Praying mantises eat other harmful insects. It is possible to purchase the egg cases of praying mantises to observe in your classroom and then release to the environment.

Construct homes for your insects. The design for your insect homes will vary depending on the nature of the insects. Children will need to find out what the insect must have to survive and thrive. Resources should be made available for this investigation and information gathering. A variety of cages can be made from common household materials (Figure 10.5).

Include in your home all of the necessities to keep your insect happy and alive: food, water, and environmental specifics. Figure 10.6 describes how to make an insect watering container.

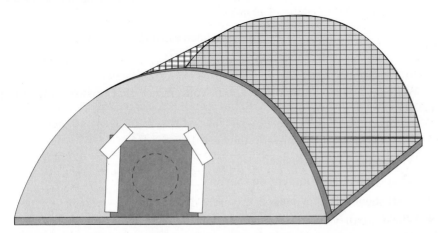

A simple cage can be constructed from scraps of wood and screening. Drill a hole in the side of the container to serve as an opening for the cage. Cover the hole with a piece of wood or heavy cardboard.

FIGURE 10.5   A sample cage.

A 35-mm film canister makes a great watering container for insects.

Cut an X in the lid of the container. Take a small strip from a cotton sock and thread it through the lid so that it protrudes from the top.

Fill the container with water. (For butterflies, a 5% sugar solution is an excellent mix.) Place the cap on the container so that the cotton strip is down in the water. The water will "wick" up the strip by capillary action. The insects can get a drink at any time and you don't have to worry that the container will fall over and spill the water.

FIGURE 10.6   Instructions for making an insect watering container.

> **Katydids**
>
> Katydids eat plant tissue. Katydids lay their eggs on plant tissue or under the ground in the fall. The eggs hatch in the spring. As the nymph grows, it will periodically shed its exoskeleton.
>
> Katydids live in trees. On summer nights, the male katydid will sing a loud sound that sounds like it is saying "katydid."
>
> They are found throughout the United States, predominantly in the East.
>
> Most katydids are green and are difficult to see because they are well camouflaged among the leaves of trees.
>
> Their antennae can be two or three times the length of their body.

Write a detailed description about your insect that answers the following questions:

- What do they eat and how do they get their food?
- What is their life cycle like?
- What type of environment do they live in?
- What sounds do they make?
- Where are they common geographically?
- What other points are of interest?

Figure 10.7 shows a report about katydids that details valuable information.

Collect a few of your insects. If possible, include both males and females. Put them in the home that you have constructed. Care for them each day, observe them, and develop a log of your observations. You and your students can write detailed reports about the insects.

2. Create an Insect and Design Its Habitat

A springboard to this exploration is to read a book together about insects. Tish Rabe's cartoon-like drawings of insects in her book *On Beyond Bugs! All About Insects* can spark a creative approach to insect construction. For a more detailed look at insects, Jen Green's *Learn About Insects* book provides actual photographs of insects, their life cycles, how they feed, their colors and camouflage, and who are their friends and foes. This book provides some accurate contexts for creating insects and their habitats.

Using common household or classroom materials, children are challenged to create an insect. For an animal to be classified as an insect, it must have certain characteristics.

Children will investigate these characteristics. They will learn that insects must have six legs and a body with three segments. It may have two or four wings. Decide what foods your insect eats and how it moves. Design a habitat to accommodate your insect's needs.

3. Bedtime Bonanza

Hang a white sheet on a clothesline. After dark, shine a spotlight on the sheet and observe what insects are attracted to the sheet. Describe how the insects are responding to each other. After a period of time, collect the insects that have landed on your sheet. How many different varieties of insects have you collected? Which is the most common or least common? Make a chart or graph displaying the data you collected. Be careful not to harm the insects.

Another bedtime bonanza could be an investigation about fireflies. Judy Hawes' book *Fireflies in the Night* offers a cultural connection to how fireflies are made good use of in the Caribbean, Cuba, Japan, and some parts of South America. Such information may spark more interest in the study of fireflies. A great companion book to Judy Hawes' book is *Ten Flashing Fireflies* by Philomen Sturges. In this book a sister and brother count to 10 as they catch fireflies in a jar. They then count backwards as they release the fireflies.

4. Plant Hotels

Select a plant from your garden or neighborhood. Observe and keep track of what insects are attracted to that plant. Your children could write a story about your plant and the insects. They might take digital photographs or videos of the insects and put them on your classroom Web site. When possible, try to observe and include the different stages of development of the insects. How does the plant react to the insects? Children should quietly observe and not disturb the insects.

5. My Life Story by Billy Beetle

Have the children tell and illustrate the life story of an insect from the egg stage to the adult stage from the perspective of the insect. Involve the plants and other animals that are involved in the life of the insect. Teachers can support this activity by providing appropriate resources for children to study. The story could be produced as a book, puppet show, video, or other descriptive process.

6. Insect Galls

Many insects deposit their eggs on the leaves of plants. As the larva matures it uses the leaf for its nutrition and its habitat. This causes the leaf to become deformed. These deformed leaves are called *insect galls*. Look in your neighborhood and identify as many galls as you can. Different types of insects select specific types of

Insect galls on a wild grape vine.

J. David Keller

plants to place their galls. Sixty percent of insect galls are found on oak trees. Other common plants where you will find galls are roses and daisies. Keep a log of your observations of these galls as the insect larvae mature.

7. Butterfly Detectives

Butterflies are wonderful insects to grow and observe with your students. Their delicate and quiet nature makes them ideal for young children. A resource for this concept exploration is the book by Dean Morris, *Butterflies and Moths*. This book has beautiful color drawings of a large variety of moths and butterflies, and it explains how they start life as tiny eggs and how they develop into caterpillars, pupae, and then butterflies and moths. This engaging book will invite young children to explore these fascinating creatures. Jen Green's book *Learn About Insects* offers directions on how to make a "Butterfly Garden." Such a project may be possible right in your own school's backyard.

The key to having butterflies common to your area is having available particular plants to which the butterflies are attracted (Figure 10.8). For example, monarch butterflies will only lay their eggs on milkweed. When the eggs hatch, the larvae feed on the milkweed.

Choose a particular common variety of butterfly and observe its movement. Track the insect for a period of time. What variety of plants is the butterfly attracted to? Describe its flight. Use a variety of methods to record your data. For instance, the children could make a map of their yards and show the different locations where the insect was spotted. They could collect a leaf from each plant each time that a butterfly was seen at the plant. The leaves could be used to produce a pictograph.

8. Interviewing Insects

Select a variety of insects that your students would like to interview. Have the class make a list of the questions that they would like to ask the insect. Using trade books, the Internet, and other common sources, have the children develop what they think would be the insects' responses. Students could produce the interview in a variety of ways. They could produce an audiotape. They could make a costume to look like the insect and make a videotape. Another option would be to develop a written interview that would be included in the school newsletter.

- **Monarch butterfly**—common milkweed, swamp milkweed
- **Zebra swallowtail**—common pawpaw
- **Spicebush swallowtail**—spicebush
- **Alfalfa and common sulfur butterflies**—red and white clover
- **Red admiral**—false and stinging nettle
- **Painted lady butterflies**—thistles, burdock, sunflowers, hollyhock, silver brocade
- **Red-spotted purple butterfly**—wild cherry, apple, hawthorn
- **Viceroy**—willows, apple
- **Eastern tiger swallowtail**—wild cherry, tulip tree
- **Great spangle fritillary**—violets
- **Black swallowtail**—rue, carrot, parsley, Queen Anne's lace, fennel
- **Cabbage butterfly**—cabbage, broccoli, cauliflower

FIGURE 10.8 Common butterflies and the plants that feed their caterpillars.

9. Ant Investigations

A great resource for this investigation is Jen Green's book *Learn About Insects*. She provides a great "Investigating Ants" project. This project will help children to design an effective approach to watching insects.

Observe a group of ants. As the ants are traveling around, observe the trail that they have formed. Follow the ant trail to identify their sources of food and shelter. You and your children could develop a map of the ant trails. List the significant features that the children identify. The children can make a pictograph identifying the types of food that the ants are collecting.

Ants mark trails to their food sources for the ant colony by depositing of a chemical substance called formic acid. After the trail has been well identified and observed by the children, you can disturb the trail by scraping off a few feet of the trail with your feet. Observe how the ants react to the problem of trying to follow the trail. How do they adapt? How do they communicate with each other?

10. Insect Picnic

In a convenient undisturbed area, place on a surface a variety of foods such as fruit, crackers, cookies, sugar, lunch meat, popcorn, and potato chips. You might invite your children to make a list of the types of food that they want to have at the insect picnic. They may theorize about what they think insects like to eat and construct the menu accordingly. Observe what types of insects are attracted to each of the foods. What types of behavior do the different varieties of insects exhibit? Do they carry away the food? How do they communicate with their kind to show where the food is?

Many ant farms are available from science and educational supply stores. You can also make your own using a gallon jar or a terrarium. Fill the container with sand. Add a few twigs for interest. Depending on the variety of ants, they can eat many common grain products or they can eat green vegetation.

How do they communicate with competing insects to keep them from eating their food?

The class can collect data in a variety of forms. They might develop a chart or graph of the types and numbers of insects that join the picnic. They could make a chart of the types of insects that eat each particular food. They could make a map showing where the insects travel. Be sure the children are respectful of the insects and that they simply observe the insects without harming them.

11. Air Explorations

Insects' flights serve many purposes. Some insects, such as the monarch butterfly, fly to migrate during the different seasons. Bees fly to collect nectar for the hive. Dragonflies are searching for other insects to eat. Some insects actually mate in flight. Invite your children to observe the flight patterns of insects. How far do they fly? How high do they get above the ground? Do they fly with great speed or do they hover? What are they attracted to in flight? Do you think they have a purpose in flying?

Invite your children to play the role of different types of insects. They could move around the classroom or playground demonstrating how the bees fly. Or they could model how a butterfly visits a garden. You might select some particular music that depicts a particular insect's flight.

12. Insect Songs

Using tape recorders, ask your students to collect as many different insect sounds as they can. Observe what times of the day and evening the different insects are most vocal. Are insects more vocal during particular weather patterns? Invite your students to describe each insect sound with different adjectives. Ask your children what they think the insects are saying. The sounds they collect could be added to your class Web site.

13. Underground Activities

Place a board or a flat rock in a remote area. Visit the site every few days for several weeks and identify any evidence of insect life you see under the board or rock. What insects do you see? Are their burrows indicating insect activity? Periodically photograph or make a sketch of the site. How did the site evolve over time? Make a chart or graph of your findings. If photographs were taken, put them in the sequence in which they were captured. Label the photographs with dates and times, as appropriate. Such sequencing helps children to seriate events over time.

Several chromo pubescents in a natural setting.

Chromo Pubescents

Chromo pubescents can be used as an excellent tool for teaching about camouflage. *Chromo pubescents* stands for "colored fuzzy things." By making small insects out of pipe cleaners and placing them along a nature trail, students will be able to differentiate between objects that are well camouflaged and those obvious to their eyes. You can make different colored chromo pubescence from pipe cleaners. Take two pipe cleaners. Cut one into three equal parts. Fold the second in half. Wrap the three short ones around the doubled pipe cleaners forming the six legs. Make about 30 of these "chromos" out of different colors.

Place each chromo pubescent along a path or the perimeter of the schoolyard where there are a variety of bushes, trees, and other plants such that they blend in with nature as best you can.

Students can mark a chart indicating what colors they found (Table 10.2). Comparisons can be made to the number that were "hidden" along the trail.

TABLE 10.2 A chart for keeping track of chromo pubescents

Chromo Pubescents Found

Black								
Blue								
Brown								
Tan								
Green								
Orange								
Purple								
Red								
White								
Yellow								
Mutants*								

*Mutants are chromo pubescents that are multicolored.

Activities in Other Explorations That Relate to Insects

Leaves (Chapter 11)

6. Insects Like Leaves Too!

Water (Chapter 17)

7. The Classroom River

10. Water's Work

Resources for Teachers

Books

Arnett, R. H., Jr., Jacques, R. L., Jr. (1981). *Simon & Schuster's guide to insects*. New York: Simon & Schuster.

Borror, D. J. & White, R. E. (1970). *A field guide to the insects of America north of Mexico*. Boston, MA: Houghton Mifflin.

Article

Raloff, J. (1996). Precollege science and math "lack focus." *Science News, 150* (16).

Web Sites

http://butterflywebsite.com/
Good general information and photographs of butterflies.

http://www.earthlife.net/insects/
General information on insects.

http://www.insectlore.com/bugfun.html
Information on a variety of insects. Particular insects and materials related to keeping insects can be ordered.

Children's Books on Insects

Allen, J. (2000). *Are you a butterfly?* New York: Kingfisher.

Allen, J. (2000). *Are you a snail?* New York: Kingfisher.

Allen, J. (2000). *Are you a spider?* New York: Kingfisher.

Allen, J. (2002). *Are you a grasshopper?* New York: Kingfisher.

Barner, B. (2004). *Bug safari*. New York: Holiday House.

Bentley, D. (1996). *If you were a bug . . .: A pop-up book about bugs and you (Pop-up books)*. New York: Random House.

Berger, M. (1997). *Flies taste with their feet: Weird facts about insects (Weird-but-true book)*. New York: Scholastic Paperbacks.

Berger, M. (2003a). *Spinning spiders*. New York: Harper Trophy.

Berger, M. (2003b). *Where did the butterfly get its name? Questions and answers about butterflies and moths*. New York: Scholastic Reference.

Berger, M., & Berger, G. (2000). *Do all spiders spin webs? Questions and answers about spiders*. New York: Scholastic Reference.

Bernhard, E. (1992). *Ladybug*. New York: Holiday House.

Carle, E. (1999a). *Grouchy ladybug*. New York: HarperCollins Children's Books.

Carle, E. (1999b). *La Mariquita malhumorada*. Econo-Clad Books.

Carle, E. (1999c). *Very clumsy click beetle*. New York: Putnam Publishing Group.

Carle, E. (2000d). *The very hungry caterpillar doll*. New York: Putnam Publishing Group.

Carle, E. (2000b). *The very quiet cricket*. New York: Putnam Books for Young Readers.

Carle, E. (2000c). *The very lonely firefly*. New York: Putnam Books for Young Readers.

Carle, E. (2001). *Honeybee and the robber*. New York: Penguin Putnam Books for Young Readers.

Carle, E. (2002). *Oruga muy hambrienta (Very hungry caterpillar)*. New York: Penguin Putnam Books for Young Readers.

Carter, D. A. (1990). *More bugs in boxes: A pop-up book about color*. New York: Little Simon.

Chinery, M. (1997) *How bees make honey*. Tarrytown, NY: Marshall Cavendish Corporation.

Chrustowski, R. (2000). *Bright beetle*. New York: Henry Holt.

Cole, J. (1997). *The magic school bus spins a web: A book about spiders*. New York: Scholastic Trade.

Cole, J. (1999). *The magic school bus gets ants in its pants: A book about ants*. New York: Scholastic.

Cole, J., & Moore, E. (2000). *The truth about bats*. New York: Scholastic Trade.

Dewey, J. O. (1997). *Bedbugs in our house: True tales of insects, bugs, and spiders discovery*. Tarrytown, NY: Cavendish.

Dussling, J. (1998). *Bugs! Bugs! Bugs! (Eyewitness Readers, Level 2)*. New York: DK Publishing.

Ehlert, L. (2001). *Waiting for wings*. New York: Harcourt Children's Books.

Facklam, M. (1999). *Bugs for lunch*. Watertown, MA: Charlesbridge Publishing.

Facklam, M. (1996). *Creepy crawly caterpillars*. Boston, MA: Little Brown & Co.

Facklam, M. (2001). *Spiders and their Web sites*. New York: Little Brown and Company.

Fowler, A. (1990). *It's good thing there are insects/Big book (Rookie Reader-about science big book)*. Children's Press.

Froman, N. (2001). *What's that bug?* New York: Little Brown and Company.

Goor, R., & Goor, N. (1990). *Insect metamorphosis: From egg to adult*. New York: Atheneum.

Green, J. (1998). *Insects*. New York: Lorenz Books.

Green, J., & Green, G. (1998). *Insects (Learn about series)*. New York: Lorenz Books.

Greenaway, T. (1998). *3D eyewitness: Insect*. New York: DK Publishing.

Greenberg, D. T. (1997). *Bugs!* New York: Little Brown & Co.

Harvey, J. (2003). *Busy bugs: A book about patterns (All abroad math reader. Station stop 1)*. New York: Grosset & Dunlap.

Haslam, A. (2000). *Insects*. Princeton: Two-Can.

Hawcock, D. (1996a). *Beetle: A read-about, fold-out, and pop-up (Bouncing bugs)*. New York: Random House.

Hawcock, D. (1996b). *Fly: A read-about, fold-out, and pop-up (Bouncing bugs)*. New York: Random House.

Hawcock, D. (1996c). *Wasp: A read-about, fold-out, and pop-up (Bouncing bugs)*. New York: Random House.

Hawes, Judy (1991). *Fireflies in the night*. New York: Harper Collins Publishers.

Hickman, P. (1999). *Starting with nature bug book*. Buffalo, NY: Kids Can Press.

Himmelman, J. (1999). *A house spider's life*. New York: Children's Press.

Johnson, J. (1997). *Simon & Schuster children's guide to insects and spiders*. New York: Simon & Schuster Children's Publishing.

Joyce, W. (1996). *The leaf men and the brave good bugs*. New York: Harper Collins Children's Books.

Julivert, A. (1992). *The fascinating world of spiders*. Hauppauge, NY: Barron's Educational Series.

Kelly, I. (2007). *It's a butterfly's life*. New York: Holiday House.

Kneidel, S. S. (1999). *More pet bugs: A kid's guide to catching and keeping insects and other small creatures*. New York: John Wiley & Sons.

Kneidel, S. S. (2000). *Stink bugs, stink insects, and stag beetles: And 18 more of the strongest insects on earth*. New York: John Wiley and Sons.

Lassieur, A. (2001). *Scorpions: The sneaky stingers*. New York: Franklin Watts.

Llewellyn, C. (1997d). *Some bugs glow in the dark and other amazing facts about insects*. Brookfield, CT: Copper Beech Books.

Llewellyn, C. (1997b). *Spiders have fangs*. Brookfield, CT: Copper Beech Books.

McDonald, M. (1995). *Insects are my life*. New York: Orchard Books.

McEvey, S. F. (2002). *Bugs*. Broomall, PA: Chelsea House Publishers.

Meister, C. (2000). *Ladybugs*. Edina, MN: Abdo Publishing.

Miller, S. S. (2001). *Beetles: The most common insects*. New York: Franklin Watts.

Miller, S. S. (2003b). *Grasshoppers and crickets of North America*. New York: Franklin Watts.

Miller, S. S. (2003d). *Ants, bees, and wasps of North America*. New York: Franklin Watts.

Morris, D. (1997). *Butterflies and moths*. Milwaukee, WI: Raintree Children's Books.

Nickle, J. (1999). *The ant bully*. New York: Scholastic Trade.

O'Neill, A. (2002). *Insects and bugs*. New York: Kingfisher.

Oppenheim, J. F. (1998). *Have you seen bugs?* New York: Scholastic Trade

Parker, N. W. (1988). *Bugs*. New York: HarperCollins Children's Book.

Pascoe, E. (2004) *Nature close-up: Bugs*. Farmington Hills, MA: Blackbirch Press.

Patent, D. H. (2003). *Fabulous fluttering tropical butterflies*. New York: Walker and Company.

Pearce-Kelly, P. (2002). *Bugs*. NY: DK Publishing.

Penner, L. (1999). *Monster bugs*. New York: Random House.

Philpot, L. (1995). *Out and about with Anthony ant*. New York: Random House.

Rabe, T. (1999). *On beyond bugs! All about insects*. New York: Random House.

Rockwell, A. (2001). *Bugs are insects*. New York: HarperCollins Children's Books.

Ross, M. E. (2000a). *Caterpillarology*. Minneapolis, MN: Carolrhoda Books.

Ross, M. E. (2000b). *Spiderology*. Minneapolis, MN: Carolrhoda Books.

Ross, M. E. (2002). *Rolypolyology*. Minneapolis, MN: Carolrhoda Books.

Rouss, S. A. (2002). *Sammy spider's first trip to Israel: A book about the five senses*. Rockville, MD: Kar-Ben copies.

Scarborough, S. (1998). *About bugs (We both read)*. Redwood City, CA: Treasure Bay Inc.

Sill, C. P. (2000). *About insects: A guide for children*. Atlanta, GA: Peachtree Publishers.

Sill, C. (2003). *About arachnids: A guide for children*. Atlanta, GA: Peachtree Publishers.

Squire, A. O. (2000). *Spiders of North America*. New York: Franklin Watts.

Still, J. (1991). *Amazing butterflies and moths*. New York: Alfred A. Knopf.

Sturges, P. (1995). *Ten flashing fireflies*. New York: North-South Books.

Swanson, D. (2001). *Bug bites*. Toronto: Whitecap Books.

Tracqui, V. (2002). *Face-to face with the ladybug*. Watertown, MA: Charlesbridge Publishing.

VanCleave, J. (1998). *Janice VanCleave's insects and spiders: Mind-boggling experiments you can turn into science fair projects*. New York: John Wiley & Sons.

VanCleave, J. (1999). *Janice VanCleave's play and find out about bugs: Easy experiments for young children*. New York: John Wiley & Sons.

Walton, R. (1995). *What to do when a bug climbs in your mouth: And other poems to drive you buggy.* New York: Lothrop Lee & Shepard Books.

Wechsler, D. (1995) *Bizarre bugs.* New York: Cobblehill Books/Dutton.

Whiting, S. (2006) *All about ants.* Washington, DC: National Geographic Society.

Zappler, G. (Ed.). (1999). *Learn about Texas insects.* Texas Parks & Wildlife Department.

Correlation of NSES Standards and NCTM Principles and Standards to Leaves Concept Exploration Activities

	1. Falling Leaves	2. Quiet Leaves	3. Leafy Lunch	4. Scratch and Sniff	5. Evergreens Also Have Leaves	6. Insects Like Leaves Too!	7. A Tribute to Transpiration	8. Leaves—Where Do They All Go?	9. Leaves—Alike but Different	10. A Rainbow Connection of Leaves	11. Leaves' Lasting Impressions	12. From a Leaf's Perspective
SCIENCE												
Inquiry	X	X		X		X			X	X		X
Physical Science				X		X			X			
Life Science	X	X		X	X	X	X	X	X	X	X	X
Earth and Space Science						X	X	X				X
Science and Technology							X					
Personal and Social Perspectives	X	X	X	X		X	X	X		X	X	X
History and Nature of Science			X					X				
MATHEMATICS												
Number and Operations	X		X				X		X	X		
Algebra	X			X	X	X			X	X		X
Geometry	X				X				X	X	X	
Measurement					X				X	X	(X)	
Data Analysis and Probability	X			X	X					X		
Reasoning and Proof							X					
Problem Solving							X					
Communication		X						X		X		X
Connections	X											
Representations	X	X				X				X		X

196

CHAPTER 11

Leaves

Tapestry of Color

Nature has a paintbrush.
I know this to be true
Because I see green colors
On leaves when spring is new
Then seasons change and leaves become
A tapestry of color—one by one
And as they wish,
They float and swish
From branches to the ground.
Nature has a paintbrush.
I know this to be true
Because the leaves and universe
Show rainbows through and through!

Genevieve A. Davis

Leaves are neat! We anticipate when the first leaves will open, signaling the beginning of spring. We watch as the different types of leaves unfold in sequence. Crocuses, daffodils, and tulips force their leaves out of the ground even when they might be coated with snow. Soon, the willow trees show their bright yellow color, then the buckeyes, maples, and fruit trees blossom. Later, the oak leaves emerge. Throughout their life cyles, leaves collect energy from the Sun and store it in the plant they're attached to. In the fall, as the amount of daylight decreases, we observe the leaves lose their chlorophyll, turn different colors, and float to the ground.

On hot days, we sit under trees because their leaves shade us from the sun. We watch leaves shimmer in the breeze on a sunlit day. As we walk in the woods, we notice that the air is much more humid because of the water transpiring from the leaves of the trees and other plants (see Concept Exploration 7). In the fall, we like to jump in a pile of leaves. We listen to them rustle as we walk through them. We eat leaves in our salads and other foods. Sibella Kraus (1993) offers many lovely ways to eat leaves in her recipe and photograph book, *Greens: A Country Garden Cookbook*. Indeed, leaves are remarkable!

SCIENCE CONCEPTS FOR TEACHERS

The Value of Leaves

Our lives would be entirely different if we didn't have leaves. In reality, we could not exist without leaves. Leaves are the manufacturing center for all plants. They collect the energy from the Sun through the process of photosynthesis and store the energy throughout the plants.

This manufacturing process basically uses the energy in sunlight to convert carbon dioxide (CO_2) from the atmosphere to organic compounds that can be utilized by the plants. In this process, not only is carbon dioxide taken from the atmosphere, oxygen (O_2) is returned into the atmosphere.

This process is critical to life as we know it, because animals, including humans, breathe in oxygen and exhale carbon dioxide through the process of respiration. In addition, all oxidation processes, such as burning gasoline in our cars and burning natural gas, coal, and oil for heat and electricity, produce carbon dioxide. This cycle is called the *carbon dioxide–oxygen cycle* and is illustrated in Figure 11.1.

The carbon dioxide–oxygen cycle acts as a buffer to keep the earth's level of carbon dioxide at a reasonably constant 0.03%. Throughout the history of the earth, the level of CO_2 has fluctuated. This fluctuation is critical, because the amount of CO_2 in the atmosphere affects the world's climate through the greenhouse effect.

We often divide plants into annuals, which live for only one year, and perennials, which live for more than one year. Many of our garden-variety flowers grow from seed to flower and die in one year. Other plants such as trees and shrubs grow for many years. Bristlecone pine trees live for as long as 3,500 years. Each year and in some cases, such as for evergreens, every two or more years, the plant will shed its leaves. In the spring of each year, new leaves will be formed.

Photosynthesis

Photosynthesis is the process by which plant cells, located predominantly in the leaves, convert carbon dioxide (CO_2) to organic material by reducing this gas to carbohydrates in a rather complex set of reactions. Energy for this process is supplied by light absorbed by plant pigments (primarily chlorophyll). The pigments absorb blue and red light. Green and yellow light are not effectively absorbed by the pigments and are reflected by leaves—this is why plants look green.

Compost

Leaves also contribute to soil development. When leaves drop in the fall, over a period of time they break down. This decomposition is caused predominantly by

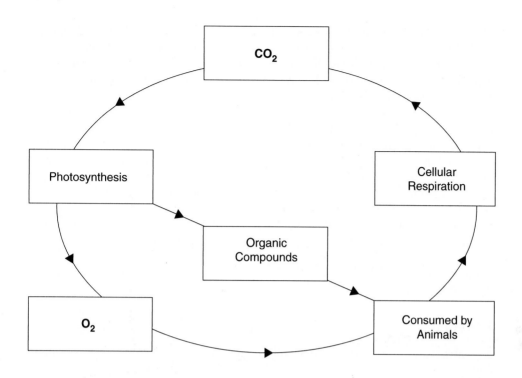

FIGURE 11.1   A simplified carbon dioxide–oxygen cycle.

microorganisms. The compost, or basic organic materials that are formed, helps plants grow. We can contribute to this process by making compost piles from grass clippings, leaves, and plant material from our garden. Information on making compost piles can be obtained from your county extension agents, books, and the Internet.

MATHEMATICS: ADDRESSING THE NCTM STANDARDS THROUGH CONCEPT EXPLORATIONS

The Concept Explorations in this chapter are designed to help children explore and investigate leaves in a way that involves many mathematical concepts and ideas.

Number and Operations and Algebra

Leaves have discernable patterns. Patterns of shape, vein structure, color, leaf grouping, and growth can be observed, described, and captured in some creative mathematical form.

As children explore leaves, they will observe similarities and differences between and among the leaves. Opportunities for counting points on the leaves and describing the attributes of the similarities and differences among the leaves should be encouraged and modeled. Children can use their own language to describe what they see, smell, feel, hear, and taste. (Keep in mind the appropriateness and safety aspects of all activities.) As descriptions are shared, an agreed-on vocabulary should be established to represent the classification schemes the children develop. These schemes can be used to identify new leaves and to serve as a means of comparing gathered leaves. Teachers should encourage creative classroom displays of these classification schemes through varied media and designs.

One of the ways young children problem solve in mathematics is through counting. You can help children count the different types of leaves they find and help them communicate the amount in some creative way. Stressing the one-to-one correspondence and the stable order in counting is important. Counting leads to the construction of a "living" graph. Actual leaves can be placed on a grid for counting and comparison. Children can see which leaves are represented the most and which the least. Children can count and count on to determine how many more of one leaf there is than another. Keeping track of these quantities helps children attach numerical meaning to their work. Asking questions about the most leaves and the least leaves, as well as the sequence of ordering from greatest amount of leaves to the least amount of leaves, gives children authentic experiences with the mathematical concepts of comparison and seriation.

Geometry

Leaf observations and explorations will provide many rich opportunities for young children to explore different geometric shapes and concepts. As children spend time looking at and collecting leaves, they will be seeing different shapes and configurations of leaves. They will be seeing symmetry in nature as they look carefully at how each leaf is constructed. As children observe leaves, they will experience the aesthetic nature of geometry and the aesthetic geometry of nature! Children can use language to describe the interesting shapes that they see, and they can create artistic representations of the leaf shapes. Certainly leaf rubbings with crayons over thin paper show the geometric structure of leaves and the vein structure beautifully.

Measurement

If appropriate, you may be comparing the leaves by size. Measurement approaches can be perceptual and holistic or mathematical and scientific. Children can compare leaves by placing them next to each other or they can compare them by means of a measuring device such as a ruler, connecting blocks, or even acorns. Children can determine a standard measuring process, such as measuring from the tip of the stem to the tallest part, or measuring from side to side at the widest point. The important aspect of measurement is the process and the approach that the children use. Tools can be standard, homemade, or improvised.

Data Analysis

Upon finding, looking at, and collecting leaves, you can help the children figure out a way to display them. The display could be a very global collage or arrangement. Or it could be in an organized format such as various collections that separate the different types of leaves based on whatever characteristic the children choose, for example, color, shape, size, or configuration. Or have children figure out a way to "graph" their wonderful finds!

Patterns and Sequencing

As children observe the growth and death of leaves, they are watching a life cycle that can be captured through photography, drawings or sketches, plays or dances, or stories written or told. In all cases, the sequence and patterns of a leaf's life are captured. Children have a sense of what happens first, what happens as a leaf grows, and what happens last.

OBSERVING WITH ALL THE SENSES

Sight

Observing leaves gives us opportunities to make comparisons. Leaves have many shapes and sizes that are interesting to see over time, from the beginning of growth to the fallen leaves. Leaves provide wonderful opportunities to compare many shades of green and other vibrant colors. Veins of leaves have intricate patterns that can be seen and felt. Surfaces of leaves often tell stories; for instance, insects can leave visible trails on the leaves. Often, we see evidence of insects' eating habits by observing the eating patterns from holes or voids along the edges of the leaves.

Sound

We can listen to leaves rustle in the wind. We can make a whistle with a blade of grass stretched between our thumbs. Walking through fallen leaves creates a symphony of crackling and schussing. Capturing these sounds on tape can provide fun opportunities for children to reflect on their experiences in nature across many seasons.

Touch

Leaves have many different textures. Some leaves feel as coarse as sandpaper; others, as soft as silk; yet others as sharp as a needle. Some leaves feel different front and back. Some leaves are difficult to tear; others fall apart on contact. In this sensory mode, we need to be cautious about leaves that can irritate and cause inflammation, such as those on poison ivy.

Smell

Many types of leaves give off odors when they are crushed. A good example is the leaf of the sassafras tree, which gives off a sweet odor or a spearmint leaf, which gives off a minty odor.

SAFETY

Care must be taken when selecting leaves for study with your children. Particular types of leaves such as poison ivy and nettles can irritate the skin. Many types of plants are poisonous to eat. More than one-half of all house plants are poisonous. Teachers need to exercise great care in this area. Only eat plants that you know are used for food.

As children collect leaves, care needs to be taken in terms of the surrounding environment. Oftentimes, insects are found on leaves and near trees. Children should be instructed to be wary of stinging or biting insects.

CONCEPT EXPLORATIONS ON LEAVES FOR YOUR CLASSROOM

These Concept Explorations examine leaves as the context for developing mathematics and science concepts and skills. Particular suggestions and opportunities are given to direct you in these explorations. The activities presented here are designed to stimulate your students' thoughts and questions and serve as a springboard for exciting explorations. As your children explore and probe their interests about leaves, the opportunities given in these explorations should stimulate their inquiries, curiosities, and ideas.

You may want to begin with a basic information book such as *Leaves* by John Farndon. In this book, children can learn a little about leaves, leaves and animals, and leaves and people.

1. Falling Leaves

In the fall one cannot keep from being affected by leaves. Whether it is the beauty of an afternoon walk in the woods observing the rich colors, the rustling sound of walking through leaves, having to rake the leaves that have blown in from your neighbor's yard, or running through and jumping on a big pile of leaves, leaves become an active and very sensory part of our lives.

Leaves provide excellent opportunities for helping children hone their observation skills. Children's interest in leaves can be a catalyst that helps them focus on particular attributes of leaves. A good way to introduce this activity is by reading David M. Schwartz's book, *Look Once, Look Again: Plant Leaves*. In this book, observation is emphasized as the author takes us on a journey looking carefully at close-up photographs of a variety of leaves. Observing and comparing characteristics of particular leaves is an important skill.

One of the most common procedures for identifying the different varieties of trees is to look for specific, genetic characteristics of their leaves. These characteristics include size, shape, type of edge, veining, and number of leaves in a grouping.

If a local site is convenient, you may take your class on a nature walk to collect leaves. Otherwise invite your children to bring in a variety of leaves from their neighborhoods.

You might laminate the leaves or use clear contact paper to preserve the leaves. Make the leaves available for a period of time so that the children can enjoy exploring the different leaves. As they explore, invite the children to use words that describe particular leaves. For instance, they might use terms such as *round, oval, sharp* or *pointy, toothed,* or *like fingers.* These terms could be written on cards and placed next to the leaves on a table, chalkboard, or bulletin board.

When the children have developed a vocabulary of descriptive terms, select one of the terms such as *toothed* and invite the children to find examples of the leaves that are toothed. You might want to select a different term each day and identify the leaves that fit that characteristic. This process can be expanded to develop the use of Venn diagrams with your students. Refer to Chapter 5 for additional information about Venn diagrams.

Once the children have developed comprehension of the basic vocabulary terms that describe the characteristics of leaves, they can use their leaves to develop a key for identifying the leaves that they have collected. Chapter 5 gives details on a process you can use with your students to develop a bimodal classification system. For leaves, the classification system can be based on the characteristics of the leaves that your children have identified, such as shape, size, color, texture, or vein structure. The children's own classification schemes then become the way the leaves are grouped and described (Figure 11.2).

For better student understanding, your classification scheme should be at the concrete level. Have specimens of each type of leaf placed on your classification chart so that the children can visualize the defining characteristics. The key that the children develop for identifying leaves should be kept very simple. Use only three to six different types of leaves and only differentiate by obvious characteristics. As you discuss the classification system with your children, encourage them to verbalize the process that they used to classify the leaves.

Your students' interest and involvement will be your best guide for knowing how far to expand this activity. If their curiosity wanes, then perhaps you have reached their limit. If you go beyond this limit, the children's attitudes toward the topic will begin to wane. You might find that a particular child or small group of children will become very involved in the activity. You can encourage such a group to expand the activity separately.

Keep in mind that as we work with young children, we are concerned with the development of the skills of observation and classification. When children can visualize organizational patterns, they will increase the retention of their skills and develop their ability to think critically and analytically. The skills that they are developing with leaves can be applied to other topics such as insects, rocks, birds, and seeds.

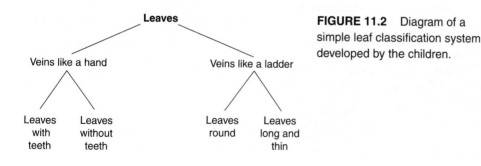

FIGURE 11.2 Diagram of a simple leaf classification system developed by the children.

FIGURE 11.3 Writing simple poems can help students express themselves. This Haiku follows the form of having three lines with 5,7, 5 syllables.

2. Quiet Leaves

Find a quiet time when you can take your class to a local site where you can watch leaves on a tree or a group of trees. Help the children capture and describe what they are experiencing and seeing. Invite them to express how they feel watching the movement of the leaves. How does a soft breeze affect the movement of the leaves? Are all types of leaves equally affected? Do some of the leaves bend toward sunlight? If there is an oncoming rain, do they tend to turn over? What descriptive words express the feelings that your children convey about the leaves? Encourage the children to tell a story about what they think the leaves are feeling during different environmental conditions. These activities can give you an opportunity to expand the concept of personification. **Personification** is the process whereby inanimate objects are given human qualities.

Another activity would be to have your students develop a simple poem, such as a haiku (Figure 11.3), to describe their observations. It is important for you to encourage children to capture their feelings and express them in many ways. Multiple forms of representation in this activity could include words both spoken and written; pictures, paintings, or sketches; and gestures, dancing, or singing. As children experience this quiet time among the leaves, they will be motivated to express their experiences in their own unique way. It is our role to support these creative expressions and capture or preserve them for later reflection.

3. Leafy Lunch

Many of the foods that we eat are leaves of various plants (Figure 11.4). Common examples include lettuce, kale, cabbage, mustard, and spinach. Other less common leafy foods include dandelion, grape leaves, and lamb's quarter, a common "weed" in

Amaranth	Chickweed
Chicory	Clover
Dandelion	Curly dock
Fireweed	Wild grape
Horsetail	Lamb s-quarters
Miner's lettuce	Mountain sorrel
Nasturtium	Nettle
Wild onion	Plantain
Purslane	Reed grass
Sheep sorrel	Shepherd's purse
Stonecrop	

FIGURE 11.4 These common wild plants have edible leaves. Information on preparing these leaves is available in numerous books and Internet sites.

many gardens. Have a "leafy lunch" with your children to invite them to try different foods that are leaves. Be sure the leaves are washed thoroughly and handled with clean hands.

Eating "leaves" provides a wonderful opportunity to learn about and experience foods from other cultures and, thus, experience a taste of a faraway land. For example, trying grape leaves, common in Mediterranean cooking, or bok choy, common in Asian cooking, can be an exciting experience for a young child. Sharing ethnic treats can open a whole new world of international cooking and eating. Children will discover the universality of eating leaves. An Asian green called tong ho is delicious when cooked in a skillet with some olive oil or another tasty, healthy vegetable oil. A good resource for types of leafy vegetables can be found at *http://www.kitazawaseed.com/seedschrysanthemum_greens_1.html*.

Another example of a cultural green is morogo, which is the collective term for various leaves of South Africa and is similar to spinach. Different African countries have their own national green leaves such as moloukia in Egypt, matapa in Malawi, cacani in Mozambique, sukuma wiki or muchicha in Kenya, and rape in Zambia and Zimbabwe (Sitole, 1999). It is interesting to know that in Thailand, banana leaves are used to wrap food for steaming, grilling and roasting (Bastyra & Johnson, 2003). Wonderful opportunities for developing cultural awareness and appreciation for nature abound in the study of leaves.

> Care must be taken to make sure that the leaves that you use in recipes are edible. Many plants are harmful. About 50% of house plants are poisonous!

Many native plants were used as principal foods for the early settlers as they traveled west. The Native Americans had excellent knowledge about which plants were edible and how to prepare them. Learning about edible (that is, safe to eat) wild foods provides opportunities for your children to learn more about ethnic foods of different cultures and about their ancestors. Your students might interview grandparents and other local seniors and ask them about leafy foods that they eat and remember eating as young children.

4. Scratch and Sniff

Many leaves have strong odors that we can smell. Herbs have strong odors and are easy to grow in pots so they can be kept in the classroom. Basil, sage, catnip, marjoram, thyme,

Anthony E. Davis

A leafy vegetable, *tong ho*, is a common Asian food. Here is the garland serrate leaved variety. It is sometimes called a chop suey green and is an edible chrysanthemum green.

and mint are good examples. Other fragrant plants that are common in gardens and in nature include the ground ivy, sassafras, wild cherry, and anise.

Rubbing the leaves and tender stems will release strong odors that the children can easily smell. Be careful to identify and know the different plants that you use. Beware of some wild plants, such as poison ivy and nettles, because they can irritate the skin and cause allergic reactions. Always accompany children as they venture into the outdoors. It is a good idea to examine the outdoor area as a precatuion before you take young children exploring.

5. Evergreens Also Have Leaves

Because most evergreens have needles instead of broad leaves, we tend to not think of them as leaves. Indeed, they are leaves, serving as the plant's collector of energy from the Sun through photosynthesis just like all other leaves. Their harder coat serves to protect the needles so that they can survive through climate changes and live for longer periods of time than one season.

Some evergreens have broad leaves. The ornamental holly shrub and the evergreen ilex are common examples in ornamental landscapes.

Invite your children to collect a variety of evergreen leaves. Make a creative display or collage using the needles. Evergreen needles also make interesting and inventive paintbrushes for students to use.

Document the different types of needles you find. The children can compare the different lengths and shapes of the needles. Needles can be displayed by length to illustrate a seriation of size.

Children can also explore different evergreens to observe how the needles cluster. Some evergreens have separate needles. Others have clusters of needles. For example, the white pine can be identified by the distinctive clusters of five needles grouped together.

As the children observe the different types of evergreen leaves, they construct their own classification systems to use.

6. Insects Like Leaves Too!

Many insects are dependent on leaves for their food and habitat. Not only do they eat leaves for their nutrition, they also lay their eggs on leaves so that the larva can feed on the leaves. Some insects, such as the katydid, even look like leaves so that they can camouflage themselves. Check the insect Concept Explorations in Chapter 10 to expand your activities relating insects to leaves.

Many economical digital cameras take both still photos and videos that your children can use to document the effects of insects or other animals on leaves. Children become much more involved when they produce the images, rather than just viewing a photo from a book. These images can be displayed in your classroom or on the class's Web site.

7. A Tribute to Transpiration

All plants transport their nutritional elements through a vascular system that runs throughout their body. The elements are transported by water. Leaves serve as the elimination system for removing the water after it has transported the elements. This process is called *transpiration*. A large tree on a sunny summer day will transpire up to 500 gallons of water. We can observe this process with a few simple clear plastic bags.

On a warm, sunny day, have your children place clear plastic bags over clusters of leaves on different types of trees in your schoolyard. After several hours, gather the bags and observe how much water has collected in each bag. Invite the children to make comparisons of the amount of water collected and the characteristics of the leaves. Your class can document and display their data in a creative way of their choosing.

8. Leaves—Where Do They All Go?

Talk with your children and explore with them where they think leaves go after they fall from the trees. After they have shared their ideas and theories, encourage them to design an experiment or process that would let them test their ideas. For example, they might like to visit a wooded area and observe how a pile of leaves on the ground changes over a period of time. They might collect a group of leaves along with a small amount of dirt with worms, small sticks, and so on, and keep them in a clear plastic container.

Many resources are available for learning how to compost leaves. Books and pamphlets are available at libraries, and the Internet has many resources that you can find by searching under "composting." Local garden centers can also be excellent resources.

9. Leaves—Alike but Different

Have each child get a leaf from a tree in the schoolyard. Invite the class to observe, discuss, and make a chart, like that shown in Figure 11.5, explaining or demonstrating the ways in which their leaves are alike and different. Encourage them to look at each other's leaves to observe the specific characteristics of them. After they have had an opportunity to make their observations, have the class make a chart identifying the characteristics that they have identified. Use the chart and their leaves to make a creative display on a bulletin board or table display.

Our Leaves	
How All Our Leaves Are Alike	**How All Our Leaves Are Different**
They are green.	They are different sizes.
They have five fingers or lobes.	Some have holes from insects.
They have veins.	Some of the veins are different.
They have a stem.	A few have big bumps on them.
They are lighter in color on the back.	The length of the stems differ.
They float to the ground.	Some have dark spots.

FIGURE 11.5 A chart can be used to help children keep track of similarities and differences among leaves.

10. A Rainbow Collection of Leaves

Collect as many different colors of leaves as you can find. In climates that have cold temperatures during the fall, a wide variety of colors of leaves can be found in nature. In addition, many house and garden plants have leaves with a wide variety of colors. Have your children create a piece of art displaying these colors. Invite your children to document the colors they find with *original*, creative names, such as "wagon red," "macaroni and cheese yellow," or "basketball brown." Have your children use their leaves to make a collage or display showing the variety of colors produced by nature.

11. Leaves' Lasting Impressions

Children can display characteristics and shapes of leaves in creative ways. Placing a leaf under a sheet of paper, children can make an impression of the leaf by rubbing the paper with a crayon. Invite the children to use different colors to make their leaf rubbings. When the rubbing is finished, they can cut out the paper in the shape of the leaf.

A second technique is to use leaves as printing stamps. Have the children coat their leaves with poster paint and place them paint side down on a sheet of porous paper. Dab the leaf with a sponge to get a good imprint. You might have the children use rubber cement, being careful of the fumes, to glue their leaves to a small piece of wood to serve as a block for them to hold when they are printing.

Children can also make imprints of their leaves by pressing their leaf on clay or Play-Doh. You can also use plaster of Paris to create a more permanent image and one that children can also paint.

12. From a Leaf's Perspective

Encourage your children to create an original story, poem, or song about the life or the nature of a leaf. Have your children display their creation in a way of their choosing. They might like to make a diorama, a picture, mobile, or collage. Or they may want to write a play or choreograph a dance to depict the life of a leaf. Multiple forms of representation are viable ways for children to share their ideas, knowledge, and theories. Their creations could also be developed for the class's Web page.

Activities in Other Explorations That Relate to Leaves

Insects (Chapter 10)

  6. Insect Galls

Light and Color (Chapter 12)

  13. Grow Plants with a Green Filter

Wind (Chapter 18)

5. Watching the Leaves Blow

Resources for Teachers

Books

Angier, B. (1967). *Free for the eating*. Harrisburg, PA: Stackpole Books.

Edlin, H. L. (1978). *The tree key: 235 species described*. London: Frederick Warne.

Farndon, J. (2006). *Leaves*. Farmington Hills, MI: Blackbirch Press.

Harlow, W. M. (1957). *Trees of eastern and central United States and Canada*. New York: Dover Publications.

Little, E. L. (1980). *The Audubon Society field guide to North American trees*. New York: Alfred A. Knopf.

Petrides, G. A. (1972). *A field guide to trees and shrubs* (2nd ed.). Boston, MA: Houghton Mifflin.

Saunders, C. (1934). *Useful wild plants of the United States and Canada*. New York: Robert McBride.

Schwartz, David. (1998). *Look once, look again: Plant leaves*. Milwaukee, WI: Gareth Stevens Publishing.

Watts, M. T. (1991). *Tree finder: A manual for the identification of trees by their leaves*. Rochester, NY: National Study Guide.

Web Sites

http://www.kitazawaseed.com/seeds_chrysanthemum_greens_1.html
Information about leafy vegetables.

http://www.cfe.cornell.edu/compost/Composting_Homepage.html
Has much information on techniques of composting.

http://www.self-reliance.net/wff.html
The School of Self-Reliance site lists wild foods that are edible.

Children's Books on Leaves

Bang, J. (1994). *One fall day*. New York: Alfred A. Knopf.

Blackby, S. (2003). *Catching sunlight: A book about leaves*. Minneapolis, MN: Picture Window Books.

Brenner, B., & Garelick, M. (1979). *The tremendous tree book*. Honesdale, PA: Boyd Mills Press.

Bridwell, N. (2000). *The big leaf pile*. New York: Scholastic.

Bulla, R. C. (1960). *A tree is a plant*. New York: HarperCollins.

Bunting, E. (2001). *Peepers*. San Diego, CA: Harcourt.

Burnie, D. (2000). *Tree*. New York: DK Publishing

Burton, J., & Taylor, K. (1997). *The nature and science of leaves*. Milwaukee, WI: Gareth Stevens Publishing.

Buscaglia, L. (1982): *The fall of Freddie the leaf*. Austin, TX: Holt Rinehart Winston.

Busch, P. (2000). *Nature projects for every season: Autumn*. Tarrytown, NY: Benchmark Books.

Christiansen, C. (1995). *Seeing science through art: Sky tree*. New York: HarperCollins.

Cook, A. E. (2001). *Fall colors across North America*. Portland, OR: Graphic Arts Center Pub.

de Bourgoing, P. (1989). *The tree.* New York: Scholastic.

Ehlert, L. (1987). *Growing vegetable soup.* Orlando, FL: Harcourt Brace.

Ehlert, L. (1991). *Red leaf, yellow leaf.* New York: Scholastic.

Florian, O. (1991). *Vegetable garden.* Singapore: Harcourt Brace.

Fowler, A. (1990). *It could still be a tree.* Chicago: Children's Press.

Gaines, I. (1999). *Doch's leaf pile.* New York: Disney Press.

Gibbons, G. (1984). *The seasons of Arnold's apple tree.* Hong Kong: South China Printing Co.

Gibbons, G. (2002). *Tell me, tree.* Boston, MA: Library of Congress.

Hall, Z. (1996). *The apple pie tree.* New York: Scholastic.

Hall, Z. (2001). *Fall leaves fall.* New York: Scholastic.

Iverson, D. (1999). *My favorite tree.* Nevada City, CA: Dawn Publications.

Johnson, S. A. (1986). *How leaves change.* Minneapolis, MN: Lerner Publications.

Kelley, M. (1998). *Fall is not easy.* Madison, WI: Zino Press Children's Books.

Knutson, K. (1993). *Ska-tat!* New York: Macmillan.

Lanner, R. (1990). Autumn leaves: A *guide to the colors of the northwoods.* Minocqua, WI: *Northword* Press.

Lauber, P. (1994). *Be a friend to trees.* New York: HarperCollins.

Lionni, L. (1992). *A busy year.* New York: Alfred A. Knopf.

Lyon, G. E. (1989). *ABCedar.* New York: Archard Books.

Maestro, B. (1994). *Why do leaves change colors?* New York: HarperCollins.

Nivola, A. (2002). *The forest.* New York: Frances Foster Books.

Ondra, N. J. (2007). *Foliage.* North Adams, MA: Storey Pub.

Packard, M. (1999). *Fall leaves.* New York: Scholastic.

Page, J. (2000). *Clifford the big red dog. The big leaf pile.* New York: Scholastic.

Pascoe, E. (2001). *Leaves and trees.* Woodbridge, CT: Blackbirch Press.

Potter, B. (1992). *The tale of Peter Rabbit and Benjamin Bonny.* London: Penguin Group.

Robbins, K. (1998). *Autumn leaves.* New York: Scholastic.

Romanova, N., & Spirin, G. (1985). *Once there was a tree.* New York: Dial Books.

Saunders-Smith, G. (1998a). *Autumn leaves.* Mankato, MN: Capstone Press.

Saunders-Smith, G. (1998b). *Leaves.* Mankato, MN: Capstone Press.

Schulz, C. M. (1998). *Leaf it to Sally Brown.* New York: Harper Horizon.

Schwartz, D. M. (1999a). *Look once, look again: Plant leaves.* Milwaukee, WI: Gareth Stevens Publishing.

Schwartz, D. M. (1999b). *Maple tree.* Huntington Beach, CA: Creative Teaching Press.

Sokl, M. E. (1993). *Look what I did with a leaf!* New York: Walker and Company.

Thomson, R. (1994). *Get set... go! Autumn.* Chicago: Children's Press.

Wheeler, C. (1982). *Marmalade's yellow leaf.* New York: Alfred A. Knopf.

Wigger, R. (1991). *Picture guide to leaves.* New York: Franklin Watts.

Correlation of NSES Standards and NCTM Principles and Standards to Light and Color Concept Exploration Activities

	1. Pinhole Projects	2. Mirrors	3. Seeing Yourself as Others See You	4. Candle Burning Under Water	5. Up Periscope	6. Doubling Your Fish	7. Reflections of a Laser Pointer	8. Magic Marker Magic	9. Combining Colors	10. Color Television Basic Colors	11. Paper Chromatography	12. Technicolor World	13. Growing Plants with Green Filter	14. Visualizing Sound with Light
SCIENCE														
Inquiry	X	X	X	X	X	X	X	X	X	X	X	X	X	X
Physical Science	X	X	X	X	X	X	X	X	X	X	X	X	X	X
Life Science												X	X	
Earth and Space Science												X		
Science and Technology	X						X			X	X			X
Personal and Social Perspectives		X	X					X			X	X		
History and Nature of Science				X							X			
MATHEMATICS														
Number and Operations		X						X	X		X	X		
Algebra		X						X	X		X	X		
Geometry	X	X	X		X	X	X							
Measurement	X												X	
Data Analysis and Probability		X						X	X	X	X			
Problem Solving		X	X	X	X	X					X		X	
Reasoning and Proof		X	X	X		X								
Communication		X	X									X		
Connections								X				X		
Representation		X				X			X		X	X		

CHAPTER 12

Light and Color

I Wanted to Play with the Sun

I didn't want the rain today.
I wanted to play with the Sun.
To chase my shadow across the lawn,
I was ready for the run.

I didn't want the rain today.
I wanted to play with the Sun.
But the skies grew dark and showers came.
That wasn't my idea of fun.

The wind played with the thunder.
Lightning announced the event.
Trees shook with laughter.
Waves clapped their content.

The Sun on the horizon entered the fray.
It wasn't willing to waste the day.
It touched the clouds with a silvery gray.
Flowers were spotlighted to a brightened bouquet.

The skies became bright.
With all colors that glow.
The Sun's rays ignited
A giant rainbow.

I didn't want the rain today.
I wanted to play with the Sun.
But the Sun and the rain made a spectacular display,
their gift for me and everyone.

J. David Keller

In our world the benefit of light and the ability to see are very important to us. Of our senses, vision is used more constantly than any other. Like all our senses, we tend to take vision for granted.

Vision is the detection of light. By understanding more about the nature of light, our students will have a greater appreciation of their vision. This appreciation will cause them to expand their visual observations.

One particular area of light that children enjoy exploring is color. The world that we see abounds with color. Children feel powerful when they can produce or manipulate colors by using filters and pigments. Studying color gives children opportunities to design their own experiments. They enjoy mixing different colors to discover what new colors will result.

SCIENCE CONCEPTS FOR TEACHERS

The science conceptual framework included here is designed to give you, as your children's teacher, information about light, and its properties. Its purpose is to give you background knowledge to assist you in your teaching. It is not intended as instructional material for the children, but instead to give you a framework to ensure that what you teach is indeed accurate and factual in nature. The greater your knowledge the more opportunities that you will recognize in the classroom for sharing your observations and ideas. Throughout your life, your knowledge will continue to grow. In addition, as scientists uncover new ideas and knowledge, we will all develop a better understanding of patterns of nature. These developments assist us in communicating ideas to our students.

Much of the physics of light and electromagnetic radiation is abstract and beyond the comprehension of young children. However, the activities given in the Concept Explorations later in this chapter will help children understand the basics of color and of vision. Before we explore those basic activities, however, you will benefit from the science conceptual framework discussed in the following sections.

What Is Light and How Is It Produced?

All matter has an internal property of energy. This energy is related to the electrons traveling in orbits around the nucleus of the atoms. As the electrons change orbital levels, energy is emitted or absorbed. For example, if we burn a sheet of paper, energy is given off, which we see as a flame. The matter in the filament of a light bulb emits light when it is excited by an electrical current.

The term that we use for emitting energy from matter is called *radiation*. Radiation is often referred to as *electromagnetic* radiation because the emitting energy has both electrical and magnetic properties.

The emitted energy is transmitted at a wavelength determined by the nature of the matter and the forces acting on it. The human eye can only detect a very small

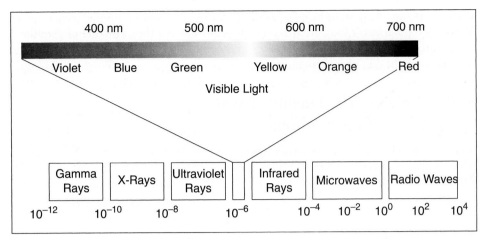

FIGURE 12.1   The electromagnetic spectrum.

range of wavelengths of radiation. What it detects we call *light*. Physicists often refer to it as *visible light*.

The electromagnetic spectrum, shown in Figure 12.1, includes the energy emitted at all wavelengths. This includes radio waves, microwaves, infrared rays, visible light, ultraviolet rays, X-rays, gamma rays, and other electromagnetic radiation of longer and shorter wavelengths.

Radio waves, which we use for AM, FM, TV, and shortwave radio, range in length from around 1 centimeter to a kilometer long. Some naturally occurring radio waves are much longer, actually thousands of kilometers long. At the opposite end of the spectrum are the gamma rays, which are radioactive and have a wavelength of less than a trillionth of a centimeter.

Note that the names given to various portions of the spectrum are arbitrary labels chosen by scientists for convenience. By setting up these artificial divisions, scientists can describe the specific nature of the waves they are examining. The various portions of the spectrum blend into one another. For example, a microwave and a radio wave at their point of contact would be identical (Chen, Kao, & Liu, 1999).

Electromagnetic radiation has three properties: wavelength, amplitude, and polarization. *Wavelength* is the length of the wave, which determines its properties. In visible light the wavelength determines the color. The *amplitude* of a wave determines the brightness of the light. *Polarization* is the angle at which the wave is vibrating.

Polarization

For us to appreciate the nature of polarization of light, we need to think in three dimensions rather than two dimensions as on a piece of paper. When we show waves on a sheet of paper, the wave is shown moving up and down. In reality, it can move at any angle from the paper. A polarized light filter such as that used on sunglasses or photographic cameras is designed to filter out the waves that are not parallel to the filter plane. This can reduce the glare off a body of water or other glaring objects. When two polarized filters are placed in front of one another, and one of the filters is rotated, that is, when the two filters become 90° apart, all of the light is filtered out and no light can pass through.

Light's Enigma: The Duality of Wave and Particle Theories of Light

Scientist have long debated whether light is a wave of energy or a particle of matter. That light demonstrates characteristics of both light and matter is accepted by most physicists. The particle characteristic of light is that particles called photons travel at the speed of light. Light is the only wave that can travel though a vacuum.

Visible Light

As previously mentioned, visible light is the small range of electromagnetic radiation that is detected by our eyes. The spectrum of visible light is further subdivided into various colors, with red having a longer wavelength and violet having a shorter wavelength. The colors are separated into the basic colors of red, orange, yellow, green, blue, and violet, ROY G. BV. Often a vowel is added to BV, making it BIV with the I standing for indigo. However, in recent years, the inclusion of indigo has been discontinued.

The Speed of Light

Visible light and all electromagnetic radiation travel at the same speed. This speed is measured by many different methods. The speed of light in a vacuum is normally rounded to 300,000 kilometers per second or 186,000 miles per second.

Light travels in a straight line. However, if it could curve around Earth, it could make more than seven trips in 1 second. Light can travel to our Moon in just over 1 second. It takes light from the Sun approximately 8 1/2 minutes to get to Earth.

Examining light from stars becomes an interesting process. Our nearest neighboring star is Proxima Centauri, which is visible in the Southern Hemisphere. Even though it is the nearest star, it takes the light from that star 4.3 years to get to Earth. Other objects in our sky, such as some distant galaxies, are so far away that it takes 13 billion years for the light to reach us. That means that we see that galaxy as it was 13 billion years ago.

The Normal Sighted Eye

The eye is an amazing organ that detects and positions light so that we can see. Our eyes collect light energy that travels through the lens of the eye and is detected by the retina (Figure 12.2). These responses are sent to the brain where they are decoded into vision.

The light receptors of the eye are of two types: cones and rods. *Cones* are specialized cells that not only detect light but also measure the wavelength so that the color of the light is recognized. Cones are concentrated at the fovea area of the retina. *Rods* detect

Cornea: The crystal clear dome that covers the front of the eye.

Lens: The crystalline lens focuses the light. It is able to change shape to allow focus on near objects. When it becomes cloudy it is called a cataract.

Iris: This is the part of the eye that gives it color (i.e., blue, green, brown).

Pupil: This is the opening in the middle of the iris. It expands and contracts to adjust for brightness. In a dark area, the pupil expands to collect more light.

Retina: This is a thin layer of nerve tissue that senses light. Specialized cells called rods and cones convert light energy into nerve signals that travel through the optic nerve to the brain. The retina is analogous to the film in a camera.

Fovea: This is the center of the retina that receives the focus of the object of regard. Nerve cells are more densely packed in this area, so images that are focused on the fovea can be seen in greater detail.

Optic nerve: This is the nerve that runs from the eyeball to the brain. It carries information from the retina to the brain for interpretation.

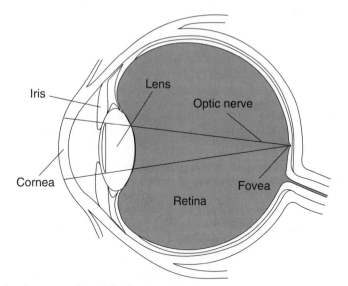

FIGURE 12.2   Cross section of the human eye.

light and are concerned with black and white vision. Because rods cover most of the retina, the objects that we see at the perimeter of our sight tend to be viewed as black and white. The objects viewed at the center of our vision tend to be more color vision.

For detecting dim objects, the rods are more critical because they do a better job of collecting light. It is interesting that observational astronomers watching stars in the nighttime sky tend to look at an object a few degrees away from the star they are viewing so that the rods come more into play than the cones. The object that they want to see will become much brighter than if they looked directly at the object.

Light and Color   217

Your eye has a blind spot at the location where the retina is attached to the optic nerve. At that point there are no rods or cones to receive light. Close your left eye and look at the circle with your right eye. Move the book in and out from your eye until the triangle disappears. You have found your blind spot. Using your left eye and closing your right, look at the triangle and the circle will disappear.

With both eyes open, we do not have the blind spots because our opposing eye sees the object at this location.

FIGURE 12.3   Find your blind spot.

Because all the photo receptor nerves of the eye collect at a central point, we each have a "blind spot" in each eye. Figure 12.3 will help you find your blind spot.

Primary Colors

The term *primary colors* can be confusing in that we often see the primary colors listed as red, blue, and yellow, and at other times as red, blue, and green. Some publications also identify magenta, yellow, and cyan as primary colors.

All primary coloring systems are based on how we detect colors with our eyes. The cones in the retina of the eye, the sensors that perceive color, are of three types. These cones are often referred to as L (long), M (medium), and S (short) wavelength cones. The L cones are sensitive to red light, the M cones are sensitive to green light, and the S cones are sensitive to blue light. The infinite colors that we perceive are formed when our brains combine all the data from the three types of cones. If we combine equal amounts of light at these L, M, and S wavelengths, we will perceive white light. Based on the physiology of the eye, the primary colors are red, blue, and green.

Additive Primary Colors

Devices that emit light energy, such as televisions and computer monitors, function with the three additive primary colors, red, blue, and green. By controlling the brightness of the red, green, and blue pixels, the different colors can be produced. Because the light being emitted is added together, these colors are said to be *additive* primary colors.

Subtractive Primary Colors

Printers and artists who work with pigments often refer to the primary colors being red, blue, and yellow because they can produce all colors of the spectrum by using red, blue, and yellow pigments. These are often referred to as the *subtractive* primary colors because they function on light being subtracted when it is absorbed by the paint.

Some printers prefer to use primary pigment colors of magenta, yellow, and cyan because they can produce better color reproductions with them. Basically all color production and pigment combinations are based on how we perceive color with the cones in the retina of our eye.

Absorption and Reflection of Light

When light strikes matter, the light can be absorbed by the matter or it can be reflected. Specific types of matter will absorb particular colors and reflect the remaining light. For instance, a leaf will absorb the red and blue parts of the spectrum and reflect the green. Since the green light is reflected, we see the leaf as being green. An object that absorbs all light will appear black. An object that reflects all colors will appear white.

Children exploring leaves at a light table.

If the object has a rough surface, the light is reflected in many directions as it is diffused. If the object is very smooth and does not absorb light, it will reflect all light without distorting it. We call these objects mirrors. If the mirror is flat, we see the object as it is. If the mirror is on a concave surface, such as the top of a spoon, we see the image enlarged. If we are too far from the mirror, the image will be inverted or upside-down. If the mirror is convex, as is the case for the bottom of a spoon or a garden reflector ball, the object appears smaller. Figure 12.4 illustrates reflection of light off of a mirror.

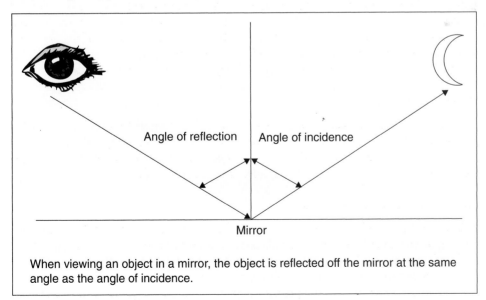

Angle of reflection   Angle of incidence

Mirror

When viewing an object in a mirror, the object is reflected off the mirror at the same angle as the angle of incidence.

FIGURE 12.4   Angle of reflection and angle of incidence.

Refraction

When light travels through a medium such as glass, the light is refracted. *Refraction* is the bending of light rays caused by the change of speed at which light is traveling (Figure 12.5). The denser the medium, the more that light is slowed down and the greater the light is refracted. A discussion of lenses and their application to refraction of light is presented in Chapter 7.

The wavelength of light is a factor in determining how much light is refracted. Red, with its long wavelength, is refracted less than violet. Thus, if white light is passed through a prism, the light will be separated out into a spectrum, or rainbow, with red being at the end that is least refracted and violet at the end that is most refracted.

The variations in the angle of refraction of different colors of light cause images to be distorted when viewed through lenses. For instance, when using an economical telescope with simple lenses, a star will not appear as a pinpoint of bright light, but as a small blur of different colors. Quality telescopes correct for this distortion by having compound lenses made of different types of glass with different densities. Each part of the compound lens refracts the light to counteract each other's distortion.

What Are Lasers and How Do They Work?

Laser is an acronym for "light amplification by stimulated emission of radiation." Basically, a laser is a devise that emits light at only one wavelength. By exciting the electrons of particular forms of matter, light of a specific wavelength is emitted. Thus,

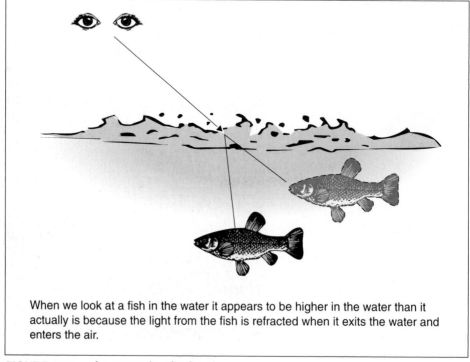

When we look at a fish in the water it appears to be higher in the water than it actually is because the light from the fish is refracted when it exits the water and enters the air.

FIGURE 12.5   An example of refraction.

laser light must be *monochromatic*, or emit only one color. Common lasers use rubies, garnets, neon, argon, carbon dioxide, and other materials. Each material results in a particular color of laser beam. For instance, a ruby emits red and argon emits green. Carbon dioxide lasers are in the far-infrared range. This area in the infrared is not visible, but it is extremely hot and can cut through steel by actually melting it.

Lasers are used in many applications. Supermarket scanners, laser printers, CD players, and smoke detectors are common examples. Lasers are also used extensively for accurate measurements and alignments. A laser beam is reflected off the Moon to measure changes in the distance between Earth and the Moon.

Most pocket laser pointers are produced with diodes and typically emit a red light. Green lasers are much more expensive but are very useful because their ray can be followed for several thousand feet. Green lasers are excellent pointers for viewing the stars.

MATHEMATICS: ADDRESSING THE NCTM STANDARDS THROUGH CONCEPT EXPLORATIONS

Color in nature and in our human-made world is amazing! Considering that there are only three primary colors, the multitude of colors that we see is incredible. Being able to mix all colors of the rainbow with just three basic colors is quite wonderful. How light and color affect our world makes for interesting and engaging Concept Explorations. Many mathematical ideas and concepts come into play as we explore light and color in our world.

Number and Operations

When children are exploring color, particularly with paint or food coloring, it is important to allow them to experiment with colors in free exploration before you help them devise experiments that are more "controlled." For example, children will see that red and blue will make purple when they are combined. At this point, posing "What if?" questions is helpful. For example, ask the children, "What if we used one drop of red and two drops of blue? Counting the drops is good practice for stable order and one-to-one correspondence. Similarly, counting out drops of one color of food coloring into a clear plastic glass of water helps children to see a gradation of color materialize from, for example, light green to very dark green.

Algebra

Sorting is the algebraic concept at play in Concept Exploration 12,

Children using palettes of color to capture their views of nature—inspiration—milkweed pods.

Technicolor World. As children describe colors in their world, they can sort them into categories. For example, they may say that they find color on plants, on clothing, on animals, in the sky, in books, and so forth. Sorting the many places that they see color helps them to think logically about classification.

Geometry

Exploring symmetry with one and two mirrors is fun. As children see the capital alphabet letters and how they are reflected, they are experiencing transformational geometry on the spot! Seeing transformational geometry in action helps children to develop skills and concepts in spatial visualization and geometric thinking.

Similarly, using mirrors to explore one's own face, we can see that our faces have a "line of symmetry." Children can look around their environment to see what else has a line of symmetry. Give each child a pipe cleaner with the ends rolled in for safety. Have them use it to delineate the middle of an object to see if one side looks just like the other side. You can then chart which objects have one or more lines of symmetry and which objects do not.

Measurement

Exploration with mixing colors calls for careful measurement skills. The children can measure paint by the teaspoon or by the drop. When mixing large amounts of paint, measuring cups can be used. Experience with tools of measurement is important for young children. As children explore mixing paint, they can record the "recipes" that make the various colors. Then as childern use the recipes, they gain experience measuring.

Data Analysis

As children explore mixing paint or food coloring, they can chart their results. For example one chart can show what happens when yellow paint and blue paint are combined in different quantities: one drop of blue and one drop of yellow; two drops of blue and one drop of yellow; three drops of blue and one drop of yellow: and so forth. Showing the resulting shades of blue colors on a chart can help children to see how to mix colors to get the desired hue.

Charting letters that have symmetry can also be done. As children see the letters and how they are reflected, they can generate categories such as "Mirror Image Looks the Same" or "Mirror Image Is Not the Same." Such a simple chart shows which letters have reflective symmetry and which do not—quite a wonderful firsthand experience with transformational geometry.

OBSERVING WITH ALL THE SENSES

Sight

Obviously, the nature of light dictates that this chapter's Concept Explorations concentrate on visual observing. Observing the characteristics of light and color provides children with many opportunities to expand their awareness of just how critical a tool vision is for learning.

Sound

Electronic light devices, such as often used in discos, can be used to convert sound to light. These devices can become valuable tools for the classroom. They can help children visualize different intensities of sound.

SAFETY

Safety should be a constant concern when working with light. Particular sources of light can cause permanent damage to the eye. Safe use of lasers must be a consideration. Lasers are classified based on their potential for biological damage. Economical laser pointers are considered hazardous only if a person tries to directly view the light beam. Other sources of bright lights should be monitored. No person should ever look directly at the Sun.

CONCEPT EXPLORATIONS ON LIGHT AND COLOR FOR YOUR CLASSROOM

These Concept Explorations direct children's interests toward the nature of light and colors. Through these experiences, several basic science processes and math concepts can be defined and developed.

As you reflect on the development and background of your students, you can select and plan specific activities from the explorations presented. Obviously, many more activities are presented here than should be delivered to you class. Be selective! Choose the activities that best fit the development and interest of your students. Alter and expand specific activities to fit your specific needs. Encourage your students to ask their own questions and to explore and expand their experiences.

As in all learning processes, your aspiration as teacher is to encourage your children to ask their own questions and to have them take part in choosing the direction and nature of the exploration. Their participation in these processes helps them feel they have ownership in their learning, and contributes to their development of basic learning skills and positive attitudes about learning. These processes also become valuable to you as a teacher in assessing the children's' background and knowledge.

You may want to read some information about light and color before you begin your explorations with the children. A good resource is the *Eyewitness Book: Light*, written by Davis Burnie in association with the Science Museum in London. This book covers basic concepts about light and how scientists study light and its effects on life.

As each exploration is completed, a summation of the knowledge, attitudes, and learning processes gained by examining the questions identified can serve as a valuable tool for assessing the development that has taken place. Such evaluations are the real basis for authentic assessment because they were developed from authentic learning experiences.

1. Pinhole Projects

Light travels in a straight line. Using this property of light, we can make a simple pinhole camera for children to see the effect of light traveling in a straight line. Take a box

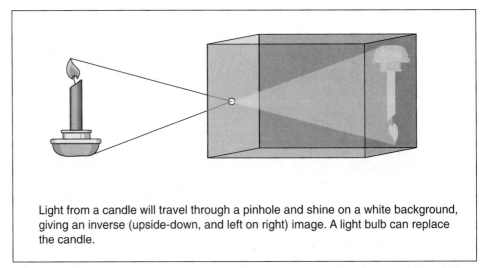

Light from a candle will travel through a pinhole and shine on a white background, giving an inverse (upside-down, and left on right) image. A light bulb can replace the candle.

FIGURE 12.6   A simple pinhole camera can demonstrate that light travels in a straight line.

and paste a sheet of white paper on the far inside wall. One the side opposite the white paper cut a small opening and tape some aluminum foil to cover the hole. Cut an opening on a side of the box so that you can open it and view the paper inside. Using a sharp point of a pencil or paper clip, make a small hole in the aluminum foil. Be careful when using sharp, pointed objects with young children. Darken the room so that light from a candle will be the only light source. View the image of the candle by looking at the white paper screen through the opening on the side of the box (Figure 12.6).

2. Mirrors

Small handheld mirrors are excellent tools for exploring the nature of light. Children enjoy manipulating the mirrors to view objects. For safety, use only plastic mirrors and be sure that the children do not reflect bright light into their eyes. Have your students print the capital letters of the alphabet on a sheet of paper. Place the mirror to the side of the letters and look at the letters through the mirror. Which letters still appear correct? Which letters now appear to be reversed? This reversal is called a *mirror image*. Have your children identify which letters they can still observe correctly in the mirror. Use only those letters to construct special messages.

Your children can also place the mirror above the letter instead of to the side. This will give a whole new set of letters. For example, when placed above the letter, now the A is upside down and the D appears to have not changed. Note that we are actually viewing all letters in their mirror image. However, some of the letters are symmetrical left and right and others, are symmetrical top and bottom. Charting these types of reflections can call attention to the different types of symmetry for each letter. Calling attention to how the letter is viewed in the reflection strengthens children's attention to careful observation and analysis. Discussion about line of symmetry can be done with the letters and their reflections.

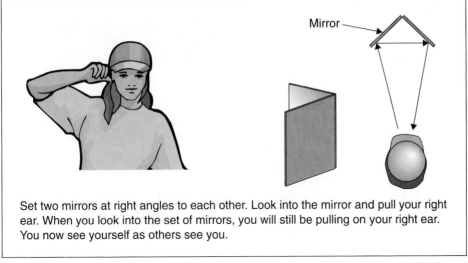

Set two mirrors at right angles to each other. Look into the mirror and pull your right ear. When you look into the set of mirrors, you will still be pulling on your right ear. You now see yourself as others see you.

FIGURE 12.7 Seeing yourself as others see you.

3. Seeing Yourself as Others See You

When we look into a mirror, our image is said to be a mirror image. For example, if we hold an object in our right hand, when we look in the mirror the person in the mirror will be holding the object in their left hand. We can see ourselves as others see us by taping two mirrors together so that they are at right angles to each other, as illustrated in Figure 12.7.

4. The Candle Burning Under Water

Place a glass of water behind a piece of glass. In front of the glass place a burning candle (Figure 12.8). Make sure that the children stay at a safe distance from the flame. Rules about not touching the candle should be given. In front of the candle, place a card so that the children cannot see the candle. When you look at the glass plate you will see the glass of water with the reflection of the candle burning in the glass of water.

5. Up Periscope

Children can make a simple periscope like that shown in Figure 12.9 with two mirrors and a mailing tube. Cut both ends of the tube at 45-degree angles. These cuts should be parallel to each other. Cut an opening at the long side of each end of the *tube*. These openings will be so that you can look into the tube at the mirror. Tape two mirrors on the ends of the tube on the 45-degree cut. When you look through the opening at one end you will see what is visualized from the other end of the tube.

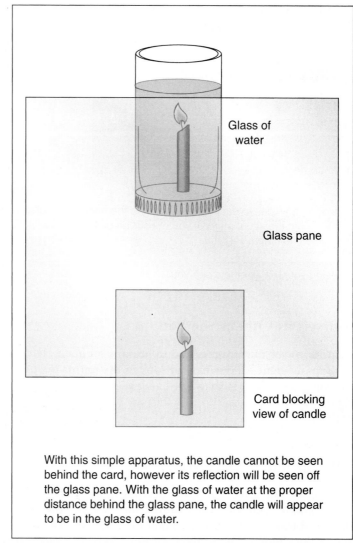

Glass of water

Glass pane

Card blocking view of candle

With this simple apparatus, the candle cannot be seen behind the card, however its reflection will be seen off the glass pane. With the glass of water at the proper distance behind the glass pane, the candle will appear to be in the glass of water.

FIGURE 12.8 How to make a candle appear inside a glass of water.

An improvement can be made by using two mailing tubes that slide over each other. This allows the children to raise and lower their periscope. In addition, the top tube can spin around so that they can see what is behind them or to the side.

6. Doubling Your Fish

Light changes speed when it travels from one medium into another medium. For instance, if light travels from air into water it slows down. This causes the light to be refracted or bent. When you look into a rectangular aquarium, the light is refracted so that objects appear to be in a different location than reality. By looking at the aquarium from a corner, you can actually see the same fish at two locations (Figure 12.10).

7. Reflections of a Laser Pointer

Economical laser pointers are valuable devices for helping children visualize basic properties of light rays. Children can reflect the rays off mirrors and alter the angles to see how the angles of incidence and reflection change. Green laser pointers are becoming more popular than red ones because the green light ray is easier to see as it travels through the air than the red one. Unfortunately, green pointers are much more expensive than red pointers.

The small laser pointers are basically safe for common use. However, care should be given to ensure that children do not point the lasers directly into their eyes. Careful monitoring of this rule is required and it must be strictly enforced.

8. Magic Marker Magic

Magic Markers (water soluble felt-tip marker) can be used in combination to create different colors. For instance, when you make an X using a blue marker for one of the lines and a yellow marker for the other line, the color where the lines cross will be green. Invite children to explore how combining the colors from the markers can make new colors.

Children can make simple color charts using water soluble magic markers. At every position where two markers cross, the color formed from the addition of the two colors will be produced (Figure 12.11).

Children can make a basic chart by producing a grid of the different colors. Make a series of vertical and horizontal lines from the basic colors. Where each combination crosses, examine the color that is produced. Children can use their grid to select color combinations for their art projects.

9. Combining Colors

Children can combine colors using common materials. Give opportunities to your children to make new colors by combining food coloring and basic art supplies. Color packs of Play-Doh are excellent for creating colors by combining the different colors in various proportions. You might challenge children to make a particular color by using the primary colors.

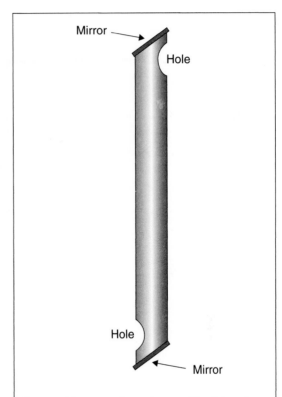

By attaching two mirrors to a mailing tube at 45 degree angles, and cutting holes for viewing we can make a simple periscope.

FIGURE 12.9 Cross section of a periscope.

FIGURE 12.10
Doubling your fish.

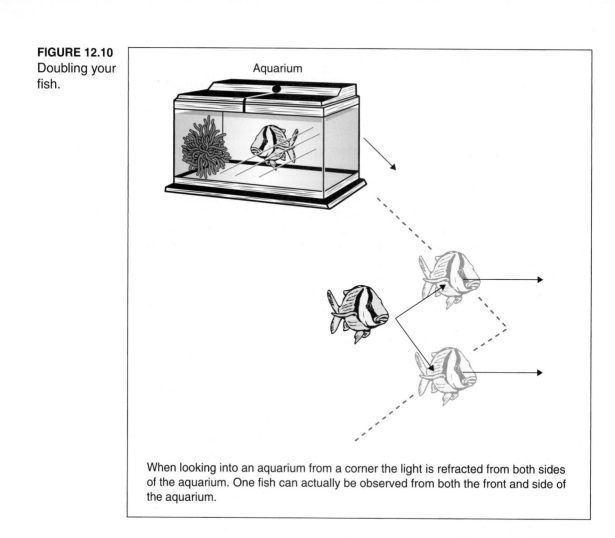

When looking into an aquarium from a corner the light is refracted from both sides of the aquarium. One fish can actually be observed from both the front and side of the aquarium.

FIGURE 12.11 Making a simple chart to show the results of combining different colors.

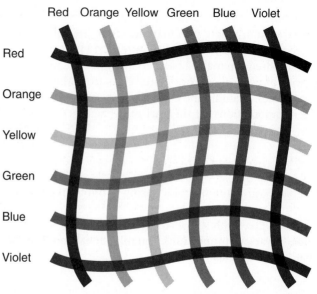

10. Color Television Basic Colors

Televisions and computer monitors produce colors from small pixels of red, blue, and green light. These pixels can be safely examined by using a 10-power jeweler's lens. When the lens is held close to the television or monitor, you can see a combination of the red, green, and blue pixels. The variations in the brightness of the pixels produce the different colors.

11. Paper Chromatography

If you touch the edge of a coffee filter (paper towels can also be used) to the surface of a glass of water, the water is absorbed up the towel by capillary action. This physical property can be used to separate the different pigments in water-soluble paint or coloring materials.

Mark a dot from a black water-soluble felt-tip pen on the paper towel about an inch from the edge. Touch the edge of the paper towel to some water in a small glass. Keep the paper towel in the water long enough that the water is absorbed up the paper towel. The pigment will be drawn up the paper towel along with the water. Black felt-tip pens are actually produced by mixing different pigments together. As the pigments are pulled up the paper towel, the individual colors will be separated, identifying the given bands of color. Children can compare different brands of black felt-tip pens and identify the different pigments used to produce the pens. After experimenting with black pens, suggest to your children that they experiment with all colors to see how different colors are produced. In fact, they can use paper chromatography to create beautiful butterflies, as described in Figure 12.12.

It is not necessary for children to understand the principles behind why the pigments are separated out. How much you try to explain to your students should be determined by their age and development. Because the cause of the separation is determined at the molecular level, the reasoning required is abstract and difficult for young children to comprehend.

The reason that the pigments are separated is determined by their molecular weight. Light molecules are pulled up with the water more easily than heavy ones. Thus, they reach higher levels on the paper towel.

12. Technicolor World

Color is a very important part of nature. Take your children out for nature walks and encourage them to observe the different natural colors they see. Your class can document the evidence of colors in nature. For instance, they can examine how animal colors are used for attracting mates and for camouflage from predators. Children can document their evidence through videotapes, photographs, drawings, or other methods. They might indicate the time of the events and the environmental conditions. Encourage your children to describe the colors they captured with three different adjectives. Relate the adjectives to the events and processes taking place. Good examples include *bright* and *soft*, *pastel* and *bold*, *light* and *dark*. Colors can set our moods and decorate our world.

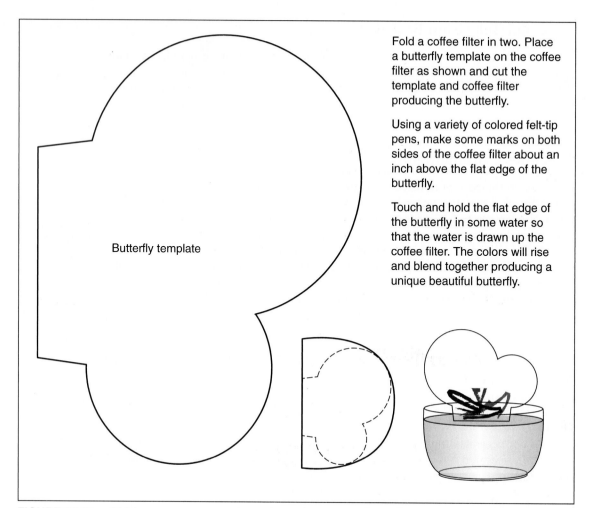

Fold a coffee filter in two. Place a butterfly template on the coffee filter as shown and cut the template and coffee filter producing the butterfly.

Using a variety of colored felt-tip pens, make some marks on both sides of the coffee filter about an inch above the flat edge of the butterfly.

Touch and hold the flat edge of the butterfly in some water so that the water is drawn up the coffee filter. The colors will rise and blend together producing a unique beautiful butterfly.

Butterfly template

FIGURE 12.12   Children can use paper chromatography to create butterflies.

Invite your class to make presentations on their findings to other classes or parent involvement events.

13. Grow Plants with a Green Filter

Plants are green because their green chlorophyll absorbs light from the blue-violet and red regions of the visible spectrum but reflects green light. This is why plants that contain much chlorophyll appear green.

If a green color filter is used, only the green light is transmitted through the filter. The light from the blue-violet and the red regions is blocked from passing through the filter to the plant. These colors are the ones absorbed by plants and used in the process of photosynthesis. Thus, if green filters are used, plants cannot survive. Children can conduct a basic experiment by growing plants in terrariums made from a two-liter beverage bottle. Place two identical plants in two terrariums. The first terrarium should be made from a clear bottle. The second should be made from a green-tinted bottle. Exercise care when working with glass. Observe the plants for a period of time and compare their growth.

14. Visualizing Sound with Light

Several electronic devices are available that convert sound waves to light. Some electronic toys include microphones and lights that flash when sound is produced.

Figure 12.13 explains how to make a simple device using a basic laser that helps children visualize sound waves. Encourage children to make different sounds at varying pitches and examine how the sounds affect the light that is produced.

Activities in Other Explorations That Relate to Light and Color

Clouds (Chapter 9)
4. How High Is a Cloud?

Leaves (Chapter 11)
10. A Rainbow Collection of Leaves

Rocks (Chapter 13)
5. Rainbow Rocks

Sun and Shadows (Chapter 15)
1. Here Comes the Sun
4. Silhouettes

Resources for Teachers

Books

Asimov, I. (1985). *Understanding physics: Light magnetism and electricity.* New York: New American Library.

Burnie, D. (1992). *Eyewitness book: Light.* New York: Dorling Kindersley Publishing.

Walden, G. (2002). *Introduction to light: The physics of light, vision and color.* Minneola, NY: Dover Publishing.

A particularly effective device that shows actual sound waves can be constructed with a cheap laser pointer, a fruit can with both ends cut off, a metal strip, a balloon, and a small chip from a mirror.

Slit open a balloon and wrap it around one end of the can using a rubber band to keep it in place. Using rubber cement, glue a 1/2-inch-square mirror to the center of the balloon. Fasten a bent metal strip to the side of a fruit can. Tape a laser pointer to the strip so that the light from the pointer strikes the mirror.

When you talk into the open end of the can with the laser pointer on, you will be able to see the sound waves produced on the far wall.

FIGURE 12.13   Children can visualize sound waves with a simple laser device.

Web Sites

http://www.bgsm.edu/eye/cornea/normall.htm
Web site of Wake Forest University Eye Center.

http://casa.colorado.edu/~ajsh/colour/primary.html
Excellent discussion of primary colors.

http://www.colorado.edu/physics/2000/applets/polarized.html
An example of the effect of a polarized filter.

http://education.jlab.org/qa/laser_01.html
Information on the basics of lasers.

http://galileoandeinstein.physics.virginia.edu/lectures/spedlite.html
An excellent history on measurement of the speed of light.

http://imagine.gsfc.nasa.gov/docs/science/know_11/emspectrum.html
A brief description of the electromagnetic spectrum.

http://kosmoi.com/Science/Physics/Light/
Basic properties of light.

http://www.nei.nih.gov/index.htm
Web site of the National Eye Institute.

http://www.thespectroscopynet.com/Educational/wave_particle_duality.htm
Discussion of the wave and particle theories of light.

Children's Books

Ardley, N. (1991). *The science book of color*. San Diego: Harcourt Brace Jovanovich.
Baber, A. (1994). *White rabbit's color book*. New York : Kingfisher Books.
Baxter, N. (1996). *Amazing colors*. Chicago: Children's Press.
Baxter, N. (1996). *Living with light*. Chicago: Children's Press.
Bennet, C., & Romig, J. (1994). *Kaleidoscopes*. New York: Workman Publishing.
Bryant-Mole, K. (1996). *Yellow*. Parsippany, NJ: Silver Press-a division of Simon & Schuster.
Bryant-Mole, K. (1997). *Green*. Parsippany, NJ: Silver Press-a division of Simon & Schuster.
Cabrera, J. (1997). *Cat's colors*. New York: Dials Books.
Carroll, C. (1996). *How artists see the weather*. New York: Abbeville Publishing Group.
Chocolate, D. (1996). *Kente colors*. New York: Walker & Company.
Crews, D. (1978). *Freight train*. New York: Greenwillow Books.
Dena, A. (1997). *Colors*. Milwaukee, WI: Garreth Stevens Publishing.
Ehlert, L. (1988). *Planting a rainbow*. San Diego: Harcourt Brace & Company.
Ehlert, L. (1990). *Color farm*. New York: HarperCollins.
Ehlert, L. (1991). *Red leaf, yellow leaf*. San Diego: Harcourt Brace Jovanovich.
Emberly, E. (1992). *The big green monster*. Boston, MA: *Little Brown & Company*.
Freeman, D. (1966). *A rainbow of my own*. New York: Viking Penguin.
Hoban, T. (1998). *Of colors and things*. New York: Greenwillow Books.
Hoban, T. (1994). *Colors everywhere*. New York: Greenwillow Books.
Inkpen, M. (1994). *Kipper's book of colors*. San Diego: Harcourt Brace & Company.
Jeunesse, G., Verdet, J., & Houbre, G. (1992). *Light*. New York: Cartwheel Books, Scholastic.
Kalman, B. (1993). *The colors of nature*. New York: Crabtree Publishing Company.
Lauber, P. (1994). *What do you see & how do you see it?* New York: Crown Publishers.
Lionni, L. (1959). *Little blue and little yellow*. New York: Scholastic.
Lionni, L. (1975). *A color of his own*. New York: Scholastic.
Lionni, L. (1985). *Frederick's fables*. New York: Alfred A. Knopf.

Mara, W. (2007). *Why is the sky blue?* New York: Marshall Cavendish.

Martin, B. Jr. (1997). *Brown bear, brown bear, what do you see?* New York: Henry Holt & Co.

McMillan, B. (1988). *Growing colors*. New York: Lothrop, Lee & Shepard.

Milich, Z. (2005). *City 1 2 3*. Toronto, ON: Kids Can Press.

Murphy, C. (1997). *Colors surprises, a pop-up book*. New York: Simon & Schuster.

Rikys, B. (1992). *Red bear*. New York: Dial Books.

Rotner, S., & Woodhull, A. L. (2007). *Every season*. New Milford, CT: Roaring Brook Press.

Rozines, R., & Roy, G. (2006). *Math all around–Patterns in nature*. New York: Marshall Cavendish Benchmark.

Rozines, R., & Roy, G. (2007). *Math all around–Measuring at home*. New York: Marshall Cavendish Benchmark.

Schroeder, P. J. (1996). *What's the big idea? Colors*. Vero Beach, FL: Rourke Publications.

Serfozo, M. (1988). *Who said red?* New York: M.K. McElderry Books.

Seuss, Dr. (1996). *My many colored days*. New York: Scholastic.

Stille, D. R. (2006). *Manipulating light reflection, refraction and absorbtion*. Minneapolis, MN: Compass Point Books.

Taylor, B. (1992). *Over the rainbow*. New York: Random House.

Vischer, P. (1997). *Junior's colors*. Nashville, TN: Tommy Nelson.

Walsh, E. S. (1989). *Mouse paint*. San Diego: Harcourt Brace Jovanovich.

Westray, K. (1993). *A color sampler*. New York: Ticknor & Fields.

Woodford, C. (2005). *Height*. Farmington Hills, MI: Blackbirch Press.

Yenawine, P. (1991). *Colors*. New York: The Museum of Modern Art. Delacorte Press.

Correlation of NSES Standards and NCTM Principles and Standards to Rocks Concept Exploration Activities

	1. Rocks Waiting to Be Found	2. Swap Rocks with Students in Other Schools	3. My Life Story by Rocky	4. Building Stones	5. Rainbow Rocks	6. Stream Sorting	7. Statues, Jewels, and Trinkets	8. Rocks—Pieces and Parts	9. Fossils	10. Graveyard Geology
SCIENCE										
Inquiry	X	X	X	X	X	X	X	X	X	X
Physical Science	X			X	X	X	X	X	X	X
Life Science						X			X	
Earth and Space Science	X	X	X	X	X	X	X	X	X	X
Science and Technology				X			X			X
Personal and Social Perspectives	X	X	X	X	X	X	X	X	X	X
History and Nature of Science			X	X					X	X
MATHEMATICS										
Number and Operations					X	X	X	X	X	X
Algebra	X		X		X	X	X	X	X	X
Geometry	X	X	X							
Measurement	X	X				X				X
Data Analysis and Probability	X			X	X	X		X	X	X
Problem Solving	X					X		X	X	
Reasoning and Proof			X							
Communication	X	X		X						
Connections	X	X								
Representation			X		X					

CHAPTER 13

Rocks

Rock in My Pocket

I have a rock in my pocket.
It brings me luck each day.
I will never lose it.
It helps me when I play.

I found this rock in the woods,
Or was it on the beach?
Oh, it's from the stream.
It was in easy reach.

Or was it from my garden?
Or was it by my tree?
Perhaps, on a hike I found it,
Or given by a friend to me?

My rock I will always treasure
from now to evermore.
I wonder how these other rocks
got on my bedroom floor?

J. David Keller

Rocks are curious things. They come in all sizes. Some are extremely small, for example, grains of sand. Others are as big as a mountain. They come in all shapes too. Some are triangular; some are spherical. Rocks have different exteriors. Some are polished smooth by wind and water. Others are jagged and can be as sharp as a knife. They come in all colors from clear as glass to obsidian black. Just about anywhere we are, there are rocks. They are the building blocks of the Earth. They are an important part of our lives.

As children spend time outdoors, they are drawn to the wonder and beauty of our natural environment. If we think back to our own childhoods and also to the time we

Ayers Rock is officially known as Uluru in honor of the Aboriginals. The rock is undoubtedly one of the most famous Australian icons. The red sandstone rock rises some 1,400 feet from the desert floor and is over 5.5 miles around at its perimeter. The rock is considered sacred and spiritually significant to the Aboriginals. The red-colored sandstone takes on various hues depending on the position of the sun.

Matthew LaRusso

spend outdoors as adults, we can remember and think about what we are drawn to. We like to feel the wind and sunshine; we like to explore the path or beach or trail as we walk along. During these excursions in the great outdoors, we will, no doubt, see rocks and minerals. How many of us have found a lucky stone or beautiful rock that we just had to bring home? How many of us have amassed our own rock collections? Sometimes, when we look at a rock that we collected a long time ago, we can easily be transported back in time and enjoy a wonderful memory.

Rocks and minerals are abundant and intriguing to all. Each rock we find has properties that make it unique, yet at the same time, it has characteristics that it shares with others. We can embrace this natural affinity for rocks as we observe, explore, and investigate the many curiosities we have about them. Allowing children to experience their world and embrace the wonders it holds is an essential part of science.

SCIENCE CONCEPTS FOR TEACHERS

The concepts and information presented here should only be presented to the children at an introductory level. For example, while your class is walking along a stream, you might point out that the rock material is being abraded and deposited in the water, and that years from now, it could be cemented into sandstone. However, it would not be appropriate to spend an inordinate amount of time trying to explain the entire rock cycle. Introductory ideas contribute to children's developing theories about rocks and the rock cycle that will be fleshed out with details in later years.

Don't Take All Rocks for Granite—What Are Minerals and Rocks?

Often, we combine discussions of rocks and minerals and just use the term *rocks*. Geologists, however, separate minerals from rocks by examining their composition.

Minerals

A commonly accepted definition of a mineral is *a naturally occurring, inorganic, homogeneous solid with a definite chemical composition and an ordered atomic arrangement.* This definition tells us that a mineral has consistent properties throughout. It will have a uniform composition and texture. Examples of minerals include diamonds, quartz, gold, agate, and topaz. Many of the common natural materials that we use each day are actually minerals. When reviewing the definition, we realize that ice actually meets all the criteria for being a mineral.

Each mineral has specific elements formed in a specific ratio and geometric crystalline structure. These properties determine the mineral's characteristics such as color, shape, and hardness.

Some common minerals.

Mineral hardness is a comparison of the scratchability of each mineral. If one mineral is rubbed against a second, the mineral that has a higher hardness level will scratch the other mineral. A standard scale of mineral hardness, the Mohs scale, shown in Figure 13.1, is used by geologists to make comparisons of the different minerals. The diamond is the hardest mineral that occurs in nature.

Rocks

A commonly accepted definition of a rock is *a naturally occurring matter variously composed, formed in masses or large quantities of minerals in the earth's crust by the action of heat, pressure, water, and so forth.*

Rocks are aggregates of minerals. Minerals are to rocks as letters are to words. For example, granite is a rock that is made from the minerals quartz, feldspar, mica, and/or hornblende.

The Rock Cycle

The rock cycle gives a succinct overview of the processes that create, modify, and destroy rocks. Rocks are commonly divided into three groups, as shown in Figure 13.2:

The Mohs Hardness Scale	
Hardness	**Mineral**
1.	Talc
2.	Gypsum
3.	Calcite
4.	Fluorite
5.	Apatite
6.	Orthoclase
7.	Quartz
8.	Topaz
9.	Corundum
10.	Diamond

FIGURE 13.1 Fredrich Mohs developed the hardness scale in 1812. The scale does not infer that there is an equal difference in hardness between each number; for example, a diamond is 1,600 times as hard as talc, not 10 times as hard.

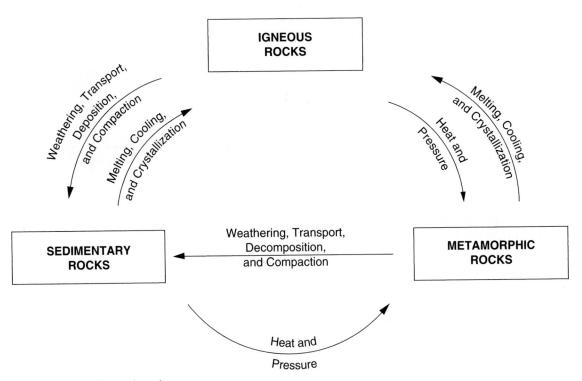

FIGURE 13.2 The rock cycle.

igneous, metamorphic, and sedimentary. These rocks can be altered and re-formed from one type to another by the natural processes occurring on and in the earth. These processes include heat, pressure, weathering, and deposition.

Igneous Rocks

Igneous rocks are formed under the surface of the Earth by extreme heat. For rock materials to melt, they must be heated to a range of 800 to 1,400 degrees Celsius (around 1,450 to 2,550 degrees Fahrenheit). This occurs deep within the Earth and at locations where two tectonic plates are colliding.

As heat is dissipated, or dispersed to the environment surrounding it, the molten rock material, called *magma*, cools and the minerals crystallize out. Different minerals crystallize at different temperatures, which sometimes causes a natural sorting of minerals into concentrated areas.

The rate at which the heat is dissipated determines the size of the mineral crystals that will eventually form rocks. The more quickly the heat is dissipated, the smaller the crystals that are formed. At times the magma cools so rapidly that the rock formed has the characteristics of glass. When magma is ejected from a volcano, the heat is dissipated very quickly and the crystals are extremely small. Thus, the basalt or rhyolite rock from a volcano has a very fine texture. The same magma, if cooled slowly over many years, would form gabbro or granite. Gabbro and granite have large mineral crystals that are easily visible to the eye without magnification.

Metamorphic Rocks

Metamorphic rocks are formed from extensive heat and/or pressure, but not to the extent that the rock material melts. Metamorphism can occur at or close to the Earth's surface in a process called *contact metamorphism*. For example, when lava from a volcano is injected into cracks in rocks, or when it travels down a slope, the rocks contacted by the lava can be altered.

Regional metamorphism is much more common. Regional metamorphism usually occurs many kilometers below the surface of the earth. For every kilometer below the surface of the earth, the temperature increases between 20 and 30 degrees Celsius. This heat and pressure is caused by a combination of the weight and pressure of the rocks above and by natural radioactive decay.

The extensive heat and pressure cause rock material to be altered. The alterations can take different forms based on the nature of the material and the processes. The crystals of particular minerals can be re-formed. For example, quartz sandstone can be metamorphosed into quartzite, a rock in which the quartz crystals are fused together. Other metamorphic rocks such as gneiss and schist have distinct banding or layering caused by the oblong crystals being lined up in a parallel orientation because of the great pressure exerted on them.

Marble is metamorphosed limestone. Limestone is formed from the compaction and cementation of millions of marine organisms. Typically, one can see many fossils of coral and animals with shells in limestone. Through metamorphic processes, the fossils are totally altered and recrystallized. Thus, marble has no fossils.

The depth at which the metamorphic rocks are formed is a determining factor in the type of metamorphic rock produced. As the depth and pressure increases, the rock material is altered to a greater degree, as shown in Figure 13.3. Thus, slate is metamorphosed less than phyllite, phyllite is metamorphosed less than schist, and gneiss is metamorphosed to the greatest extent.

Some geologists debate whether granite should be considered a well-metamorphosed rock or an igneous rock. They debate whether, during its formation, it actually became a fluid molten magma or just underwent incomplete recrystallization.

Sedimentary Rocks

Sedimentary rocks are formed by weathering, deposition, precipitation, and/or organic processes. The most common types of sedimentary rocks are formed by deposition. Over millions of years, rock materials are weathered and abraded, or ground, into small particles. These particles are transported by water, ice, or wind.

Sedimentary rocks formed by deposition are classified into categories based on the size of the particle deposited. Whatever the composition of the rock material, after it is deposited it is compacted by the weight of sediment above it. Water percolates through the material, and over a period of time chemicals are dissolved, transported, and reprecipitated between the rock particles, cementing the particles into a solid rock. Figure 13.4 lists some particle component sizes and the resulting sedimentary rocks.

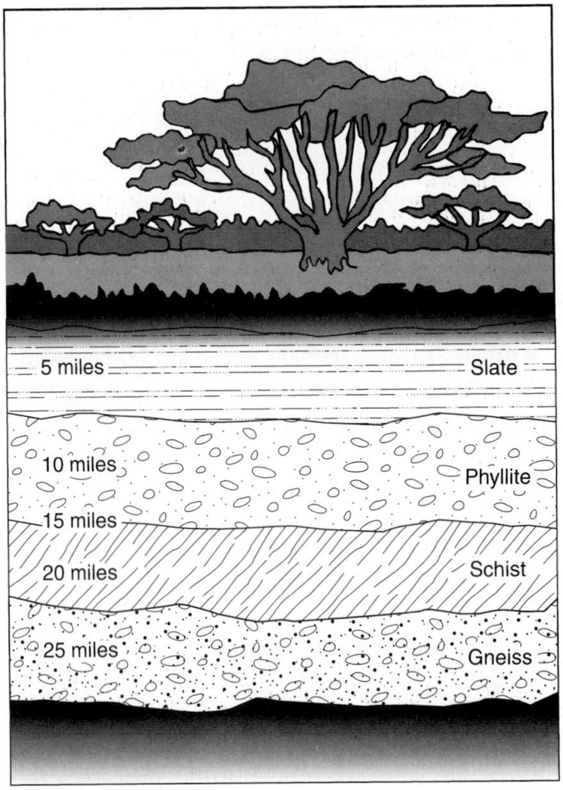

FIGURE 13.3 The depth at which metamorphic rocks are formed determines the type of rock produced.

Rock Components	Consolidated Rockate
Clay	Shale
Silt	Siltstone
Sand	Sandstone
Pebbles and rocks	Conglomerate
Organic material, plant fragments	Coal
Animal shells	Limestone

FIGURE 13.4 Some common rock components and the resulting sedimentary rocks.

Sedimentary rocks can also be formed by chemical solutions and precipitation processes. For example, chemically precipitated limestone can be formed in warm seas, hot springs, and saline lakes. The hot water is rich in calcium carbonate. As the water slowly cools and evaporates, the calcium carbonate precipitates out in a crystalline form. The resulting rock that is formed often will have irregular voids and color differentiations from being stained by chemical impurities. This limestone is often called *travertine*.

Bedrock containing sedimentary rocks is easy to identify because it has obvious layering. Bedrock containing igneous and metamorphic rocks tends to appear more massive without laminar, or layered, surfaces.

In regions that have had glacial activity, one can typically find a wide variety of rocks, making them excellent sites for collecting. Over long periods of time, glaciers tend to move great distances. As they travel, glaciers pick up rock debris and transport it as part of the glacier. As the glacier melts, these rocks are deposited in a random fashion. Much of the northern United States was glaciated.

The region in which you live determines the nature of the types of rocks that are found in your vicinity. Mountainous areas tend to be rich in igneous rocks. The plains tend to have sedimentary rocks.

MATHEMATICS: ADDRESSING THE NCTM STANDARDS THROUGH CONCEPT EXPLORATIONS

Many mathematical ideas are utilized when children study rocks, beginning with basic observation, organization, and classification of collected rocks and minerals, to counting and seriating them according to specific criteria such as amount, size, color, texture, or mass. Children can view the patterns on rocks and minerals and also begin to have an awareness of the sequence of the rock cycle.

Number and Operations

As children gather and collect rocks and minerals, they can classify them into categories of their choosing. Counting the number of rocks in each category will yield a frequency count. Rational counting in this activity gives children practice with the stable order principle of counting as well as one-to-one correspondence.

Algebra

As children become "backyard geologists" and find an exciting variety of rocks and minerals, they should be given opportunities to describe and classify them according to many attributes. As children begin to collect and examine these rocks and minerals, they are naturally engaging in algebraic thinking when they sort and classify them by many properties. Encouraging children to sort and re-sort a collection strengthens their ability to think logically and apply reasoning to new classification schemes.

Geometry

When children discover the wonderful variety of rocks and minerals that can be found in their own backyards, they can begin to describe their shapes in their own words. The language of geometry can help children expand their mathematical vocabulary. For example, if a rock is very round, they may say it is "round" or "spherical." Helping children with accurate mathematical terms is important. Some rocks may be "triangular" in shape or have "straight" edges, whereas others may be "oval" in shape and have "curved" edges. Looking to see if there is any symmetry in the rocks can heighten awareness of looking for patterns in the rocks. Interesting designs can be replicated using a variety of

Many minerals *cleave* (break) along planes forming geometric shapes. Halite cleaves into cubes.

media such as clay, salt dough, watercolor, sketching, or coloring with crayons. Mixing paint to mimic the colors the children see in nature is a wonderful experience with fractions and ratios as colors are tweaked by adding drops of pigment to a color.

During this time of exploration and observation children can also develop and use terms for location to explain where they found their rocks. Some rocks may be found "north" of school, whereas others may be found "in front of" their house or under a bush. Recording this kind of information supports children's development of important geometric ideas for location and navigation.

Measurement

In addition to the richness that can be gained by describing the physical characteristics of the rocks and minerals, another useful way to describe them is by size. Measurements of each rock can be taken; they can be weighed and seriated according to their weight. They can also be seriated according to their texture, ranging from very smooth to very rough. Interesting notions can be made about density as children see that some smaller rocks can weigh more than some larger rocks, depending on their density.

Data Analysis

Rock collections provide wonderful opportunities for sorting and for constructing charts and graphs of all types. After a collection of rocks has been sorted by the children's chosen categories, they can be arranged on a graphing mat. A graphing mat is a large grid made on chart paper, a window shade, or a shower curtain. The grid should be constructed large enough to fit the items being graphed.

Using a graphing mat, the children place one rock in each "box" so that comparisons of the number of rocks are accurate. A graphing mat can easily be made with a window shade or a shower curtain liner and masking tape of a bright color. The masking tape is used to make the horizontal and vertical lines on the grid. Visual comparisons are easy for children to make. You can count the boxes to attach a cardinal property to each set of rocks. Making comparisons by using the concepts of *more* and *less* are easy to do with a graphing mat. Questions such as "How many more?" or "How much more?" encourage the process of counting-on to solve problems. Using the language of comparison and seriation is a natural way for children to describe data. For example, seeing the "most", the "least", and the same in a collection and all the sequencing in between is a good way for young children to organize data according to numbers.

Another interesting way to display the different rocks is with a "living" people circle graph. After the children decide how to classify the rocks, each child holds his or her own rock. Children group themselves together according to the agreed-on classification schemes. For example, all of the children who have sedimentary rocks stand together. Then they line up and join the other groups, such as the igneous and metamorphic rock groups, forming a circle. To separate the different groups, stretch some yarn between the groups to the center of the circle. The visual display of how the circle is segmented tells the children which group has the most rocks. The language of fractions or percents can be used as appropriate.

The same data can be displayed in a "living" people graph. In this model, the children simply line up in their groups and count off to determine the magnitude of each group. Counting-on in this context is very easy to do.

OBSERVING WITH ALL THE SENSES

Rocks are valuable resources for exploring with the senses. Giving children opportunities to use multiple senses in their explorations enhances the investigations and increases their retention of these experiences.

Sight

The eye can detect much detail. Rocks have ideal characteristics that encourage critical observations. Each rock is unique. Viewing a rock such as a piece of granite gives children opportunities to examine specific crystals within the granite. Children can compare various samples of the same types of rocks to examine similarities and differences.

Rocks are ideal for observing with optical aids. Many hand lenses are available for use by children. It is recommended that children utilize large hand lenses rather than microscopes. Young children do not have the fine-motor skills needed to make fine adjustments to microscopes. Large free-standing tripod lenses are available for young children to use. Such a structure can be a permanent part of a science center. Many objects can be placed under the lens for exploration and observation. Additional details on using optical aids are provided in Chapter 6.

Viewing fossils with the aid of hand lenses can be a valuable experience. Children can make predictions about the nature of the organism that has been fossilized and the type of environment in which it lived.

Touch

Rocks have different textures, which makes them excellent materials for children to handle for many reasons. For example, feeling the different textures and creating descriptions from their observations is important for children's vocabulary development.

Obviously rocks are available in most all regions. Rocks provide opportunities for children to become involved in "hands-on" activities. They can become involved in collecting and gathering, as well as sorting and classifying.

Some rocks are very coarse and rough. Others are as smooth as glass. The surface of the rock can be studied to infer what forces created the surface features of the rock. Smooth surfaces are produced when the rock is tumbled in a stream or water current. If a rock is in a windy area where sand blows constantly, it can, over a long period of time, be polished. Rich language experiences can unfold as children use words to describe the many textures and surfaces of rocks. Children can put rocks in order from the roughest to the smoothest, thus engaging in an experience with seriation—that is, putting things in ascending or descending order based on some characteristic.

Sound

Rocks make characteristic sounds when scratched or struck. Rocks with a tight crystalline structure make a ringing sound. Other rocks that are weathered, or not well cemented, have a lower pitched, muted sound. Care must be taken to use eye protection any time you or the children use a hammer to strike rocks.

SAFETY

Safety should be a constant concern when working with rocks. Rocks contain many minerals and should never be put in the mouth. Often these minerals contain elements such as lead and mercury, which can produce long-term illnesses if they are absorbed into the body. Teachers need to exercise great caution and do a great deal of preliminary work to ensure children's safety when handling and observing of rocks and minerals.

CONCEPT EXPLORATIONS ON ROCKS FOR YOUR CLASSROOM

The following Concept Explorations use children's experiences with rocks to examine several basic science processes that are supported by basic math skills. The nature of your local geological history obviously could be a controlling factor for some explorations.

1. Rocks Waiting to Be Found

A wonderful introduction to this exploration is to read a book about rocks. A great choice is Peggy Christian's *If You Find a Rock*. In it are beautiful photographs of children finding rocks in a variety of places. Her use of prose helps us to connect to the process of rock finding and collecting.

Children will be much more involved when the rocks that they explore are their own. You might introduce rocks by giving each child one rock that they can call their very own or having them bring in one special rock that they have found. This introduction can be a motivator for children to go on a "rock hunt." You may plan and take your students on short nature walks to collect rocks for their studies. Good locations for collecting rocks include shallow stream beds, recently tilled soil, and sand and gravel pits. Often piles of gravel can be found around construction sites. Careful planning needs to be completed to make your trips beneficial and safe. (Chapter 6 includes guidelines for conducting safe field trips.)

Children can also explore the surroundings at and near your school. Rocks are in all the usual and unusual places. Children may even be excited to see what rocks they can find at home or on a family outing. Encourage your children to bring into the classroom the rocks that they collect. Children appreciate the ownership they have when they collect rocks from their neighborhood and from their travels.

One natural thing to do with rocks and minerals is to look at them, feel them, and, of course, wonder about them. We can begin our initial investigation of rocks and minerals by simply describing them. We can use and encourage rich language as children tell about their treasures. As we share these descriptions, we can chart our information. Using large chart paper works well for this activity.

Charts like the one shown in Figure 13.5 can vary in sophistication depending on the developmental level of the children. Younger children might make line drawings and sketches to represent visual and tactile characteristics. Photographs can also be taken of each child's rock. The photos can be put together to make a book. Each child can share information about her or his rock in written form. Such a compilation becomes a class photographic journal about rocks.

My Rock	Texture	Shape	Size	Where I Found It

FIGURE 13.5 Charts can be used to help children record their observations of rocks.

Smooth	Sandy
Jagged	Sharp
Coarse	Rough
Ouchey	Hard
Shiny	Dark
Heavy	

FIGURE 13.6 Terms often used by children to describe rocks.

Your class could also develop Web pages on which to share their projects. Web pages are valuable resources in that your children can share their experiences with friends, extended family, and other children around the world.

This process of collecting, observing, organizing, and describing enables children to develop and clarify many vocabulary terms that not only relate to rocks and minerals, but also to characteristics of many common materials around them.

Having collected a variety of rocks, encourage the children to separate the rocks into groups based on characteristics identified by the children. Encourage the children to name their groups based on the terms that they used to describe their rocks (Figure 13.6). It is important for children to negotiate the classification scheme to use in their organizational work with rocks.

Once the groups have been identified and the rocks sorted, children can form subgroups for each category. What characteristics the children select is not important. It is more important that the children have ownership of their decisions and that these decisions are based on their descriptive terms. Typically the children will identify characteristics of rocks not unlike geologists. Indeed, young children are scientists!

When appropriate, reference books can be made available for children to use. Having a classroom library available to your students is an important tool in giving children ownership of their learning. Locating their rocks in resource books can help children develop skills in observing, sorting, and identifying characteristics of rocks. Having real rocks around serves as a motivator to explore books.

2. Swap Rocks with Students in Other Schools

Collect some rocks of interest that are indigenous to your school's location. By using the Internet or by e-mailing other schools, you can offer to trade some of your rocks to schools in different geographic areas. For instance, if you are in an area that has interesting fossils, you could trade some of your rocks for volcanic rocks from Hawaii.

Activities in locating and collecting rocks provide opportunities to expand experiences in developing maps and expanding geography skills. For example, a wall map of the United States could be developed to indicate the location of specific rocks that the children have received.

Information on rocks of local interest can be obtained from many sources. Earth science teachers in your community can be excellent resources. Many local communities have rock and gem societies whose members may be interested in sharing their interests. Local natural history museums also have geologists who can be excellent resources. Rock stores are also good places to visit. Proprietors of such stores are usually experts about the rocks that they have on display and for sale.

3. My Life Story by Rocky

As children are examining rocks, discussion might develop on how the rocks were formed. Select a rock or a small number of rocks and write a story telling the different stages that it/they went through including formation, weathering, and transportation.

Details on the actual processes of the rock cycle are difficult for young children to understand because the concepts involved are very abstract. Children have a difficult time understanding processes that take millions of years since they have little understanding of large numbers in general. In addition, because many of the rock-forming processes occur deep underground, they are not easily visualized.

The processes that took place millions of years ago to form the rocks that the children have collected are the same processes that are going on today. This principle is often called the *uniformitarian principle*. Briefly, this principle states that "the present is the key to the past." For example, a sandstone bedrock that we see on a road cut might show particular layering that is identical to the layering that we can see on a beach today. This helps us understand the nature of formation of rocks.

Comparing the processes that create sedimentary rocks to some of the local processes that children might observe along a stream deposition or erosion area will contribute much to children's understanding.

4. Building Stones

Because of the variety, durability, and the natural beauty of many types of rocks, rocks are often used in the construction of buildings. Granite is often used for countertops and building faces. Limestone, marble, and travertine are used for decorative flooring, counters, and walls. Sandstones are used for building walls, sidewalks, and other features. In some community buildings, one can find benches formed from a variety of rocks. Slate shingles on roofs will last for more than 100 years. In older schools, slate is the standard for chalkboards.

Visit buildings in your community to observe examples of rocks used in construction, both inside and outside. Identify whether the rocks are sedimentary, igneous, or metamorphic. How has it been prepared? Has it been polished? If possible, try to find out where the rock came from.

5. Rainbow Rocks

The color of different rocks is determined by the minerals from which they are made. The color of the minerals can vary depending on the elements within the minerals. For example, quartz mineral can be as clear as glass or it can be purple, rose colored, yellow, or white. The color of quartz is determined by trace elements within the quartz. Feldspar, the main mineral in granite, can vary in color from white to gray, black, or pink. A great resource for looking at the materials that rocks are made from—minerals—is Chris Oxlade's book *Rocks*. This book has beautiful photographs of the many patterns of color, shape, and design found on rocks. This book also displays how rocks are used in construction, architecture, and art—a great springboard to rock exploration.

Collect a variety of rocks and try to sort them by color to form as many colors of the rainbow as possible. Display the rocks in a way that shows their differences. Try to replicate the colors by experimenting with mixing paint.

6. Stream Sorting

Water has a great sorting ability. The activity of the water will separate rock particles depending on the action of the water. After a heavy rain, when the stream flow increases, small particles of sand and silt will be carried downstream. These particles will later be deposited as water movement decreases.

By comparing different locations along a small stream, particle sorting can be identified. The water flow tends to be more active on the outside of a stream bend. Thus, smaller particles are found on the inside of a stream bend and larger particles are found on the outside.

Visit a small stream and observe the rocks. Look for examples of how the water has sorted the rocks. Observe areas where sand congregates. How does the water flow at these areas? Observe areas where larger rocks are found. What are the characteristics of these areas?

7. Statues, Jewels, and Trinkets

Stone can be carved into statues, but natural materials are also often used for smaller items of beauty. Jewelry is based on gems, both precious and semiprecious. Other examples of rocks being used for common items of beauty include paperweights, bookends, wall hangings, and clocks.

Collect small items that include rock materials. If possible keep and display the items. Otherwise take photographs of the objects. Make a variety of classification systems based on the use of the objects and by examining the characteristics of the rocks and minerals used to form the objects.

8. Rocks—Pieces and Parts

Collect a variety of small rocks about the size of a quarter. Wrap each rock in a paper towel or a thin cloth; then place it in a zippered plastic bag. Using a hammer, break the rock into as many small pieces as possible. The teacher may need to do the hammering if the children are too young to swing to a target. Make sure whomever does the hammering wears safety glasses. Observe the particles using a hand lens. Sort each piece into categories. What particles are most common? Which types were more difficult to break? Compare the combination of particles for each rock that you break.

9. Fossils

Fossils can be found in many sedimentary rocks. Limestone, sandstone, siltstone, and shale are good sources for fossils. Often, limestone gravel will have fossils that can be used for investigation. Find as many rocks as you can that have evidence of life. This could include shells of animals; imprints of plants; or grooves, holes, or footprints of animals formed by animals boring through soil or moving on the surface. From the evidence of the fossil, try to analyze what the animal was like and the environment in which the animal lived.

10. Graveyard Geology

Local graveyards are rich sources for learning about the history of your community. Dates on tombstones can give much information about early development in your community. Cemetery records are kept by local officials and religious organizations. These can provide much data for the formation of charts and graphs.

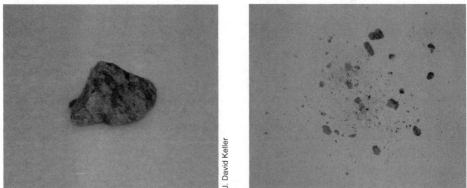

By viewing the individual particles that form rocks, like the granite pictured here, it is easier to understand their formation.

The types of gravestones that are displayed in the cemetery can also provide much information. Typically stones formed from varieties of granites are common. Some tombstones are also formed from marble. Children could compare the rates of weathering that have occurred for the different rocks. They could also see if preferences for the different types of rocks have changed over time.

Visit a neighborhood graveyard. Examine the different varieties of tombstones. How many varieties of rocks can you find? How old is the oldest tombstone? Which types of rocks weather most quickly? Does the variety of rock vary during different periods of history?

Students can learn much about the nature of rocks by examining gravestones.

Activities in Other Explorations That Relate to Rocks

Water (Chapter 17)

10. Water's Work

Resources for Teachers

Books

Atwood, F. D. (1997). *Rocks and minerals: A portrait of the natural world.* New York: Smithmark.

Barnes-Svarney, P. L. (1991). *Born of heat and pressure: Mountains and metamorphic rocks* Hillsdale, New Jersey: Enslow Publishers.

Caduto, M. J., & Bruchac, J. (1997). *Keepers of the earth: Native American stories and environmental activities for children.* Golden, CO: Fulcrum.

Cheney, G. A. (1985). *Mineral resources.* New York: Franklin Watts.

Gans, R. (1984). *Rock collecting.* Illus. by H. Keller. New York: HarperCollins.

Hoban, T. (1995). *Animal, vegetable, or mineral?* New York: Greenwillow Books.

Hunt, J., Selsam, H. E., & Hunt, J. (1984). *A first look at rocks.* Illus. by H. Springer. New York: Walker and Company.

Kerrod, R. (1994). *The world's mineral resources.* New York: Thomson Learning.

Oxlade, C. (2002). *Rocks.* Chicago: Heinemann Library.

Parker, S. (2002). *Rocks and minerals.* Milwaukee, WI: Gareth Stevens.

Pellant, C. (2002). *Rocks and minerals.* New York: Dorling Kindersley.

Rhodes, F. H. T., Shaffer, P. R., Zim, H. S., & Perlman, R. (1962). *Fossils: A guide to prehistoric life.* New York: Golden Press.

Symes, R. F., & Staff of the Natural History Museum of London. (1988). *Eyewitness books: Rocks and minerals.* New York: Alfred A. Knopf.

Zim, H. S., & Shaffer, P. R. (2001). *Rocks, gems and minerals: A guide to familiar minerals, gems, ores and rocks.* New York: St. Martin's Press.

Web Sites

http://www.geolab.unc.edu/Petunia/IgMetAtlas/mainmenu.html
An atlas of igneous and metamorphic minerals.

http://webmineral.com
Excellent mineral database.

http://volcano.und.nodak.edu/vwdocs/vwlessons/lessons/Slideshow/Slideindex.html
A slide show of rocks and minerals.

http://volcano.und.nodak.edu/vw.html
Information on volcanoes.

http://www.fi.edu/tfi/units/rocks/rock.html
Information on rocks and minerals.

http://www.fi.edu/fellows/fellow1/oct98/create
How rocks are formed.

http://www.science.ubc.ca/~geo1202/rockcycle/rockcycle.html
Information on the rock cycle.

http://www.bbc.co.uk/education/rocks/rockcycle.shtml
Experiments related to rock cycle.

http://www.rocksandminerals.com/rockcycle.htm
The rock cycle.

http://www.fi.edu/fellows/fellow1/oct98/create/sediment.htm
How sedimentary rocks are formed.

http://www.uh.edu/~jbutler/physical/chapter7.html
Sedimentary rocks.

http://www.fi.edu/fellows/fellow1/oct98/create/metamorph.htm
How metamorphic rocks are formed.

Children's Books on Rocks

Arnold, C. (1996). *Stories in stone: Rock art pictures by early Americans*. New York: Clarion Books.

Barnes-Svarney, P., & Svarney T. E. (2004). *The handy geology answer book*. Detroit, MI: Visible Ink Press.

Baylor B. (1974). *Everybody needs a rock*. New York: Simon & Schuster.

Bingham, C. (2004). *Rocks and minerals*. London, New York: DK Publishing.

Brown, M. (1947). *Stone soup*. New York: Charles Scribner's Sons.

Cefrey, H. (2003). *Igneous rocks*. New York: PowerKids Press.

Cefrey, H. (2003). *Metamorphic rocks*. New York: PowerKids Press.

Christian, P. (2000). *If you find a rock*. San Diego, CA: Harcourt.

Cole, J. (1987). *The magic school bus: Inside the earth*. New York: Scholastic.

Fowler, A. (1993). *It could still be a rock*. Chicago: Children's Press.

Gallant, R. A. (2000). *Rocks*. New York: Tarrytown, New York: Benchmark Books.

Gans, R. (1997). *Let's go rock collecting*. New York: HarperCollins.

Harshman, M., (1991). *Rocks in my pockets*. New York: Cobblehill Books/Dutton.

Hooper, M., & Coady, C. (1996). *The pebble in my pocket: A history of our earth*. New York: Viking.

Leonni, L. (1994). *On my beach there are many pebbles*. New York: Mulberry Books.

Lye, K. (1993). *Rocks and minerals*. Austin, TX: Raintree Steck-Vaughn.

Marrin, A. (2002). *Secrets from the rocks: Dinosaur hunting with Roy Chapman*. New York: Dutton Children's Books.

Marzollo, J. (1998). *I am a rock*. New York: Scholastic.

Murphy, S. J. (2000). *Dave's down-to-earth rock shop*. New York: HarperCollins.

Pellant, C. (2000). *The best book of fossils, rocks, and minerals*. New York: Kingfisher Press.

Polacco, P. (1995). *My ol' man*. New York: Philomel Books.

Ricciuti, E. R. (2001). *Rocks and minerals*. New York: Scholastic.

Richardson, A. O. (2002). *Rocks*. Mankato, MN: Capstone Press.

Rosinsky, N. M. (2003). *Rocks: Hard, soft, smooth and rough*. Minneapolis, MN: Picture Window Books.

Steig, W. (1969). *Sylvester and the magic pebble*. New York: Simon & Schuster.

Tocci, S. (2002). *Experiments with rocks and minerals*. New York: Scholastic.

Zoenfeld, K. W. (1995). *How mountains are made*. New York: HarperCollins.

Correlation of NSES Standards and NCTM Principles and Standards to Seeds Concept Exploration Activities

	1. Eating Seeds Is Fun!	2. What Foods Do We Eat?	3. What Do Our Animal Neighbors Eat?	4. Seeds Growing in Nature	5. The Germination Race	6. Trees Grow from Seeds	7. Flower Seeds to Flower Seeds	8. Pop Corn, Indian Corn, Sweet Corn	9. Let's Be Gentle!	10. All Quiet on the Stage!	11. Lights, Camera, Action	12. Story Time	13. Seed Mosaics
SCIENCE													
Inquiry	X	X	X	X	X	X	X	X	X	X	X	X	X
Physical Science			X		X	X	X	X	X		X		
Life Science	X	X	X	X	X	X	X	X	X	X	X	X	X
Earth and Space Science				X			X	X					
Science and Technology				X		X		X	X	X	X		
Personal and Social Perspectives	X	X	X	X	X	X	X	X	X	X	X	X	X
History and Nature of Science	X	X	X	X		X	X	X					
MATHEMATICS													
Number and Operations	X	X	X	X	X	X	X	X	X	X	X	X	X
Algebra	X	X	X	X			X						
Geometry													X
Measurement				X	X	X	X		X				X
Data Analysis and Probability	X	X	X	X	X		X	X			X	X	
Problem Solving	X	X	X	X	X	X	X		X				
Reasoning and Proof				X									
Communication	X	X									X		X
Connections	X	X	X			X	X						
Representation	X	X	X	X	X		X	X			X	X		X

CHAPTER 14

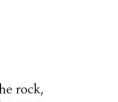

Seeds

> One for the rock,
> One for the crow,
> One to die, and
> One to grow.
>
> *Old English saying*

Seeds demonstrate the magic of life—we can take a small "lifeless" seed; add water and a warm environment; and, in a short while, the seed sprouts into a living plant. This is an amazing phenomenon to witness. However, we experience this process of seeds growing into plants so commonly throughout our lives that this magic often becomes taken for granted. But, indeed, the process continues to be a miracle.

It is incredible to think of a small buckeye seed holding within itself the power to become a towering, abundant tree producing thousands more buckeyes. Similarly, a tamarind tree, which can grow to be 80 feet tall with a spread of 20 to 35 feet, begins with a tiny seed. The tamarind evergreen tree is native to Asia and eastern Africa but grows in southern California and Mexico to smaller heights of 10 to 25 feet. Its unusual fruit is encased in seed pods that protect the large, glossy dark brown seeds embedded in the tasty pulp. An interesting fruit to eat!

Even our largest trees, like the giant redwoods, started as tiny seeds weighing 1/7,500 of an ounce. Seeds of lotus plants that had been in jars along with the Dead Sea scrolls for 2,000 years germinated when planted. Dandelion seeds can be transported for thousands of miles by the wind. Other seeds, such as coconut seeds, can float on an ocean current for years to a faraway island where they will germinate.

Seeds are the necessary basis for the continuation of most plant life. Without seeds we would have no food. Even the meat we eat can only exist because most animals

> Bad seed is a robbery of the worst kind: for your pocket-book not only suffers by it, but your preparations are lost and a season passes away unimproved.
>
> George Washington

Anthony E. Davis

Here we see the long, irregularly curved seed pods of the tamarind tree, a native of Asia and eastern Africa. One seed pod has been cracked open to show the edible pulp, enclosed by strands of fiber; and some glossy dark brown seeds.

Helanna Bratman, City Seeds of the Poughkeepsie Farm Project

A harvest of dill seeds at the Poughkeepsie Farm Project's urban agriculture program, City Seeds.

used for meat eat plants. Teachers can locate local resources to help children understand the importance of seeds for growing food to sustain the world. For example, in Poughkeepsie, New York, the Poughkeepsie Farm Project is a nonprofit organization working toward growing and sustaining food in the area. This organization provides a wealth of information about farming. Finding similar organizations in your own area will prove a valuable resource as children understand their role in keeping the earth a place where food can be grown to benefit all living creatures.

Seeds are everywhere in the world where there is life. Seeds are a very real and natural part of every child's world. Children blow dandelion seeds into the air dreaming about where the seeds might land and what it would be like to be attached to the seeds and floating about in the air. They watch the maple seed "propeller" twirl from the sky. Seeds stick to their clothes when they walk through a field. They wish that watermelons didn't have seeds, but they are glad that the seeds are easy to see so they can be separated from the fruit.

Children love to watch animals collect seeds from trees. Squirrels are industrious creatures when they are collecting seeds. Where do they take the seeds? How do they manipulate the seeds to eat them? How do they crack the seed pod? Children often have had the experience of watching a gerbil or guinea pig eat sunflower seeds. They maneuver the seed with great skill to get to the meat.

We all eat seeds. We plant them and watch them grow into the beautiful flowers and vegetables in our garden. We collect them in jars to decorate our homes. We use them as counters for games. Seeds are a common and very important part of our lives.

Seeds have many attributes that make them ideal for children to observe and grow. They are plentiful and economical. There are many varieties—too numerous to count. They are easy to handle. They germinate and grow quickly. Seeds give children opportunities to develop responsibilities for caring for life. The process of seeds germinating and growing fosters children's interest in observing change. They gain firsthand information about the sequence of growth, the cycle of life. Observing the seeds change causes children to ask questions and to try different experiments and activities with them. Teachers can support children's developing knowledge and concepts about seeds by providing interesting and informational materials and resources for children to examine and study.

SCIENCE CONCEPTS FOR TEACHERS

The Nature of Seeds

Seeds are the product of the reproduction of plants. Plants produced by seed are typically divided into two groups: the *gymnosperms*, or naked seed plants, and the *angiosperms*, the flowering plants. Gymnosperms include the conifers, or cone-bearing plants, such as pines, cedars, and firs. Cone-bearing trees have been around since the Permian period, 290 million years ago. Angiosperms have been around for about 75 million years.

Seeds are produced in the flowers of plants (Figure 14.1). Flowers contain long tubes called *stamens*. The *anther* at the end of the stamen contains pollen sacs. The sacs release pollen. Pollen is transported by the wind or by insects to the stigma of another flower or the same flower. The *stigma* is covered with a sticky substance to which the pollen grains adhere. The pollen grains grow down the style to the *ovary* where they attach to the *ovule*. The silk in an ear of corn is an example of the style. There is one strand of silk for each kernel of corn. The fertilized ovule becomes the seed.

Parts of a Seed

All seeds have basic parts that contribute to the development of a plant from the seed. Each part varies based on the nature of the seed, but each part is critical for the germination of the seed.

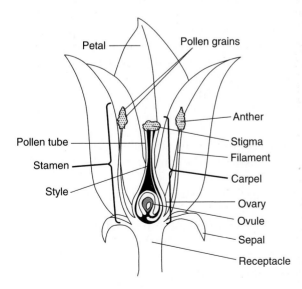

FIGURE 14.1 The flower is the center of seed reproduction.

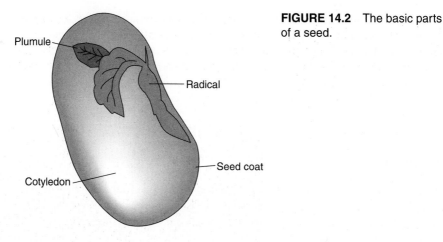

FIGURE 14.2 The basic parts of a seed.

Figure 14.2 shows the basic parts of a seed. The *seed coat*, sometimes called the *testa*, protects the seed. For some seeds, such as the seed of a honey locust tree, the seed coat is very hard and impervious to water. A honey locust seed might weather for as long as 15 years before it germinates.

The *cotyledon* is the energy storage system for the embryo. When a seed such as a lima bean germinates, the cotyledons appear to be the first leaves of the plant. The *radical* is the part of the embryo that becomes the root. The *plumule* is the part of the embryo that becomes the shoot or the stem of the plant.

Seed Germination

When seeds sprout, the process is called *germination*. When a seed is dormant, it is very difficult to determine whether the seed is alive, because the metabolic processes are extremely slow.

The germination process is initiated when the seed is placed in the proper environment to grow and produce a plant. The proper environmental characteristics include moisture and warm temperature. Some seeds, such as lettuce, also need light.

Seed Transportation

Each species of plant, over time, has developed specific attributes that contribute to the transportation of their seed. This helps ensure the continuation and propagation of the species.

Seeds are dispersed in any of five ways: wind, water, animal, explosions, and fire. Seeds that are dispersed by wind are very light. We have all enjoyed blowing dandelion seed "parachutes" and watching the seeds float in the breeze and wondering how many miles the parachute would travel. Seeds that are dispersed by water will float along with the current of the water, depositing themselves at various spots along the water's path. Two examples are water lilies and coconuts.

Seeds that are dispersed by animals have fruits that are edible. The seeds pass through the animal's digestive tract after the fruit is digested. We can often see in open fields lines of wild cherry trees that were produced by birds sitting on a pre-existing fence. Years later the fence is gone, but the seeds dropped by the birds have germinated and grown into large trees.

Other animals such as squirrels transport and bury nuts and forget to reclaim them. A year or two later, the nuts germinate and trees are naturally propagated.

We have all walked through fields to find that when we were finished, many seeds had attached to our clothing. Many plants have hooks that attach to an animal, so that the seed can be carried away from the parent plant and dropped at another location. Velcro was actually inspired when its inventor was walking through a field and noticed seeds on his clothing.

Seeds are dispersed by explosions when pods burst as they ripen. This is how members of the "impatient" family got their name. The seedpods of the common jewelweed, sometimes called touch-me-nots, will "explode" when ripe, causing the seeds to be ejected away from the parent tree. This process assists the plant in expanding its territory.

Seeds that are dispersed by fire have special adaptations that keep the seeds protected until a certain temperature is reached. When that temperature is reached, the fire melts the protective covering and allows the seeds to be released and germinate.

Jim Raco/National Park Service

The 1988 fires at Yellowstone National Park destroyed entire forests of lodgepole pines. However, lodgepole pinecones remain tightly sealed until the surrounding temperature reaching around 300 degrees Fahrenheit. The pinecone has a delaying mechanism that causes the seed cone to open *after* the fire, releasing the seed.

If you collect pinecones from lodgepole pines or jack pines and place them on a cookie sheet in an oven at 300 degrees Fahrenheit, the cones will open up and you can plant the seeds.

MATHEMATICS: ADDRESSING THE NCTM STANDARDS THROUGH CONCEPT EXPLORATIONS

Seed investigations and explorations provide children with rich opportunities to use a variety of mathematical concepts and ideas involving counting; sequencing and patterns; observing, analyzing, and sorting data; graphing; and measuring.

Number and Operations

Counting seeds helps children practice rational counting and counting-on with real objects. As children construct simple charts and graphs, their ability to count with meaning will help them to describe data sets with their cardinal property. Concepts of *more* and *less*, of comparison and seriation, and of sequence can be emphasized in these explorations. When seeds are very tiny, you can make groupings of them that are easy for children to count, such as groupings of twos, fives, tens, or twenty-fives. This experience in multiplicative thinking helps develop the concepts and skills necessary for multiplication and division. It is important for children to see items in groups or collections.

You can construct a number book with each page showing one, two, three, four, five seeds, or more; or you can have each page show a group of seeds in multiples to show skip counting ideas or multiplication. For example, page 1 could have a group of five seeds, page 2 then would have two groups of five seeds, and so forth.

Algebra and Patterns

As children collect and observe seeds, they can see patterns on the seeds themselves and in the seedpods. For example, the design of seeds in a sunflower is lovely to look at. The seeds are arranged in the sunflower in a spiral pattern. The spirals are patterns that the eye sees, with "curvier" spirals appearing near the center of the flower and flatter spirals appearing the farther out we go. We can encourage children to examine these seeds with hand lenses. The spirals that we see are called *Fibonacci spirals*. Pinecones also show the Fibonacci spirals clearly as we examine them. It is a beautiful sight to see such organization in nature. For more information on Fibonacci spirals and Fibonacci numbers, see the link provided in the end-of-chapter Web sites list. Other links can be found by searching for "Fibonacci."

Although the complex, mathematical nature of Fibonacci numbers and spirals is quite advanced for young children, teachers should be aware of how mathematics exquisitely describes natural phenomena. Our awareness can help us to guide our children's observational experiences and enhance their appreciation of nature and mathematics. Seeing patterns of seeds alone can provide a lens to the aesthetic aspect of Mother Nature. Children can certainly enjoy the these pleasing patterns without understanding the complex mathematics that describes them.

Classifying and sorting seeds help children develop the abilities to reason and to think critically. These tasks also help them expand their language and vocabulary. Seed collections provide so many opportunities for children to sort and re-sort. Numerous sorting categories can be easily generated as children

J. David Keller

Children can sort varieties of bean seeds by shape, color, size, and texture.

observe and collect seeds. Attributes such as size, mass, texture, shape, growth pattern, and origin are some of the ways children will be able to sort the seeds. Children should be encouraged to determine their own classification categories. Finding out how scientists classify seeds can support this experience. Trade books, Web sites, or community garden club members can supply this type of information.

Geometry

As children examine seeds and experiment with sorting and classifying, you may want to ask them to construct works of art such as mosaics with the seeds. Opportunities to think about number, symmetry, shape, perspective, and direction can help to describe and define the artistic work.

Measurement

Children observe seeds as well as their cycles of growth. Measuring and charting the growth rate of germinating seeds provides children with opportunities to see sequences and patterns in nature and to learn about seriation and the attributes of measurement. Measuring length and temperature of germinating seeds gives children multiple experiences using a variety of measuring devices.

Data Analysis

Graphing the sorted categories of seeds can be done in many ways. Seeds can be displayed on paper plates, in plastic jars, or on paper. Charts can be constructed with the actual seeds or a more abstract bar graph can be constructed. Refer to Concept Exploration 5, The Germination Race, for more ideas about graphing. Children make connections across many areas of mathematics as they carefully examine and investigate seeds in their world.

OBSERVING WITH ALL THE SENSES

Seeds give excellent opportunities to explore using our senses.

Sight

Seeds have wide varieties of shapes, sizes, textures, and colors. Identifying these characteristics gives students opportunities to observe and sort. Characteristics that can commonly be identified include color, shape, texture, and size. Children also use visual skills as they observe the growth cycle of seeds and how seeds are dispersed.

Touch

Seeds have many textures that give us opportunities to compare touch sensations. Some seeds, like most acorns, are very smooth to the touch. Others, like cockleburs, feel like a ball of needles. Some seeds, like the propeller seeds of maple trees, have ribs or veins.

Sound

Although we normally do not think about seeds making sounds, some seeds make noise when they pop open. One of the joys of popcorn is actually hearing the explosions of each kernel. Actually popcorn is not unique. Other plants actually eject their seeds by a popping process. The pinecones of some pine trees release their seeds in the spring by popping. On the first warm spring day when the temperature gets to around 75 degrees Fahrenheit, the pinecones will pop open their seed coat. Increasing pressure from the sap returning up the branches and the wax becoming warm enough to melt cause the pinecone to "pop" during the germination process.

We can also compare the sounds that seeds make by making shakers containing seeds. Some gourds when dried become good shakers, as well as some seed pods. Shakers can also be made by putting seeds in a cardboard container such as that used for snacks. Such a sensory observation can spark interest in making homemade shakers with different types of seeds. Shake and listen!

Taste

Seeds give children an excellent opportunity to observe and try different foods. By identifying seeds, children can recognize that many of the foods that they eat come from seeds. In many cases, such as corn, peas, sunflowers, and nuts, children can recognize the seeds as they eat them. In other cases, such as wheat ground into flour, children may not be aware that they are eating seeds. Opportunities for cooking and baking can be taken into account based on your particular classroom facilities. Simple recipes such as preparing sunflower or pumpkin seeds for eating provide fun ways to engage children in cooperative projects that everyone can enjoy.

Smell

Particular types of seeds in a natural setting can have a distinct odor. Many fruits from nut trees have a distinct odor when roasted. For example, roasted chestnuts have a very pleasant odor. Children can compare the smells of unpopped popcorn and popped corn as well as other seeds that can be smelled in both their uncooked and cooked states.

SAFETY

Care must be taken when children are invited to taste any food. Some children are allergic to particular foods, for example, peanuts and walnuts. When possible, check your children's medical history. If you are going to have a seed-tasting event, notify parents first to see if there are any children who should not participate. In some cases, this might be the first time the children have tasted a particular food. If a child should happen to have a reaction, notify medical and school authorities immediately.

Care also needs to be taken when using seeds produced for plantings. Often, seeds are treated with different chemicals to protect them from organisms in the soil. Goggles can be worn and, if necessary, thin rubber gloves.

CONCEPT EXPLORATIONS ON SEEDS FOR YOUR CLASSROOM

The following Concept Explorations use children's experiences with seeds to examine several basic science processes and utilize basic math skills.

Activities that help children to recognize that our food include a wide variety of seeds help them appreciate the cycles in nature that are critical for life. It is important that children enter into discussions about where their food comes from. They need to have more understanding than to say food comes from the grocery store. Understanding that food comes from nature helps foster a curiosity and respect for our environment. The universality of food in nature helps children see the interconnectedness that all cultures have with their environment. *Roots, Shoots, Buckets and Boots*, a book by Sharon Lovejoy, gives rich information about Native American gardening as children explore cultural traditions of planting, harvesting, and eating!

1. Eating Seeds Is Fun!

Many of the foods that we eat are seeds (Figure 14.3). Often we can recognize the type of seeds that we eat. We see the seeds we are eating when we eat beans, corn, and peas. Sometimes the seeds are altered so that we might not recognize the food as a seed, such as when we eat popcorn. At other times, we might not recognize that the food is from seeds such as when we eat a slice of bread made from ground wheat.

Invite your children to collect a variety of foods that come from seeds. Have a seed-eating party and sample the different seeds that the children collect. Caution should be exercised for possible and existing allergies in your children. Explore creative ways that you can collect, organize, and display your seeds. Invite your students to identify different categories that could be used to classify their different types of seeds. Encourage them to explain how they identified and developed these attributes. Children should come to a consensus about the classification schemes that are generated. This agreed-on scheme can be used to sort newfound seeds, providing good experiences with analysis, reasoning, and critical thinking.

Common Seeds That We Eat	
Beans	Peanuts
Corn	Pumpkin seeds
Peas	
Foods That Include Seeds	
Cucumber	Tomatoes
Okra	Breads
Squash	
Herbs and Spices from Seeds	
Pepper	Poppy seeds
Caraway seeds	Dill

FIGURE 14.3 Children may not realize that many of the foods we eat are seeds or contain seeds.

2. What Foods Do We Eat?

Have your children make a list of all the foods that they eat for a period of 3 days. Invite your class to make a chart classifying the foods into categories that they select such as meats, vegetables, fruits, cereals, breads, and dairy products. Divide the food categories into groups that are seeds, are made from seeds, or are made by animals that eat seeds.

Children might also divide the foods grown from plants into foods that come from roots, leaves, and fruits. Fruits, by definition, are the seed-producing part of a plant. With many common fruits, such as peaches, oranges, apples, mangoes, and plums, we discard the seed. With others such as bananas, raspberries, and strawberries, we eat the seed as part of the fruit. There is a special fact about the strawberry—its seeds are on the outside. Can you find any other fruit with this characteristic? When we eat nuts such as walnuts, pecans, and chestnuts we are actually eating the seeds. These seeds are protected by a covering that varies in hardness.

3. What Do Our Animal Neighbors Eat?

Ask the children to observe the animals that live in their neighborhood and where these animals forage for their food. Make a list of the animals and their food. How many of these foods are seeds? What role do these animals play in transporting seeds? Care should be exercised to respect and not bother the animals during observation.

Your children can document their observations through any option of their choosing. They might take some digital photographs of the animals for a bulletin board, or they could make a videotape or use a live video-cam to show a feeding station in the school yard.

4. Seeds Growing in Nature

While your class is taking a fall nature hike, invite a couple of children to walk through a field wearing a heavy white cotton sock over their shoe on one foot. After the hike, observe the seeds that have become attached to the socks. Collect and sort the seeds into groups. How many varieties did your children find? Sort the seeds by size.

How did the seeds stick to the sock? Invite the children to look through a hand lens to observe the surface and contours of the seeds.

Place the sock with the seeds attached on a shallow tray. Add sufficient water so the water can wick up the sock and keep it moist. Put the tray in an area that gets good indirect sunlight. Add water as needed. Find a creative way to display the different types of plants that grow on your sock. As the seeds germinate, you might transplant the seedlings into a small flower pot or nature garden.

5. The Germination Race

Another aspect of seeds that children enjoy observing is the process of change. As seeds germinate, they can observe seeds change and grow. Many types of seeds have characteristics that make them good for classroom use. Lima beans are large and the parts of the seed are easy to identify. Radish seeds germinate quickly. When given moisture and warmth [approximately 27 degrees Celsius (80 degrees Fahrenheit)], a radish seed can germinate in less than 24 hours.

Collect packets of seeds and test their germination by putting 10 seeds on a wet paper towel in a covered petri dish (Figure 14.4). Place the seeds in a warm, well-lit area. Compare the number of seeds that germinate and how many days it takes for them to germinate.

Plastic disposable petri dishes can be purchased from science supply houses in large quantities. A second convenient way to germinate seeds is to use small freezer-strength baggies, as illustrated in Figure 14.5.

Teachers can ask for free outdated seeds from local garden centers to use with your students. These seeds will function well for your classroom projects. Ask for the seeds in the fall using your school letterhead to make the request.

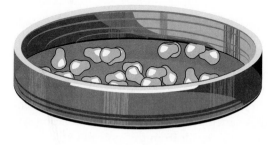

FIGURE 14.4 Children can use their counting skills to determine how many days it takes to germinate seeds in a petri dish.

1. Place a paper towel in the bag.

2. Staple the bag and the paper towel across the bottom of the bag about one and a half inches from the bottom of the bag.

3. Put several seeds in front of the paper towel so that they are above the staples.

4. Pour water into the bag so that it is in the bottom 1 inch of the bag. The water will wick up the paper towel and keep the seeds moist.

5. Staple the bag to a bulletin board, keeping the bag unzipped so that air can get in the bag. Observe the changes that take place over a period of time.

6. Keep the water level constant throughout the observation.

Notice that the roots will grow downward and the stem grows upward. This process in which plants respond to gravity is called *geotropism*.

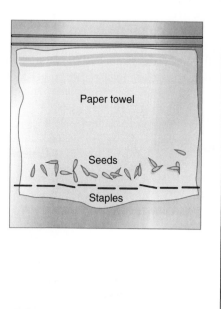

FIGURE 14.5 A bulletin board for observing germinating seeds. Freezer-strength zippered plastic bag are excellent for observing seeds germinate because we can see each part of the seed as it grows.

Seed germination also provides an excellent opportunity for children to collect data and make graphs. Graphs of numbers or percentage of seed germination can be constructed by your children using a variety of techniques that vary from the concrete to the abstract. For example, at the concrete level, children can glue the number of seeds of each variety that germinated to a poster board in different columns. When it is possible and easy to count seeds, use compatible numbers of seeds for analysis, such as multiples of 2, 5, 10, or 25.

At the semiconcrete level, the children could draw a representation of each type of seed or use pictures or photos of the seed. At the semiabstract level, the children could make a chart, bar graph, or circle graph.

6. Trees Grow from Seeds

During the fall take a nature walk to observe the different types of trees and the seeds that have grown during the summer. Figure 14.6 lists some common trees you might find. Collect samples of the seeds from different types of trees. Many of the seeds are large and easy to spot. Your children might want to compare the types of seeds that they collect. What type of a seed coat do they have? How do they feel? Are they rough or smooth? Are they big or little? Have your children identify different attributes of the seeds they collect and use these attributes to develop a classification system. Concepts of comparison and seriation can result from this type of exploration. Ordering the seeds by texture or size can be a great activity. Determining the ordering, or the seriation, of how the seeds feel from very smooth to very rough helps children with their sensory observational skills.

Citrus fruit seeds are an excellent type of seed to grow in your classroom. Most seeds will germinate very easily. Perhaps you have even noticed that when you cut open a grapefruit, some of the seeds have started to sprout. Collect seeds from different citrus fruits, such as oranges, lemons, limes, and grapefruit. Germinate the seeds using the moist paper towel method in bag (see Figure 14.5) or plastic petri

FIGURE 14.6 During a nature walk, have the children look for trees with seeds.

Types of Trees That Have Obvious Seeds	
Oak	Acorns
Buckeye, horse chestnut	Large black fruit
Maple	Propellers
Sycamore	Spiny buttons
Dogwood	Hard-shelled red seeds
Apple tree, pear tree	Large fruit
Pine tree	Pinecones
Cherry tree	Variety of fruits
Beach tree	Small nuts
Locust tree	Pods ranging from a few inches to more than a foot long
Citrus tree	Varieties of citrus fruits

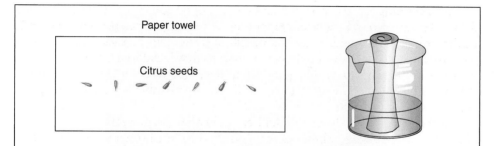

Paper towel

Citrus seeds

Seeds of citrus fruits are interesting seeds to germinate and grow.

1. Collect the seeds from the fruits.

2. Fold a paper towel in triplicate and place the citrus seeds on it about 2 inches apart. Roll up the paper towel.

3. Place the paper towel in a beaker or glass. Add about an inch of water to the glass. Keep the water at that level for the next few weeks.

4. The seeds will germinate within 3-4 weeks. Once the trees have started to grow they can be transplanted into a pot with good potting soil. They can be part of your classroom for years.

FIGURE 14.7 Growing citrus trees: Seeds of citrus fruits are interesting seeds to germinate and grow.

dishes and then transplant them to some potting soil. Compare the growth and other characteristics of the trees that develop.

Some of the seeds will quickly germinate when placed in the proper surroundings. Most seeds will prosper in a warm, moist environment. Children can test to see which types of seeds will germinate by placing a few seeds in a paper towel, as demonstrated in Figure 14.7.

Be aware that seeds from particular species of trees have built-in characteristics that regulate their germination. Some seeds such as the honey locust need to have the seed coat scarified or scratched so that the moisture can enter the embryo to initiate germination (Figure 14.8). Others, such as the red oak, need to go through a cold, dormant period before they germinate. Thus, the acorns can be in the soil throughout the winter and then germinate when the soil warms in the spring. It is interesting that acorns from white oaks will germinate without a dormant period. A wonderful resource for this exploration is Ken Robbins' book, *Seeds*. The photographs in this book give children a wonderful glimpse of seeds that may not be available in their geographic area.

7. Flower Seeds to Flowers

Many types of flowers germinate from seeds and grow to mature flowers in short periods of time. This gives children an opportunity to observe the entire cycle of life in a short period.

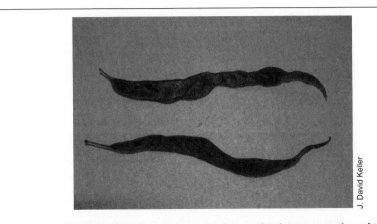

Honey locust seed pods have many aspects that assist the propagation of the honey locust tree.

Honey locust trees get their name because the seed pod is very sweet and is a delicious fruit for animals such as deer. When a deer eats the honey locust seed pod, the seeds travel through the digestive tract. The seeds, ready to germinate, are then deposited in a supply of manure perhaps miles away from the parent tree.

The seeds have a hard impermeable seed coat that cannot be digested by animals. In nature, they can lie unaltered for 15 years.

You can germinate honey locust seeds in the classroom. Because the seed coat is so hard, you need to soften it. You can do this by scoring the seed coat with a file. A second process is to drop the seeds into some boiling water. Remove the boiling water from the source of heat, add your seeds, and let the water cool down. The seeds can then be wrapped in a paper towel and kept moist for a few weeks while they germinate. You can then plant your honey locust tree. Note: Exercise caution around boiling and hot water.

FIGURE 14.8 Honey locust seed pods.

Tell your children that they need to grow flower seeds that will be used for next year's class. Give each child a few seeds to plant in a small container with potting soil. Small zinnias are excellent for classroom use in that they grow from seed to seed in approximately 6 weeks. *Note:* Be careful to not use a hybrid variety of flower. Most hybrids grow sterile seeds that will not germinate.

Have the children observe the plants grow through the various stages of development: seed germination, plant and leaf development, blossom development, and flower maturity. When the flowers mature and dry up your children can break open the seed pods and collect the seeds that can be used for the next year's class.

Your children might select a variety of different environments that they would like to use to plant their seeds. The children can make a series of digital photographs of their plants over a period of time. Photographs in Gail Saunders-Smith's book, *Seeds*, give children an accurate look at real seeds and how they germinate and grow.

These photographs could be used for bulletin boards, scrapbooks, Web pages, journal covers, or stationery. Children could also develop a Web video-cam for their plants to share the constant progress of their flower. Observing this entire growth cycle beautifully shows the important patterns of growth in nature.

8. Popcorn, Indian Corn, Sweet Corn

Corn is an easy seed for children to grow. Particular types of corn can be very fascinating for young children. Children have a particular fascination with popcorn because of its exploding personality and great taste. Popcorn is easy to germinate and can be grown in a small plot of land. Indian corn is also interesting because of the variety of colors of the different kernels. When the corn matures, collect the ears and hang them to dry. After the corn dries, you can shell the corn. With the Indian corn, have your students sort the kernels by the different colors. Which colors are most common? Children can make a chart or graph of their data.

9. Let's Be Gentle!

Research at North Carolina State University examined germination of seeds that were handled roughly. Is it possible to affect the germination rate by abusing seeds?

Have your students take some lima beans and sort them into three or four equal groups. Have the children drop the seeds onto a hard floor from a variety of heights. A hallway stairwell might serve well for the seed drop experiment. Set one group of seeds aside for the control.

Germinate the seeds using the procedure discussed in Concept Exploration 5, The Germination Race. Does germination decrease when seeds are handled roughly?

10. All Quiet on the Stage!

Children enjoy reading books related to plants and seeds. After the class has had opportunities to read a variety of trade books (see list at end of chapter), ask the children which book was their favorite. Invite the students to put on a play based on their favorite book. For example, if they choose Eric Carle's *The Tiny Seed*, they could reenact the events of the tiny seed as it takes its incredible journey.

Their play could be developed using several different formats. For example, a puppet show could be given. Or, if some of the children have a background in dance, they could perform a dance showing how seeds germinate and grow.

Their presentation might include songs about the growth of a seed. Hand gestures and body movements can represent the stages of development of the seed. Experiences using physical movements often help children to remember processes and sequences more easily.

11. Lights, Camera, Action

Students can develop a television show related to seeds and gardening. Episodes might answer these questions: How do we start seeds for the garden? What do seeds need to grow? What conditions are best for starting plants? What are some of the attributes of different types of seeds? What are some good recipes for eating different types of seeds? Teachers and families can support this investigation by supplying easy-to-follow recipe books. The children might also include commercials that advertise the values of different foods that come from seeds.

12. Story Time

Invite your students to write stories about seeds. They might base their story on seeds that they germinated. Children can share their stories using drawings, paintings, cutouts, song, dance, photographs, or other creative techniques.

13. Seed Mosaics

Seed pictures can be created by gluing seeds of different sizes, shapes, and colors to a poster board, or to other interesting materials, to construct a mosaic. Supply some basic seeds that are a variety of bright colors such as corn, peas, and pinto beans. You might also stain some seeds with food coloring to create special effects.

Encourage children first to examine the seeds that are available and then to sketch out a plan or map of the mosaic they envision unfolding with the seeds. Using multiple forms of representation, help children become abstract thinkers. Along with this artwork, children might also write poems to describe their seed mosaics.

Activities in Other Explorations That Relate to Seeds

Birds (Chapter 8)

2. Feed the Birds

4. Food Preferences of Birds

Resources for Teachers

Books

Burton, J., & Taylor, K. (1999). *The nature and science of seeds*. Milwaukee, WI: Gareth Stevens Publishing.

Morgan, S. (1996). *Flowers, trees and fruits*. New York: Kingfisher Publications.

Peterson, R. T., & McKenny, M. (1996). *A field guide to wildflowers: Northeastern and north-central North America*. Boston, MA: Houghton Mifflin.

Venning, F. D. (1984). *Wildflowers of North America*. New York: Golden Press.

Article

Romme, W. G., & Despain, D. G. (1989, November). The Yellowstone fires. *Scientific American*, pp. 37–46.

Web Sites

http://www.appleseeds.org
Provides quotations and short stories from eclectic sources that promote positive attitudes about plants.

http://www.bonsaisite.com/germinate.html
Tips on germinating tree seeds.

http://www.burpee.com
Lists varieties of seeds and information on germinating seeds.

http://cityseeds.org
Web site for City Seeds, a collaborative project of the Poughkeepsie Farm Project and the Cornell Cooperative Extension–Focus on urban agriculture.

http://www.crfg.org/pubs/ff/tamarind.html
Provides information about the tamarind fruit, native to Asia and eastern Africa.

http://www.davesgarden.com.html
Information about gardening and gardening terms.

http://www.ext.vt.edu/departments/envirohort/articles2/sdgrmtmp.html
Information on temperature variations for seed germination.

http://www.farmproject.org
Poughkeepsie Farm Project site, a nonprofit organization that works toward sustainable food systems in the mid-Hudson Valley, New York.

http://www.farmersteve.com/corn.htm
Live Web video-cam of popcorn growing.

http://mdmd.essortment.com/indoorgardeningrjgx.htm
A good site for gardening techniques for children. Here you will find information about house-plants; kitchen gardening; and how to plant citrus, date, mango, avocado, and pomegranate seeds.

http://www.mcs.surrey.ac.uk/Personal/RKnott/Fibonacce/fibnat.html
Information about the Fibonacci spirals and Fibonacci numbers in nature.

http://ohioline.osu.edu/hyg-fact/1000/1228.html
A Web site about growing sunflowers and their uses.

http://www.seedman.com/welcome
Unusual and exotic fruit and nut plant seeds from around the world.

Children's Books on Seeds

Anthony, J. (1997). *The dandelion seed*. Nevada City, CA: Dawn Publications.
Barton, B. (1993). *The little red hen*. New York: HarperCollins.
Berenstain, J., & Berenstain, S. (1996). *The Berenstain bears grow it*. New York: Random House.
Brown, R. (2001). *Ten seeds*. London: Andersen Press.
Bulla, C. R. (1998). *The poppy seeds*. Prince Frederick, MD: Recorded Books.
Burnie, D. (1992). *Flowers*. New York: DK Publishing.
Carle, E. (2001). *The tiny seed*. New York: Aladdin Paperbacks. Scholastic.
Cole, J. (1995). *The magic school bus: Plants, seeds*. New York: Scholastic.
Cowley, J. (1999). *The rusty, trusty tractor*. Honesdale, PA: Boyds Mill Press.
dePaola, T. (1978). *The popcorn book*. New York: Holiday House.
Dieckmanm, M. (1994). *The sunflower*. Niwot, CO: Roberts Rinehart Publishers.
Dunrea, O. (1993). *Noggin and Bobbin in the garden*. Glenview, IL: Scott, Foresman, and Company.
Dunrea, O. (2006). *Hanne's quest*. New York: Philomel Books.
Eclare, M. (2000). *A handful of sunshine*. Brooklyn, NY: Ragged Bears.
Ehlert, L. (1987). *Growing vegetable soup*. San Diego, CA: Harcourt Brace Jovanovich.
Ehlert, L. (1988). *Planting a rainbow*. San Diego, CA: Harcourt Brace Javanovich.
Fowler, A. (1994). *Corn—On and off the cob*. Canada: Children's Press.

Gibbons, G. (1991). *From seed to plant*. New York: Holiday House.

Goodman, S. (2001). *Seeds, stems and stamens*. Brookfield, CT: Millbrook Press.

Hall, Z. (1998). *The surprise garden*. New York: Blue Sky Press.

Hearn, D. D. (1994). *Anna in the garden*. New York: Silver Moon Press.

Hickman, P., & Collins, H. (1997). *A seed grows*. Toronto: Kids Can Press.

Hillert, M. (1966). *The magic beans*. Columbus, OH: Modern Curriculum Press.

Jordan, H. (1992). *How a seed grows*. New York: HarperCollins.

Kite, P. L. (1998). *Dandelion adventures*. Brookfield, CT: Millbrook Press.

Krauss, R. (1973). *The carrot seed*. New York: Harper and Row.

Krementz, J. (1991). *A very young gardener*. New York: Dial Books.

Kuchalla, S. (1982). *Now I know all about seeds*. Mahwah, NJ: Troll Associates.

le Tord, B. (1984). *Rabbit seeds*. New York: Four Winds Press.

Lobel, A. (1992). *Pierrot's ABC garden*. New York: Golden Books.

Lovejoy, S. (1999). *Roots, shoots, buckets and boots*. New York: Workman.

Maestro, B. (1992). *How do apples grow?* New York: HarperCollins.

Marzollo, J. (1996). *I'm a seed*. New York: Scholastic.

McPhail, D. (1998). *A bug, a bear, and a boy*. New York: Scholastic.

Medearis, A. S. (1999). *Seeds grow*. New York: Scholastic.

Mockford, C. (2000). *What's this?* New York: Barefoot Books.

Morton, J. F. (1971). *Exotic plants*. New York: Golden Press.

Pascoe, E. (1997). *Seeds and seedlings*. Woodbridge, CT: Blackbirch Press.

Pattou, E. (2001). *Mrs. Spitzer's garden*. San Diego, CA: Harcourt.

Pfeffer, W. (2002). *From seed to pumpkin*. New York: HarperCollins

Posada, M. (2000). *Dandelions: Stars in the grass*. Minneapolis, MN: Carolrhoda Books.

Richards, J. (2002). *A fruit is a suitcase for seeds*. Brookfield, CT: Millbrook Press.

Robbins, K. (2005). *Seeds*. New York: Atheneum Books.

Saunders-Smith, G. (1998). *Seeds*. Mankato, MN: Capstone Press.

Sloat, T. (1999). *Patty's pumpkin patch*. New York: Putman's.

Titherington, J. (1986). *Pumpkin pumpkin*. New York: Greenwillow Books.

Worth, B. (2001). *Oh say can you seed?* New York: Random House.

Correlation of NSES Standards and NCTM Principles and Standards to Sun and Shadows Concept Exploration Activities

	1. Here Comes the Sun	2. I Saw the Sun Move	3. Me and My Shadow	4. Silhouettes	5. Exploring the Shapes and Sizes of Shadows	6. Photo Opportunities	7. Shadow Games	8. The Warmth of the Sun	9. The Sun Is a Spotlight	10. Mythology and the Sun
SCIENCE										
Inquiry	X	X	X	X	X	X	X	X	X	X
Physical Science	X	X	X	X	X	X	X	X	X	X
Life Science								X	X	X
Earth and Space Science	X	X	X			X		X	X	X
Science and Technology						X				X
Personal and Social Perspectives	X	X	X	X	X	X	X	X	X	X
History and Nature of Science	X									X
MATHEMATICS										
Number and Operations	X	X	X					X		
Algebra	X	X	X			X		X		
Geometry	X	X	X	X	X	X			X	
Measurement	X	X	X		X				X	
Data Analysis and Probability	X	X	X					X		
Problem Solving	X	X			X	X			X	
Reasoning and Proof		X	X		X	X				
Communication			X	X			X	X		
Connections					X					X
Representation	X	X	X	X	X	X	X		X	X

CHAPTER 15

Sun and Shadows

My Shadow

I have a little shadow that goes in and out with me,
And what can be the use of him is more than I can see.
He is very, very like me from the heels up to the head;
And I see him jump before me, when I jump into my bed.
The funniest thing about him is the way he likes to grow—
Not at all like proper children, which is always very slow;
For he sometimes shoots up taller like an India-rubber ball,
And he sometimes goes so little that there's none of him at all.
He hasn't got a notion of how children ought to play,
And can only make a fool of me in every sort of way.
He stays so close behind me; he's a coward you can see;
I'd think shame to stick to nursie as that shadow sticks to me!
One morning, very early, before the sun was up,
I rose and found the shining dew on every buttercup;
But my lazy little shadow, like an arrant sleepy-head,
Had stayed at home behind me and was fast asleep in bed.

Robert Louis Stevenson

The Sun is the center of our existence. Earth, and all the life that Earth supports, receives its energy from the Sun. Children can see the effects of the Sun everyday. Even when the skies are cloudy, our daylight is filtered through the clouds to us. But the consistent miracles of life, as we know them, are taken for granted; we do not usually direct our attention to the Sun. We need to take advantage of daily opportunities to notice the effect of the Sun on our lives. Helping children understand the importance of the Sun can be very exciting and illuminating!

The apparent movement of the Sun, as it travels through our sky from sunrise to sunset, causes changes in our local temperature. The soft light of the morning that causes the dew to glisten becomes replaced by the searing heat of a summer afternoon followed by the red hue of the sunset.

Understanding the nature of the Sun and its daily and seasonal patterns permits us to expand our enjoyment of the Sun's processes. It also assists us in exploring many other processes in the world around us that are controlled by the Sun.

Accompanying the Sun are its constant companions, shadows. Shadows fascinate young children. When children first see their own shadows, their exploration almost becomes a game. They try to manipulate their shadows, changing the shape or causing them to move. They might try to hide from their shadows or try to shake them off or run away from them, but to no avail. Observing shadows can provoke valuable learning experiences. Shadows help us understand more about the nature of light; that light travels in a straight line. Observing changes in shadows also helps us understand more about the nature of the apparent movement of the Sun. As the day progresses, the shadows seem to shorten and then lengthen again in the evening.

Obviously, the Sun is a major part of children's world. Exploring the Sun can be an excellent vehicle for children to learn about their world and about themselves.

SCIENCE CONCEPTS FOR TEACHERS

These Concept Explorations use children's experiences involving the Sun and the properties of light to examine several basic science processes and utilize basic math skills. The concepts and information presented here should only be presented to the children at an introductory level. For example, your children might explore the movement of the shadows on the sundial; however, young children do not yet have the cognition to understand how the tilt of the axis and Earth's orbit around the Sun cause day and night and the seasons.

It could be said that the Sun is an average, ordinary star. There are many other stars similar to our Sun. The stars that are much bigger than the Sun are called *red giants* and *super red giants*. Consider this: If the Earth were the size, of a BB, the Sun would be the size of a basketball, and the super red giants would be as big as the basketball arena.

The Sun Is a Nuclear Furnace

The energy that the Sun gives off is the result of a constant nuclear reaction. Nuclear reactions are divided into two types: fission and fusion. Fission is the process in which atoms are broken apart. For example in fission, atoms of uranium give off particles, breaking the atom down into simpler elements.

2007/04/11 00:00

Solar and Heliospheric Observatory

The Sun.

Fusion is the process in which atoms are combined to form heavier atoms. For example, in fusion, hydrogen atoms combine to form helium atoms. The nuclear reaction that happens on the Sun is fusion. The Sun contains mainly hydrogen; in fact, more than 92% of the atoms are hydrogen.

Because of the massive amount of matter on the Sun, the gravity pulling toward the center of the Sun is immense. This force causes the atoms to be squeezed together. This pressure causes a great amount of heat—the center of the Sun reaches around 15 million kelvin. At this temperature, hydrogen atoms fuse to form helium. In this process, a small amount of matter is changed into energy. This is the energy that we receive from the Sun.

In a nuclear reaction, in which matter is converted to energy, a small amount of matter produces a tremendous amount of energy. According to Einstein's equation, $E = mc^2$, the amount of energy (E) that is created is equal to the amount of mass (m) times the speed of light (c) (186,000 miles per second) squared. Simply what this means is that if you exchange 1 gram of matter (1 millimeter of water), enough energy is produced to keep a 100 watt light bulb burning for 3.5 million years.

Each second, the Sun transforms approximately 5,000,000 tons of matter (equivalent to a 30-car train) into energy. The energy from the Sun is dissipated in all directions. Thus, Earth only receives an extremely small portion of this energy.

We do not fully understand how the Sun and its planets were formed. We do know that stars such as our Sun form when gravity causes large clouds of gas (mainly hydrogen) to contract. The Sun formed approximately 4.6 billion years ago. It is expected that the Sun will last for another 5 billion years.

The Earth's Revolution and Rotation Determine the Earth's Seasons

Earth continuously makes two distinct motions: rotation and revolution. *Rotation* refers to the spinning of Earth around its axis. This spinning causes our days and nights, and each rotation takes 1 day. *Revolution* refers to Earth's movement around the Sun. Each revolution takes 1 year. These two distinct motions of Earth cause our seasons and our climates.

The Sun in Our Sky

The cause of the seasons of the year is one of the most misunderstood concepts in science. Many people mistakenly think that the seasons of the year are caused by variations in the distance of Earth to the Sun. Actually, Earth's orbit is very close to circular. The variation is very slight, with Earth being closest to the Sun on January 4, and farthest from the Sun on July 4. The cause of the seasons is the tilt of Earth's axis at a 23.5-degree angle. This causes the rays of energy from the Sun to concentrate on either the Northern Hemisphere or the Southern Hemisphere.

The rays of light from the Sun strike perpendicularly at one location on Earth. If you were at that point, the Sun would appear to be at the *zenith*, or the point directly overhead. Because Earth is a sphere, as you move away from that point, the Sun's angle from the horizon decreases. The further away you travel, the lower the Sun would appear to be in the sky. At a 90-degree angle, the Sun would appear to be at the horizon.

As we know, Earth revolves around the Sun once each year. Earth acts as a giant gyroscope. As it spins, the axis continues to point at the same direction. The result is that as Earth travels around the Sun, the latitude at which the Sun shines directly on the surface varies (Figure 15.1). On the first day of summer in the Northern Hemisphere (called the summer solstice), the Sun shines directly at 23.5° North Latitude. The circle at this latitude is called the Tropic of Cancer. North of this line, the Sun never shines at the zenith. If you were at the North Pole, the sun would shine all day with the Sun circling you 23.5° above the horizon. You could travel southward 23.5° and you would continue to have 24 hours of daylight. The circle at 23.5° south of the North Pole is called the Arctic Circle. This day is also the first day of winter for the Southern Hemisphere.

On the first day of winter in the Northern Hemisphere (called the winter solstice), the Sun shines directly at 23.5° South Latitude. The circle at this latitude is called the Tropic of Capricorn. South of this line, the Sun never shines at the zenith. On the first day of winter, the sun would be at the horizon at the Arctic Circle. North of that circle, you would have 24 hours of darkness. This day is also the first day of summer for the Southern Hemisphere.

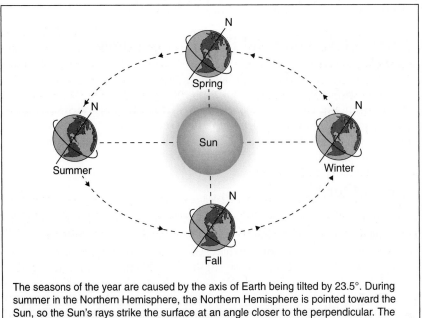

The seasons of the year are caused by the axis of Earth being tilted by 23.5°. During summer in the Northern Hemisphere, the Northern Hemisphere is pointed toward the Sun, so the Sun's rays strike the surface at an angle closer to the perpendicular. The Southern Hemisphere is pointed away from the Sun, so the rays strike at an angle closer to the horizon. Thus, the Southern Hemisphere is in winter. Six months later the system is reversed. The Northern Hemisphere is in winter and the Southern Hemisphere is in summer.

FIGURE 15.1 Seasons in the Northern Hemisphere.

On the first day of spring (called the vernal equinox) and the first day of fall (called the autumnal equinox), the Sun shines directly on the equator. The Sun would be at the horizon at both the North and South Poles.

Observing the Daily and Annual Motion of the Sun in Our Sky

The apparent motion of the Sun each day is caused by Earth's counterclockwise motion (when viewed from above the North Pole). For locations in the middle northern latitudes, as Earth spins, the Sun rises above the eastern horizon and during the morning, moves into our southern sky. At noon it is at its highest point. During the afternoon, the Sun moves into the western sky where it sets in the evening.

The difference in the position of the Sun in our sky during the different seasons is how high the Sun moves from the horizon. During the spring and summer, the Sun is higher in the sky than it is during fall and winter. This causes the Sun's rays to shine more directly on us giving us more energy from the Sun. It also means we have more daylight hours each day.

MATHEMATICS: ADDRESSING THE NCTM STANDARDS THROUGH CONCEPT EXPLORATIONS

Many mathematical concepts are used as children explore and investigate sunshine and shadows. Many of the activities in these Concept Explorations involve patterns and sequencing; geometry; measurement; and data collection, organization, and analysis. As you engage in these creative investigations and explorations with your students, be aware of the wonderful opportunities that present themselves to infuse creative and thoughtful observation, thinking, and communication about sunshine, shadows and the feelings they inspire.

Number and Operations

Anytime we attach counting to an activity, we are helping children practice one-to-one correspondence and stable order. As children learn to describe phenomena with numerical information, they are learning that mathematics is the language of science.

Algebra

Children are using algebraic thinking when they sort, classify, and order things by size and other properties. As they observe shadows and begin to classify them as large or small, they are beginning to understand the patterns in their world. As they attach language to their observations, for instance, when describing the sequence of change in a growing or shrinking shadow, they are learning how to describe qualitative change, another important algebraic process. The mathematical language of comparison and seriation such as tall, taller, tallest, is important to model and use.

Geometry

Shadow exploration with young children will provide many rich opportunities for them to explore patterns and geometric concepts. Children experience spatial concepts as they explore the dynamic nature of shadows and their movements. As they watch shadows change and move with the movement of the Sun, they are exploring ideas involved with shape, position in space, symmetry, and transformations. Sundials, in particular, give children opportunities to see the dynamic nature of changing angles as the gnomon on the sundial casts ever changing angle sizes indicating the passage of time. As children continue to spend time investigating and exploring the Sun's effect on shadows, they will continue to make new discoveries and develop new theories about the relationships they are exploring.

In addition, as children explore their own movements and see how they can construct and change a shadow, they are beginning to analyze how patterns are generated and changed. Keeping track of how these changes are made helps children understand their role in this cause-and-effect relationship.

Using the language of space and shape helps children to deepen their level of descriptions as they observe shadows. For example, using geometric words such as *circular, round, oval, rectangular,* and so forth, makes children aware of the many ways they can describe the interesting phenomena of nature. Similarly, they should be encouraged to use language of relative position in space such as over, under, up, down, above, below, together, near, far, top, bottom, next to, in front of, behind, in between, and so forth. As they attach this descriptive language to their observations, they will be expanding their mathematical vocabulary in meaningful and creative ways. These concepts should be extended through conversations and storytelling. Using the language of sequence, navigation, and movement in natural ways strengthens a child's ability to make sense of his ever-changing, dynamic world.

Multiple forms of representation can also be used to capture the patterns and shapes that are cast by shadows. Sketches, tracings, photographs, videos, paper cutouts, paint and crayon renderings, or three-dimensional replicas of clouds can be constructed.

Opportunities for describing the attributes of the similarities and differences among shadows and of how shadows change can also be given. Looking for these similarities and differences between and among the shadows is also important for sound development in building and understanding classification schemes. Children can use their own language to capture what they see and feel.

Measurement

Measurement is an important tool for documenting the existence and dynamic nature of shadows and the movement of the Sun. Children can explore creative ways of measuring the Sun's movement and engage in interesting activities and experiments to determine how fast the Sun moves or how much a shadow has changed in length or height. Children can create artistic representations of shadow configurations with many different techniques. Children can be asked what materials they think would be best to use to capture their shadows.

The construction of simple sundials helps children capture their observations of the Sun's movement in the sky as they watch the changing length of the shadow cast by the gnomon. The sundial exploration in this chapter (Concept Exploration 1) helps children use time and elapsed time to describe the Sun's movement across the span of a day. Children can pose interesting questions about measuring size, height, and movement of shadows as they construct the sundial. Support for this exploration can be provided with watches, clocks for measuring and keeping track of time, and standard and nonstandard measuring tools for measuring the lengths of shadows. Children should be given many opportunities to use the tools and to examine carefully the attributes they are measuring.

Inherent in sundial explorations and construction are opportunities for language development and record keeping. Modeling and validating appropriate language utilizing words that relate to comparison and seriation should be encouraged. The sundial will show a seriated sequence of shadow lengths as they are cast by the gnomon. Having children become fully engaged in this exploration helps them to generate theories about the apparent movement of the Sun.

Data Analysis

Graphing can be used to document the effects of the Sun's movement on how shadows "grow" and "shrink." Much of the exploration involved in observing shadows and in constructing the sundial can be documented through creative graphing. Organizing these data can be a creative collaboration as the children choose their own ways in which to represent the changing shadows. It is important for children to design ways of collecting, representing, and displaying their data. Teachers can provide a variety of media for the children to explore in the construction of tables and graphs.

OBSERVING WITH ALL THE SENSES

Sight

The Sun is the brightest object in our sky and our constant companion. The Sun gives us many opportunities to observe its continuous changes. Observations related to the Sun must be indirect. **No person should ever look directly toward the Sun.** Galileo became virtually blind by trying to observe sunspots on the Sun. Fortunately, there are many indirect techniques that we can use with our children to observe changes in the position of the Sun.

During a short observation period, we can observe changes in the position of sunlight and the shadows produced from the sunlight entering our classroom windows. The "window box" will travel across the floor. Measurable changes will occur in just a few minutes. For example, you could place a small stuffed animal in the sunlight so that the animal can be warm. When you return around an hour later, the animal might now be out of the "window box." Making informal observations of these movements at frequent intervals throughout the year gives children a general sense of the motion of the Sun.

On the playground we can observe changes in the position of the Sun with a sundial or by simply observing the shadow from the school flagpole. To verify movements of the flagpole shadow, you can place markers or stakes in the ground identifying the time that the shadow was at that location.

Techniques for Looking at the Sun

You can use some simple techniques to observe the Sun and its features. One simple technique is to make a type of pinhole camera, as illustrated in Figure 15.2. This is accomplished by making a fine pinhole on the side of a cardboard box. This is best done by cutting a small square out of the box, covering the square opening that is left with some aluminum foil, and then making a pinhole in the aluminum foil. On the opposite side of the box, place a white sheet of paper to serve as a screen. When the sunlight shines through the pinhole, it will appear as a small circle on the screen. This technique is often used to observe the Sun during solar eclipses.

Many Web sites have live cameras for viewing the features of the Sun (refer to the end-of-chapter Web site list for some specifics). The photos taken daily by these cameras can be used to observe sunspots, solar flares, and many other features.

Exploring Shadows

Young children find shadows very interesting. When they first discover shadows, they explore different things that they can do; for example, they try to hide from their shadows or cause their shadows to disappear. This exploration is very valuable because, through this process, they are examining basic properties of light, such as "light travels in a straight line." If light did not travel in a straight line, we would not be able to see the distinct shadows that we do see.

Children also enjoy observing the shadows of different objects. For instance, the shadows of branches of trees move with the branches in the wind. The shadow of a small white cumulus cloud will travel across a field toward them.

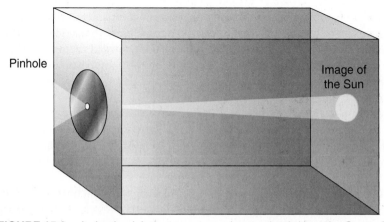

FIGURE 15.2 A simple pinhole camera can be used to look at the Sun safely.

Touch

Our sensitive body can detect changes in temperature very quickly. When we walk into a sunny area, we quickly can feel the warmth of the Sun on our body.

We can also detect this heat from the Sun using other techniques. One technique utilizes a simple device that demonstrates the greenhouse effect. Cover a box or container with a clear sheet of plastic or glass.

The rays of light radiated by the Sun are transmitted through the glass and are absorbed by the box. The box also radiates heat. However, because the box is at a much lower temperature than the Sun, the box radiates heat at a much longer wavelength. The glass cannot transmit these longer rays, thus the heat is trapped and the box warms up.

We observe the greenhouse effect on sunny days with our car. The Sun's heat is trapped in the car, often heating the car by 30 to 40 degrees Fahrenheit. This can be extremely dangerous for young children or pets that are left in the car even for short periods.

A technique for indicating the amount of heat that is absorbed is to place thermometers on different surfaces. For example, if you place one thermometer on a white surface and a second thermometer on a dark surface, the thermometer on the white surface will be cooler because the white surface will reflect more of the Sun's rays. The dark surface will absorb more of the rays from the Sun.

SAFETY

Extreme safety should be a constant concern when observing the Sun or any bright light. Damage that occurs to the eye when looking at the Sun is permanent. Caution should also be exercised in protecting children's skin from the harmful rays of the Sun by using sunscreen.

CONCEPT EXPLORATIONS ON SUN AND SHADOWS FOR YOUR CLASSROOM

The following Concept Explorations use children's experiences with the Sun to examine several basic science processes and utilize basic math skills. Utilizing some of the books listed at the end of this chapter is a great way to invite interest and imagination as you plan the activities to follow. Joseph Sherman's book, *Sunshine: A Book About Sunlight*, offers interesting facts about sunshine, weather, rainbows, sunsets, and moonlight and provides an appropriate advanced look at what will unfold in these explorations.

1. Here Comes the Sun

Sundials are fascinating devices. Sundials come in all shapes, styles, and sizes and can be as little as a wrist watch or as large as a building, or as simple as a stick in the ground. Sundials are known to have existed for thousands of years.

As Earth spins on its axis, the Sun appears to rise in the east and over the day move toward the western sky, setting in the evening. Sundials document this movement by recording the shadow movement.

This sundial in Japur, India, is over 500 years old.

J. David Keller

Have your children design and make a sundial. You might initiate the experience by having the children observe how the Sun's shadows are constantly changing. The sunlight entering the classroom window leaves a pattern on the floor or wall that is constantly moving. A small piece of paper or a pencil placed along the edge of the shadow on the floor can mark the position. In just a few minutes your children can see the movement of the shadow.

On a larger scale children can use small stakes to mark the shadow created by the school flagpole. During the school day, they will be able to see that the shadow moves to the opposite side of the flagpole.

After your children have experienced the changes in the shadows produced by the sunlight, this experience can be personalized by having the class make their own sundials.

Basically, a sundial is a column or pin, called the *gnomon*, that is supported by a base. The purpose of the gnomon is to cast the shadow of the sunlight. The base can be marked with lines indicating the different times of day that the shadow of the gnomon will pass through. In this sense, a wooden spoon set upright in a piece of clay serves the purpose.

On a simple sundial, the gnomon is vertical. More often, the gnomon is at an angle pointing to the north celestial pole. (The gnomon in reality is parallel to the axis of Earth.) The angle of the gnomon is determined by the latitude of the location that the sundial is located. If your latitude is 40°, the gnomon would be set at an angle of 40° pointing northward. Document that your sundial works by taking photographs, making drawings, or recording markings on paper with times indicated or any other techniques that you would like to use.

These experiences also provide children with opportunities to explore and measure angles. As the children record the movement of the shadows around the gnomon, different angles are produced.

2. I Saw the Sun Move

Mark the position of the Sun's shadow and see how long it takes before you can document that the shadow moved. Can you reposition the object or choose a different object that will decrease the time for movement to be noticed? What object do you find that works the best? What characteristics do these objects have?

This activity is very valuable to children because it allows them to explore the effect of size. The shadow of a large object such as a building produces a big shadow. The shadow of a small object such as a pencil produces a small shadow. As they explore these relationships, they will discover that they can document the movement of the large shadow more quickly than the movement of the small shadow.

3. Me and My Shadow

Children enjoy exploring their own shadows. You can help children explore their shadows using a bright light such as an overhead projector. Cut out the children's shadows on black paper and place them on a bulletin board. Children should look for unique characteristics so that they can recognize each member of the class.

Children can work as teams to mark their shadows on the sidewalk with chalk. Suggest that they measure the size of the students' shadows during different times of the day. Devise a way to record the shadows and discuss the results.

4. Silhouettes

Children can explore shadows by creating silhouettes. For example, they might cut out figures on tag board. Using a bright light they could use their shadow puppets to produce shadows on a wall, or they could shine the images on a white sheet. Similarly, they can cast silhouettes with hand and body movements on the wall or a screen.

These experiences give children opportunities to experiment with shape and movement as well as express themselves by telling stories or carrying on conversations. They might tell their favorite fairy tale or they could tell riddles.

5. Exploring the Shapes and Sizes of Shadows

This exploration gives children experiences that assist them in their development of spatial awareness. Shadows provide opportunities for children to explore two-dimensional geometric shapes. As they manipulate objects, they can change the shape of the shadow that is produced. For example, they can manipulate a square piece of paper to produce a square, rectangular, or line segment shadow.

These manipulations also give children opportunities to explore size. How can they manipulate a card to produce the largest shadow? How can they produce the smallest shadow? What generalizations can they make about producing the different shapes and sizes?

6. Photo Opportunities

Give your children a simple digital camera and ask them to explore their shadows. For activities of this nature, it is best to give children specific objectives that they should accomplish. You might suggest that they take photographs that show angles, or they might be challenged to find the smallest shadow. If the weather conditions are right, they might photograph the shadow of a small cloud. Encourage the children to analyze the differences and similarities that they capture in their pictures.

A video camera can also be a valuable tool in this investigation. Video cameras have the benefit of showing movement. For example, shadows of branches and leaves on a tree being buffeted by the wind can produce interesting shapes on the ground. Particular areas of sunlight will seem to expand and contract as the leaves are blown around.

7. Shadow Games

Invite your children to design a game or activity using shadows. For instance, they might play shadow tag. They might try to toss a ball into the air to produce a shadow of the ball on a target on a wall. They might use their shadows to produce the letters of the alphabet on the ground. You might suggest that two or more students work as a team to produce different shadow figures. They might try to cause their shadows to "touch" without their bodies touching each other.

8. The Warmth of the Sun

Nothing is more pleasant than feeling the warmth of the Sun on a cool spring day. On the other hand, we seek shade from the burning Sun in August. Invite your children to compare how they feel when they move in and out of sunshine and shadow. What parts of their body are most sensitive to these changes? You might place a black and a white or light-colored teddy bear in the sunlight and compare which one feels the warmest.

J. David Keller

These bushes have protected the snow, in their shadow, from the sunlight. The snow that was in the sunlight has melted. Invite your students to observe other examples of differential heating caused by Sun and shade.

An extension of this might be to suggest that your children explore to see which animals seek sunlight and which animals try to hide from the Sun. Why does a garter snake seek the Sun? Why do worms try to stay away from the Sun?

The effect of the Sun can also be examined by observing inanimate objects. After a heavy frost, the sunlight melts the frost, clearly identifying areas in shadow. Likewise, sunlight might "dry out" portions of a sidewalk after a rain. Encourage your children to identify changes that take place. How many different ways can they document the work of the Sun?

9. The Sun Is a Spotlight

Your children might use a camera to photograph objects that are enhanced by the sunlight. For example, photograph the morning dew sparkling like diamonds on a spider's web, or the glistening glow of a puddle stretched out in the sunshine.

One of the benefits of activities of this nature is to expand children's vocabulary skills. For each photograph, encourage your children to identify five adjectives that describe the significance of the photograph.

10. Mythology and the Sun

Throughout ancient times, many mythological stories developed around the Sun. The Sun is critical for basic life, so it is not surprising that the Sun had major significance and took on mythological and religious roles. Many civilizations have developed stories about the Sun.

Probably the earliest stories about the Sun came from Egypt and China. Many stories can also be found in the well-known Greek and Roman mythology. However, most other early cultures also had mythological stories related to the Sun. These include the Mayan, Indian, Native American, and Viking cultures.

Identify some mythological stories about the Sun and share them with your children. Encourage your children to use some form of representation or medium to depict the story. For example, they might use dioramas, paint, song, dance, or drama.

> According to Norse mythology, Sol was the daughter of Mundifari. She was stolen away from her father by the gods who put her to work in the heavens. She drives the chariot that carries the Sun across the heavens.

Activities in Other Explorations That Relate to Sun and Shadows

Leaves (Chapter 11)

7. A Tribute to Transpiration

Resources for Teachers

Books

Canduto, M. J., & Bruchac, J. (1988). *Keepers of the night: Native American stories and nocturnal activities for children.* Golden, CO: Fulcrum.

Canduto, M. J., & Bruchac, J. (1989). *Keepers of the Earth: Native American stories and environmental activities for children.* Golden, CO: Fulcrum.

Greeley, R. (1997). *The NASA atlas of the solar system.* Cambridge, MA: Cambridge University Press.

Rohr, R. (1996). *Sundials: History, theory and practice.* New York: Dover Publications.

Article

Suplee, C. (2004). A stormy star. *National Geographic*, pp. 2–33.

Web Sites

http://www.alumni.ca/~wongj/index.htm
Information on the birth, life, and death of stars.

http://aa.usno.navy.mil/data/docs/UpcomingEclipses.html
Upcoming eclipses of the Sun and Moon.

http://aa.usno.navy.mil/faq/docs/seasons_orbit.html
Information about seasons and Earth's orbit.

http://www.conservation.state.mo.us/nathis/backyard/sundial
Simple plans for constructing sundials.

http://home.att.net/~tangents/tech/astrocal.htm
An astronomical calendar of events.

http://www.mts.net/~sabanski/sundial/sotwl.htm
Sundials of the world.

http://seds.lpl.arizona.edu/nineplanets/nineplanets/sol.html
Basic information on the Sun.

http://sohowww.nascom.nasa.gov
Gives daily activities and data on the Sun.

http://umbra.gsfc.nasa.gov/images/latest.html
Has several photographs of the Sun taken daily using a variety of filters.

Children's Books on Sun and Shadows

Anno, M. (1987). *Anno's sundial*. New York: Philomel Books.
Armstrong, J. (1995). *Sunshine, moonshine*. New York: Random House.
Asch, F. (1985). *Bear shadow*. New York: Scholastic.
Asch, F. (2000). *The Sun is my favorite star*. San Diego, CA: Harcourt Brace.
Ashwell, M., & Owen, A. (1999). *Sunshine*. Chicago: Heinemann Library.
Branley, F. M. (2002). *The Sun, our nearest star*. New York: Harper Collins.
Branley, F. M. (2005). *Sunshine makes the seasons*. New York: Harper Collins.
Bulla, C. R. (1994). *What makes a shadow?* New York: Harper Collins.
Burke, J. S. (2000). *Sunny days*. New York: Children's Press.
Chorao, K. (2001). *Shadow night*. New York: Dutton.
Desimini, L. (1999). *Sun and Moon*. New York: Blue Sky Press.
Dorros, A. (1990). *Me and my shadow*. New York: Scholastic.
Fiarotta, P., & Fioratta, N. (1999). *Great experiments with light*. New York: Sterling Publishing Co.
Freeman, D. (2000). *Gregory's shadow*. New York: Viking.
Gibbons, G. (1983). *Sun up, Sun down*. New York: Harcourt Brace Jovanovich.
Goor, N., & Goor, R. (1981). *Shadows: Here, there, and everywhere*. New York: Thomas Y. Crowell.
Grackenbach, D. (1983). *Mr. Wink and his shadow, Ned*. New York: Harper and Row.
Hendra, S. (1996). *Oliver's wood*. Cambridge, MA: Candlewick Press.
Hines, A. G. (1999). *What can you do in the Sun?* New York: Greenwillow Books.
Hoban, T. (1990). *Shadows and reflections*. New York: Greenwillow Books.
Hoban, T. (1993). *White on black/black on white*. New York: William Morrow & Company.
Kaner, E. (2007). *Who likes the Sun?* Toronto, Ontario: Kids Can Press.
Kent, J. 1992. *The biggest shadow in the zoo*. New York: Parents Magazine Press.
Lodge, Y. (2001). *A book about day-time: A pop-up book about sundials.* London: Brown Wells & Jacobs.
Mahy, M. (1989). *The boy with two shadows*. New York: J.B. Lippincott.
Moore, P. (1995). *The Sun and Moon*. Brookfield, CT: Copper Beech Books.
Nankivell, A. S., & Jackson, D. (1999). *Science experiments with light*. New York: Franklin Watts/Grolier Publishing.
Narahashi, K. (1987). *I have a friend*. New York: Margaret K. McElderry Books.
Orii, E., & Orii, M. (1989). *Simple science experiments with light*. Milwaukee, WI: Garrett Stevens Children's Books.
Palazzo, J. (1982). *Our friend the Sun*. Mahwah, NJ: Troll Associates.
Paul, A. W. (1992). *Shadows are about*. New York: Scholastic.
Petty, K. (1997). *The sun is a star*. Brookfield, CT: Copper Beech Books.
Richards, J. (1999). *Light and sight*. Brookfield, CT: Copper Beech Books.

Rosinsky, N. M. (2003). *Light: Shadows, mirrors, and rainbows*. Minneapolis, MN: Picture Window Books.

Royston, A. (2002). *My world of science light and dark*. Chicago: Heinemann Library.

Saunders-Smith, G. (1998). *Sunshine*. Mankato, MN: Capstone Press.

Sayre, A. P. (2002). *Shadows*. New York: Henry Holt.

Simon, S. (1985). *Shadow magic*. New York: Lothrop, Lee, and Shepard.

Stevenson, R. L. (1999). *My shadow*. Cambridge, MA: Candlewick Press.

Swinburne, S. R. (1999). *Guess whose shadow?* Honesdale, PA: Boyds Mills Press.

Tafuri, N. (1997). *What the Sun sees*. New York: Greenwillow Books.

Taylor, B. (1990). *Shadows and reflections*. New York: Warwick Press.

Taylor, B. (1991). *Seeing is not believing: The science of shadow and light*. New York: Random House.

Tocci, S. (2001). *Experiments with lights*. New York: Lothrop, Lee, and Shepard.

Tompert, A. (1984). *Nothing sticks like a shadow*. Boston, MA: Houghton Mifflin.

Tresselt, A. R. (1949). *Sun up*. New York: Lothrop, Lee, and Shepard.

Webb, P. H., & Corby, J. (1991). *Shadowgraphs anyone can make*. Philadelphia, PA: Running Press.

Winter, S. (1994). *My shadow*. New York: Bantam Doubleday Dell.

Zimmermann, E. (1990). *Shadow puppets for children*. Beltsville, MD: Gryphon House.

Correlation of NSES Standards and NCTM Principles and Standards to Toys and Tools Concept Exploration Activities

	1. Toy Festival	2. How Many Simple Machines Can You Find?	3. Rulers and Pencils	4. Strings and Things	5. The Toy Factory	6. Toys of Different Countries	7. The Human Machine	8. Invention Convention	9. The Ball Olympics
SCIENCE									
Inquiry	X	X	X	X	X	X	X	X	X
Physical Science	X	X	X	X	X	X	X	X	X
Life Science		X				X	X		
Earth and Space Science									
Science and Technology	X	X			X	X		X	X
Personal and Social Perspectives	X	X			X	X	X	X	X
History and Nature of Science		X			X				
MATHEMATICS									
Number and Operations	X	X		X		X			X
Algebra	X					X			X
Geometry					X			X	X
Measurement			X	X				X	X
Data Analysis and Probability	X	X	X	X		X			X
Problem Solving			X	X	X		X	X	X
Reasoning and Proof		X	X	X	X		X		X
Communication	X		X			X	X	X	X
Connections	X						X	X	X
Representation		X							X

CHAPTER 16

Toys and Tools

My Bouncing Friend

My ball is something special,
It is my favorite toy.
I play with it so often,
It always brings me joy.

I drop it out my window,
It bounces very high.
When I throw it on the pavement,
It rebounds to the sky.

I rolled it down a real long hill,
It jumped from here to there.
It bounded over rocks and grass,
and continued on with flair.

It splashed into the pond
and sailed across the sea.
It seemed to know just where to go,
It must have liked being free.

I'm glad I crossed the bridge,
To gather my bouncing friend.
It seems to chuckle with me,
It makes my spirit mend.

J. David Keller

Balls are wonderful toys. Other than a rattle, they are probably most children's first real toy. In fact, it is one of the first words that many children say, sometimes even before *Mama* and *Dada*. They enjoy watching a ball roll around. Babies enjoy having someone roll a ball to them. They enjoy causing a ball to deflect or bounce. Playing with large balls is an early source for developing hand–eye coordination and gross motor skills.

Balls introduce children to the nature of toys. Balls are critical for helping children learn that they can manipulate and control objects around them and, in doing so, can manipulate their experiences and their environment.

As children develop they learn that they can create other objects that will interact with toys. They can roll a ball off a box or a ramp. They can hit the ball with a stick or bat. They might even use a ball to interact with their dog or cat.

People really never lose this affinity for balls. We become more selective, however, choosing to play with a golf ball, tennis ball, football, or baseball. Regardless, balls continue to be an important part of our lives.

As children continue to develop, they identify many other toys that they can manipulate. Blocks take many forms. How high can we make a tower? How long can we make a road or train track? These toys are important not only for developing motor skills, but also for developing basic living experiences. Children will spend hours designing and building train tracks. They move around all the furniture and people in a doll house.

These activities help children develop skills in interacting with people. These activities are also critical for developing the concept of sequence. Should they build the bridge before or after the road? Should they serve cookies or tea first at the tea party? Using basic toys with children has many positive aspects. When we use toys in the classroom we are using the child's world.

With children, there is a close relationship between play and work. As they play, they imagine that they are working; that they are doing adult things. A preschooler once said, "I am going to 'little-work.'" He said this as he was arriving at his preschool. He knew that adults go to work, so he made the connection that he was going to work too! But because he was not as big as the adults, he framed his destination for the day as 'little-work.' As we mature into adults this reverses. We wish we could be playing, rather than having to "work."

Did you ever stop to think that perhaps the only difference between toys and tools is the age of the user? As a child we spend hours pulling our wagon or pushing our toy car up a ramp of blocks. Toys are a child tool for imagining about being an adult. As adults we select "tools" to accomplish a task.

Consider the old saying, "The only difference between men and boys is the price of their toys!" Perhaps the only real difference between toys and tools is the perspective of the user.

The Concept Explorations in this chapter examine how we can use basic toys and tools to give children experiences in exploring physical and mechanical events. In physics, mechanics is the study of forces on matter. We study how we can construct simple machines to help us do work. We look for ways to reduce friction, or to move objects.

By incorporating toys and basic tools into learning, we are able to introduce the science of mechanics to children as part of their world.

SCIENCE CONCEPTS FOR TEACHERS

As mentioned, *mechanics* is the study of the effect of forces on matter. Each day we use tools to do hundreds of basic tasks that change matter. These tasks include opening a door, stepping on a gas pedal, climbing stairs, and cutting with scissors. By understanding how these tools function, we can better understand when and how we can use them.

Simple Machines

Simple machines are devices that help us do many daily basic tasks. We use these simple machines because they make our tasks easier. All simple machines are based around two basic functions: effort and resistance. The *effort* is the force applied to the device. For instance, to raise the handles of a wheelbarrow, you might need to use a force of 20 pounds. Thus, the effort is 20 pounds. The *resistance* for this example would be the weight of the material in the wheelbarrow and the weight of the wheelbarrow itself. For the case of the wheelbarrow, the resistance might be 100 pounds. By using a wheelbarrow as a simple machine, we can move a 100-pound resistance with a 20-pound effort.

Simple machines make our tasks easier because they perform in one of three ways to reduce the amount of effort required to move the resistance:

1. Many simple machines can change the direction of a force. Often it is easier for us to pull down on an object than it is to lift up an object. For instance, if we push down on a car jack to lift up a car, we can use the force of gravity and our body weight to help us, which is much easier than trying to lift up an equal weight.

2. Some simple machines can increase the force on the resistance. For example, it would be extremely difficult to split a wood log in two with our hands. But by using an ax, we can easily split the wood. The ax has increased our ability to apply effort.

3. Some simple machines can increase the distance an object moves. We use a golf club because as we swing the golf club, the head of the club travels much more quickly through the ball. This impact causes the ball to travel much further than if we had tried to throw the ball.

Simple machines are based on these three properties. Some simple machines can change the direction of the force while increasing either the distance moved or the force applied. However, no simple machine can increase both force and distance.

It is not critical for young children to identify the specific simple machine that they are using. It is more important that they recognize opportunities to use and manipulate the basic devices. We need to give children as many opportunities as possible to manipulate simple machines. As they mature, they will be able to use these concrete experiences to recognize and differentiate between the different simple machines.

For us as teachers it is important that we be able to recognize these simple machines so that we can point out to our students that they are using simple machines to make their tasks easier.

Simple machines are usually divided into six categories: lever, inclined plane, wedge, wheel and axle, screw, and pulley (Figure 16.1). Let's examine the basic characteristics of each.

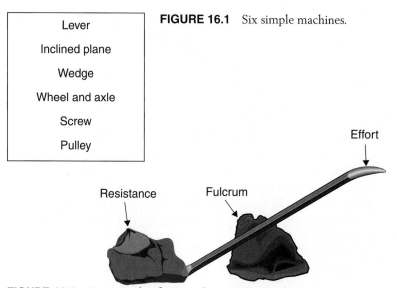

FIGURE 16.1 Six simple machines.

| Lever |
| Inclined plane |
| Wedge |
| Wheel and axle |
| Screw |
| Pulley |

FIGURE 16.2 An example of using a lever to move a large object.

Lever

Levers include many basic objects that we use every day, for example, pry bars, doors, golf clubs, and hammers. All levers have three basic common characteristics. They must include a *fulcrum*, or a solid point on which the lever pivots. They must have resistance; (for example, an object that needs to be moved). A lever must also include a force, often called the effort, to move the lever. When we push on a lever, we are supplying the force or effort.

If one were moving a rock with a long pry bar, as shown in Figure 16.2, the rock would be the resistance, because basically the rock doesn't want to move. By placing the pry bar against the rock and also placing another object such as a smaller rock near the base of the pry bar, and pushing down on the opposite end of the pry bar, we can move the rock.

Some very basic events occur during this process. For the example of the rock, the critical aspect is that we must move the end of the pry bar much farther than the distance that the rock moves. But by doing so we might be able to move a rock that weighs several hundred pounds. When we push on the pry bar, the pry bar might move 3 feet, whereas the rock might only move a few inches. We have sacrificed distance to gain force. With a lever, we can push on the pry bar with a force of, say, 50 pounds and move a rock that weighs 500 pounds.

The positions of the fulcrum, the resistance, and the effort are critical when designing levers for particular tasks. Movement of the fulcrum from one end toward the middle of the lever alters the amount of resistance that can be moved and the effort that will be needed. If the fulcrum is closer to the effort, we can increase the distance the resistance will move.

Levers are divided into three classes, as shown in Figures 16.3, 16.4, and 16.5, based on the position of the fulcrum, resistance, and effort. Each class of lever has properties that make it useful for particular situations.

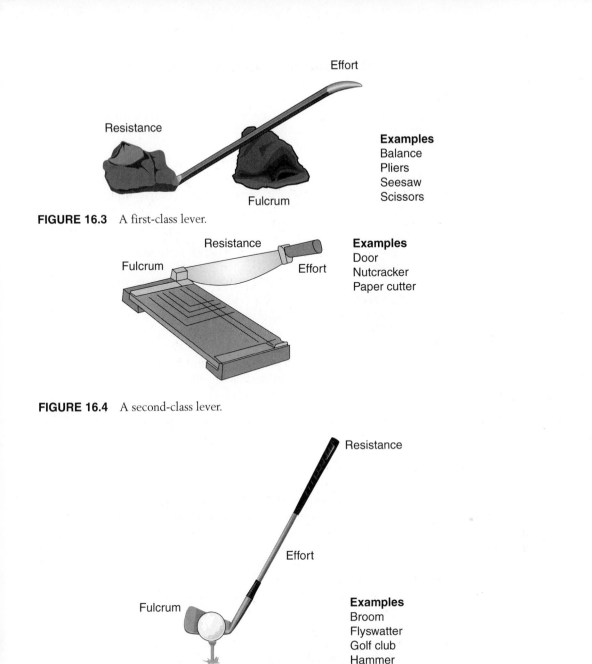

FIGURE 16.3 A first-class lever.

Examples
Balance
Pliers
Seesaw
Scissors

Examples
Door
Nutcracker
Paper cutter

FIGURE 16.4 A second-class lever.

Examples
Broom
Flyswatter
Golf club
Hammer

FIGURE 16.5 A third-class lever.

A first-class lever has the fulcrum in the middle with the resistance at one end and the effort at the other. First-class levers are designed to change the direction of the force. You can push down on a first-class lever and the resistance will go up. Depending on the location of the fulcrum, the force can increase or the distance the resistance moves can increase. Scissors have first-class levers. Because they also have a sharp cutting edge, which is an example of a wedge, scissors are considered compound machines.

A second-class lever has the fulcrum at one end, the resistance in the middle, and the effort at the other end. Second-class levers are used to increase the force.

We often do not think of a door as a lever. However, by placing the doorknob at the side away from the hinge, it is easier for us to open the door. Imagine what it would be like to have a doorknob on the side close to the hinge. We would have to use a much greater force to open the door.

A third-class lever has the fulcrum at one end, the resistance at the opposite end, and the effort in the middle. An ax is a third-class lever; however, because it has a wedge-shaped cutting edge, like scissors, it is considered a compound machine.

Inclined Plane

Inclined planes are simple machines that help us change from one level to another. Probably the most common example of an inclined plane is stairs. Stairs make it easier to go from one level to another. Instead of trying to climb vertically directly up a ladder, it is easier to walk up a fight of stairs.

Inclined planes have a slope that determines the difficulty for traveling up a ramp. The greater the slope, the more difficult it is to travel up an inclined plane.

With all simple machines, however, there must be a sacrifice for the benefit of the machine. In the case of the inclined plane, we benefit by decreasing the force or effort applied. For example, it is easier to push a wheelbarrow up an inclined plane than it is to lift the wheelbarrow to a higher level. The sacrifice is distance. By traveling up an inclined plane you must push the wheelbarrow a much greater distance, as illustrated in Figure 16.6.

Wedge

Many consider a *wedge* to be a variation on an incline plane. If you place two inclined planes back to back, you will have the shape of a wedge. Inclined planes are used to decrease forces necessary to move objects. Wedges are used to increase force that can be applied to an object. A good example is that of a wedge used to split wood. The wedge can be pounded into a log for several inches and split the wood just a small amount. However, this small amount is sufficient to break the fibers in the wood so that the log splits.

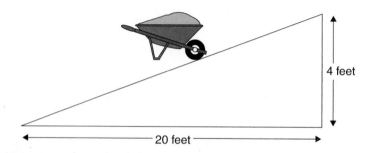

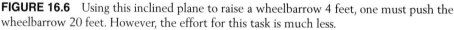

FIGURE 16.6 Using this inclined plane to raise a wheelbarrow 4 feet, one must push the wheelbarrow 20 feet. However, the effort for this task is much less.

FIGURE 16.7 Common devices that are wedges.

Wedge Device	Combined with
Nail clipper	Second-class lever
Scissors	First-class lever
Paper cutter	Second-class lever
Hatchet	Third-class lever
Can opener	Wheel and axle
Circular saw	Wheel and axle
Wood screw	Screw

FIGURE 16.8 Wedges are often used in combination with other simple machines.

Dial on radio	Steering wheel
Doorknob	Waterwheel
Screwdriver	Windmill

FIGURE 16.9 Common devices that are simple wheel-and-axle machines.

We use wedges constantly. Figure 16.7 lists some common wedges. Knives are common examples of wedges. The sharp blade permits us to apply a greater force to a very small area. This makes it possible to cut an item that we would not ordinarily be able to cut.

Wedges are often used in combination with other simple machines, as listed in Figure 16.8.

> A sharp knife makes all the difference. The sharper the knife, the smaller the contact area. This increases the force at the entry position and makes the cut easier.

Wheel and Axle

The *wheel and axle* is one of the most often used and also the most misunderstood simple machine. Every time we turn a knob on our stereo, twist our doorknob, or wind our watch, we are using a wheel and axle. The steering wheel on our car is a wheel and axle as are the wheels themselves. Other examples are listed in Figure 16.9.

We use many devices that have wheels and axles; however, that does not make them simple machines. To have a simple wheel-and-axle machine, the wheel and the axle must be attached and frozen together. By turning either the wheel or the axle, the other part must turn with it.

The value of the wheel and axle is that you can gain either force or distance moved. For example, try to open a doorknob with only the stem. The stem is the axle of the doorknob. The doorknob is the wheel. The stem has a circumference of around 1 inch.

Pizza cutter	Wagon
Roller skate	Wheelbarrow
Rolling pin	

FIGURE 16.10 Examples of items with a wheel on an axle that are not simple wheel-and-axle machines.

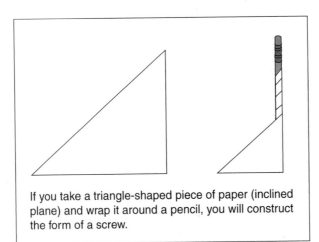

FIGURE 16.11 Forming a screw from an inclined plane.

If you take a triangle-shaped piece of paper (inclined plane) and wrap it around a pencil, you will construct the form of a screw.

Container cap
Jar lid
Nut and bolt

FIGURE 16.12 Common devices that are simple screw-type machines.

The circumference on the doorknob is around 6 inches. The force necessary to turn the stem is too great for us. However, when we add the knob, we have no difficulty. As we spin the doorknob, the outside of the doorknob will move a greater distance than the stem. We have to move the knob a greater distance than the stem (so we sacrifice distance), but we gain the force on the stem and we can turn the stem easily. Consider what it would be like to steer a car with just the stem instead of the steering wheel.

A screwdriver is actually a wheel and axle as well. The screwdriver is effective because the handle of the screw driver is much wider than the steel rod with the slotted or Phillips end. This increases the force that can be applied to the screw. *Caution:* When you open a paint can with your screwdriver, the screwdriver has become a first-class lever.

Many devices have a wheel on an axle with bearings that are lubricated so that the wheel can easily spin on the axle. This reduces the friction and makes objects easier to use. However, this does not fit the definition of a wheel-and-axle simple machine. Figure 16.10 lists some more items that do not qualify as simple wheel and axles.

Screw

The *screw* is an interesting form of a simple machine. Its main use is to increase force. Note that some people believe that the screw is a derivative of the inclined plane. Indeed, an inclined plane that continuously circles develops a screw (Figure 16.11).

A common example of a screw is a screw lid for a container such as toothpaste; other examples are listed in Figure 16.12. By twisting the cap, the cap tightens down

| Awnings |
| Curtains |
| Flagpole |
| Venetian blinds |

FIGURE 16.13 Common devices that use simple pulley-type machines.

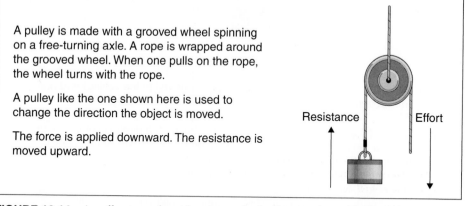

A pulley is made with a grooved wheel spinning on a free-turning axle. A rope is wrapped around the grooved wheel. When one pulls on the rope, the wheel turns with the rope.

A pulley like the one shown here is used to change the direction the object is moved.

The force is applied downward. The resistance is moved upward.

Resistance · Effort

FIGURE 16.14 A pulley is made with a grooved wheel spinning on a free-turning axle. A rope is wrapped around the grooved wheel. When one pulls on the rope, the wheel turns with the rope.

on the tube of toothpaste. We twist the cap a greater distance than the distance the cap moves toward the toothpaste tube. This causes a tighter seal. This same screwing action is used for many jars and other containers. Some lids are made with a broad cap and a small screw opening. This can develop a very tight seal since this device uses properties both of a screw and a wheel and axle.

Screw devices are often used for fine-tuning the position of objects. For instance, by turning a screw a half turn, the contact point for a control device might change only 1/100 of an inch. For some electrical and temperature control devices, this distance might be critical.

Pulley

Pulleys are simple machines that can be used to change the direction of the force. Common devices that use pulleys are listed in Figure 16.13. By using a combination of pulleys, you can also increase the force on an object (at the sacrifice of distance) or increase the distance an object moves (causing one to apply a greater force). Figures 16.14 and 16.15 illustrate two different types of pulleys.

Mechanical Advantage

Mechanical advantage is a term often used in relationship to simple machines. The mechanical advantage is seen in the relationship between the effort and the resistance. For instance, we might use a car jack (a first-class lever) to lift the front end of a car. The force that we press on the car jack (the effort) might be 50 pounds.

FIGURE 16.15

A pulley system.

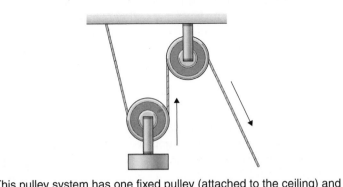

This pulley system has one fixed pulley (attached to the ceiling) and one movable pulley.

The fixed pulley permits the operator to change the direction of the force so that the operator can pull downward on the pulley to raise an object.

The movable pulley is used to decrease the force necessary to pull up the object. Note that half of the weight (one of the two supporting ropes) is supported by the ceiling. The operator can pull with one-half the force and still lift the object. Note, however, that the operator must also pull the rope twice as far as the object is lifted.

Gyroscopes have a heavy mass spinning around an axis. Once the gyroscope is put into motion, its angular momentum will keep it spinning along the same plane.

Andy Crawford © Dorling Kindersley

The resistance of the car being lifted might be 500 pounds. Thus, the mechanical advantage would be 10 to 1, because for every pound we use in the effort, we are able to move 10 pounds. Obviously, there is always a payback. In this case the car will be raised only one-tenth the distance that we move the jack handle.

Inertia

Inertia is a basic property of matter related to how matter moves. Inertia is defined as follows: "When an object is at rest, it tends to stay at rest. When an object is in motion, it tends to stay in motion."

When an object is stationary, it takes an initial force to get the object moving. The greater the mass of the object, the harder it is to initiate any movement. Perhaps you have had to push a car. You know how difficult it was to start the car moving. However, once the car was in motion, it wanted to keep moving and hopefully you could apply breaks to stop it. This forward motion of an object is called *momentum*.

Gyroscopes are excellent examples for demonstrating inertia. Gyroscopes are designed to have a heavy mass that will spin around an axis with bearings to reduce friction.

It takes a strong pull on the string to initiate the spinning of the wheel of a gyroscope. However, once the gyroscope is spinning, it will continue for an extended period. Because the inertia on the wheel is spinning in a circle, it is often referred to as *angular momentum*. We can observe angular momentum with many common objects including a spiraling football, tires on a bicycle, wheels on a roller skate, or a yo-yo.

Center of Gravity

All objects have what is referred to as a *center of gravity*. The center of gravity of an object is the point at which the force of gravity acts on the object. For example, a cube of wood would have the center of gravity in the middle of the object. An irregularly shaped object such as a golf club has its center of gravity down toward the head of the club because that is where most of the mass is.

Center of gravity is important because it determines the stability of an object. For example, it is easy to set a block of wood on a table and have it stay there because the center of gravity is within the *base* of the block. It is extremely difficult to balance a golf club on the end of the handle because the center of gravity would have to fit within the small area at the end of the handle. Center of gravity is critical for many items. For example, a car with a low center of gravity will not overturn as easily as a car with a high center of gravity. A swing seat designed like a bucket for a child to sit in will not overturn as easily as a flat seat.

Friction

Friction is the resistance to a force caused by two objects rubbing against each other. The greater the resistance, the greater the amount of friction that is produced. The result of friction of objects is the production of heat. When you rub your hands together, the resistance to the motion causes friction. The result is heat.

Friction can be reduced by using lubricants such as oil. Air can also reduce friction as is observed when playing at an air hockey table.

Mass and Weight

Mass and *weight* are two terms that are often confused. *Mass* is an actual measurement of the amount of matter an object has. The mass of an object does not change depending on its location. For example, the mass of a person on Earth is the same as the mass of that person on the Moon or in a space capsule.

Weight is the measured force of gravity on an object. A person on Earth might have a weight of 200 pounds which is a unit of weight. That means that Earth is pulling on him with a force of 200 pounds. If that person went to the Moon, the Moon's force of gravity on him would be much less. His weight would only be around 33 pounds.

Mass and weight are particularly confusing because the customary measurement in United States is pounds. In the metric system the customary unit is grams (or kilograms), which is a measurement of mass. Thus, it is not proper to convert from pounds to kilograms. As long as we are on Earth, the values are equivalent. However, once we leave Earth, the values would be incorrect.

MATHEMATICS: ADDRESSING THE NCTM STANDARDS THROUGH CONCEPT EXPLORATIONS

Mathematics for young learners is most effective if it is integrated and interwoven into their world. The NCTM standards are designed to help teachers see how the integrated nature of mathematics relates to the world of young children. Many of the mathematics standards can be used as children explore the fascinating and intriguing world of toys and tools.

Number and Operations

In many of the Concept Explorations in this chapter, rational counting can take place. As children engage in the Toy Festival; How Many Simple Machines Can You Find?, and Strings and Things Concept Explorations, they are given opportunities to gather and observe a variety of toys and tools. Taking count of these items requires rational counting with one-to-one correspondence, stable order and keeping track. Frequency counts are generated by careful one-by-one counting or possibly counting in groups of twos or fives or tens. Tallies can be used for counting by fives and is appropriate for primary-aged children. Determining the cardinal property of a set is an important beginning to communicating mathematically.

Part of the conversation about cardinal property can also lead to using words of comparison and magnitude such as *more, less,* and *same*. Putting the set of numbers, which define each set, in size order helps children with sequencing and seriating from least to most or from most to least.

Algebra

As children gather examples of toys and tools, they can sort them into their own self-selected categories. Asking children to sort items helps them to focus on the similarities and differences between and among the items. A specific example is given in Concept Exploration 6, Toys of Different Countries. Venn diagrams can be generated showing the similarities and differences between and among the toys that may have common characteristics. Toys can be sorted by the country they are from or by type and function.

Another concept in algebra, at this level, is having children describe change, both qualitative and quantitative. As children engage in the Ball Olympics Concept Exploration, they have many opportunities to do this. For example, if they are seeing which ball rolls down a ramp the fastest, they may experiment with the height of the ramp. Observing and keeping track of the results allow them to see and make generalizations about the relationship between the height of the ramp and the speed of the ball. Other relationships involving qualitative or quantitative change can be observed in other events, defined by the children, in the Ball Olympics.

Geometry

Children can use geometric language when describing toys and tools. Words such as *curved, straight, triangular, square,* or *oval* can be used when telling the specific characteristics of the toy or the tool. Using these geometric characteristics, children can define a classification scheme for sorting the toys and tools into categories. For example, you could have a group of toys that have curves or are triangular shaped, rectangular shaped, or have symmetry. Analyzing the items geometrically gives children experience with looking carefully for specific geometric properties.

As children experiment with the events in the Ball Olympics, they can see geometric relationships, the height and steepness of the ramp for rolling balls. As they construct apparatus for the events, they are experiencing shape, form, and structure.

Measurement

Measurement can be experienced in many of the Concept Explorations involving toys and tools. As children collect and observe toys and tools, they can use attributes of measurement to describe them. From the simple notion of big and small, children can begin to measure the toys and tools to see which ones are the biggest and smallest. Using nonstandard or standard tools for measurement is a wonderful experience for young children to have as they explore relationships.

In the Ball Olympics, measuring will be important as children design and develop events in which their balls will compete. For example, if they are going to see which ball bounces the highest, they will need to decide and measure a height from which the balls are dropped. Then, they will need to see how high the ball bounced. This event requires a lot of careful measuring. Even if the children put a piece of tape along a wall to show how high the ball bounced, they are experiencing the concept of measurement. Using attributes of length, whether inches or centimeters, helps children see how mathematics can describe an event.

Data Analysis and Probability

In the Concept Explorations of Toy Festival, How Many Simple Machines Can You Find?, and Strings and Things, children are given opportunities to collect and observe a variety of toys and tools. After taking count of these items, children can organize them and construct graphs to show the specific defined attributes. Putting the toys or tools on a grid helps keep the one-to-one correspondence easy to see. Ideas such as *most*, *least*, and *same* can be visually seen and discussed. Using the language of comparison helps children with communicating mathematically.

Specific to the Ball Olympics is the notion of prediction. As children experiment with each ball's performance in the events, data can be gathered. From these data, children can predict which other balls they think will perform similarly. Asking the children questions such as "Do you think it is likely that this ball will bounce as high as your ball?" "Do you think it is unlikely that this ball will roll as far as your ball?" "Is it likely or unlikely that this ball will float?" will help them to focus their attention on the analysis of completed events. Giving a rationale for their predictions helps them to focus on attributes of the ball and the structure and design of the event.

OBSERVING WITH ALL THE SENSES

Using toys and tools gives children many opportunities for tactile experiences. Giving children opportunities to use multiple senses in their explorations increases their retention of these experiences.

Sight

The eye can detect much detail. Many of the experiences children have with their toys and tools lead to making careful and critical observations. Some of the visual observations encourage careful measurement. Children can compare different varieties of toys and tools to examine similarities and differences.

Touch

Toys and basic tools give excellent tactile experiences. Manipulation of tools often gives children a chance to learn about forces such as those caused by motion, gravity, and angular momentum. Developing descriptions of the different textures of the surfaces of a variety of items from their observations is important for their vocabulary development.

Sound

Many toys and tools produce a variety of sounds that attract children's interests. Encourage children to examine these sounds and suggest why the sounds are made. For example, how does the friction caused by tightening a nut on a bolt cause a squeaking sound?

Children can compare the sounds that different balls produce when they are bounced. What do these different sounds indicate about the properties of the balls?

SAFETY

Safety should be a constant concern when working with mechanical items. Most tools should be either used by children under close adult supervision or demonstrated by an adult. Learning about simple machines provides excellent opportunities to discuss good safety habits when using common materials. Choose examples that are safe for children to use.

CONCEPT EXPLORATIONS ON TOYS AND TOOLS FOR YOUR CLASSROOM

The following Concept Explorations provide a wide variety of activities that are appropriate for young children. Although these activities focus on children using basic toys and tools, the processes of science that are incorporated are universal. You may want to review some of the references cited at the end of this chapter to spark your imagination and creativity for working with toys and tools. Neil Ardley's *The Science Book of Motion* offers many simple experiments with motion that primary children can do, under supervision, in the classroom.

Battery-operated toys	Pull toys
Erector set	Tinker Toys
Friction cars	Toys with ramps and tracks
Frisbee	
K'NEX	Windup toys
Marble drops	Yo-yo
Mouse Trap game	

FIGURE 16.16 Examples of action toys that demonstrate basic properties of physics.

1. Toy Festival

Invite your children to bring in their favorite toy. Suggest that they select a toy that has action, such as those listed in Figure 16.16. As each child demonstrates how her or his toy operates, discuss how the toy demonstrates basic properties such as inertia, friction, or center of gravity.

Many action toys utilize simple machines, either individually, such as a seesaw (first-class lever), or in combination such as a push toy that usually operates using a wheel and axle and different types of levers. Classifying these toys into student-determined categories can lead to sorting and the construction of Venn diagrams. Children can explain how they sorted the toys by the way they work.

Help each child recognize how their toys are based on simple machines. It is not critical for the children at this age to identify specific simple machines. It is more valuable for them to recognize that the items that they use each day have properties that make them function. As the children mature, the identification of the specific simple machines will become better developed.

An excellent extension to this exploration would be to invite the children's grandparents to bring in a toy that they played with as a child. Comparisons could be made to demonstrate that few of their toys used batteries or any electronics.

2. How Many Simple Machines Can You Find?

Set aside a bulletin board or wall area to collect examples of simple machines that we use each day. Depending on the age and development of your class, you might divide the display into the six areas representing the specific simple machines. Encourage the children to contribute photos, drawings, or pictures from magazines that can be placed on the display.

As children identify and use simple machines they will undoubtedly come into contact with devices that have sharp edges such as scissors and knives. Other devices such as pliers and nut crackers can also become dangerous if not used correctly. Monitor your students' use of all tools. Help them learn how to hold and use tools safely.

3. Rulers and Pencils

Rulers and pencils are excellent simple tools that you can use in the classroom to help children understand the simple nature of levers. By placing a ruler on a pencil

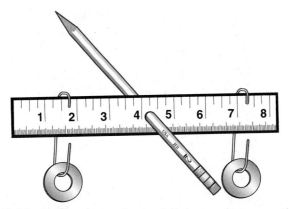

FIGURE 16.17 Children can make simple balances using a pencil, ruler, and paper clip. Washers make excellent weights.

that serves as the fulcrum and pushing on either end of the ruler, they can experience the cause-and-effect relationship of pushing down on one side of a lever and having the other side move in the opposite direction.

When a weight is placed on one end and children push on the opposite end, they can get a feel for the forces involved. Suggest to the children that they move the pencil toward one end of the ruler and examine how that affects the force necessary to move the object and also the change in the distance moved by the weight.

Students can also place a pencil through the center hole of a ruler, as shown in Figure 16.17. The ruler will spin on its central axis. Hook paper clips on both sides of the ruler. Attach a variety of weights to the clips. Invite the students to balance the ruler.

4. Strings and Things

Wrapping strings around dowel rods or other objects can duplicate the effect of pulleys. In classrooms where pipes extend from the ceiling, a string can be wrapped over a pipe. Children can see how the direction of force can be changed by pulling down on their string and lifting up an object tied to the other end of the string.

As long as the weights are not too heavy, causing friction between the dowel rods and the string, the nature of a pulley can be demonstrated. Pulleys should be used as often as possible to accomplish daily tasks to help children understand what a pulley is and recognize its basic parts.

As you demonstrate the nature of pulleys, relate the pulleys to ones that children see and use each day such as flagpoles and classroom curtains and blinds. When two or more pulleys are used in combination to increase force or distance, we call the system a *block and tackle* (Figure 16.18). Teachers can demonstrate the effect of a block and tackle by tying a rope to one broomstick handle and then loosely wrapping it around two broomsticks. Invite four children to hold the broomsticks, with two children holding either side of each broomstick. You will pull on the rope. Have them try to pull the broomsticks apart. They will have a hard time doing so. However, you can pull on the rope and easily pull the sticks together because of the mechanical advantage of the block and tackle.

FIGURE 16.18 A homemade block and tackle can be used to demonstrate how we can use tools to gain a mechanical advantage.

5. The Toy Factory

Turn your classroom into a toy factory. Have your students make some simple toys that utilize the basics of simple machines. Some basic examples that children can easily make include spinning and flipping devices.

You might make one of the toys shown in Figures 16.19 and 16.20 for each child in the class and then invite them to make additional toys to give to their friends.

Tops are excellent toys for demonstrating the nature of inertia. Once a top is given its initial spin, its moment of inertia keeps it in motion. Small disks made out of cardboard or plastic lids can be glued to toothpicks and used to make simple tops. Another type of simple top children can make is the button-and-string top shown in Figure 16.21.

Children can experiment to see what variables they can use to keep the top spinning the longest. How does the surface of the table affect the top? How do the size and weight of the disk

Tops are excellent toys for demonstrating the moment of inertia. Shown here are tops from Japan.

Anthony E. Davis

FIGURE 16.19 Children enjoy making and playing with color spinners. Spinners are examples of a simple wheel-and-axle machine.

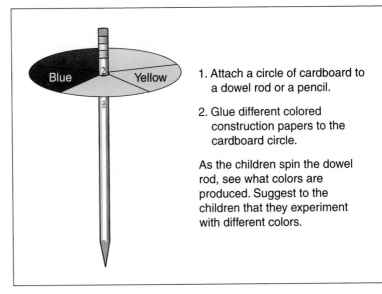

1. Attach a circle of cardboard to a dowel rod or a pencil.

2. Glue different colored construction papers to the cardboard circle.

As the children spin the dowel rod, see what colors are produced. Suggest to the children that they experiment with different colors.

FIGURE 16.20 Simple bird-in-the-cage toy.

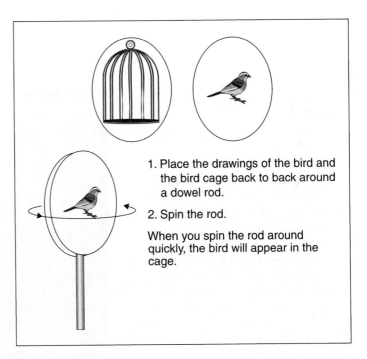

1. Place the drawings of the bird and the bird cage back to back around a dowel rod.

2. Spin the rod.

When you spin the rod around quickly, the bird will appear in the cage.

affect how long it spins? What can they use other than a toothpick to make a top that spins longer? Simple toys that give children opportunities to manipulate objects are good for developing hand–eye coordination, as shown in Figure 16.22.

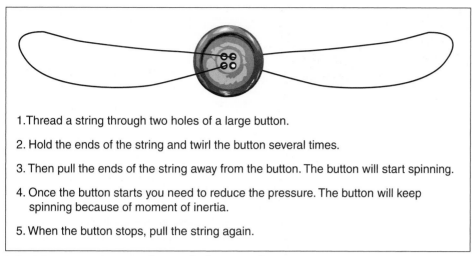

1. Thread a string through two holes of a large button.

2. Hold the ends of the string and twirl the button several times.

3. Then pull the ends of the string away from the button. The button will start spinning.

4. Once the button starts you need to reduce the pressure. The button will keep spinning because of moment of inertia.

5. When the button stops, pull the string again.

FIGURE 16.21   One type of top is the button-and-string top.

6. Toys of Different Countries

Make a collection of toys from different countries. Compare how the toys are similar and how they are different. How do these toys utilize the different simple machines? What characteristics do they have that indicate they are from a particular culture? Often toys are a basis for children's stories about a country's culture.

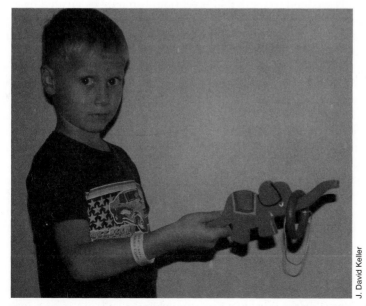

J. David Keller

FIGURE 16.22   Simple toys that give children opportunities to manipulate objects are good for developing hand-eye coordination. Actually this toy is a variety of a third class lever.

FIGURE 16.22 Sample student lever competition activities.

7. The Human Machine

The human body is a system of levers. Our hands, feet, arms, and legs are good examples of complex systems of levers. Each joint can be considered a fulcrum for a lever. Explore the nature of how these levers help us. For example, having legs gives us mobility. The movement of our arms gives us balance. Having long arms also helps us throw a ball farther.

Our jaw is also a lever that gives us a greater force for breaking down and chewing foods. Even our ears have miniature levers that detect sound vibrations.

Explore with your students how these levers assist us in our daily functions. You can set up some activities, such as those listed in Figure 16.22, to see how well we utilize these levers. Invite the children to design the events for the competition. For each event, the students must identify how they use their body as a system of levers.

8. Invention Convention

Unfortunately we tend to think that inventions can only be created by a few professional inventors. Actually each of us can create new devices and procedures that help us do daily tasks. Having an Invention Convention in your classroom is an excellent way to help students understand the simplicity of inventing.

You might introduce inventions by having an invention warm-up. Introduce a simple task that you challenge the students to do either individually, in small groups, or as a class. For example, ask them to design a device to catch flies. Or, they might design a way to measure the height of a tree. Or, they might design a way to communicate with students in a different wing of the school. As you present these options, encourage the students to suggest their own tasks that they might prefer to do. Indicate to the class that this is how inventions are created.

Invite your students to each make their own invention. Tell them that an invention is simply a device that they design that does something different or better than what they currently use. At first, students feel that this will be extremely difficult. However, by presenting them with the questions related to daily tasks and frustrations that are shown in Figure 16.23, they will begin to think of simple solutions.

9. The Ball Olympics

As we mentioned in the introduction to this chapter, balls are of keen interest to children of all ages. The Ball Olympics gives children an opportunity to explore the characteristics of balls that makes them so interesting.

1. Identify something that you do every day.

2. Identify something that you find difficult to do.

3. Identify something that often breaks.

4. Identify something that you put off to another day.

5. Identify something difficult to carry or hold.

6. Identify something that you think cost more than it should.

7. Identify a way that you often get injured.

8. Identify a task that takes longer than it should.

9. Identify something that does not last as long as it should.

10. Identify something that would help your pet.

FIGURE 16.23 Invention questionnaire.

Tell your students that they must each bring a ball to school. Do not give any explanations or suggest what type of a ball they should bring.

The Ball Olympics is divided into two stages. During the first stage, children will examine specific characteristics of balls. During the second stage, children will conduct their own Ball Olympics in the classroom.

During the first stage, balls are used as a classification tool. (Review the section on classification in Chapter 5.) First, have the children form a line holding their ball so that the smallest ball is at one end of the line, and the largest ball is at the other. You can then also line up the balls by other characteristics such as weight. The characteristics of size and weight are examples of seriation. (Review the section on seriation and gradation in Chapter 5.)

From the children's discussion, notice that not all characteristics of the balls will define a serial, or seriated, pattern. For example, when comparing the children's balls, some will have stitches, while others will not. Another characteristic is that some balls will have writing, while others will not. These are referred to as *discrete* attributes.

Children can quickly identify several obvious discrete attributes for balls such as balls for sports and balls not for sports, balls with holes and balls without holes, and balls with air inside and solid balls.

Discrete characteristics are excellent for developing classification systems because the items either have a discrete characteristic or they don't. (Note that a seriation characteristic is more difficult to use in that the characteristic is relative. For example, a baseball is big compared to

J. David Keller.

Children competing in the Ball Olympics.

Toys and Tools   **309**

a golf ball, but it is small when compared to a basketball. This relative evaluation makes classification inconsistent.)

Discrete characteristics of balls can be used to develop classification keys such as the classification of balls developed by a third-grade class, as shown in Figure 1.2 on page 13. This same procedure can be used by children to classify other objects such as keys, buttons, insects, and rocks.

The Ball Olympics gives children an opportunity to test properties of their ball in an enjoyable way. Divide your class into approximately five groups. Challenge each group to design an Olympic event in which their balls will compete. Each event must be based on the balls competing on their own merit. For example, an event designed around who can throw a ball the farthest would test the person throwing the ball and not the ball itself. Thus, the events need to be designed so that the balls are released in a consistent way.

The events that children typically design include how far a ball will role, how high it will bounce, how well it floats, and how many bottles a ball can knock down. However, some groups will also see which balls will sail across a basin or examine how much water the ball can displace. Encourage each group to design an event that is not similar to any of the other groups' events.

Inform the students that they will not be able to enter their own ball into the event that they design. This will keep them from designing an event for which their ball has the proper characteristics.

Conduct each event one at a time so all students can observe all events. As your students conduct each event, help them recognize the physical properties that affect the ability to perform. Characteristics such as *mass, weight, buoyancy, inertia,* and *rebound* become needed vocabulary terms.

The Ball Olympics requires children to develop measurement techniques to evaluate the performances of the balls. It also gives children opportunities to make charts and diagrams of the data they collect.

Activities in Other Explorations That Relate to Toys and Tools

Birds (Chapter 8)

13. Egg Incubators
14. How Much Does a Bird Weigh?

Insects (Chapter 10)

1. Let's Build an Insect Zoo
2. Create an Insect and Design Its Habitat

Light and Color (Chapter 12)

1. Pinhole Projects
5. Up Periscope

Sun and Shadows (Chapter 15)

1. Here Comes the Sun

Water (Chapter 17)

8. Drip, Drop, Tick, Tock

Wind (Chapter 18)

2. Capture the Wind
3. Let's Go Fly a Kite
4. Construct a Maximum Wind Gust Measuring Device
7. Using Wind to Do Work

Resources for Teachers

Books

Ardley, Neil (1992). *The science book of motion*. San Diego: Harcourt Brace Jovanovich.

Khanna, S., Wolf, G., & Ravishankar, A. (1999). *Toys and tales with everyday materials*. Chennie, India: Tara Publishing.

Nelson, J. R. (1998). *American folk toys—Easy-to-build toys for kids of all ages*. Newton, CT: The Taunton Press.

Article

Keller, J. D., & Brickman, B. (1998). The Ball Olympics: Up and down, all around. *Science and Children*, pp. 26–31, 56.

Web Sites

http://www.rube-goldberg.com
A Web site exploring the ideas involved in Rube Goldberg's inventions with opportunities for student interaction and involvement.

http://museumsandpublicschools.org.
This Web site provides teachers with ideas for science projects and lesson plans.

Children's Books on Toys and Tools

Ardley, N. (1992). *The science book of machines*. San Diego, CA: Harcourt Brace Jovanovich.

Ardley, N. (1995). *How things work*. Pleasantville, NY: Reader's Digest association.

Armentrout, P. (1997). *A pulley*! How can I experiment with simple machine? Vero Beach, FL: Rourke Press.

Auerbach, S. (1999). FAO Schwarz *Toys for a lifetime: Enhancing childhood through play*. New York: Universe Publishing.

Ayo, Y. (1995). *Eyewitness books—Africa*. New York: DK Publishing.

Baquedano, E. (1993). *Eyewitness books—Aztec, Inca, & Maya*. New York: Random House.

Beech, L. (1995). *The magic school bus in the haunted museum: A book about sound*. New York: Scholastic.

Branley, F. M. (1996). *What makes a magnet?* New York: HarperCollins.

Cooper, J. (2002). *Sound (science secrets series)*. Vero Beach, FL: Rourke Press.

Dahl, M. (2006). Pull, lift and lower: A book about pulleys. *Pulleys*. Minneapolis, MN: Picture Window Books.

Darling, D. (1991). *Sounds interesting: The science of acoustics*. New York: Dillon Press.

Davenport, Z. (1995). *Toys (words for everyday)*. New York: Ticknor and Fields.

Fowler, A. (2001). *Rookie read-about science series: Simple machines*. New York: Grolier Publishing.

Fowler, A. (2001). *Simple machines*. New York: Children's Press.

Frey, T. (1994). *Toy bop: Kid classics of the 50's & 60's*. Murrysville, PA: Fuzzy Dice Productions.

Gardner, R. (2000). *Science projects about the physics of toys and games*. Berkeley Heights, NJ: Enslow Publishers.

Geisert, A. (2002). *The giant ball of string*. Boston, MA: Houghton Mifflin.

Glover, D. (1997). *Simple machine series: Pulleys and gears; springs; screws; levers; wheels and cranks; ramps and wedges*. Chicago: Rigby Education.

Golding, V. (1999). *Traditions of Africa*. Austin, TX: Raintree Steck-Vaughn Company.

Harper, C. M. (2001). *Imaginative inventions: The who, what, where, when, and why of roller skates, potato chips, marbles, and pie (and more!)* Boston, MA: Little Brown.

Harvey, M. (1998). *Look what came from China*. New York: Grolier Publishing.

Harvey, M. (1998). *Look what came from Egypt*. New York: Grolier Publishing.

Hewitt, S. (1998). *Machines we use*. New York: Children's Press.

Hodge, D. (1998). *Simple machines*. Toronto, Ontario: Kids Can Press.

Jacobs, D. (1992). *What does it do: Inventions then and now*. Milwaukee, WI: Raintree Publishers.

Jones, C. F. (1991). *Mistakes that worked*. New York: Doubleday.

Kalman, B., & Schimpky, D. (1995). *Old time toys*. New York: Crabtree Publishing.

Lafferty, P. (1992). *Force and motion*. New York: DK Publishing.

Lampton, C. (1991). *Sailboats, flagpoles, cranes: Using pulleys as simple machines*. Brookfield, CT: Millbrook Press.

Lohf, S. (1990). *Building your own toys*. Chicago: Children's Press.

Lunde, A. (1992). *Whirligigs for children, young and old*. Randor, PA: Chilton Book Co.

Markel, M. (2000). *Cornhusk, silk, and wishbones: A book of dolls from around the world*. New York: Houghton Mifflin.

Murdoch, D. (1995). *Eyewitness books—Native American Indians*. New York: DK Publishing.

Murrell, K. (1998). *Eyewitness books—Russia*. New York: DK Publishing.

Marshall, J. (1995). *Energy and action: Working machines*. Vero Beach, FL: Rourke Book Company.

Murrell, K. B., & Murdorch, D. (1998). *Eyewitness books—Russia/Eyewitness books—North American Indian*. New York: DK Publishing.

Nankivell-Aston, S., & Jackson, D. (2000). *Science experiments with simple machines*. New York: Franklin Watts.

Oxlade, C. (1998). *Machines (young scientist concepts & projects)*. Milwaukee, WI: Garth Stevens Publishing.

Oxlade, C. (2003). *Useful machines: Levers*. Chicago: Heinemann Library.

Oxlade, C. (2003). *Useful machines: Pulleys*. Chicago: Heinemann Library.

Parker, S. (2005). *The science of forces: Projects with experiments on forces and machines*. Chicago: Heinemann Library.

Pfeffer, W. (1999). *Sounds all around*. New York: HarperCollins.

Pickering, D., Turpin, N., & Jenner, C. (1999). *The ultimate Lego book*. New York: DK Publishing.

Potter, J. (1998). *Science in seconds with toys: Over 100 experiments you can do in ten minutes or less*. Brevard, NC: Wiley.

Steele, P. (2000). *Toys and games*. New York: Scholastic.

Stover, C. (2002). *Small dolls of the 40s and 50s: Identification & value guide*. Paducah, KY: Collector Books.

Tocci, S. (2002). *Experiments with gravity*. New York: Children's Press.

Walker, S. M., & Feldmann, R. (2002). *Pulleys*. Minneapolis, MN: Lerner Publications.

Ward, A. (1991). *Experimenting with sound*. New York: Chelsea House Publications.

Weiss, H. (1983). *Machines and how they work*. New York: Thomas Y. Crowell.

Welsbacher, A. (2001). *Pulleys*. Mankato, MN: Bridgestone Books.

Wood, R. W. (1997). *Mechanics fundamentals (fantastic science activities for kids)*. Philadelphia, PA: Chelsea House.

Wulffson, D. L. (2001). *The kid who invented the trampoline: More surprising stories about inventions*. New York: Dutton Children's Books.

Correlation of NSES Standards and NCTM Principles and Standards to Water Concept Exploration Activities

	1. Splish Splash	2. Water, Water, Everywhere	3. How Much Water Do We Use in a Day?	4. Don't Drown Lincoln	5. Little Water—Big Water	6. Water Resources and Water Treatment Plants	7. The Classroom River	8. Drip, Drop, Tick, Tock	9. Water Words	10. Water's Work	11. Sequencing Water Processes	12. I Scream! You Scream! We All Scream for Ice Cream!
SCIENCE												
Inquiry	X	X	X	X	X	X	X	X	X	X	X	X
Physical Science	X	X	X	X	X	X	X	X	X	X	X	X
Life Science		X			X	X	X			X	X	
Earth and Space Science		X			X		X			X	X	
Science and Technology		X	X			X				X		X
Personal and Social Perspectives	X	X	X	X	X	X	X	X	X	X	X	
History and Nature of Science					X	X	X	X		X		
MATHEMATICS												
Number and Operations	X	X	X	X	X			X	X			X
Algebra	X											
Geometry	X								X			X
Measurement	X	X	X		X			X	X		X	X
Data Analysis and Probability	X	X	X	X	X			X	X			X
Problem Solving	X		X	X	X			X	X			X
Reasoning and Proof			X									
Communication	X	X	X		X	X			X	X		X
Connections			X		X	X	X	X	X	X	X	X
Representation									X		X	

CHAPTER 17

Water

Water Is Wonderful

Water is good and it quenches our thirst,
It falls from the clouds in droplets to Earth.
It nourishes flowers, it falls in the sea,
It sometimes can fall on you and on me.
We can jump in its puddles and swim in it, too,
When it gets cold enough, it's called ice, yes, it's true.
Water is wonderful, wouldn't you say?
What else can you learn about water today?

Elizabeth A. Davis

Water is indeed wonderful! Colorless, odorless, and tasteless, water is the only material that is commonly found in nature as a solid, liquid, and gas. Its ubiquitous nature causes us to view water as a simple material that we need and use. Every day of our lives we are directly involved with water: We drink it. We bathe in it. We cook with it. We water our garden and our pets. Water is a great playmate, whether we are running by a sprinkler, swimming, boating, or playing in a bathtub.

Our common relationship with water causes us to accept water as a convenient, necessary compound—one that we very much take for granted. Just as people who live in New York don't visit the Empire State Building, and people who live in Paris don't visit the Eiffel Tower, we constantly use water, but never really think about its properties and characteristics.

The Concept Explorations in this chapter give us opportunities to examine and experience, with our children, some of the characteristics of water. Before we get to the Concept Explorations, however, let's study some of the physical and chemical properties of water. Although much of the information given in the following sections is beyond the comprehension of your students, it provides valuable background information that assists you in understanding water better and helps you relate the fascinating nature of water to your class. In addition, this information is just neat. Water is truly fun to play with and learn about.

SCIENCE CONCEPTS FOR TEACHERS

Water Cycle

As mentioned earlier, in this chapter, water is the only naturally formed matter that is common in all three states: solid, liquid, and gas. This unique property of water is critical for our planet to function as it does. Indeed, life could not exist without water occurring in all three states.

Scientists believe that the water on the earth has been here for more than a billion years. Some believe that the water came from comets hitting the planet over millions of years. Every time we take a drink of water, we are drinking water that has been around for several hundred millions of years. Molecules of the water we drink were drank by George Washington, a saber-toothed tiger, or perhaps a *Tyrannosaurus rex*. The amount of water on our planet has not changed significantly throughout this period. Water travels around the world, changing states between solid, liquid, and gas. It takes temporary residence in animals and plants. It "travels" in a large, continuous cycle. We call this the *water cycle* or the *hydrologic cycle* (*hydro* means "water").

Figures 17.1 and 17.2 present two different diagrams of the water cycle. The first is a simplistic diagram that you can use with your students. The second includes

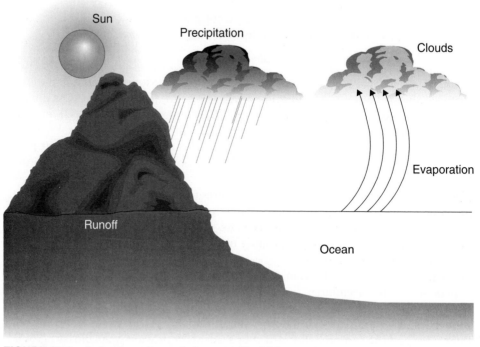

FIGURE 17.1 A simple water cycle for use with children.

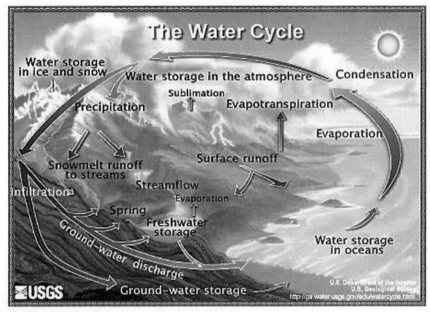

FIGURE 17.2 A detailed water cycle for teachers.

additional details that give teachers a much greater understanding of the many processes that take place in the water cycle.

A simple version of the water cycle (see Figure 17.1) demonstrates the process that transports water around the earth. Because it is a "cycle," there is no starting or ending point. Water collects in the oceans. The water at the surface of the oceans evaporates and becomes part of the atmosphere. As the air in the atmosphere cools, the water vapor condenses, forming precipitation in the form of rain, snow, or ice. The precipitation falls back to the surface of the earth. This water can infiltrate into the soil, or it can run off into lakes or streams. Eventually this runoff flows back to the oceans, completing the water cycle.

A Detailed Water Cycle

Figure 17.2 describes in more detail the processes that contribute to water transportation and the transitions that water undergoes. Its purpose is to give teachers a more solid background about the water cycle. Some aspects of this discussion are beyond the scope of understanding of most primary classes. We next examine separately each of the five stages of the water cycle: evaporation, condensation, precipitation, infiltration, and runoff.

Evaporation

Evaporation is the process by which water changes state from a liquid to a gas. Evaporation is usually divided into two categories. The first we refer to as simple evaporation.

Simple evaporation is the direct process of water changing from a liquid to a gas. Approximately 71% of the earth is covered with oceans. The wind causes the water at the ocean's surface to form waves. When large enough, these waves form *whitecaps*, which cause droplets of water to spray in the air. These droplets evaporate and are transported into the atmosphere.

Oceans are amazing forms of nature that are very interesting to study. You may want to share some readings about oceans with your students. Sheila Rivera's book *Ocean* and Katy Pike and Maureen O'Keefe's book *Ocean Facts—Oceans* are two wonderful books that have beautiful photographs of the various oceans of the world, coasts, waves, tides, currents, and life in the ocean.

Evaporation also occurs at the surface of all water. We can observe water evaporating from a pan of water or a wet sidewalk. A good, quick way for children to observe water evaporate is to use a sponge to wipe water on your classroom chalkboard. The children can observe the board dry in just a few minutes.

Children also experience water evaporating when they go swimming or take a bath. When they get out of the water they can feel "the shivers" because the water evaporating from their skin absorbs heat from their body, causing them to feel cold. We discuss this concept later in the section on latent heat.

A specialized form of evaporation is termed *transpiration*. Transpiration is evaporation caused by plants that transport water through their vascular system, carrying the nutrients needed for life. When the water reaches the leaves in the plant, the water evaporates and exits the plant through small pores called *stomata* on the underside of the leaves. An activity on transpiration, Concept Exploration 7, is included in Chapter 11.

Condensation

Condensation is a process by which water changes state from a gas to a liquid. The primary cause for water condensing in air is a change in the air temperature. The cooler the air, the less water vapor the air can hold. At a particular temperature, the air will be saturated with water vapor. Any additional water vapor or cooling of the air will cause water to condense into small particles of water that make up clouds.

Water tends to condense by being attracted to small particles in the air. These particles are called *hygroscopic particles*. *Hygroscopic* means "to attract water." A majority of the particles are actually molecule-sized particles of salt. When the water in the ocean spray evaporates, the salt dissolved in the ocean water is lifted into the atmosphere and travels around the world.

Many different particles in the atmosphere can serve as hygroscopic particles. At particular times in industrial and/or congested areas, pollution from combustion or other chemical processes can increase the percentage of particular types of hygroscopic particles. This can cause the resultant rainwater to be polluted, which is what occurs with acid rain.

Precipitation

The process of *precipitation* is a continuation of the process of condensation. When the particles of water become so large that they cannot be transported in the air, they will fall as rain, sleet, hail, or snow.

Rain   Rain occurs when the air temperature is above the freezing point of water (32 degrees Fahrenheit or 0 degrees Celsius). The greater the reduction in temperature of the air and the greater the size of the cloud, the heavier the rainstorm will be.

Sleet   Sleet occurs when water droplets form as rain and then freeze.

Hail   Hail is formed by a fascinating process that occurs during extreme storm conditions. When a cold front is replacing an area of warm air, the density of the cold air causes the warm air to rise. The updraft can be very strong with vertical winds around 80 miles per hour (Crook, Dowell, & Sun, 2003). As the air rises it cools, causing the moisture in the air to condense into water droplets and, if sufficiently cold, freeze. These ice pellets will fall toward the base of the cloud, collect moisture on their surface and, if caught by an updraft, will be whisked up thousands of feet to freeze again with the new layer of ice. This process can be repeated numerous times causing the size of the hailstone to become as large as a softball. Obviously, hailstones can cause significant damage.

Snow   Snow is formed when the water vapor changes directly from a gas to a solid crystal of ice. Snowflakes are formed by the ice particles accumulating on the crystal. Depending on the changes in air temperature and the amount of water vapor available, the snowflake can be very small or large. On average, 10 inches of snow is equivalent to 1 inch of water. Many areas rely on snow as their main source of water. Melting snow in the spring can cause runoff and flooding of rivers.

You may want to read an engaging book about snow with the children. Nikki Bundey's book *Snow and People* offers a photographic view of snow and how people and animals exist in snowy places such as the Arctic and Antarctic.

Dew and Frost   Dew and frost are types of precipitation that occur directly on any solid object. Objects such as grass become colder during the nighttime than does air. As the air comes in contact with the solid object, the water vapor condenses on the solid object. If the temperature of the object is above 32 degrees Fahrenheit (0 degrees Celsius), dew will form. Below freezing, frost will form.

Infiltration

Infiltration is the process by which water infiltrates into soil and bedrock. Water that infiltrates into the earth is called groundwater. It is the source for all well water.

The various factors listed in Figure 17.3 affect the amount of precipitation that will infiltrate into the ground. The percentage can vary from close to 0 (with a cement parking lot) or close to 100 for sandy areas.

Runoff

Runoff is the process by which water that cannot be absorbed into the soil flows along the surface. It is the water that collects in the streams, rivers, and lakes. Eventually, runoff flows back to the oceans. Runoff carries with it eroded soil and dissolved minerals from the ground.

What happens to precipitation?

It has been estimated that approximately 75% of precipitation reenters the atmosphere by way of transpiration through all types of plants. Ten percent of precipitation enters the soil by infiltration, and 15% runs off the surface back to the oceans.

Ground cover—Soil that is covered with vegetation will tend to contain the water, giving it a greater opportunity to infiltrate into the soil.

Slope—The gradient of the terrain affects the amount of infiltration. The greater the slope, the more quickly the water will tend to run off.

Permeability—In terms of soil and rock, permeability is the rate at which water can flow through soil. The size of the particles of Earth material determines the permeability. The smaller the particles, the slower the rate of permeability. Clay is much less permeable than sand.

Porosity—In terms of soil and rock, porosity is the available volume (pores) in rock material. It is the nooks and crannies between the rock particles.

Saturation—When significant rain has occurred over recent periods, the soil can become saturated (that is, unable to hold any more water), causing the water to run off.

Type of rain—A slow, steady rain will infiltrate more than a quick, heavy downpour.

FIGURE 17.3 Factors that influence percentage of infiltration.

If beings from other planets examined the Earth, our planet would be referred to as the water planet. Seventy-one percent of the earth is covered by the oceans.

NASA

The Water Planet

The Earth is truly the "water planet"! Seventy-one percent of the surface of the Earth is covered by the oceans. As shown in Table 17.1, the oceans contain 97.24% of all water on the Earth. The average depth of the ocean is approximately 16,000 feet, or about 3 miles. The oceans contain approximately 300 million cubic miles of water.

The water in the oceans contains salts of sodium, calcium, potassium, and magnesium. Each liter of seawater contains approximately 35 grams of salt. The salt in the oceans is sufficient to cover the land area of the Earth with a layer 500 feet thick.

The water available for human consumption and use in the streams, freshwater lakes, and groundwater is approximately 0.7%.

The Curious Nature of Water

Water has physical characteristics that make it unique. Without these unique characteristics, life as we know it could not exist.

TABLE 17.1 Sources of Water on the Earth

Water Source	Water Volume (Cubic Miles)	Percentage of Total Water
Oceans	317,000,000	97.24
Icecap glaciers	7,000,000	2.14
Groundwater	2,000,000	0.61
Freshwater lakes	30,000	0.009
Inland seas	25,000	0.008
Soil moisture	16,000	0.005
Atmosphere	3,100	0.001
Rivers	300	0.0001
Total water volume	326,000,000	100%

Sources: Nace, U.S. Geological Survey, 1967, and *The Hydrologic Cycle* (pamphlet), U.S. Geological Survey, 1984.

There have been 60 anomalies of water identified (see Web site listing of Martin Chaplin at end of chapter). Let's look at just a few of these that are critical for life.

Water Expands at Lower Temperatures

All matter, except water, contracts the colder it gets. Water is unique in that it contracts until it reaches 40 degrees Fahrenheit (4 degrees Celsius). When the temperature gets below 4 degrees Celsius, water starts to expand. When water freezes at 0 degrees Celsius, the ice that forms is approximately 10% less dense than water. This causes ice to float. About 90% of an iceberg's volume is below the water level.

This simple fact seems innocent at first, but it is critical for life. If ice were denser than water, it would freeze at the bottom of lakes and streams and expand until it solidified the body of water. All of the fish and other forms of life would freeze. But because ice is less dense than water, it freezes at the surface, forming an insulating cover for the water, which stays at about 4 degrees Celsius throughout the winter.

That ice expands is also critical for soil formation. Water seeps into rocks and other permeable surfaces such as cement. When this water freezes, the expansion causes hairline fractures at first. After many subsequent freezing and thawing cycles, these cracks expand and actually break the rocks apart. This is called *weathering*. We get exasperated because of the pot holes in our streets and cracks in our sidewalk that form from this process, but it is critical for the breakdown of rock material to form soils.

Water—The Universal Solvent

More substances dissolve in water than in any other liquid. Surprisingly, water dissolves more types of matter than even sulfuric acid. This property makes it possible to transport minerals. For example, the human body contains approximately 70% water. As the water is transported around our body, it transports the minerals and nutrition to all cells of our body. On a larger scale, minerals are dissolved and transported in streams, lakes, and oceans over the surface of the Earth.

Heat Capacity and Latent Heat

Heat capacity is the amount of heat that is absorbed by matter. Water has the highest heat capacity of any liquid or solid except ammonia. This is critical property: Because water can absorb tremendous amounts of heat, the temperature of the oceans does not vary as much as do land surfaces. Thus, water acts like a heat buffer for the Earth. This characteristic also holds true for the human body. The high heat capacity also keeps our body temperature within a small range.

    Latent heat is the heat energy that is needed to change matter from a solid to a liquid or a liquid to a gas. To melt 1 gram of ice, 80 calories are required. This is the same amount of energy required for water to change from 0 to 80 degrees Celsius. To vaporize 1 gram of water, 540 calories are required. This is significant for humans because it serves as the air conditioner for the human body. When our body "sweats," the water on our skin evaporates. The heat energy to vaporize the water comes from our body, cooling us off.

High Surface Tension

Water has a very high *cohesive* property, which means that water has the ability to adhere to itself. It is interesting to observe a drop of water "bubble up." Water tends to be sticky. It sticks to itself and it tends to stick to other surfaces. This "stickiness" is often referred to as *surface tension*.

    A high surface tension is critical for plants because it permits water to be transported *up* the vein structures of plants because water will adhere to the tissue of the veins.

MATHEMATICS: ADDRESSING THE NCTM STANDARDS THROUGH CONCEPT EXPLORATIONS

The Concept Explorations with water engage children in many good applications of mathematics. Many of these activities involve counting; algebra, patterns, and sequencing; mapping; measurement; and data collection, organization, and analysis. As you engage in these interesting explorations with children, be aware of the many opportunities to connect mathematical thinking and concepts to scientific study.

Number and Operations

As children engage in many of these explorations, they will have opportunities to practice rational counting. As they explore how many drops can stay on a penny without overflowing, they are counting and keeping track of quantities. Also, as they experiment with containers at the water table, they are gaining experience with counting how many of one container it takes to fill another. Containers that are volumetrically related, such as measuring cups, are helpful as children begin to explore these ratios and relationships.

    As children chart the uses of water or the words used to describe water, they can "count the ways" and record them. Such counting yields frequency counts of data—a cardinal property of "how many?" Tallies can sometimes be used with primary-aged children to keep track of the same data.

Algebra, Patterns, and Sorting

In the early years of a child's schooling, algebraic ideas involve sorting, classifying, finding patterns, and sequencing of qualitative and quantitative change. In the Concept Explorations in this chapter, all of these ideas come into play. For example, as children explore the many uses of water or the many words used to describe water, they can begin to sort these into categories. When describing uses of water, categories such as growing plants; washing things; drinking for people and pets; or playing in the ocean, river, or lake can be generated.

Documenting how things change as a result of water helps children examine and capture qualitative and quantitative change. The Concept Exploration "The Classroom River" provides such opportunities. Photos can be taken and then sequenced on an experience chart or panel poster. Numbering the sequence defines the ordinal property of the events. This documentation can capture how water makes its way through a pile of sand or dirt; or how water can change the colors created with water-soluble markers.

Geometry

Geometric ideas concerned with mapping can be utilized in some of the Concept Explorations. As children learn about water resources and water treatment plants, they can find these places on local maps. Determining directions to the sites such as a reservoir or water treatment plant helps children with the concept of north, south, east, and west.

Measurement

As children explore at the water table in Concept Exploration 1, "Splash, Splash," they are beginning to use informal means of measuring. They happily pour water from container to container and experiment with measuring cups and spoons. These particular measuring tools help children to figure out simple measurement ratios, such as four quarter-cup-size containers can fill the 1-cup container.

As children explore timing devises in "Drip, Drop, Tick, Tock," they are keeping track of drops with time intervals. Such experimenting leads to charting data into creative and informative graphs.

Data Analysis

Charting and graphing the data collected in these Concept Explorations can be fun. For example, as the children experiment with "Don't Drown Lincoln," they can chart each person's results of how many drops they were able to fit on their penny.

As children explore the various ways in which water is used, they can create simple charts with specified headings. They can first sort the uses of water into their own categories. They can use these classification schemes as headings for their chart. They may have headings such as Washing and Cleaning, Drinking, Plants, and Playing. Then, they can simply put the examples under the appropriate heading. As new data are gathered, they can simply be added to the chart.

Similarly, in gathering words that are used to describe water, children can chart them under their own specified headings.

OBSERVING WITH ALL THE SENSES

The ubiquitous nature of water makes water a valuable tool for exploring the five senses. Giving children opportunities to use multiple senses in their daily explorations increases their retention of the basic properties of water.

Sight

Water has ideal characteristics that encourage critical observations. Observing a small amount of water causes children to carefully look into the basic properties of water. Observing how a water droplet beads up helps children understand the nature of surface tension. Observing large quantities of standing water such as in a wading pool or basin helps children better understand the formation of waves. Watching running water such as along a stream or curb gives children opportunities to observe the force of water on other objects.

Touch

The nature of water invites children to explore. Having children play with water helps develop different characteristics of touch. Water can feel soft when it flows gently over our hands. Water can feel hard if we smack the water with our hand.

That water exists in different states gives children opportunities to feel the varying properties of water. As a solid, we can feel the hard and at times sharp nature of an icicle. But we can also sense the softness of a snowflake. Children can also feel the warm, wet nature of water by placing their hand safely above a pan of hot water and feeling the water vapor condense on their hand.

Water also becomes a useful tool for sensing different temperatures. The body senses changes in temperatures. The sense of water being warm or cold is relative to the previous environment the body occupied. For instance, if a person places one hand into ice water and her other hand into warm water and leaves them in the water for a period of time and then places both hands into a third container with water at room temperature, one hand will think the water is warm and the other hand will think the water is cold.

It is interesting to note that humans are better at detecting changes in temperature than we are at estimating specific temperatures. At times, observations by different people tend to contradict each other. This is why sometimes one person in a room will complain that the room is too warm, while a second person will complain that the room is too cold.

Sound

The movement of water creates many enjoyable sounds. Water dropping into a basin creates a pleasant dripping sound. Bubbling water produces a restful rippling sound that is very relaxing. Water can also make an intense sound when it is moving in volume such as over a dam or waterfall. Encourage your children to explore the various sounds of water.

Taste and Smell

Pure water is colorless, tasteless, and odorless. However, we all know that water has various tastes. That is because water will dissolve many different minerals that it absorbs from nature. In addition, treated water may contain chlorine and other chemicals that are added to purify water. We tend to get used to the water we drink daily, and cannot detect distinct properties. If we travel to different locations, however, we notice that the water is different. At times, water can have a distinct odor caused by chemicals that vaporize out of the water.

SAFETY

Safety should be a constant concern when working with water. Water from a safe water supply should give no concern. However, if your children collect water from other sources such as streams or lakes, they should not taste the water and their contact with it should be limited. If the children do touch the water, they should thoroughly wash their hands at the end of the activity.

Care should be given to the nature of water used for tasting experiments. Never have children taste samples of water for which you do not know the sources. Be sure to explain that we should only drink water that is from the faucet, water fountain, or a prepared water bottle.

As children engage in the following Concept Explorations, be sure that water temperatures are safe to feel. Too cold or too hot water temperatures can damage tender skin.

CONCEPT EXPLORATIONS ON WATER FOR YOUR CLASSROOM

The nature of water makes it an ideal material to use with our children. It is always available, causes little harm in our classroom, and is, in general, safe (see section on safety). In reality, nobody is allergic to water.

The nature of water encourages exploration. Our activities can encourage children to experiment and play with water. This involvement develops and expands their curiosity and questioning. In addition, these explorations give the children experiences in using and understanding measurement and the characteristics of volume. Children also can sense the hot and coldness of water, which makes it valuable in examining basic scientific properties and measurement of temperature. Activities incorporating water can also be valuable tools for demonstrating the relevance of mathematics in daily experiences. Identify specific mathematics skills that your students need to develop and correlate them to specific explorations that utilize those skills.

1. Splish, Splash

Set aside an area for playing with water. Use a small portable swimming pool or a basin. Supply a number of containers and/or toys for the children to manipulate. Identify some projects that will cause kids to play with and manipulate the water. For instance, you might ask how many small containers of water it takes to fill a larger container. Observe how the children develop and construct their projects. You might place a white board or an easel next to the basin and write down the different adjectives and terms that the children use while playing with the water.

Make available to the children containers that have a variety of shapes. Encourage the children to transfer water back and forth between the different containers. Children need multiple hands-on manipulations of volumes of water to develop a sense of volume. By using containers that measure units of volume such as cups and liter, children obtain a broad understanding of how big the different units are.

2. Water, Water, Everywhere!

Invite your children to document each time that they observe water being used. You may want to read Robin Nelson's book *We Use Water* as a way to invite discussion about how children think about how water is used in their daily lives. Document the events by having the children make a drawing, cut a picture from a magazine, or write a description or poem. Identify a bulletin board or available wall area that can be designated for identifying uses of water, as shown in Figure 17.4.

3. How Much Water Do We Use in a Day?

Most water supply sources bill for their water based on the amount of water used by their consumers. Invite your school custodian to talk with your class about where the water supply for the school enters the building. If possible have the children see the water meter and learn how to read the meter. Ask the children to make daily readings at the same time of day and measure the amount of water used each day. If the children have sufficient math skills, the students should calculate the average amount of water used for each student, teacher, and other persons in the school.

An expansion of this activity could be to read the meter each hour of the day. Children could make bar graphs of their data, like that shown in Figure 17.5, and compare the graph to the activities of the students.

4. Don't Drown Lincoln

How many drops of water can you put on a penny? Give children a paper towel, penny, eyedropper, and a small container of water. Invite the children to predict how many drops of water they can put on the penny before it spills over the side. Make a histogram of the children's predictions. (See the discussion of histograms in Chapter 5.) Give the children an opportunity to experiment and see how many drops of water they can place on their penny.

How We Use Water	
Give my dog water	Wash chalkboard
Water my plants	Squirt my water gun
Fill my fish bowl	Wash my bike
Wash my hands	Make soup

FIGURE 17.4 Display the children s suggestions about how they use water on a bulletin board.

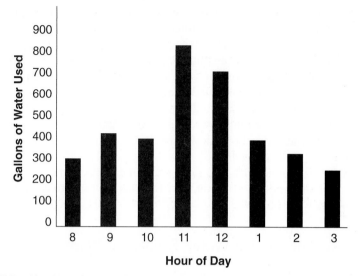

FIGURE 17.5   Number of gallons of water used at our school on April 17.

Invite children to guess how many drops of water they can put on a penny before the water spills over the side.

After your children have completed their experiments, make a second histogram showing their actual results. Invite the children to compare the two histograms to examine why their predictions were probably too low.

This activity provides a great opportunity to discuss the surface tension of water. Surface tension is the ability of a liquid to stick to itself. This property is sometimes call *cohesion*. (See "The Curious Nature of Water" section earlier in this chapter.)

Here is a sneaky little teacher's trick! As the children are experimenting with how many drops of water they can fit on a penny, rub a few of the children's pennies with some soapy water. The soap will reduce the surface tension and greatly reduce the number of drops that they can get on their penny.

An alternative activity is to fill a glass to the brim with water and invite children to see how many pennies they can drop in the glass before the water spills over the side.

5. Little Water—Big Water

Water is so much a part of our lives that we often take it for granted or overlook opportunities to notice that water is constantly around us. For instance, perhaps we can see a small puddle or some dew drops on a spider's web. We might also see a drop of water on a leaf after a rain. We can often feel the wetness of water that has condensed on a glass of ice water on a humid day. Encourage your children to observe water in its smallest quantities. Children can take digital photographs of the water they observe. You can read a couple of "Read About Science" books such as *Where Do Puddles Go?* by Fay Robinson or *It Could Still Be Water* by Allan Fowler to spark interest in the amazing amount of water there is on our planet.

Children can also observe water in large quantities. If you live by a river, you can discuss the amount of water that flows by each day. After a heavy rain you can discuss the amount of water that flows down a gully. Look for photographs in the newspaper after floods have occurred.

Develop a wall mosaic with two categories: one for documenting the observation of a very small amount of water, and the second for situations where large amounts of water were observed.

6. Water Resources and Water Treatment Plants

From a child's point of view, water comes from a spigot. There is not much thought about what is on the other side of the spigot. Likewise, water just disappears down the drain never to be thought of again.

> Each drop of water in the Ohio River is used an average of four times by the cities along its path.

Children will become much more responsible water users when they understand that the water that they use has a source and that this water must be returned to nature in a responsible way. Set up field trips to your local water treatment plants and/or sewage treatment plants.

7. The Classroom River

A classroom "stream table" can be an enjoyable release for curious children. Commercial stream tables are available from science supply sources, or you can develop one using a small portable swimming pool.

Place some clean sand in the table with the sand being higher at one end. Connect a small hose to the high end of the table. The hose can be connected to a water source or could function as a siphon attached to a bucket of water. Water at the lower end can be collected with similar techniques.

As the water flows from the tube into the sand, it will seek its lowest level. As it travels through the sand, it will transport the sand, forming a river bed. Changing the amount of water flowing down the river can indicate periods of flooding and dry spells. Children can observe the river channel form and transform. The classroom river can be observed over an extended period. Children might form lakes by adding a small barrier to the stream.

By carefully using a trowel or other basic instrument such as a table setting knife or a sliff plastic spatula you can cut a cross section along the stream bed and observe how the sand particles are aligned in the bed. If you happen to have some sandstone in your classroom, children can make comparisons to the layering in the stream bed and the sandstone. This exploration requires basic classroom safety considerations one would use when children are active around water and sand.

8. Drip, Drop, Tick, Tock

Many early timing devices were based on flowing water. The period of time that it would take for water to drop through a pinhole in a large container to fill a can would be considered a basic unit of time.

Other devices were based on levers with weights at one end and a bowl at the other. As water poured into the bowl, it would cause the lever to flip and the bowl would empty. The weighed end would again pull the lever down to initiate the process again. Devices of this nature are often found at water gardens today.

Invite your children to make simple devices that could be used to measure time in a nonstandard way.

9. Water Words

Dedicate an area on a bulletin board, chalkboard, or wall where children can add words that describe water (Figure 17.6). Discuss how each of the terms infers an attitude about the nature of water and how we can view the nature of water much differently in varying circumstances.

10. Water's Work

Water causes many changes in our environment. In nature, we can see the effect of water and ice on sidewalks and roadways because of the action of water freezing and thawing. We can also see how rock and other objects can be transported by water currents. There are even documented cases where steam locomotives have been washed down rivers during floods.

Mankind also uses water to accomplish great tasks. Dams to control water flow are connected to generators that produce electricity. Early society dammed up streams to turn water wheels for power for many basic tasks such as grinding grain into flour and sawing logs. Water canals were also constructed to transport produce and people more efficiently and economically.

Collect evidence of changes that have occurred because of water. The evidence might be photographs or a chip of cement that was heaved up from a sidewalk. Ask your students to sort their events by whether they were caused by nature or by people.

Words Describing Water			
Wet	Sloppy	Splashy	Glassy
Loud	Bubbly	Drippy	Strong
Squishy	Cold	Hot	Muddy

FIGURE 17.6 Capture children's descriptions of water on a bulletin board.

Or, they could separate the events by whether the water was moving or stationary. What other characteristics could be used to classify the actions of water?

11. Sequencing Water Processes

Using a camera, invite your children to take five or more photographs of a water-related event. Each photograph should document the process of movement of water. Develop a puzzle that requires students to put the photographs in the proper sequence.

12. I Scream! You Scream! We All Scream for Ice Cream!

Children love everything about ice cream. Obviously they love to eat it. They also love to make ice cream. Making ice cream in the classroom is a great way for children to observe the high heat capacity and latent heat properties of water. (See the discussion of heat capacity and latent heat earlier in this chapter.) Making ice cream in the classroom gives children an opportunity to observe transfer of heat in a concrete way. With an ice cream maker, you start with a warm ice cream mix and lots of ice and transfer the heat from the ice cream to the ice. You will end up with frozen ice cream and water.

Simple ice cream makers can be created by using a large coffee can and a smaller jar (a peanut butter jar works well), as shown in Figure 17.7. The ice cream mix is poured into the jar and the jar is tightly sealed. Leave an air space at the top of the jar because the ice cream mix will expand as it freezes. Place the jar in the center of the coffee can and surround the jar with ice. (Snow works well also!) Add a handful of rock salt to the ice and place the lid tightly on the can. The children can roll the

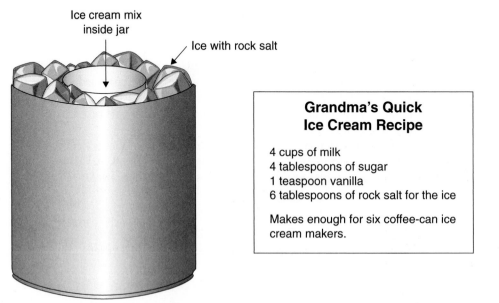

Ice cream mix inside jar

Ice with rock salt

Grandma's Quick Ice Cream Recipe

4 cups of milk
4 tablespoons of sugar
1 teaspoon vanilla
6 tablespoons of rock salt for the ice

Makes enough for six coffee-can ice cream makers.

Coffee can

FIGURE 17.7 Making ice cream provides children with a good example of the process of heat transfer.

can back and forth from one to another to mix their ice cream. Check to see if the process is complete after about 15 minutes.

When salt is added to ice it lowers the freezing point of ice. Freshwater freezes at 32 degrees Fahrenheit (0 degrees Celsius). Saturated saltwater freezes at approximately 0 degrees Fahrenheit (-18 degrees Celsius). The salt causes the ice to melt. The saltwater solution becomes much colder. It takes as much heat to melt a gram of ice as it takes to heat a gram of water to 80 degrees Celsius. The heat to melt the ice comes from the ice cream mix causing it to become much colder. Because the mix has no salt, it freezes at around 32 degrees Fahrenheit.

Activities in Other Explorations That Relate to Water

Clouds (Chapter 9)
3. Catch Your Breath

Leaves (Chapter 11)
7. A Tribute to Transpiration

Light and Color (Chapter 12)
6. Doubling Your Fish
11. Paper Chromatography

Seeds (Chapter 14)
5. The Germination Race

Resources for Teachers

Books

Carroll, C. (1996). *How artists see the weather*. New York: Abbeville Publishing Group.

Crook, N. A., Dowell, D., & Sun, J. (2003). *Wind and thermodynamic retrievals in a supercell thunderstorm: 4DVar Results*. Boulder, CO: National Center for Atmospheric Research.

Hulme, J. N. (1991). *Sea squares*. New York: Hyperion Books.

Mason, J. (2006). *Ocean commotion: sea turtles*. Gretna, LA: Pelican Publishing.

Milich, Z. (2005). *City 1 2 3*. Toronto, ON: Kids Can Press.

Pallotta, J. & Bersani, S. (2005). *Ocean counting: odd numbers*. Watertown, MA: Charlesbridge.

Rotner, S. & Woodhull, A. L. (2007). *Every season*. New Milford, CT: Roaring Brook Press.

Roy, J. R., & Roy, G. (2006). *Math all around—Patterns in nature*. New York: Marshall Cavendish Benchmark.

Roy, J. R., & Roy, G. (2006). *Math all around—Sorting at the ocean*. New York: Marshall Cavendish Benchmark.

Roy, J. R., & Roy, G. (2007). *Math all around—Measuring at home*. New York: Marshall Cavendish Benchmark.

Trefil, J. (1992). *1001 things everyone should know about science*. New York: Doubleday.

Woodford, C. (2005). *Height*. Farmington Hills, MI: Blackbirch Press.

Journal

Weiss, P. (2004). Wet wild. *Science News, 165(10)*, 58–60.

Web Sites

http://www.epa.gov/surf
Find your watershed.

http://ga.water.usgs.gov/edu
Excellent resource on water.

http://ga.water.usgs.gov/edu/mwater.html
Excellent site for water characteristics and resources.

http://kids.earth.nasa.gov/droplet.html
Shows the water cycle from the aspect of a water droplet through cartoon figures.

http://www.lsbu.ac.uk/water/anmlies.html
A 2007 Web site; Martin Chaplin.

http://www.ocean98.org/fact.htm
Information on the water in the oceans.

http://www.oceansonline.com/waterprops.htm
Basic information on water.

http://water.usgs.gov/watuse
Information on how much water we use.

http://ww2010.atmos.uiuc.edu/(Gh)/guides/mtr/cld/home.rxml
An excellent resource on clouds and precipitation; sponsored by the University of Illinois.

Children's Books on Water

Ardley, N. (1991). *The science book of water*. Orlando, FL: Harcourt Brace Jovanovich.
Arnosky, J. (1994). *All night near the water*. New York: G. P. Putnam's Sons.
Asch, F. (1995). *Water*. San Diego, CA: Harcourt Brace & Company.
Atwell, D. (1999). *River*. Boston, MA: Houghton Mifflin.
Baines, J. (1993). *Water*. New York: Thomson Learning.
Bittinger, G. (1993). *Exploring water and the ocean*. Everett, WA: Warren Publishing House.
Brandenberg, A. (1993). *My visit to the aquarium*. New York: HarperCollins.
Branlex, F. M. (1986). *Snow is falling*. New York: Crowell.
Broekel, R. (1982). *Aquariums and terrariums*. Chicago: Children's Press.
Bundey, N. (1998). *In the water*. Minneapolis, MN: Carolrhoda Books.
Burningham, J. (1977). *Come away from the water, Shirley*. New York: Thomas Y. Crowell.
Cole, J. (1986). *The magic school bus at the waterworks*. New York: Scholastic.
Cole, J. (1987). *The magic school bus: Ups and downs*. New York: Scholastic.
Cole, J. (1996). *The magic school bus wet all over*. New York: Scholastic.
Cooper, J. (1992). *Water*. Vero Beach, FL: The Rourke Corporation.
de Paola, T. (1975). *The cloud book*. New York: Scholastic.
Dorros, A. (1991). *Follow the water from brook to ocean*. New York: Harper Collins.
Dunrea, O. (2002). *It's snowing*. New York: Farrar, Straus & Giroux.
Fowler, A. (1992). *It could still be water*. Chicago: Children's Press.
Fowler, A. (1994). *All along the river*. Chicago: Children's Press.
Fowler, A. (1996). *Life in a pond*. New York: Children's Press.
Georges, D. V. (1986). *Glaciers*. Chicago: Children's Press.

Gordon, M. (1995). *Simple science: Float and sink*. New York: Thomson Learning.

Graber, M. (1994). *A raindrop's journey*. New York: Creative Advantage, Owens Corning.

Graham, B. (1991). *Rupert's big splash*. New York: Galley Books.

Hest, A. (1995). *In the rain with baby dusk*. Cambridge, MA: Candlewick Press.

Holl, A. (1965). *The rain puddle*. New York: Lothrop, Lee & Shepard.

Houghton, E. (2000). *Rainy day*. Minneapolis, MN: Carolrhoda Books.

Inkpen, M. (1994). *Kipper's book of weather*. San Diego, CA: Red Wagon/Books–Harcourt Brace & Company.

Inkpen, M. (1998). *Little Kipper's splosh*. San Diego, CA: Red Wagon/Harcourt Brace.

Jackson, S. (1998). *The old woman and the wave*. New York: ADK Ink Books.

Jarnow, J. (2000). *Splish! Splash!* New York: Grosset & Dunlan.

Jonas, A. (1995). *Splash!* New York: Greenwillow Books.

Jones, R. C. (1991). *Down at the bottom of the deep dark sea*. New York: Bradbury Press.

Kalman, B., & Schwab, J. (1992). *Wonderful water*. New York: Crabtree Publishing.

Komaiko, L. (1995). *Just my dad and me*. New York: Harper Collins.

Kuskin, K. (1995). *James and the rain*. New York: Simon & Schuster.

Locker, T. (1987). *The boy who held back the sea*. New York: Dial Books.

Locker, T. (1997). *Water dance*. San Diego, CA: Harcourt Brace & Company.

London, J. (1997). *Puddles*. New York: Viking Press.

London, J. (2001). *Sun dance, water dance*. New York: Dutton Children's Books.

MacPhail, D. (1997). *The puddle*. New York: Farrar Straus Giroux.

Martin, B. Jr., & Archambault, J. (1988) *Listen to the rain*. New York: Henry Holt & Co.

Marzollo, J. (1996). *I am water*. New York: Scholastic.

Maynard, C. (1996). *Why are there waves?* New York: DK Publishing.

Morrison, G. (2006). *A drop of water*. Boston, MA: Houghton Mifflin Company.

Nelson, R. (2003). *We use water*. Minneapolis, MN: Lerner Publications.

Parker, J. (1999). *The science of water*. Milwaukee, WI: Gareth Stevens Publishing.

Ramsay, H. (1997). *Rivers and lakes*. London, NY: Children's Press.

Rauzon, M. J., & Overbeck, B. C. (1994). *Water, water everywhere*. San Francisco, CA: Sierra Club Book for Children.

Reidel, M. (1981). *From ice to rain*. Minneapolis, MN: Carolrhoda Books.

Ricciuti, E. (1996). *Ocean*. New York: Marshall Cavendish.

Robbins, K. (1994). *Water*. New York: Henry Holt & Company.

Robinson, F. (1995). *Where do puddles go?* Chicago: Children's Press.

Schaefer, M. L. (2000). *A rainy day*. Mankato, MN: Pebble Books.

Shannon, D. (2000). *The rain came down*. New York: Blue Sky Press.

Schmid, E. (1989). *The water's journey*. New York: North-South Books.

Serfozo, M. (1990). *Rain talk*. New York: Margaret K. McElderry Books.

Stangl, J. (1993). *The little scientist: An activity lab*. Blue Ridge Summit, PA: TAB Books.

Swinburne, R. S. (1998). *Water for one, water for everyone*. Brookfield, CT: The Millbrook Press.

Taylor, B. (1991). *The science of water: Sink or swim*. New York: Random House.

Tresselt, A. R. (1947) *white snow, bright snow*. New York: Lothrop, Lee and Shepard Co.

Van Allsburg, C. (1982). *Ben's dream*. Boston, MA: Houghton Mifflin.

Volkmann, R. (2001). *Curious kittens*. New York: Doubleday House.

Ward, A. (1992) *Water and floating*. New York: F. Watts.

Wellington, M. (1989). *All my little ducklings*. New York: E. P. Dutton.

Westberg, P. L. (1991). *Water's way*. New York: Arcade Publishing.

Wick, W. (1997). *A drop of water*. New York: Scholastic Press.

Wyler, R. (1989). *Raindrops and rainbows*. Englewood Cliffs, NJ: J. Messner.

Zolotow, C. (1952). *The storm book*. New York: Harper & Row.

Books About Rain

Agell, C. (2000). *Up the mountain*. New York: DK Publishing.

Albee, S. (2003). *The perfect picnic*. New York: Random House.

Barrett, J. (1978). *Cloudy with a chance of meat-balls*. New York: Atheneum.

Bogachi, T. (1997). *Cat and Mouse in the rain*. New York: Farrer, Straus and Giroux.

Carle, E. (1996). *Little cloud*. New York: Philomel Books.

Christian, S. (1997). *Can it really rain frogs?* New York: John Wiley & Sons.

Davies, K., & Oldfield, W. (1990). *Rain rain*. Austin, TX: Raintree Steck-Vaugh Publishers.

Dundon, C. (1994). *The yellow umbrella*. New York: Simon & Schuster.

Eagle, K. (1994). *It's raining, it's pouring*. Boston, MA: Whispering Coyote Press.

Gardner, R. (1997). *Science project ideas*. Springfield, NJ: Enslow Publishers.

Graham, H. (1983). *Down comes the rain*. New York: HarperCollins.

Greene, C. (1982). *Rain! Rain!* Chicago: Children's Press.

Gretz, S., & Sage, A. (1987). *Teddy bears stay indoors*. New York: Four Winds Press.

Henderson, K. (1999). *The storm*. Cambridge, MA: Candlewick Press.

Henley, C. (1993). *Stormy day*. New York: Hyperion Books.

Hesse, K. (1999). *Come on, rain!* New York: Scholastic.

Hoban, J. (1989). *Amy loves the rain*. New York: Harper & Row.

Johnson, R.L. (2001). *A walk in the rain forest*. Minneapolis, MN: Carolrhoda Books.

Kahl, J. D. (1992). *Weatherwise: Learning about the weather*. Minneapolis, MN: Lerner Publications.

Kalan, R. (1993). *Rain*. New York: Green Willow Books.

Keats, J. E. (1968). *A letter to Amy*. New York: Harper & Row.

Krupp, E. C. (2000). *The rainbow and you*. New York: Morrow Junior Books.

Malan, J. (1997). *How it works: Wacky weather*. New York: Simon & Schuster.

Markies, S. (1993). *A rainy day*. Orchard Books.

Mayer, M. (1990). *Just a rainy day*. Racine, WI: Western Publishing Company.

McPhail, D. (1997). *The puddle*. Farrar, Straus & Giroux.

Medears, A. S. (1995). *We play on a rainy day*. New York: Scholastic.

Polacco, P. (1990). *Thunder cake*. New York: Philomel Books.

Radley, G. (1992). *Rainy day rhymes*. Boston, MA: Houghton Mifflin.

Reay J., & Gon, A. (1995). *Bumpa Rumpus and the rainy day*. Boston, MA: Houghton Mifflin.

Roche, H. (1996). *Pete's puddles*. New York: De Agostini Editions.

Saunders-Smith, G. (1998). *Rain*. Mankato, MN: Pebble Books.

Shannon, D. (2000). *The rain came down*. New York: Blue Sky Press.

Skofield, J. (1984). *All wet! All wet*. New York: Harper & Row.

Spier, P. (1982). *Rain*. New York: Doubleday.

Stojic, M. (2000). *Rain*. New York: Crown Publishers.

Tresselt, A. R. (1946). *Rain drop splash*. New York: Lothrop, Lee, & Shepard.

Tuxworth, N. (1999). *Splish, splash: A very first picture*. Milwaukee, WI: Gareth Stevens Publishers.

Wyler, R. (1989). *Raindrops and rainbows*. Englewood Cliffs, NJ: J. Messner.

Yashima, T. (1977). *Umbrella*. New York: Puffin Books.

Books About Snow

Bauer, C.F. (ed.). (1986). *Snowy day: Stories and poems*. New York: Lippincott.

Branley, F. M. (2000). *Snow is falling*. New York: HarperCollins.

Brett, J. (1989). *The mitten*. New York: Putnam Sons.

Bundey, N. (1998). *In the snow*. Minnneapolis, MN: Carolrhoda Books.

Carle, E. (2000). *Dream-snow*. New York: Philomel Books.

Carlstrom, N. W. (1992). *The snow speaks*. New York: Boston, MA: Little Brown & Company.

Dorros, A. (1991). *Animal tracks*. New York: Scholastic.

Ehlert, L. (1995). *Snowballs*. San Diego, CA: Harcourt Brace & Company.

Grossnickle, H. A. (1999). *What can you do in the snow?* New York: Greenwillow Books.

Keats, E. J. (1962). *The snowy day*. New York: Viking Press.

Keller, H. (1988). *Geraldine's big snow*. New York: Greenwillow Books.

Kirk, D. (2000). *Snow family*. New York: Hyperion Books.

Martin, J. B. (1998). *Snowflake Bentley*. Boston, MA: Houghton Mifflin.

Marzollo, J. (1988). *I am snow*. New York: Scholastic.

Poydar, N. (1997). *Snip, snip . . . snow!* New York. NY: Holiday House.

Prelutsky, J. (2006) *It's snowing! It's snowing!: Winter poems*. New York: HarperCollins.

Sabuda, R. (1999). *The blizzard's robe*. New York: Atheneam Books.

Sanfield, S. (1995). *Snow*. New York: Philomel Books.

Schaefer, C. L. (2000). *Snow pumpkin*. New York: Crown Publishers.

Tresselt, A. R. (1947). *White snow bright snow*. NewYork: Lothrop, Lee & Shepara Co.

	1. See the Wind	2. Capture the Wind	3. Let's Go Fly a Kite	4. Construct a Maximum Wind Gust Measuring Device	5. Watching the Leaves Blow	6. Animals Using the Wind	7. Using the Wind to Do Work	8. Water Evaporation	9. Micro and Macro
SCIENCE									
Inquiry	X	X	X	X	X	X	X	X	X
Physical Science	X	X	X	X	X	X	X	X	X
Life Science					X	X			X
Earth and Space Science	X	X	X	X	X	X	X	X	X
Science and Technology		X		X			X		X
Personal and Social Perspectives	X	X	X		X	X			
History and Nature of Science		X					X		
MATHEMATICS									
Number and Operations					X				X
Algebra					X				X
Geometry		X	X	X			X		
Measurement	X			X			X		
Data Analysis and Probability					X				X
Problem Solving		X	X	X		X	X	X	X
Reasoning and Proof				X					
Communication	X		X						
Connections	X		X						
Representation	X					X	X		

CHAPTER 18

Wind

An' little Orphant Annie says, when the blaze is blue,
An' the lamp-wick sputters, an' the wind goes woo-oo!
An' you hear the crickets quit, an' the moon is gray,
An' the lightnin' bugs in dew is all squenched away. . . .

From Little Orphant Annie, James Whitcomb Riley (1885).
Indianapolis Journal

We can't see it, but we can feel it. We can't catch it, but it will catch a kite. It has no muscles, but it can be very strong. It can't cause seeds to grow, but it determines where they should be planted. It's called the *wind!*

The wind is like a friend. It lets us know when it's around. On a warm day, a gentle breeze cools us. On a winter day, it chills us. At times, it warns us of an oncoming storm. Sometimes it appears to be angry and blows the roof off a structure.

As children experience the outdoors, many of their activities will be influenced by the wind. A gust of wind can blow their papers from the table into the air. The wind can tug on their balloons or kites. The waves on the lake caused by the wind move the float on their fishing lines. The wind knocks over the cardboard fortresses they construct. It pulls the dandelion seeds from the pods in their hands. Each of these experiences causes children to react and to respond. These experiences cause children to learn how to manipulate and control the environment around them. They think: "Put a rock on my papers." "Hold the balloon tightly." "Recognize that not all movements on the fishing line tell me I caught a fish." These natural experiences help children to learn to predict the effect of the wind.

SCIENCE CONCEPTS FOR TEACHERS

The science conceptual framework is included here to give teachers the background knowledge and information necessary to investigate wind.

What Is Wind?

Wind is simply the movement of air. Our atmosphere is made up of nitrogen (78%), oxygen (21%), and other elements and compounds, as listed in Figure 18.1.

If we view a square inch on the surface of the earth and take the column of air above it, the air would weigh approximately 15 pounds. We refer to this as *air pressure*, as illustrated in Figure 18.2.

Air changes temperatures based on the heat that it absorbs directly from the Sun and the heat dissipated from the Earth. The concentration of energy that a particular location receives from the Sun depends on its latitude and the season of the year. As illustrated in Figure 18.3, if the Sun's rays shine at a high angle, the rays are more concentrated, and more heat is absorbed. If the Sun's rays are low in the sky, the rays are spread across a greater area and less heat is absorbed.

The amount that air is heated is controlled by the nature of the land features. Some land features will collect more heat from the Sun than others. This phenomenon is based on the types and amounts of vegetation present and the nature of the bedrock. Land features will rise in temperature more quickly than water. This is because just the top few inches of the soil will collect the day's heat from the Sun. Water will collect the same amount of heat, but because it is fluid, the heat is absorbed throughout the depth of the water. The surface temperature of water will not be altered as much as that of land features. As a result, during the day, the land features will be warmer and bodies of water will be cooler.

Because the heat of land features is concentrated at the surface, it tends to dissipate more heat during the nighttime than do bodies of water. Thus, during the night,

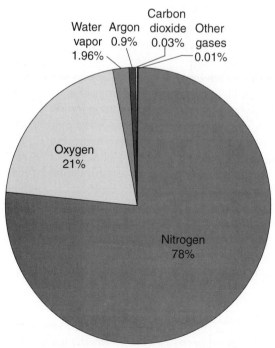

Nitrogen	78%
Oxygen	21%
Water vapor	1.96%
Argon	0.9%
Carbon dioxide	0.03%
Other gases	0.01%

FIGURE 18.1   Gases in the earth's atmosphere.

FIGURE 18.2 The column of air for every square inch on the surface of the Earth weighs approximately 15 pounds.

FIGURE 18.3 Because the Sun is much higher in the sky during the summer, the Sun's rays strike the Earth over a smaller area. During the winter, because the Sun is low in the sky, the rays cover a much larger area. The result is that during the summer much more heat is absorbed than during the winter.

land features become cooler than water. Because the water's heat is absorbed to a much deeper level, it dissipates less heat and the air above the water will tend to be warmer than that on the land.

Air temperature is controlled by two main sources: by the heat dissipated from the Earth, and by the heat it absorbs directly from the Sun's rays. Variations in the Earth's features cause the air at different locations to be heated to varying amounts. The result is that the temperature of air varies at different locations.

Air expands and contracts as it is heated or cooled. When air is heated it expands, making it less dense. When air is heated it also becomes lighter. When air is cooled, it contracts, making it denser; it also becomes heavier. This change in the weight of a volume of air results in a change in air pressure.

The atmosphere is constantly adjusting to equalize air pressure. This movement of air is called *wind*. The greater the difference in air pressures at two related locations, the greater the speed of the movement of air. The variations of intensity of the wind are indicated by the Beaufort scale shown in Figure 18.4. The Beaufort scale is a convenient scale for quantifying wind speed. The Beaufort scale was introduced in 1806 by Admiral Sir Francis Beaufort (1774–1857) of the British navy. The Beaufort scale describes wind effects on a fully rigged sailing vessel and

Beaufort	Average Miles per Hour	Average Kilometers per Hour	Surroundings
0 (calm)	0	0	Smoke rises vertically and the sea is mirror smooth.
1 (light air)	1.2–3	2–5	Smokes moves slightly with breeze and shows direction of wind.
2 (light breeze)	3.7–7.5	6–12	You can feel wind on your face and hear the leaves start to rustle.
3 (gentle breeze)	8–12.5	13–20	Smoke will move horizontally and small branches start to sway. Wind extends a light flag.
4 (moderate breeze)	13–18.6	21–30	Loose dust or sand on the ground will move and larger branches will sway; loose paper blows around; and fairly frequent whitecaps occur.
5 (fresh breeze)	19.3–25	31–40	Surface waves form on water and small trees sway.
6 (strong breeze)	25.5–31	41–50	Trees begin to bend with the force of the wind and causes whistling in telephone wires and some spray on the sea surface.
7 (moderate gale)	32–38	51–61	Large trees sway.
8 (fresh gale)	39–46	62–74	Twigs break from trees, and long streaks of foam appear on the ocean.
9 (strong gale)	47–55	75–89	Branches break from trees.
10 (whole gale)	56–64	90–103	Trees are uprooted, and the sea takes on a white appearance.
11 (storm)	65–74	104–119	Widespread damage.
12 (hurricane)	75+	120+	Structural damage on land and storm waves at sea.

FIGURE 18.4 The Beaufort wind scale.

was originally based on observing the waves of water on the open ocean. It has been modified to include descriptions of effects common on land features as well.

Your students might choose to design their own scale based on their school yard. For instance, they could relate the scale to the school flagpole and trees in the yard; or they could examine how much wind it takes to cause the playground swings to sway back and forth.

Wind Chill

The wind chill temperature indicates how cold people and animals feel when they are outside. The stronger the wind and the colder the air, the more difficult it is to maintain body heat. As the wind increases, it draws heat from the body, driving down skin temperature and eventually the internal body temperature. Therefore, the wind makes you feel much colder than the actual temperature would indicate. If the temperature is 0 degrees Fahrenheit (−18° Celsius) and the wind is blowing at 15 mph, the wind chill is −19 degrees Fahrenheit (−28° Celsius). At this wind chill temperature, exposed skin can freeze in 30 minutes (see Figure 18.5).

Wind chill is only a factor with live animals. It has no effect on inanimate objects. For example, an automobile will be no colder because of the wind than if there was no wind at all. The only variation that will occur because of the wind will be that the car will *cool* to the air temperature more quickly.

MATHEMATICS: ADDRESSING THE NCTM STANDARDS THROUGH CONCEPT EXPLORATIONS

Many of the activities designed to explore and observe the effects of the wind involve observation and classification, patterns, geometry, measurement, and data collection and analysis. As children use mathematics to describe what they

Temperature (°F)

Calm	40	35	30	25	20	15	10	5	0	−5	−10	−15	−20	−25	−30	−35	−40	−45
5	36	31	25	19	13	7	1	−5	−11	−16	−22	−28	−34	−40	−46	−52	−57	−63
10	34	27	21	15	9	3	−4	−10	−16	−22	−28	−35	−41	−47	−53	−59	−66	−72
15	32	25	19	13	6	0	−7	−13	−19	−26	−32	−39	−45	−51	−58	−64	−71	−77
20	30	24	17	11	4	−2	−9	−15	−22	−29	−35	−42	−48	−55	−61	−68	−74	−81
25	29	23	16	9	3	−4	−11	−17	−24	−31	−37	−44	−51	−58	−64	−71	−78	−84
30	28	22	15	8	1	−5	−12	−19	−26	−33	−39	−46	−53	−60	−67	−73	−80	−87
35	28	21	14	7	0	−7	−14	−21	−27	−34	−41	−48	−55	−62	−69	−76	−82	−89
40	27	20	13	6	−1	−8	−15	−22	−29	−36	−43	−50	−57	−64	−71	−78	−84	−91
45	26	19	12	5	−2	−9	−16	−23	−30	−37	−44	−51	−58	−65	−72	−79	−86	−93
50	26	19	12	4	−3	−10	−17	−24	−31	−38	−45	−52	−60	−67	−74	−81	−88	−95
55	25	18	11	4	−3	−11	−18	−25	−32	−39	−46	−54	−61	−68	−75	−82	−89	−97
60	25	17	10	3	−4	−11	−19	−26	−33	−40	−48	−55	−62	−69	−76	−84	−91	−98

Wind (mph) (vertical axis label)

FIGURE 18.5   A wind chill chart.

observe and experience, they are gaining a valuable understanding of the use of mathematics to communicate discoveries.

Geometry

As you engage in kite construction with young children, there will be rich opportunities to explore geometric shapes. Children can design interesting kites and try flying their creative geometric constructions. In constructing and flying their kites, children can make adjustments and redesign their kites for better soaring or launching.

Identifying kites that are symmetrical will be an important skill because symmetrical kites fly better than unsymmetrical ones. Children can investigate which geometric shapes fly better: Do kites that are basically "kite" shaped (four-sided figure with adjacent sides congruent and opposite sides parallel) fly better than other shaped kites such as rectangular or oval kites?

Measurement

Measurement will be an important tool for documenting the evidence of the wind. Children can explore creative ways to measure the wind's force and engage in interesting activities to determine distance and time. Support for these activities can be provided with stopwatches and nonstandard measuring tools such as craft sticks, footstep strides, or lengths of blocks. Children should be given many opportunities to use the tools and to examine carefully the attributes they are measuring.

Data Analysis

Does the length of string used to launch the kite make a difference in the kite's liftoff and flight? Much of the exploration involved in capturing and seeing the wind can be documented through creative graphing. It is important for children to pose their own questions about the wind and to design ways of collecting data. Children should also have an active part in determining how to organize and display the data. Teachers can provide a variety of media for the children to explore in the construction of the graphs.

Children can be supported as they interpret data recorded on their graphs and make predictions. For example, if they are graphing the force of the wind by watching fabrics move in the wind, they may make predictions about similar fabrics. If silk moves with very little wind or a gentle breeze, what would happen to a piece of nylon? Is nylon likely or not likely be affected by a gentle breeze? What fabrics are less likely to be affected by a gentle breeze? Graphing the fabrics according to agreed-on criteria will be a good activity. For example, headings on such a graph could be "Moves with Little Wind" and "Moves with a Lot of Wind." This graph could be expanded into three categories, thus beginning a seriation of wind strength by fabric weight.

OBSERVING WITH ALL THE SENSES

The wind is an excellent tool for exploring the five senses.

Sight

The eye is a great tool for sensing motion. A still photograph would not pick up the shimmering of a leaf, but our eyes do. A hawk has difficulty seeing an animal at rest. But when a rabbit moves, the hawk can detect it at a great distance.

Sight is a great tool for indirectly seeing the evidence of the wind. Though air is invisible, it causes motion that is easily detected by our eyes. We can see dust picked up by a gust of wind. We can see sand dunes and infer the accomplishments of the wind. We can see snowdrifts and water rippling across a pond. All of these events show us the power of the wind.

Sound

The sounds of the wind give children wonderful opportunities to differentiate sounds. Some sounds are soft, like the leaves rustling on a tree, the hum of the wind on a telephone line, or the flapping of a paper blowing across a football field. How many different sounds caused by the wind can your students identify? Can they relate some of the sounds they hear to some of the observations that they were able to see?

Touch

The sense of touch is very complex. The primary purpose of touch is to feel differences in objects. We can tell if something is hard like a metal plate or soft like a cotton ball. Our body will also tell us if something is hot or cold. This sensing of differences in temperatures is very important to us in detecting the wind. When the wind blows against our skin, it causes any moisture on our body to evaporate. This evaporation draws heat from our body. Evaporating 1 gram of water requires more than five times the heat needed to heat the same water from the freezing temperature to the boiling point. This is why we feel so cold when we get out of a swimming pool. This is also why a soft breeze feels so good on a hot day.

At times, the wind becomes so strong that we turn our back to it because it evaporates the moisture on our eyes and causes them to become uncomfortable.

Smell and Taste

We can all remember the pleasant odors from a bakery or pizza shop when "the wind is just right." Smell and taste are interrelated. When you eat foods such as pizza, some of the flavor enters our nostrils. This combination of taste and smell helps us denote specific flavors.

Smell and memory are also interrelated. Smells can bring back wonderful memories of a place, a person, or an earlier time in your life. Maybe the smell of a certain food reminds you of your grandparents or of a different time in your life when that particular smell was common. We remember those smells even if we haven't smelled them for a long, long time.

Our senses of smell and taste also help us determine if something is no longer good to eat or drink. Sour milk does not have an appetizing smell nor does moldy cheese or rotten eggs. These smells waft to us with air currents the same way as do lovely smells from the bakery or pizza shop.

SAFETY

As children explore the effects of the wind, they may be a target for blowing dust. Caution children about flying dust particles in the air. If necessary, children can wear plastic safety goggles.

Kite flying is great fun. The caution exercised has to do with the string. Be sure that string does not get wrapped around fingers, wrists, or other body parts.

Pinwheels and fans have their own set of dangers. Keeping a safe distance from rotating surfaces is a must. Children should be watched carefully when using any type of propelling machine such as a fan.

CONCEPT EXPLORATIONS ON WIND FOR YOUR CLASSROOM

The following Concept Explorations on wind provide many opportunities for children to ask questions and to investigate their interests. You may want to read books related to wind such as Helen Frost's *Wind*. This short book has photographs and text that tell children about the nature of wind, kinds of wind, how wind helps us, and examples of windy weather. Kite flying and current-day windmills are also featured in this book.

Trees that grow in areas where there are strong prevailing winds become deformed by the forces of the wind.

1. See the Wind

We often talk about seeing the wind. In reality, we cannot see the wind, but we can constantly see the result of the wind's action, whether the movement of leaves from a quaking aspen or dust "kicked up" from a baseball diamond.

Help your students creatively document the evidence of the wind. Complete this documentation by making photographs, drawings, or paintings; by constructing models; or by using other methods to record the effects of the wind's presence. Indicate the time of the event and the weather conditions.

Documenting events affected by the wind gives children very realistic experiences in utilizing their observation skills. The wind is ideal for exploring all five of the senses. Often, we can hear the effect of the wind and feel the effect of the wind before we can see the effect of the wind. We often can smell odors or even taste the air when the wind blows over a field of hay.

Documenting the evidence of the wind gives wonderful opportunities to develop vocabulary skills. For example, for each of the experiences documented, the children could identify different adjectives or adjectival phrases that describe the event. The wind might be "soft as a ball of cotton" or as "loud as a locomotive." These actions give the children opportunities to openly express their feelings and capture their thoughts about the wind. They encourage children to make comparisons of different events affected by the wind. Their descriptions might lead to seriations that rank the magnitude of the wind.

2. Capture the Wind

Children enjoy constructing many things. They want to share items they produce with all of their friends and family. These constructions take on greater significance when the children's products are used as part of the classroom experience of problem solving.

Many devices can be designed and made to capture the wind. For example, wind vanes, wind chimes, windmills, pinwheels, and wind socks each can be used to not only document particular properties of the wind, but to also utilize the different senses.

Encourage your children to be original. Often, by starting with a basic design, children can come up with a unique characteristic for their device by using different materials that they collect. Recycling materials can be used for this purpose.

The development of these constructs can be used as a catalyst for further exploration. Can their device be used to measure the wind? How little change can occur in the wind before their device will notice the alteration? What type of device can

A wind chime made from shells collected at the ocean can extend the memories of travel.

they construct that will indicate the changes? How can they record the effectiveness of their wind-measuring device? How do scientists measure the wind's power? It is important for children to wonder and think about the wind. They can share their theories and pose questions to explore and research.

The items that the children construct also can be a catalyst for skills in language arts. Children might be encouraged to describe their invention by using poetry or by writing a song.

3. Let's Go Fly a Kite

The design and construction of kites provide excellent opportunities for children to explore and experience the power of the wind. Kites come in all sizes and shapes.

Kites are used in many places around the world. Exploring cultural connections to kite flying can open a door to the wide and windy world.

Before beginning this exploration, you should review the guidelines listed in Figure 18.6 for safely flying a kite.

Design and construct a kite. Discuss what is needed to build a kite. Have some materials available for children to examine. Plan an approach for construction and carry it through. Does the children's kite stay together? Do they think it will fly? Discuss an approach to its flight. Field test and record the children's experiences. How did the kite fly? Ask the children to think about how they might change the kite to improve its flight. Create the plan and make the changes. Identify the changes and adjustments that are made to improve the kite. How did the adjustments alter the kite's performance?

Kites present an excellent opportunity to discuss the different geometric shapes with your children (Figure 18.7). Kites can have many geometric shapes including triangles, squares, and diamonds. What geometric shape makes the sturdiest kite? Kites can be two dimensional or three dimensional. Kites are also made in the shape of creatures such as fish, birds, and dragons. One critical aspect of constructing kites

---

Remember that safety is the responsibility of the flyer, not the spectator! Here are some important guidelines for you and your student, to follow when flying kites:

- Keep away from overhead power lines.
- Don't fly kites close to roads. A kite or kite string in a roadway could cause a serious accident.
- Don't fly kites near airports. There are federal laws against flying things near airports.
- Do not stand under the landing (or crashing) area for your kites.
- Don't have small children try to hold a large kite in a strong wind.

FIGURE 18.6 Safety in kite flying.

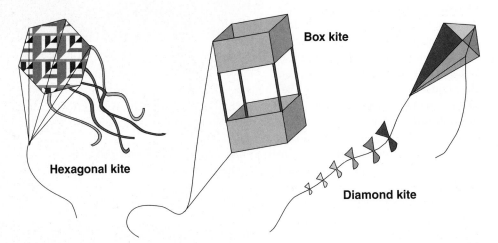

FIGURE 18.7 Kites present an excellent opportunity to discuss geometric shapes with children.

so that they will fly is that the kite must have symmetry. That means the kite needs to have a centerline with equivalent sides. Otherwise the kite will constantly pull to one side and drop out of the sky.

Kites are valuable tools for observing the nature of the wind in your area each day. The wind need not be strong for flying kites. For ease of flying, the critical factor is that the wind is constant. A constant wind will cause your kite to steadily rise. A gust of wind will cause your kite to rise quickly and be very active; however, as soon and the gust dies, so does your kite.

Kites also provide opportunities to explore different cultures. For example, in Asian countries such as China and Japan, kite constructing and flying is an ancient art. In China kites were flown over 3,000 years ago. Kite flying had mythological and religious significance. In Japan, kites are flown on special days. Over time, kite flying expanded throughout Asia and to Europe and Australia.

Kites have also been used for scientific and utilitarian purposes. Kite experiments were conducted by Benjamin Franklin and Alexander Graham Bell. In the late 1800s and early 1900s, kites were used in the military for observing enemy forces. Around this time, box kites were also used for measuring wind velocity, temperature, barometric pressure, and humidity in the atmosphere. Kites have also been used for fishing by using the kite to fly the bait far out into the water.

4. Construct a Maximum Wind Gust Measuring Device

We have all watched as a gust of wind has picked up an object and transported it, sometimes causing great damage. The power of a hurricane can destroy anything in its path. A tornado can sustain winds of several hundred miles per hour.

Have your children design simple instruments that will indicate a gust of wind. The devices that your children design can be used for developing a variety of mathematics skills. A square sheet of cardboard attached with tape and hanging from some playground equipment will move from the vertical position because of air currents. Similar materials can be hung to show the same force. Children can estimate the angle of deflection. Right angles or, as they are sometimes called, square angles are easy for children to identify. The angles can be estimated relative to the right angle. For example, angles greater than or less than 90 degrees can be easily determined. Children can also make simplistic charts and graphs based on the data they collect. The charts can be as simple as having a classification scheme with these headings: "Greater Than a Right Angle," "Right Angle," and "Less Than a Right Angle."

J. David Keller

Stack several empty beverage cans on top of each other. The stronger the wind, the lower the stack that will be blown over.

In an earlier section, we discussed the Beaufort scale, which is a standard way to indicate the velocity of the wind. Children could use their observations to develop their own scale for measuring the wind.

5. Watching the Leaves Blow

Leaves are a common, natural part of a child's world. They can be observed to flutter on trees, and they will appear to travel in unison along the ground. Leaves of some species of trees will flutter more than others. For example, leaves on an aspen tree will "quake" because the stem of the leaf is flattened, causing it to have little strength.

In the fall, blowing leaves can give indications of the blowing wind. By looking along fences, children can make "guesstimations" about what direction the wind has been blowing. Which side of the fence has the most leaves? You can simulate this activity indoors by using leaves, a homemade fence, and a simple hair dryer.

Birds use rising air currents to soar.

6. Animals Using the Wind

The wind plays an important role in many animals' lives. Many animals such as hawks, eagles, and vultures benefit from the wind by using thermals (rising air currents) to soar.

At other times, the wind can be detrimental to some animals. Insects and birds can be blown off course by strong winds. Natural shelters in trees can be destroyed by strong winds or by forest fires augmented by the wind.

Have your children develop a scenario, or story, based on how the wind affects their favorite animal. Document how the wind affects the life of that animal. Is the effect positive or negative? How does the animal adapt to the factors of the wind? Encourage the children to use songs, poetry, and art to tell their story.

7. Using the Wind to Do Work

Can we harness the wind's power and make it work? In physics, work is defined as the force needed to move an object times the distance the object is moved: Work = Force × Distance. Anytime the wind moves an object, it is doing a form of work. For example, when the wind moves a sailboat, it is doing work. When the wind moves the arms of a windmill, it is also doing work.

Recently, the use of wind power has been expanded both for industry and recreation. Wind farms have large banks of wind turbines that produce electrical energy. Sail devices have been attached to surfboards and also used for cross-country skiing.

Encourage your children to design a device that will do work. For example, they could make a sailboat to sail on a wading pool. (Use a fan to produce the wind.) Or they could make their own windmill to lift a small object. Tinker Toys, K'NEX, and other building materials can be used to guide students in their discoveries.

8. Water Evaporation

The wind increases the normal rate of water evaporation. The more air that contacts the surface of water, the more rapidly the water will evaporate. We can watch evaporation occur very easily in our classroom when we wash the chalkboard. Other examples of evaporation can be seen on sidewalks when the sun appears after a rain or after the kitchen table is wiped off with a sponge. We can see how to hasten the drying process by blowing on the wet surface.

Encourage your children to document, by using a camera or other means, how the wind increases the rate of evaporation of water from common places and items such as soil, a clothesline, a table, or a puddle.

9. Micro and Macro

What is the smallest object that you can find that is affected by the wind? What is the largest object? Design a tool or use a common device that is altered by the most gentle air currents. What device can you make that will detect the smallest movement of air possible? For example, collect some dandelions seed balls and release the seeds to the wind. Can you follow their trip? What other plants use the wind to transport their seeds?

What about different fabrics hung outside on a clothesline? Watch what happens to a strip of gauze, silk, polyester, corduroy, denim, or burlap. Which ones move first with a gentle breeze? How much wind does it take to get the burlap to move or the denim? Make predictions and watch. You can help this experiment along with a fan. Try to discover why what you observe is happening.

You could also place a series of objects of differing masses on a flat surface to see which ones blow off in the breeze most easily. Find natural items such as a pinecone, stone, blade of grass, leaf, or seashell to use in your experiments.

After conducting these types of experiments and exploration, children can think about structures in their environment. We can direct their attention to things they see on a daily basis. For example, how are some large objects such as road signs and buildings designed to withstand strong winds? Why do architects need to understand the wind? Have your students identify items in their community that need to withstand strong winds. How can one prepare for severe weather conditions such as tornadoes and hurricanes?

Activities in Other Explorations That Relate to Wind

Birds (Chapter 8)

1. How High Do Birds Fly?

Clouds (Chapter 9)

1. How High Is a Cloud?
2. What to Do with the Weather
3. I've Looked at Clouds from Both Sides Now
4. Which Way Are You Going?

Leaves (Chapter 11)

1. Quiet Leaves

Resources for Teachers

Books

Canduto, M. J. (1997). *Keepers of the earth: Native American stories and environmental activities for children.* Golden, CO: Fulcrum.

Watts, M. (2000). *Water and wind power.* Buckinghamshire, UK: Shire Publications.

Woelfe, G. (1997). *The wind at work: An activity guide to windmills.* Chicago: ChicagoReview Press.

Websites

http://www.aka.kite.org/
Site of the American Kite Fliers Association.

http://www.awea.org/
American Wind Energy Association Web site.

http://www.clem.freeserve.co.uk/
Guidelines on making simple kites from newspaper.

http://www.eere.energy.gov/wind/
U.S. Department of Energy Web site.

http://www.geocities.com/Colosseum/4569/home.html
Excellent site for kite design, construction, and flying information.

http://www.kites.org/jo/beaufort.html
Information about the Beaufort Wind Scale for land and water.

http://www.nrel.gov/wind/
National Wind Technology Center Web site.

http://www.nws.noaa.gov/om/windchill/index.shtml
Wind chill temperature index.

Children's Books on Wind

Allaby, M. (1995). *How the weather works: 100 ways parents and kids can share the secrets of the atmosphere.* New York: Reader's Digest Association.

Allen, O. E. (1983). *Atmosphere.* Time-Life Books.

Birmingham, M., Bledsoe, E. K., & Halls, M. K. (2000). *365 outdoor activities.* Publications International.

Brooks, L. (1999). *Windmills.* New York: Metro Books.

Burda, C. (1999). *Wind toys that spin, twirl and whirl.* New York: Sterling Publishing. Co.

Calhoun, M. (1987). *Jack and the whoopee wind*. New York: William Morrow & Co.

Carle, E. (2005). *The tiny seed*. New York: Little Simon.

Cannon, J. (1993). *Stellaluna one word*. San Diego, CA: Harcourt Brace & Co.

Carlstrom, N. W. (1993). *How does the wind walk?* New York: Macmillan.

Cooper, J. (1992). *Science secrets: Wind*. Vero Beach, FL: The Rourke Corporation.

Cosgrove, B. (1991). *Weather*. New York: Alfred A. Knopf.

Cox, J. D. (2000). *Weather for dummies*. Forest City, CA: IDG Books. Worldwide.

Crews, D. (1995). *Sail away*. New York: Greenwillow Books.

Dabcovich, L. (1990). *Ducks fly*. New York: Dutton Children's Books.

Davies, K., & Oldfield, W. (1995). *See for yourself: Wind*. Austin, TX: Raintree Steck-Vaughn.

Davis, L. (1997). *P. B. Bear catch that hat!* New York: DK Publishing.

Disney, W. *Disney's animal stories—Dumbo the biggest ears ever*. New York: *Scholastic*.

Dorros, A. (1989). *Feel the wind*. New York: Crowell.

Eastman, P. D. (2000). *Flap your wings*. New York: Beginner Books.

Ets, M. H. (1963). *Gilberto and the wind*. New York: Viking Press.

Fowler, A. (1995). *When a storm comes up*. Chicago: Children's Press.

Frost, H. (2004). *Wind*. Mankato, MN: Capstone Press.

Gibbons, G. (1989). *Catch the wind! All about kites*. New York: Little, Brown & Co.

Ginsburg, M. (1992). *Asleep, asleep*. New York: Greenwillow Books.

Glover, D. (1993). *Flying and floating*. New York: Kingfisher Books.

Grady, J. (1980). *Catch the wind*. New York: Coward, McCann & Georghegan.

Harshman, M. (1991). *Rocks in my pockets*. New York: Cobblehill Books/Dutton.

Hoban, J. (1988). *Amy loves the wind*. New York: Harper & Row.

Hooker, J. (1990). *In praise of windmills*. New York: Jeremy Hooker, Circle Press Publications.

Hutchins, P. (1974). *The wind blew*. New York: Macmillan.

Kalman, B., & Schaub, J. (1993). *The air I breathe*. Niagra-on-the-lake, Ontario: Crabtree Publishing Co.

Karas, G. B. (1998). *The windy day*. New York: Simon & Schuster.

Kennedy, D. M. (1998). *Make things fly: Poems about the wind*. New York: Margaret K. McElderry Books.

Kerrod, R. (1990). *Air in action*. Tarrytown, New York: Marshall Cavendish.

Lafferty, P. (1989). *Wind to flight*. London: Alladin Books.

Lipson, M. (1994). *How the wind plays*. New York: Hyperion Books for Children Co.

MacDonald, E. (1992). *The very windy day*. New York: Tambourine Books.

Marzollo, J. (1996). *I'm a seed*. New York: Scholastic.

McKee, D., S. (1998). *Elmer takes off*. New York: Lothrop, Lee & Shepherd.

McKissack, C. P. (1988). *Mirandy and Brother Wind*. New York: Alfred A. Knopf.

McPhail, D. (1997). *A bug, a bear, and a boy plant a garden*. New York: Scholastic.

Munsh, R. N. (1984). *Millicent and the wind*. Willodale, Ontario: Annick Press.

Rey, M. (1958). *Curious George flies a kite*. Boston, MA: Houghton-Mifflin.

Root, P. (1996). *One windy Wednesday*. Cambridge, MA: Press.

Schaefer, L. M. (2000). *A windy day*. Mankato, MN: Pebble Books.

Shearer, A. (1998). *Professor Sniff and the lost spring breezes*. New York: Orchard Books.

Steele, P. (1991). *Wind: Causes and effects*. New York: Franklin Watts.

Stolz, M. (1994). *The weeds and the weather*. New York: Greenwillow Books.

Tibo, G. (1991). *Simon and the wind*. Plattsburgh, New York: Tundra Books.

Tocci, S. (1988). *Experiments with air*. New York: Children's Press.

Walpole, B. (1987). *Fun with science—air*. New York: Warwick Press.

Winer, Y. (2001). *Butterflies fly*. Watertown, MA: Charlesbridge.

Yolen, J. (1988). *The emperor and the kite*. New York: Philomel Books.

Zolotow, C. (1995). *When the wind stops*. New York: HarperCollins.

APPENDIX

NCTM Process Standards

NCTM does not delineate process standards for individual grade bands; the standards listed here address expectations for grades prekindergarten through 12. The Concept Explorations in this book involve all of the NCTM Process Standards. Teachers are encouraged to review these standards and utilize as many of them as possible with their young learners as they explore the many concepts found in this book.

PROBLEM SOLVING STANDARD

Instructional programs from prekindergarten through grade 12 should enable all students to—

- build new mathematical knowledge through problem solving;
- solve problems that arise in mathematics and in other contexts;
- apply and adapt a variety of appropriate strategies to solve problems;
- monitor and reflect on the process of mathematical problem solving.

REASONING AND PROOF STANDARD

Instructional programs from prekindergarten through grade 12 should enable all students to—

- recognize reasoning and proof as fundamental aspects of mathematics;
- make and investigate mathematical conjectures;
- develop and evaluate mathematical arguments and proofs;
- select and use various types of reasoning and methods of proof.

COMMUNICATION STANDARD

Instructional programs from prekindergarten through grade 12 should enable all students to—

- organize and consolidate their mathematical thinking through communication;
- communicate their mathematical thinking coherently and clearly to peers, teachers, and others;
- analyze and evaluate the mathematical thinking and strategies of others;
- use the language of mathematics to express mathematical ideas precisely.

CONNECTIONS STANDARD

Instructional programs from prekindergarten through grade 12 should enable all students to—

- recognize and use connections among mathematical ideas;
- understand how mathematical ideas interconnect and build on one another to produce a coherent whole;
- recognize and apply mathematics in contexts outside of mathematics.

REPRESENTATION STANDARD

Instructional programs from prekindergarten through grade 12 should enable all students to—

- create and use representations to organize, record, and communicate mathematical ideas;
- select, apply, and translate among mathematical representations to solve problems;
- use representations to model and interpret physical, social, and mathematical phenomena.

References

Bastyra, J., & Johnson, B. (2003). *Thai: The essence of Asian cooking*. London: Annes Publishing.

Berk, L., & Winsler, A. (1995). *Scaffolding children's learning: Vygotsky and early childhood education*. Washington, DC: National Association for the Education of Young Children.

Berk, L. (2006). *Child development*. Boston: Pearson-Allyn and Bacon.

Bruner, J. (1966). *Toward a theory of instruction*. Cambridge, MA: Harvard University Press.

Bruning, R. H., Schraw, G. J., Norby, M. N., & Ronning, R. R. (2004). *Cognitive psychology and instruction*. Upper Saddle River, NJ: Pearson, Merrill Prentice Hall.

Chaille, C., & Britain, L. (1997). *The young child as scientist: A constructivist approach to early childhood science education*. Boston: Allyn & Bacon.

Chen, G., Kao, J., & Liu, T. (1999). *A survey of the nature of light*.

Conezio, K., & French, L. (2002). Science in the preschool classroom: Capitalizing on children's fascination with the everyday world to foster language and literacy development. *Young Children*.

Crook, N. A., Dowell, D., & Sun, J. (2003). *Wind and thermodynamic retrievals in a supercell thunderstorm: 4D Var results*. Boulder, CO: National Center for Atmospheric Research.

Dewey, J. (1938). *Experience and education*. New York: Colliers Books.

Dewey, J. (1959). *Art as experience*. New York: Capricorn Books. (Original work published 1934)

Dewey, J., & Dewey, E. (1915). *Schools of tomorrow*. New York: E. P. Hutton.

Edwards, C., Gandini, L., & Forman, G. (Eds.). (1998). *The hundred languages of children: The Reggio Emilia approach to early childhood education* (2nd ed.). Norwood, NJ: Ablex.

Edwards, C., Gandini, L., & Forman, G. (1998). *The hundred languages of children*. Westport, CT: Ablex Publishing.

Gallas, K. (1995). *Talking their way into science: Hearing children's questions and theories, responding with curricula*. Columbia, NY: Teachers College Press.

Gonzalez-Mena, J., & Widmeyer Eyer, D. (2001). *Infants, toddlers, and caregivers*. Mountain View, CA: Mayfield Publishing Company.

Gordon, A. M., & Williams Browne, K. W. (2004). *Beginnings and beyond—Foundations in early childhood education*. Clifton Park, NY: Delmar.

Harlan, J. D., & Rivkin, M. S. (2004). *Science experiences for the early childhood years—An integrated affective approach* (9th ed.). Upper Saddle River, NJ: Merrill Prentice Hall.

Honig, A. S. (2003, January/February). Supporting curiosity: Offering infants and toddlers choices. *Scholastic Early Childhood Today*, 34–40.

Isenberg, J., & Quisenberry, N. (2002). Play: Essential for all children. *Childhood Education*, 79(1), 33–39.

Kamii, C. (2000). *Young children reinvent arithmetic*. New York: Columbia University.

Katz, L., & Chard, L. (2000). *Engaging children's minds: The project approach*. New York: Ablex.

Keller, J. D. (1993). Go figure! The need for manipulative in problem solving. *Contemporary Education*, 65(1), 12–15.

Keller, J. D., & Brickman, B. (1998). The Ball Olympics: Up and down, all around. *Science and Children*, 26–31, 56.

Kolb, D. A., Rubin, I. M., & McIntyre, M. (1984). *Organizational psychology* (4th ed.). Englewood Clifs, NJ: Prentice Hall.

Kolb, D. A., Rubin, I. M., & McIntyre, J. M. (1984). *Organizational psychology* (4th ed.). Englewood Cliffs, NJ: Prentice Hall.

Kraus, S. (1993). *Greens: A country garden cookbook.* San Franciso: HarperCollins.

Kuhn, T. S. (1996). *The structure of scientific revolutions.* Chicago: The University of Chicago Press.

National Committee on Science Education Standards and Assessment, National Research Council. (1996). *National science education standards.* Washington, DC: National Academies Press.

National Council of Teachers of Mathematics. (2000). *Principles and standards for school mathematics.* Reston, VA: NCTM.

National Research Council. (1996). *National science education standards.* Washington, DC: National Academy Press.

Newmann, F. M., & Wehlage, G. G. (1993). Five standards of authentic instruction. *Educational Leadership, 50(3)*, 8–12.

Noddings, N. (1995). *Philosophy of education.* Harper Collins: Westview Press.

Piaget, J. (1952). *The origins of intelligence in children.* New York: Norton.

Piaget, J. (1954). *The construction of reality in the child.* New York: Basic Books.

Piaget, J. (1963). *The child's conception of the world.* Patterson, NJ: Littlefield, Adams.

Piaget, J., & Garcia, R. (1989). *Psychogenesis and the history of science.* New York: Columbia University Press. (Original work published 1983)

Pluckrose, H. (1994). *Walkabout seashore.* Chicago: Children's Press.

Polya, G. (1971). *How to solve it: A new aspect of mathematics method* (2nd ed.). Princeton, NJ: Princeton University Press.

Polya, G. (1971). *How to solve it: A new aspect of mathematics method* (2nd ed.). Princeton, NJ: Princeton University Press.

Poole, C. (1998). The path to math developmental ages and stages. *Early Childhood Today, 12(4)*, 13–16.

Raloff, J. (1996, October 19). Precollege science and math 'lack focus.' *Science News, 150*(16).

Raths, L. E., Wasserman, S., Jonas, A., & Rothstein, A. (1986). *Teaching for Thinking.* New York: Teachers College Press.

Rogers, C. S., & Sawyers, J. K. (1992). *Play in the lives of children.* Washington, DC: National Association for the Education of Young Children.

Rousseau, J. J. (1957). *Emile.* New York: Dutton.

Sitole, D. (1999). *Cooking from Cape to Cairo—A taste of Africa.* Singapore: Tien Wah Press.

Smith, D. V., & Margolskee, R. F. (2001, March). Making sense of taste. *Scientific American.*

Story, R. D., & Carter, J. (1992, December). Why The Scientific Method?: Do we need a new hypothesis? *The Science Teacher*, pp. 18–21.

Trepanier-Street, M. (2000). Multiple forms of representation in long-term projects—The garden project. *Childhood Education, 77(1)*, 18–25.

Vygotsky, L. S. (1978). *Mind and society: The development of higher mental processes.* Cambridge, MA: Harvard University Press. (Original works published 1930, 1933, and 1935)

Vygotsky, L. S. (1986). *Thought and language.* Cambridge, MA: MIT Press. (Original work published 1934)

Index

Mathematics
  communicating and sharing ideas
    in, 60–68
  conceptual framework for, 98–109
    identifying resources in, 98–99
    stations for sight in, 106–109
    stations for sound in, 104–106
    stations for the sense of smell in,
      102–103
    stations for the sense of taste in,
      103–104
    stations of the sense of touch in,
      100–101
    using the five senses in, 99–100
  data organization for, 70–84
  development of, 9–14
    classifying in, 12–13
    comparing in, 12
    object permanence in, 11
    one-to-one correspondence in,
      13–14
    pattern in, 9
    sequence in, 9–10
    seriation in, 10–11
    sorting in, 11–12
    spatial relationships in, 11
  language and learning of, 6–8
  National Standards in Mathematics
    and Science, 19–20
  science and, 50, 92–93
  solid mathematics content,
    88–89
  solving problems in, 43
Me and my shadow, 283
Mean statistical value, 79
Measurement
  approaches and techniques of,
    55–57
  astronomy exploration and,
    122
  benefits of, 49
  birds observation and, 144
  of changing things, 51–52
  cloud observation and, 164
  communicating mathematical ideas
    through, 60–68
    developing referents for
      measurement, 64–68
    group sharing and discussion
      format, 60–61
    journaling, 61
    making a book, 61
    modeling mathematical and
      scientific language, 61–62
    providing discrete items to
      count, 62–64

  relating rational counting
    of units, 62
  for documenting evidence
    of, 164
  for documenting wind, 342
  ideas for teaching children, 60
  importance of, 50–51
  insects observation and, 181
  instructional psychology for
    teaching, 60
  introduction to, 49–51
  leaves observation and, 200
  light and color observation and, 222
  National Standards concerning,
    57–59
  rocks observation and, 241
  seeds observation and, 259
  Sun and shadows observation and,
    278–279
  toys and tools observation
    and, 301
  using senses and, 51
  water observation and, 323
Measuring tools, standardized,
  58
Mechanical advantage, 287–298
Mechanics, defined, 290
Median statistical value, 79
Memory, 1
Mercury (planet), 125
Metamorphic rocks, 239
Meteorites, 132
Metric system, 59
Micro and macro, 349
Micro-meteorites, collecting,
  131–132
Migratory patterns, of birds, 143,
  153–154
Minerals, description of, 236–237
Mirrors, 224
Model, role in classroom, 31
Mode statistical value, 79
Mohs, Fredrich, 237
Momentum, 298
Monochromatic light, 221
Moon, causes and phases of, 128
Moon watching, 128–129
Motion of the sun, 277
Mount or tripod, in telescopes, 120
Multiculture books, 111
Multimodal distribution, 79
Multiple-column chart, 72
Musical instruments, 105–106
My life story by Billy Beetle, 187
My life story by Rocky, 246
Mythology and the Sun, 285

National Association for the
  Education of Young Children
  (NAEYC), 98
National Council of Teachers of
  Mathematics (NCTM), 2
  on concept explorations and
    standards, 121–122, 143–145
  on mathematics development, 8
  *Measurement standard 1 for grades
    pre-k–2*, 58–59
  National Standards, 110–111
  *Principles and Standards for
    School Mathematics*, 19, 88,
    110, 212
  on problem solving, 18, 37
  on process standards through grade
    12, 352–353
  Teaching Children Mathematics
    (Journal), 98
  vision of, 22
National Research Council (NRC),
  2, 20
National Safety Council, 24
National Science Education Standards
  (NSES)
  concept exploration, 110
  content standards K–12, 58
  explanation of inquiry, 29
  *Principles and Standards for School
    Mathematics*, 19–20
*National Science Education Standards
  Publication*, definition of
  inquiry, 44
National Science Teachers Association
  (NSTA), 20, 22, 98
National Standards concerning
  measurement, 57–59
National Standards in Mathematics and
  Science, 19–20
Natural exploration, in classroom,
  28–29
Nature, seeds growing in, 262
NCTM. *See* National Council of
  Teachers for Mathematics
  (NCTM)
NCTM process standards through
  grade 12, 352–353
Nebula, defined, 118
Neptune, 121
Neutron star, defined, 118
Newness, experiencing, class
  environment and, 28–30
Newton, Isaac, 116
Noddings, Nel, 22
Northern Hemisphere, seasons in, 276
North Pole. *See* Arctic Circle

Where to Find NCTM Standards Addressed in This Book

The National Council of Teachers of Mathematics (NCTM) Principles and Standards for School Mathematics describes a set of goals for mathematics instruction. The first five Standards present goals in the mathematical content areas of number and operations, algebra, geometry, measurement, and data analysis and probability. The second five describe goals for the processes of problem solving, reasoning and proof, communication, connections, and representation. (For a full list of NCTM's Process Standards, see the Appendix on pages 352–353.) Together, the Standards describe the basic skills and understandings that students will need to function effectively in the twenty-first century.

The chart lists the Standards for prekindergarten through grade 12 (left column) and the Expectations for primary learners, kindergarten through grade 2 (second column). The Concept Explorations chapters and topics follow.

Instructional programs from prekindergarten through grade 12 should enable all students to—	EXPECTATIONS In prekindergarten through grade 2 all students should—	CHAPTER 7 ASTRONOMY AND SPACE SCIENCE	CHAPTER 8 BIRDS	CHAPTER 9 CLOUDS	CHAPTER 10 INSECTS	CHAPTER 11 LEAVES	CHAPTER 12 LIGHT AND COLOR	CHAPTER 13 ROCKS	CHAPTER 14 SEEDS	CHAPTER 15 SUN AND SHADOWS	CHAPTER 16 TOYS AND TOOLS	CHAPTER 17 WATER	CHAPTER 18 WIND
NUMBER AND OPERATIONS													
Understand numbers, ways of representing numbers, relationships among numbers, and number systems	• count with understanding and recognize "how many" in sets of objects;	X	X	X	X	X	X	X	X	X	X	X	X
	• use multiple models to develop initial understandings of place value and the base-10 number system;	X			X		X						
	• develop understanding of the relative position and magnitude of whole numbers and of ordinal and cardinal numbers and their connections;	X				X	X		X	X	X	X	
	• develop a sense of whole numbers and represent and use them in flexible ways, including relating, composing, and decomposing numbers;				X				X		X		
	• connect number words and numerals to the quantities they represent, using various physical models and representations;	X	X	X	X	X	X	X	X	X	X	X	X
	• understand and represent commonly used fractions, such as 1/4, 1/3, and 1/2.		X		X						X	X	X

Instructional programs from prekindergarten through grade 12 should enable all students to—	EXPECTATIONS In prekindergarten through grade 2 all students should—	CHAPTER 7 ASTRONOMY AND SPACE SCIENCE	CHAPTER 8 BIRDS	CHAPTER 9 CLOUDS	CHAPTER 10 INSECTS	CHAPTER 11 LEAVES	CHAPTER 12 LIGHT AND COLOR	CHAPTER 13 ROCKS	CHAPTER 14 SEEDS	CHAPTER 15 SUN AND SHADOWS	CHAPTER 16 TOYS AND TOOLS	CHAPTER 17 WATER	CHAPTER 18 WIND
Understand meanings of operations and how they relate to one another	• understand various meanings of addition and subtraction of whole numbers and the relationship between the two operations;				X								
	• understand the effects of adding and subtracting whole numbers;				X	X			X		X		
	• understand situations that entail multiplication and division, such as equal groupings of objects and sharing equally.				X								
Compute fluently and make reasonable estimates	• develop and use strategies for whole-number computations, with a focus on addition and subtraction;		X				X				X		
	• develop fluency with basic number combinations for addition and subtraction;												
	• use a variety of methods and tools to compute, including objects, mental computation, estimation, paper and pencil, and calculators.	X	X								X		

ALGEBRA

Instructional programs from prekindergarten through grade 12 should enable all students to—	EXPECTATIONS In prekindergarten through grade 2 all students should—	CHAPTER 7 ASTRONOMY AND SPACE SCIENCE	CHAPTER 8 BIRDS	CHAPTER 9 CLOUDS	CHAPTER 10 INSECTS	CHAPTER 11 LEAVES	CHAPTER 12 LIGHT AND COLOR	CHAPTER 13 ROCKS	CHAPTER 14 SEEDS	CHAPTER 15 SUN AND SHADOWS	CHAPTER 16 TOYS AND TOOLS	CHAPTER 17 WATER	CHAPTER 18 WIND
Understand patterns, relations, and functions	• sort, classify, and order objects by size, number, and other properties;	X	X	X	X	X	X	X	X	X	X	X	
	• recognize, describe, and extend patterns such as sequences of sounds and shapes or simple numeric patterns and translate from one representation to another;		X	X	X	X	X		X	X	X	X	
	• analyze how both repeating and growing patterns are generated.	X		X	X	X			X	X	X	X	

(continued)

Instructional programs from prekindergarten through grade 12 should enable all students to—	EXPECTATIONS In prekindergarten through grade 2 all students should—	Ch. 7 ASTRONOMY AND SPACE SCIENCE	Ch. 8 BIRDS	Ch. 9 CLOUDS	Ch. 10 INSECTS	Ch. 11 LEAVES	Ch. 12 LIGHT AND COLOR	Ch. 13 ROCKS	Ch. 14 SEEDS	Ch. 15 SUN AND SHADOWS	Ch. 16 TOYS AND TOOLS	Ch. 17 WATER	Ch. 18 WIND
Represent and analyze mathematical situations and structures using algebraic symbols	• illustrate general principles and properties of operations, such as commutativity, using specific numbers;												
	• use concrete, pictorial, and verbal representations to develop an understanding of invented and conventional symbolic notations.												
Use mathematical models to represent and understand quantitative relationships	• model situations that involve the addition and subtraction of whole numbers, using objects, pictures, and symbols.				×				×		×		
Analyze change in various contexts	• describe qualitative change, such as a student's growing taller;	×	×	×	×	×	×		×	×	×	×	
	• describe quantitative change, such as a student's growing two inches in one year.	×	×		×		×		×	×	×	×	×
GEOMETRY													
Analyze characteristics and properties of two- and three-dimensional geometric shapes and develop mathematical arguments about geometric relationships	• recognize, name, build, draw, compare, and sort two- and three-dimensional shapes;	×	×			×					×		
	• describe attributes and parts of two- and three-dimensional shapes;		×						×		×		×
	• investigate and predict the results of putting together and taking apart two- and three-dimensional shapes.		×						×		×		×

Instructional programs from prekindergarten through grade 12 should enable all students to—	EXPECTATIONS In prekindergarten through grade 2 all students should—	CHAPTER 7 ASTRONOMY AND SPACE SCIENCE	CHAPTER 8 BIRDS	CHAPTER 9 CLOUDS	CHAPTER 10 INSECTS	CHAPTER 11 LEAVES	CHAPTER 12 LIGHT AND COLOR	CHAPTER 13 ROCKS	CHAPTER 14 SEEDS	CHAPTER 15 SUN AND SHADOWS	CHAPTER 16 TOYS AND TOOLS	CHAPTER 17 WATER	CHAPTER 18 WIND
Specify locations and describe spatial relationships using coordinate geometry and other representational systems	• describe, name, and interpret relative positions in space and apply ideas about relative position;	×	×	×	×	×	×	×	×	×	×	×	×
	• describe, name, and interpret direction and distance in navigating space and apply ideas about direction and distance;	×	×	×	×	×	×	×	×	×	×	×	×
	• find and name locations with simple relationships such as "near to" and in coordinate systems such as maps.	×	×	×	×	×		×	×	×	×	×	×
Apply transformations and use symmetry to analyze mathematical situations	• recognize and apply slides, flips, and turns;	×	×	×	×	×	×	×	×	×	×		×
	• recognize and create shapes that have symmetry.					×	×			×			×
Use visualization, spatial reasoning, and geometric modeling to solve problems	• create mental images of geometric shapes using spatial memory and spatial visualization;	×	×	×	×	×	×		×	×	×		×
	• recognize and represent shapes from different perspectives;	×	×	×		×	×		×	×	×		×
	• relate ideas in geometry to ideas in number and measurement;	×				×		×	×	×	×		×
	• recognize geometric shapes and structures in the environment and specify their location.	×	×	×	×	×			×	×	×	×	

(continued)

CHAPTERS AND TOPICS

Instructional programs from prekindergarten through grade 12 should enable all students to—	EXPECTATIONS In prekindergarten through grade 2 all students should—	CHAPTER 7 ASTRONOMY AND SPACE SCIENCE	CHAPTER 8 BIRDS	CHAPTER 9 CLOUDS	CHAPTER 10 INSECTS	CHAPTER 11 LEAVES	CHAPTER 12 LIGHT AND COLOR	CHAPTER 13 ROCKS	CHAPTER 14 SEEDS	CHAPTER 15 SUN AND SHADOWS	CHAPTER 16 TOYS AND TOOLS	CHAPTER 17 WATER	CHAPTER 18 WIND
MEASUREMENT													
Understand measurable attributes of objects and the units, systems, and processes of measurement	• recognize the attributes of length, volume, weight, area, and time;	X	X	X	X	X	X	X	X	X	X	X	X
	• compare and order objects according to these attributes;	X	X	X	X	X	X	X	X	X	X	X	X
	• understand how to measure using nonstandard and standard units;	X	X	X	X	X	X	X	X	X	X	X	X
	• select an appropriate unit and tool for the attribute being measured.	X	X	X	X	X	X	X	X	X	X	X	X
Apply appropriate techniques, tools, and formulas to determine measurements	• measure with multiple copies of units of the same size, such as paper clips laid end to end;	X	X	X	X	X		X	X	X	X	X	X
	• use repetition of a single unit to measure something larger than the unit, for instance, measuring the length of a room with a single meterstick;	X			X				X		X		
	• use tools to measure;	X	X	X	X	X	X	X	X	X	X		
	• develop common referents for measures to make comparisons and estimates.	X	X	X	X	X	X	X	X	X	X	X	X